Urban Politics and Administration

From
Service Delivery
to Economic Development

Elaine B. Sharp
University of Kansas

Longman
New York & London

URBAN POLITICS AND ADMINISTRATION: FROM SERVICE DELIVERY TO ECONOMIC DEVELOPMENT

Copyright © 1990 by Longman.
All rights reserved.
No part of this publication may be reproduced,
stored in a retrieval system, or transmitted
in any form or by any means, electronic, mechanical,
photocopying, recording, or otherwise,
without the prior permission of the publisher.

Longman, 95 Church Street, White Plains, N.Y. 10601

Associated companies:
Longman Group Ltd., London
Longman Cheshire Pty., Melbourne
Longman Paul Pty., Auckland
Copp Clark Pitman, Toronto

To Bob, for his patience and support.

Senior editor: David J. Estrin
Production editor: Linda Carbone
Cover design: Tom Slomka/THOMAS WILLIAM DESIGN
Production supervisor: Priscilla Taguer

Library of Congress Cataloging-in-Publication Data

Sharp, Elaine B.
    Urban politics and administration : from service delivery to
economic development / Elaine B. Sharp.
      p.   cm.
    ISBN 0-8013-0170-X
    1. Municipal government—United States. 2. Municipal employees—
United States. 3. Municipal services—United States. 4. Economic
development. I. Title.
                                                    89-36783
                                                    CIP

ABCDEFGHIJ-MA-99 98 97 96 95 94 93 92 91 90

Contents

Preface

Several years ago, I found myself complaining to a colleague about the lack of a suitable book for classroom use in my course on Urban Politics and Administration in the urban management track of the MPA program. Basic textbooks on urban politics, several covering introductory materials in excellent and imaginative ways, were readily to be found. Any one of these could be counted on to provide necessary background on such topics as the nature of governing institutions at the local level (particularly the history and consequences of the reform movement), the intergovernmental context for local governance, debates over the distribution of power in American communities, and patterns of metropolitan development. However, there seemed to be no single volume that provided a comprehensive synthesis and discussion of important research developments on what I consider to be the two key roles of local government: service delivery and economic development.

For MPA students and upper-division undergraduates, it seemed to me necessary to go beyond the basics of urban politics to a thorough consideration of what we have learned about local governments' performance of those two roles. This is especially the case since so many of the more controversial and contentious topics within the field of urban politics fit under one or the other of these two topics. For example, substantial sets of research findings and debate have been generated around the issues of privatizing local government services, equity of service delivery in cities, and public policy strategies for economic development. I wanted to expose my students to those research results and to the sometimes heated debates about them among professional scholars of urban affairs.

My colleagues' response to my complaints about the lack of such a book was: Why don't you write it? That suggestion planted the seed that has ultimately grown into this volume.

As the foregoing comments suggest, this book differs in important ways from traditional urban politics texts. First, it presumes knowledge of most of the basics covered in traditional texts. For many purposes, such as upper-division courses in urban politics or planning, I have assumed that this book would be used in conjunction with a solid introductory text. Second, the book has a topical, issue-oriented approach rather than organizing material around governmental institutions or key actors. As a result, institutions or features of urban governance that might traditionally be treated in chapters of their own (for example, the states and the federal government) emerge instead in a variety of issue chapters where they are relevant. Finally, the book deliberately attempts to synthesize the best of contemporary research on a variety of topics, leaving an ample bibliographic trail for interested students to follow. Above all else, the book should be viewed as an invitation—an invitation to students and colleagues to join in a dialogue about the problems facing urban governments and the prospects for their resolution.

CHAPTER 1

Urban Services and Economic Development: An Introduction

This book focuses on two core functions of urban governments: service delivery and economic development. Service delivery, covering a diverse array of traditional municipal activities from streetsweeping to policing, may sometimes appear to be the more mundane and routine of the two functions. Although service delivery is routinized, however, it is far from trivial in terms of either dollars or human consequences, and it is frequently the focus of substantial political conflicts that make urban governance a challenge.

The economic development function encompasses a broad variety of strategies and programs by which local governments attempt to stimulate the local economy, attract new jobs and tax base, and maintain opportunities for the level and type of private sector activity deemed appropriate in the community. Although recent developments have propelled the economic development function to center stage, it is by no means a new function for local governments. In the period 1815 to 1870, many cities competed for locational advantages as canal or railroad termini because of the economic benefits expected, and in the "great city era" of 1870 to 1929 cities borrowed heavily to finance major infrastructure projects critical to their economic growth.[1]

If service delivery and economic development are two long-standing functions of urban government, however, the two have perhaps been on different trajectories in the 1980s. Traditionally the heart of urban management, urban service delivery has more recently been subject to challenges by those who argue for more privatization and hence a reduced role for traditional urban bureaucracies and public sector managers. On the other hand, urban officials are being asked to do more and more with respect to economic development, including forging creative approaches to revitalization and fostering

1

public-private partnerships reminiscent in their extensiveness of the 1880s period of public underwriting of private expansion.

Although they are on different trajectories, both service delivery and economic development remain core functions of urban management. In fact, there are interesting complementarities and conflicts between them. Much of what local government does with respect to basic urban services can have extremely important implications for economic development. For example, the availability of high-quality city services (at reasonable tax rates) can in itself be a crucial factor in the locational decisions of firms. This suggests that excellence in service delivery and success in economic development go hand in hand. On the other hand, there is the potential for conflict as well. Resources used for economic development, whether in the form of tax abatements or actual expenditures, can be seen as competing with needs for immediate service improvements. Economic development policies can pit business interests against neighborhood interests.

Before exploring these conflicts and complementarities further, this chapter provides overviews of both the service delivery function and the economic development function, with special attention given to the diversity of activities encompassed within each function. The chapter concludes with a discussion of the relationships, conflictual and complementary, between the two functions.

SERVICE DELIVERY

On July 21, 1986, twelve thousand blue-collar municipal workers went back to work in Philadelphia after a three-week strike. During those three weeks, thousands of tons of garbage piled up, and city officials feared violence as citizens living near emergency garbage collection sites became frustrated with the rats and smell. The contract settlement that got the garbage trucks rolling again was estimated to add $91 million in payroll and benefit costs to the city's budget.[2]

For Wilson Goode, the mayor of Philadelphia, the strike was yet another challenge in a period of severe strain on his administration. A special investigating commission named by the mayor had judged him "grossly negligent" in his handling of an incident the preceding year. In that incident, city officials were confronted by the radical group MOVE, which had barricaded itself in a house in a middle-class black neighborhood. Police dropped a bomb on the MOVE house, and in the resulting fire eleven people were killed and 250 houses were consumed, thus decimating the neighborhood.[3]

In July 1986, as Philadelphia residents grew impatient with the problems of uncollected garbage, residents of Rochester, New York, had to contend with a different problem. Small amounts of fecal coliform bacteria had been found in the city's water system, and until the source of the contamination could be located, city residents remained under "the great water alert." The city's population of more than 241,000 was having to boil any tap water used or else avoid using it altogether, hotels were bringing in ice from elsewhere, and hospitals were distilling water for their use. Amid the complaints and inconvenience as residents entered their second week of such conditions, some citizens were claiming that flawed municipal sewer projects were responsible for the contamination.[4]

Rochester's problems pale by comparison with those of Clairton, Pennsylvania, however. In the fall of 1985, this old-time steel city in the Pittsburgh area was laying off its entire remaining police force of fourteen officers, its ten-member fire department, and its clerical staff, and many street lights had been turned off. Virtually no street paving was being undertaken. These drastic moves became necessary because of a lack of resources to pay for these services—a lack of resources resulting from the scaling down of the giant United States Steel Corporation plant, which had served as the primary employer and taxpayer for years. In place of the municipal police force, residents now rely on state police patrol and on those laid-off fire fighters who have stayed on call.[5]

These stories of dramatic failure and drastic cutback remind us of the significance of urban services and the important impacts that routine municipal activities can have on everyday life. As with most things taken for granted in normal times, we can best see how important something is when it is no longer available, or no longer functioning as smoothly as usual, or when a mistake disrupts regular operations. As long as pure water flows from the tap, garbage disappears from the curb, a police car reassuringly rolls through the neighborhood, streets appear smooth and clear of snow, and so forth, most citizens are unlikely to think very much about city services, except perhaps when the tax bill comes due and they stop to wonder what they are getting for their money (see Box 1.1).

What *are* the citizens getting for their money? The answer, of course, varies considerably from one city to the next because different cities offer different ranges of service. These differences are partly due to different state laws governing the division of responsibility between local governments and state government.[6] Similarly, large, diverse cities usually provide a more complex set of services than very small municipalities. Furthermore, even cities of similar population size and with similar contexts of state law may offer different mixes of services because local political cultures differ, and decisions about the provision of city service reflect such political cultures. Williams, for example, suggests that in some communities conservative political attitudes and a low tax tradition mean that city government is limited to providing only the basic services in a no-frills manner.[7] In such "caretaker" communities, police and fire protection, street maintenance, and garbage collection may constitute virtually all that city government does. By contrast, in other communities there is a prevailing view that city government should provide many services to support a full and rich lifestyle. In such "amenities" communities, city government

---

BOX 1.1   A Case Example of Extraordinary Service Delivery

Although examples do not as quickly come to mind, the significance of municipal services is also highlighted on those occasions when service delivery is unusually impressive. Such perhaps was the case in New York City during and after the Fourth of July weekend in 1986. On that "Liberty Weekend," in which extravagant celebration accompanied the unveiling of the refurbished Statue of Liberty, municipal services were strained to deal with the problems and needs of the many millions of people who were in the city for the festivities. The New York City Fire Department had 5,000 employees working that weekend, responding to 2,318 calls, including 1,351 fires. It was, according to a department spokesman, "the busiest day of the 121-year history of the Fire Department." Sanitation Department and Parks and Recreation Department workers and volunteers swept through the city like an army, cleaning up the tons of refuse from each of three days of record crowds. The police department set up and maintained 5,778 police barriers, and by Sunday of the holiday weekend had handled 308 requests for help, 29 water rescues, 9 boat accidents and 2 fires, and 66 bomb threats, in addition to the normal range of preventive patrol, crime call, and arrest duties throughout the city. By the end of the holiday weekend, Mayor Koch was beaming at the success of the city's handling of supportive services and the image it would provide of a city that works, saying: "I would think that the best salesperson, male or female, for the city of New York is an out-of-towner who comes here, goes home and dispels all the mythology as it relates to New York City." The city's euphoria was marred somewhat when, on Tuesday, a homeless Cuban refugee went on a rampage with a sword on the Staten Island Ferry, which was still crowded with out-of-town visitors. Two were killed and several wounded in this incident. But a retired policy officer emerged as a hero after subduing the killer on the ferry.

Sources: Todd S. Purdum, "Police Blanket of Blue Fosters a Safe Festival," *New York Times,* July 7, 1986, p. 13; Deirdre Carmody, "Cleanup Added to List of Liberty Superlatives," *New York Times,* July 8, 1986, p. 12.

---

may be involved in the provision of elaborate recreational facilities and in regulation to prevent the intrusion of land uses that interfere with a high-quality residential atmosphere.

    A look at one medium-sized city illustrates the sometimes surprising range of activities that fall under the rubric of city services. Kansas City, Missouri's 1986/87 budget shows, for example, that in 1984/85 (the most recent year for which final figures are available), the city Parks and Recreation Department repaired or laid 10,000 square feet of pavement, graded 150 ball diamonds, mowed 3,032 acres of park land, planted 98,000 plants or bulbs, pruned 5,659 trees, planted 1,255 trees and provided storm-damage maintenance for 2,680 others, inspected and serviced 650 park buildings, repaired or serviced 3,600 pieces of equipment, managed a zoo for 501,040 visitors, provided recreational programs at community centers for more than 20,000 school age children and almost 13,000 adults, handled more than 230,000 users of the city's various swimming or wading pools, maintained four eighteen-hole golf courses and two driving ranges, and provided for numerous park concerts, theatrical events, and festivals.

This, of course, is only a listing of the sorts of services provided by a single department. Table 1.1 illustrates some of the services provided by a few other departments in Kansas City, Missouri. Whether services such as these are the services citizens want, whether cities provide them in the most efficient, effective, and responsive manner, and what issues of fairness surround service delivery are questions that will be taken up in later chapters of this book.

TABLE 1.1. SELECTED SERVICES PROVIDED BY FOUR CITY DEPARTMENTS IN KANSAS CITY, MISSOURI, FISCAL YEAR 1984/85

Department	Service Activities
Neighborhood Development	1,608 inspections of dangerous buildings
	200 dangerous building demolitions
	6,022 rodent complaints investigated
	6,638 premises baited for rodents
	56,081 properties inspected for weed problems
	9,210 inspections of property maintenance problems (nuisances, environmental hazards)
	850 houses painted (Neighborhood Paint-Up)
Health	12,306 births registered
	5,000 blood pressure problem screenings
	6,200 people screened for sickle cell anemia
	1,155 client-days of alcohol detoxification
	271 refugee health examinations
	2,900 pregnancy tests
	6,539 food industry inspections
	208 noise complaints investigated
Transportation	3,130 street light problems handled
	451 miles of street lines repainted
	14,600 street signs repaired/reinstalled
	15,480 illegally parked/stolen/abandoned cars towed
	210,631 passenger trips in a low cost transportation program for disabled/elderly
Fire	6,311 inspections for fire hazards
	679 investigations of fire causes
	22,860 fire incidents responded to
	9,950 home and building inspections
	16,495 fire hydrant inspections

Source: City of Kansas City, Missouri, *Budget: Fiscal Year 1986/87.*

The Nature of Urban Services

We have been speaking about urban services as though there were no doubt or confusion about what they are. In fact, there is a generally accepted notion that urban services consist of such things as policing, snowplowing, and the like that are provided to citizens by local governments. However, as some commentators have noted, this understanding is an overly fuzzy conceptualization.[8] This section provides a more formal definition. In the process, some important features of urban services are highlighted, and some key distinctions between urban services and other activities and functions are drawn.

Traditionally, economists have drawn a distinction between *services* and *goods,* where goods are tangible commodities (loaves of bread or shoes) and services are intangible things (education or housecleaning) that provide benefits to the recipient.[9] An incredible array and volume of services are provided by private sector firms in the United States. In fact, sociologists such as Daniel Bell have observed that the United States is no longer functioning as an industrial society but as a postindustrial society, with one of the key features of postindustrialism being the fact that "the majority of the labor force is no longer engaged in agriculture or manufacturing but in services."[10]

It would seem fairly simple, then, to define urban services as those services produced for citizens by local government. However, as Chapter 5 shows, many services that once were produced by government agencies have been given over to private firms, either under contract to a local government or under some other arrangement. Other chapters show that links between government and the nonprofit sector as well as proliferation of special quasi-governmental organizations make it difficult to characterize particular service production arrangements as either private or public. The line has been substantially blurred.

So what, then, is an urban service? Clearly, it does not involve *every* service available to city residents, for then we would be discussing dry cleaning and housepainting, neither of which is what we really mean by urban services. Yet if we include only those services produced by local government, we would fail to consider those interesting situations in which local governments have attempted to come up with more creative arrangements for service production. It becomes easier to define urban services if we acknowledge the distinction between service provision and service production.[11] *Service production* involves actual service delivery—that is, the operating, delivering, running, doing, selling, administering. A city government that *produces* residential garbage collection service is one with some sort of sanitation department whose employees do the work of garbage collection under the supervision of supervisors who are also government employees. *Service provision* involves decisionmaking and arranging for services. It may include the decision to institute in-house service production and, hence, decisions about financing such a unit; or it may involve franchising private sector producers, regulating private sector producers, purchasing service from private sector producers, and the like.[12]

With this distinction between service provision and service production in hand, we can now more easily define the scope of what we mean by urban services. They are the services that local government *either* produces *or* provides for. Hence, our subject matter not only includes the political and administrative issues involved when city government runs a service delivery operation; it also includes the political and administrative issues that emerge when city governments, in their service *provider* role, become involved in sometimes complex relationships with private firms, nonprofit organizations, and other entities.

This line of argument brings us to the definition of urban services offered by Baer:

> [A]n urban service is one which serves the public interest by accomplishing one or more of the following purposes: preserving life, liberty and property; and promoting enlightenment, happiness, domestic tranquility and the general welfare. It is provided by one or more of the sectors in the economy through government regulation, co-production, or direct provision.[13]

Notice that Baer's definition sets a number of lofty goals for urban services. However, even high-quality urban services would not in and of themselves bring about the realization of those goals. For example, recreational services contribute to happiness, but many other factors do so as well; similarly, police services contribute to the preservation of property, but the security of one's property is ultimately the result of many other factors beyond the control of police departments.

This principle of partial impact is related to the two-stage process of service production suggested by Jones.[14] In the first stage of the production process, resources (service inputs) are used by the service production organization to create service activities (service outputs). For example, a streets and sanitation department spends its budget on sanitation workers, garbage trucks, and rights to landfill space (service inputs). These resources are used to generate sanitation service activities, such as a particular frequency of curbside trash collection and landfill disposal (service outputs). In this first stage of the production process, government has a relatively high level of control over what happens, and it can readily be held to account. For example, if poor-quality workers are hired or a lack of fleet maintenance leads to frequent breakdowns of garbage trucks and resulting delayed garbage pickup, citizens would be quite right to direct their displeasure to city officials.

In the second stage of the production process, service outputs are expected to have an effect on the problems for which they are designed or to help achieve the goals to which they are relevant (service impacts). Sanitation service is a response to problems such as rats, other public health menaces, unsightliness, and nuisance odors that would plague citizens if garbage were left to pile up. However, even with the best of service outputs, the goal of a clean, pest-free, sanitary community may not be met. If citizens litter or allow garbage to accumulate at the back of the house or in apartment building stairwells, the positive impact of sanitation service outputs will nevertheless not yield total goal attainment. In short, local government's control over impact is typically less than its control over service inputs and service outputs.

Table 1.1 gave a small taste of the great diversity of activities that are likely to be included under the topic of urban services. This diversity, of course, limits the number of general statements and across-the-board characterizations of urban services that can be made. What is true of environmental code enforcement, for example, may not be true of street paving, and knowing about policing may not necessarily mean that one has a good understanding of snowplowing. Rather than throw up our hands in frustration at the diversity of activities involved, we can identify several key dimensions that provide conceptually useful ways of distinguishing various *types of service* from one another. These include (1) scale of the service target, (2) regulatory versus distributive characteristics, (3) human services versus physical services, and (4) capital-intensive versus labor-intensive services. Each of these differences is described in the following pages along with suggestions about the implications of each difference.

Scale of Service Target. Some services are delivered directly to individuals whereas others must be delivered either to groups or, more often, to geographical entities. For example, burglary investigation service is in some sense provided directly to the relevant individuals—victims of burglary. These are the individuals with whom police officials will interact, they are the individuals who directly benefit from the efforts of the police, and they are the individuals in the best position to know how well the police have done. By contrast, there are services, such as preventive police patrol, that must be delivered to areal aggregations of individuals, like neighborhoods, rather than to individuals. Squad cars for patrol must be assigned to some zones or areas (typically called *beats*), and whatever frequency and quality of service a given zone receives is shared by all who live or have a business in that zone. Finally, some services are by nature delivered or provided to even larger aggregations, perhaps even jurisdiction-wide or not at all. For example, a jurisdiction with a single, centralized municipal sewage treatment facility in some sense delivers to all citizens the level and quality of sewage treatment that this facility permits (although differences in sewage pipe size, age, and level of maintenance may in fact mean that the sewage handling service does differ in quality from one neighborhood to another).

For several reasons, the scale of the service target is an important basis for describing urban service differences. As we will see in Chapter 7, certain arrangements, such as asking actual recipients to pay a fee for the service they use, are possible when the service is provided directly to individuals but less feasible when the service is provided to an areal aggregate. In addition, the scale of the service target has an important bearing on how services should be evaluated. For example, a survey asking all citizens to rate the quality of police burglary investigation service will generate much less valid and reliable information than will a survey of citizens who have recently contacted police about a burglary incident. More generally, the scope and character of political conflicts that erupt over urban services depend in part on the scale of the service target. Services that are directed at geographical entitites like neighborhoods often enough become the subject of a classic form of urban political conflict in which organizations representing those neighborhoods struggle with city hall, usually over their treatment vis-à-vis other neighborhoods. By contrast, when the service target is the jurisdiction as a whole, so that every area receives the same service outcome, political conflicts may erupt over the propriety or quality of the service, but the conflict will not be over subarea differences.

Regulatory and Distributive Services. Urban services are by and large directed at solving or at least ameliorating problems. In some cases, problems can be remedied by providing helpful resources to those who are experiencing the problem. Thus, for example, a local government may spray certain low-lying swampy areas in order to remove a mosquito problem that would otherwise plague residents of nearby neighborhoods. Similarly, cities provide park facilities in various areas that solve problems for parents who do not want to see their children playing in the streets. Drawing on part of a classic typology offered by Theodore Lowi, we might refer to these sorts of services as distributive ones—valued, problem-solving resources are given out to various constituencies that will benefit from those resources.[15] Obviously, the key conflicts over distributive services will involve the basic who-gets-how-much questions.

Many urban problems, however, result when the activities of some individuals adversely affect other individuals. Left to their own devices, some citizens would allow brush piles to accumulate on their property, thus attracting rodents to the entire area, and some restaurants have been known to sacrifice cleanliness (and therefore their patrons' health) in favor of cost savings. In any basic course in welfare economics, concepts such as *negative externalities* are introduced to describe such situations and to provide a theoretical justification for state intervention. To solve such problems, governments often use regulation. When local government regulates, it invokes what is traditionally referred to as its *police power,* which is the general authority granted to it by the state to act to ensure public safety, health, and general welfare. Regulation involves authoritative decrees such as laws or ordinances that (1) make some behaviors mandatory and others illegitimate, and (2) specify sanctions for noncompliance. In many cases, monitoring or enforcement of compliance is also part of the regulation package.[16]

Regulatory activity is not always considered to be a form of service delivery, but it is. It is a problem-solving or ameliorating activity that yields benefits for those citizens who are protected from the negative externalities that they might otherwise have to endure. One observer of urban affairs argues that cities are increasingly using regulatory and other "staff powers" to accomplish objectives that might historically have been approached through provision of a traditional service by a public agency.[17] For example, cities traditionally finance and construct roads, sewer systems, schools, and the like. Recently, however, many cities have accomplished these purposes by adding to the land use regulations that govern private development. In order to be granted the necessary permits to build a new residential complex, a developer might be asked to put in a street system that links the development to existing roads, dedicate land for a new school, and pay fees to defray the costs of added capacity of the sewage treatment system.

A considerable portion of local government activity falls into the category of provision of regulatory services. This includes zoning enforcement, building code enforcement, much (but not all) of the activity of the police department, enforcement of noise ordinances, inspections of the food industry, abatement of environmental nuisances and hazards on private property, and many other activities. In contrast with distributive services, local government plays a coercive role in providing regulatory services. Conflicts over regulatory services can involve the same sorts of who-gets-how-much issues that surround distributive services. For example, one of the standard public criticisms of agencies charged with enforcing the building code is that some neighborhoods receive too little attention from the inspectors.[18] On the other hand, regulatory services also tend to embroil city officials in a very different form of controversy, those involving basic conflicts over the scope of government and the propriety of government constraints on private individuals (see Box 1.2).

Larger issues and basic value conflicts underlie these and many other cases of conflict over cities' regulatory-based services. By regulating problems such as trash piles, cities provide service to citizens who might otherwise be subject to health hazards and other nuisances. However, when regulatory policies extend into matters that are less obviously connected to health or safety concerns, regulation may be viewed as unnecessary imposition of the aesthetic views of the majority on minority groups. Especially when such regulatory policies have adverse economic impacts on some groups, vitriolic community controversy is possible.

Human Services and Physical Services. A common distinction used in describing services is that which distinguishes "human" services from "physical" services. Actually, all services are ultimately human services in the sense that they are of benefit and value to individual citizens. Sometimes, the term *human services* is used to refer primarily to income maintenance programs and closely related welfare and family support services. Here, however, the term is used more broadly to refer to all those services that involve relatively high levels of personal interaction, and often interaction designed to yield developmental changes in the service recipient. Education, for example, entails changing levels of skill, understanding, and competence on the part of the student; with-

---

BOX 1.2   Conflict over City Government's Regulatory Role

A "prairie patch" owned by one resident of Lawrence, Kansas, and a carpet store owned by another exemplify the sorts of conflicts that often revolve around regulatory services.

With regard to the prairie patch: Mr. Almon of Lawrence keeps his yard maintained in a somewhat unorthodox manner—that is, about half the yard mowed and the other half covered with "large sections of unmowed bluegrass, a wildflower garden, a berry patch, other wild edibles, and some fruit and nut trees." This arrangement is a natural form of landscaping that, according to Almon, is more effective than traditional mowing as well as being more beautiful than the usual, plain-mowed yard. Comparing the areas that have been mowed to the unmowed bluegrass, Almon argues "Any area you see that I do mow generally reverts into plants that are very much more invasive, such as crabgrass, foxtail and buckhorn. But I have beautiful bluegrass. I have a solid stand of bluegrass and if I mowed it, then I wouldn't have it anymore." Despite Almon's logic and esthetic preferences, he has become the subject of regulatory service delivery. Every year an anonymous caller files a complaint about the yard. In June 1986, Almon was again cited for violating the weed ordinance.

In 1982, Almon "challenged the wording and intent of the weed ordinance" but the city commission refused his request for a variance and his suggestion that the ordinance be rescinded. Almon is not the only citizen to object to the city's regulations in this area. In 1979 another citizen filed a lawsuit against the city for allegedly cutting weeds and trees on his property when they should not have. And according to Almon, several organizations, including the Appropriate Technology Center, the Kansas Area Watershed Council, and the Lawrence Community Gardening Association, are compiling recommendations for a revised Lawrence weed ordinance.

Like the weed ordinance, the city of Lawrence sign ordinance has also generated its share of controversy. One case in point was Bob's Carpet Store. The owners had painted the exposed side of the building in splashy red, white, and blue tones along with the name of the store. The city's sign ordinance, like those of many communities, restricts the size of commercial signs. When city officials concluded that the entire side of the building was serving as a sign, it was obvious to them that it exceeded the size limits. The owners objected vehemently, and another conflict was underway. Just as city officials had been forced into a discussion of "what is a weed" over challenges to the weed ordinance, so here officials became embroiled in discussion over what constitutes a sign.

Source: Bonnie Dunham, "Controversy Grows on Prairie Patch" *Lawrence Journal-World,* August 24, 1986, p. 3A.

---

out such changes, education cannot be said to have been provided. Similarly, various health services require that there be change in the client or patient's behavior, such as change in diet, exercise, or personal hygiene.[19] These interdependencies between service providers and service recipients will be examined further when we turn to the topic of coproduction in Chapter 4.

By contrast, physical services entail changes in the physical environment of citizens. Such services may be performed without behavioral change from beneficiaries (although behavioral change on the part of beneficiaries can assist service delivery agents enormously, as Chapter 4 explains). Street paving, snowplowing, and garbage collection are classic examples of physical services. In contrast with human services, physical services need not involve direct, personal interaction between a service delivery agent and a citizen-client. Although it is difficult to imagine education, health care, welfare, and even some police services being provided without some face-to-face interaction between recipients (often referred to as *clients* in this context) and service professionals or paraprofessionals, physical services can be provided without any direct interaction between citizens and those producing the service. Very few citizens ever speak with street-paving crews, snowplow operators, and the like. Sanitation workers sometimes claim that they take a lot of abuse from disgruntled citizens, but in fact direct interaction with citizens is not essential to the performance of their work, as is the case with many human service agents.

This difference is important to keep in mind because it frames the types of issues that are likely to surround each type of service. Physical services typically become the focus of conflict over some effectiveness or efficiency issue, although sometimes these are implicitly equity debates, too (as when citizens of a particular neighborhood claim that their streets are poorly maintained compared to other areas). Physical services also occasion many controversies over locational decisions. For example, decisions about the siting of solid waste landfills evoke the NIMBY (not-in-my-backyard) syndrome as residents fight to keep the landfill away. Rarely, however, do physical services become controversial because of service agents' alleged treatment of individual citizens. Human services are quite another matter. During the 1970s, for example, urban service bureaucracies came under fire for being remote, rude, and unresponsive to the public. Human services were often the focal point of these criticisms, perhaps because the direct interaction with the public that is entailed in these services provided the setting for the conflicts and perceived abuses that were at issue. Intense pressures sometimes occur when service delivery agents, functioning as the visible representatives of government authority, deal directly with citizens, a fact well documented by Lipsky's analysis of these "street-level bureaucrats."[20] The kinds of individuals recruited to these roles, the mechanisms for supervision and management of their discretion, and the continuities and changes in their relationships with the public they serve are considered in Chapter 2.

Capital-Intensive versus Labor-Intensive Services. Baer argues convincingly that scholars have underemphasized the important differences between capital-intensive services (i.e., those involving relatively heavy amounts of non-personnel costs) and labor-intensive services (i.e., those involving relatively heavy amounts of personnel costs).[21] In fact, Baer argues, such scholarship about urban services focuses on services that are labor intensive rather than those that are capital intensive. This focus has important consequences for our understanding of urban services because the two types have very different features and often involve very different decisionmaking issues. As Baer says:

> Those services which are labor intensive . . . are typically routine, repetitive, and recurrent, of short duration, easily divisible, and revisable or even reversible if change is desired in current delivery patterns. Police patrols, street cleaning and repair, garbage collection, and housing inspection are examples. Capital intensive services . . . are more typically extraordinary (in terms of financing and frequency of provision), continual, long-lived, lumpy, and nonreversible. Examples include police stations, street construction, and disposal dumps.[22]

In this book, most of the issues raised in Chapters 2 through 6 are relevant to labor-intensive services. Chapter 8 turns to the public works issues that are a key to capital-intensive services.

Key Features in the Study of Urban Services

The preceding sections outlined a number of the important differences across urban services. Acknowledging these differences helps us to appreciate the diversity of what urban service delivery entails and sensitizes us to the various issues and processes that are likely to characterize various types of services. Similarly, some important general features of urban services should be noted because they help to show the connections between the study of urban services and several basic questions of political science and public administration.

Urban Services and the Politics-Versus-Administration Question. First, urban services are a matter of both policymaking and administration. They are, as a result, the focal point for the sometimes strained and sometimes smooth relationships between elected politicians and the bureaucracy. Whether it is proper to envision a clear dichotomy between politics and administration is a classic question in public administration theory and one that periodically bubbles to the surface whenever specific qualms about the role of the bureaucracy are brought to light. Basically, the concept of a politics-administration dichotomy traces to early public administration writings outlining a model of democracy in which elected officials monopolize policymaking through their legislative powers, whereas the bureaucracy serves as a neutral servant for the execution of those policies, free of political interference as it carries out its administrative role. As Jones rightly notes, there is a confounding of "political" and "policymaking" in all this.[23] Early writers saw the legislative branch as the proper arena for both politics (i.e., relationships with the public based on electoral accountability) and policymaking (i.e., decisions about the role and scope of government activities).

On several counts this purist model rather quickly strains at the seams in practice. On the one hand, administration virtually always involves important, substantive decisions because legislatively created policies are rarely detailed and precise enough to allow for off-the-rack implementation. Depending on how vague the legislation is and how much filling in the bureaucracy has to do, the administrative side may involve either large or small amounts of functional policymaking power. At the extreme, Lowi criticizes those situations in which there are huge and inappropriate delegations of legislative function to the bureaucracy.[24]

Others note the ways in which bureaucratic actors play influential roles in the policymaking process, largely because of their control of information and expertise but also because of their close links with constituency groups important to elected officials. This view of the bureaucratic role in policymaking is embodied in descriptions of the policymaking process as dominated by "iron triangles" consisting of those sets of interest groups, bureau heads, and legislative committees with a stake in a particular substantive policy area.[25]

If the barrier between policymaking and administration is breached by these bureaucratic involvements in policymaking, it is also sometimes breached by elected officials' playing influential roles in administration. Where reform structures and principles have not totally squeezed out patronage practices, administrative interference by politicians may come in the form of influence over who gets certain city jobs. But patronage considerations in the process of recruiting city workers is only one form of interference, and a relatively extreme form at that. More subtle forms of interference can occur if elected officials attempt to run interference for citizens complaining about city services or demanding special treatment. Greene shows that this is a definite source of strain between service delivery bureaucrats and elected officials.[26] Seventy-five percent of the administrators he interviewed thought it was inappropriate for elected officials to act as intermediaries for citizens, and about 60 percent said that they would respond more favorably to contacts directly from citizens than to requests and demands carried by elected officials.

On the other hand, service delivery operations sometimes become extremely controversial, leading to the intensive involvement of elected officials. This can occur if corrupt practices in city operations are exposed, thus forcing elected officials into a legislative oversight role. It can also occur if community controversy erupts over service delivery, as when equity questions are raised about certain service practices of the city. Under these circumstances, the fine distinction between the macropolicy concerns of legislators and the micropolicy concerns of administrators break down because both are enmeshed in political controversy over an ostensibly minute matter of administrative procedure.

These many observed violations of a pure politics-administration dichotomy in practice have created a revisionist perspective in public administration that emphasizes the interpenetration of politics and administration. But if these two spheres sometimes overlap, there are still important differences between them, both theoretically and in practice. In describing his study of Department of Buildings officials in Chicago, for example, Bryan Jones notes: "The administrators I have interviewed distinguished situations in which they made policy and those in which they administered it, and they were usually appropriately cautious in policy-making situations."[27] Similarly, although elected officials may occasionally attempt to get service delivery responses on behalf of particular constituents, they too are presumably cautious about pressing too far. When due care is not exerted, misunderstandings and conflict occur. Many a city manager's tenure has been cut short over just such matters as these.

In short, definition of the appropriate sphere in which politicians should act and the appropriate sphere for administrative autonomy is an ongoing process. The process of urban service delivery is an interesting microcosm of practices, belief patterns, adaptations, and strains that are involved in the ever-shifting grounds of practical and theoretical debate over the scope of these two spheres.

Community Power and Urban Services. The study of urban services is also relevant from a perspective of community power because power relationships are manifested, at least in part, in who gets what in the service delivery process. Stated another way, urban services constitute some of the important benefits that can be distributed by local government, so the pattern of their distribution should reveal something about the "responsiveness bias" of local government.[28] Conflicts over services become occasions for assessing who has influence.

Even when there are no overt conflicts over service delivery, it is possible to assess patterns of bias in influence and responsiveness by tracking patterns of service distribution. The notion here is that city governments may be able to quietly favor some groups over others, and that this would be revealed through systematic examination of actual patterns of service distribution. By and large, research in this vein has not found the patterned inequalities that were suspected.[29] But that research is open to criticism on several fronts, and many questions remain.[30] In the courts, meanwhile, equalization litigation has fallen on hard times after an initial flurry of attention created by the case of *Hawkins* v. *Shaw.*[31] In that case, racially patterned inequalities in service delivery were extreme and readily documentable. Later cases have been less clear-cut, and decisions have presented obstacles to future litigation. Both in social science inquiry and in the courts, then, the question of distributional equity has fallen victim to a series of thorny issues of measurement and interpretation. Service distribution and equity issues are considered more fully in Chapter 6.

ECONOMIC DEVELOPMENT

The preceding sections provide an overview of the diversity of activities encompassed by the term *service delivery* and introduce key characteristics and questions associated with the study of urban service delivery. Similarly, the economic development function comprises a wide variety of activities and has some key features that contrast in important ways with the service delivery function.

Varieties of Economic Development Activity

In the latter 1970s, St. Paul, Minnesota, created the Department of Planning and Economic Development within city government to deal with problems of a declining inner city and a stagnating economy. In its first six years of operation, that department orchestrated a $100 million downtown office-retail project, provided $111 million to assist small businesses, garnered 15 Urban Development Action Grants from the federal government for development projects, used tax-exempt revenue bonds to generate $218 million for new housing development, created a $2.25 million Neighborhood Partnership Program fund that neighborhood groups can apply to for projects, and helped with a variety of other neighborhood and commercial revitalization projects. Local officials are pleased with their in-house approach to economic development, arguing that local government can hire people "who can relate both to the needs of the public and the goals of the private developer—just as a private or nonprofit entity would have to do."[32]

Although they are often less comprehensive and multifaceted than in the St. Paul case, economic development activities are also crucial in much smaller communities. For example, Columbus, Nebraska, a town of about seventeen thousand people, used a Community Development Block Grant of $980,000 as leverage to get a manufacturer of electrical fixtures to locate in the city in 1986. The resulting 500 new jobs are a significant addition to the local economy and an important economic development coup for the community.[33] Sometimes the efforts are much more symbolic but no less focused on the desire for economic development. Ottumwa, Iowa, for example, instituted a campaign in which anyone over age ten can be fined 25 cents for saying anything negative about the community.[34] The local Chamber of Commerce supports the campaign, which is in response to sagging spirits created by agricultural crisis and the shutdown of a local meatpacking plant. Local officials and residents are said to hope that "the new positive attitude will help persuade developers to build a new mall nearby and persuade companies to move into the area."[35]

Economic development need not refer only to industrial development. Commercial development projects also abound, such as the commercial revitalization efforts conducted by New Haven's Office of Economic Development.[36] New Haven links public improvement decisions to merchants' revitalization commitments. First, merchants in a neighborhood must create a revitalization district, with over half of the merchants or property owners agreeing to renovate their property subject to the guidance of a design review committee. Owners are eligible for matching grants from the city, and the city's Economic Development office provides technical assistance as well. Once half of the buildings in the district have been renovated, the district is eligible for public improvements and special assistance grants from the city. In the first four to five years of this program, the city has used $500,000 in rehabilitation grants and $1 million in public improvements to generate about $5 million in private investment in two special districts.

Economic development efforts are not always unequivocal success stories, of course. A community group in Providence, Rhode Island, for example, is criticizing the community's Industrial Development Bond (IDB) program, which has given loans to over 165 firms since 1967.[37] The group claims that firms receiving the loans fell 10,400 jobs short of the job creation goals promised in their applications, yielding a total of only 4,700 new jobs across all 165 firms. Much of the net addition of new jobs is in fact attributable to the Electric Boat Company, which generated 6,000 new jobs according to the group; if that firm is excluded from the analysis, all other firms involved in the IDB program generated a net *loss* of 1,300 jobs.

Yet despite occasional critiques such as this, communities are using a variety of fiscal incentives and other tools to pursue economic development goals, especially when private sector decisions place the burden of economic revitalization in the hands of local government. In Youngstown, Ohio, for example, city officials are using a $1 million low-interest loan and tax abatement as incentives in their efforts to find a buyer for a large, abandoned lamp manufacturing plant now owned by General Electric.[38] General Electric is in effect unloading the plant, which is economically inefficient for its original use, by making it available to the city at little or no cost. The city will be advertising the availability of the plant and accompanying financial incentives and taking responsibility for finding a manufacturing concern to replace the local jobs lost as GE bows out of the picture.

Characteristics of Economic Development

The foregoing examples illustrate several important characteristics of the economic development function and several important contrasts between economic development and the service delivery function. First, economic development activities are largely *nonroutine* activities, in contrast with the predominantly routinized world of urban service delivery. While many communities institutionalize the economic development function in either a special city department or a combined public-private organization, the activities of these institutions are not readily described in the regular case-processing or line operations terms that describe urban service delivery. Instead, economic development often involves special projects, crisis responses to events like plant closings or scrambling to take advantage of unique opportunities.

In a related vein, the economic development function typically has much less of the bureaucratic flavor of service delivery.[39] The quality of urban service delivery is much affected by the discretionary activities of street-level bureaucrats[40] and urban service policymaking is an amalgam of politics and administration, with department heads often playing significant roles. Economic development by contrast is a much more centralized activity. Mayors, chief executive officers, and their immediate staff (including specialized economic development staff) are central figures in deal making in economic development, along with their counterparts in the private sector. The results of a 1984 survey of cities by the International City Management Association shows the extent of centralization of economic development activity. When asked where the economic development function is housed within city government, two-fifths of the respondents say that it is within the office of the city manager or chief administrative officer; 25 percent of the respondents indicate that economic development is even more centralized—that is, it is part of a larger community economic development agency. Only 12 percent of the respondents say that economic development activity is carried out by individual line departments.[41]

This more centralized, top-leadership aspect of economic development is a direct result of the nonroutine nature of economic development activity. Economic development ventures often involve unique problem-solving situations and negotiated arrangements with private sector firms, sometimes with substantial public sector resource commitments at stake. In this occasionally high-stakes world of nonincremental decisionmaking, it is not surprising that top leadership plays a central role while the bureaucratic politics of service delivery decisionmaking recedes into the background.

The economic development function is, furthermore, one that places cities in the position of competing with one another. Questions of who gets what and assessments of the winners and losers in economic development tend to focus on city-to-city comparisons (and state and regional comparisons as well), in contrast with urban service delivery, where questions of who gets what are more typically focused on differing subgroups or neighborhoods within a community.

This is not to say that all groups within a city benefit equally from economic development initiatives, nor is it to say that there are no important interlocal conflicts involving service delivery, especially in metropolitan areas. The nature of economic development conflicts and the patterns of local politics that result are the focus of Chapter 11.

The more visible and articulated form of city-to-city competition also involves issues of economic development. Sometimes there is direct and overt competition, as in the flurry of communities bidding to be chosen as the site for General Motors' new Saturn plant or in the head-to-head competition between Fort Wayne, Indiana, and Springfield, Ohio, to have the International Harvester truck assembly plant when IH announced that operations in the two cities would be consolidated into one.[42] In a broader sense, it has been argued that because cities cannot control the mobility of taxpayers, firms, and capital, the interests of each city always lie in the development of policies that will "maintain or enhance the economic position, social prestige, or political power of the city" relative to other cities.[43]

There are, however, numerous examples of cooperative ventures, especially involving collaborative relationships among smaller communities within a state, with the state playing a leadership role. Despite these, the dominant theme is competitive, not cooperative. Whether direct and visible or indirect and low-key, the economic development imperative pits communities (and regions) one against the other and forces local officials into an entrepreneurial, risk-taking role that contrasts with the more traditional roles of urban service policymaking and administrative oversight.[44]

Finally, the economic development function generates public-private relationships that contrast in important ways with those that obtain in the service delivery realm. It is true that privatization is very much an issue with respect to service delivery. Public officials are being challenged to provide services more cheaply by turning them over to private sector firms for production under contract. As we will see in Chapter 5, however, the boundary between the public sector and the private sector can still be quite clear under a contracting arrangement, and expectations on the part of both parties to the contract need not be particularly confused. By contrast, economic development initiatives have come to involve the public and the private sector in a host of complex, collaborative arrangements. The distinctiveness of the public sector role becomes less clear under such arrangements, as public and private actors assume new roles and responsibilities. This intermingling of public and private roles is an important theme in Chapter 10, which reviews various strategies and policies that local governments are using to achieve their economic development goals. As we will see, the intermingling of public and private is both a strength of many economic development initiatives and a source of conflict and problematic expectations.

NOTES

1. Robert L. Cook Benjamin, "From Waterways to Waterfronts: Public Investment for Cities, 1815-1980," in *Urban Economic Development,* ed. Richard D. Bingham and John P. Blair (Beverly Hills: Sage, 1984), pp. 23-46.
2. Rodd Zolkos, "Philadelphia's Costs Pile Up," *City & State,* August 1986, p. 1.
3. Lindsey Gruson, "Philadelphia Services Strike a Challenge for the Mayor," *New York Times,* July 2, 1986, p. 8.
4. Robert O. Boorstin, "Rochester Copes with the Great Water Alert," *New York Times,* July 14, 1986, p. 1.
5. Lindsey Gruson, "Steel Towns Discharge Police and Reduce Services Sharply," *New York Times,* October 6, 1985, p. 1.
6. Roland Liebert, *Disintegration and Political Action* (New York: Academic Press, 1976).
7. Oliver Williams, "A Typology for Comparative Local Government," *Midwest Journal of Political Science* 5 (1961): 150-164.
8. William C. Baer, "Just What Is an Urban Service, Anyway?" *Journal of Politics* 47 (August 1985): 881-898.

9. Richard Lipsey and Peter Steiner, *Economics,* 5th ed. (New York: Harper & Row, 1978).
10. Daniel Bell, *The Coming of Post-Industrial Society* (New York: Basic Books, 1976).
11. Ted Kolderie, "The Two Different Concepts of Privatization," *Public Administration Review* 46(July/August 1986): 285–291.
12. Ibid., p. 286.
13. Baer, "Just What Is an Urban Service?" p. 886.
14. Bryan Jones, *Governing Urban America* (Boston: Little, Brown, 1983). pp. 350–351.
15. Theodore Lowi, "American Business Public Policy: Case Studies and Political Theory," *World Politics* 16(June 1964): 677–715.
16. B. Guy Peters, *American Public Policy* (Chatham, NJ: Chatham House, 1986).
17. Baer, "Just What Is an Urban Service?" p. 887.
18. Bryan Jones, *Governing Buildings and Building Government* (University, AL: University of Alabama Press, 1985).
19. For further discussion of this point, see Gordon Whitaker, "Coproduction: Citizen Participation in Service Delivery," *Public Administration Review* 40 (May/June 1980): 240–246.
20. Michael Lipsky, *Street-Level Bureaucracy: Dilemmas of the Individual in Public Services* (New York: Russell Sage, 1980).
21. Baer, "Just What Is an Urban Service?" p. 890.
22. Ibid.
23. Jones, *Governing Buildings and Building Government,* pp. xiii–xiv.
24. Theodore Lowi, *The End of Liberalism,* 2nd ed. (New York: Norton, 1979).
25. Harold Seidman, *Politics, Position, and Power,* 2nd ed. (New York: Oxford University Press, 1976).
26. Kenneth Greene, "Administrators' Reactions to Elected Officials' Contacts: Avoidance or Cooperation," paper presented at the 1982 Annual Meetings of the Southwestern Political Science Association, San Antonio, Texas, March 17–20, 1982.
27. Jones, *Governing Buildings and Building Government,* p. xiii.
28. Paul Schumaker and Russell Getter, "Structural Sources of Unequal Responsiveness to Group Demands in American Cities," *Western Political Quarterly* 36 (March 1983): 7–29.
29. Robert Lineberry, *Equality and Urban Policy: The Distribution of Municipal Public Services* (Beverly Hills: Sage, 1977).
30. Rodney Hero, "The Urban Service Delivery Literature: Some Questions and Considerations," *Polity* 18(Summer 1986): 659–677.
31. Ralph Rossum. "The Rise and Fall of Equalization Litigation," *The Urban Interest* 2 (Spring 1980): 2–10.
32. Ruth Knack, James Bellus, and Patricia Adell, "Setting Up Shop for Economic Development," in *Shaping the Local Economy,* ed. Cheryl Farr (Washington, D.C.: ICMA, 1984).
33. *City & State,* August 1986, p. 16.
34. *Economic & Industrial Development News* 5, no. 11 (June 2, 1986): 8.
35. Ibid.
36. Lawrence Hall, Robert Lurcott, Karen LaFrance, and Michael Dobbins, "No Lost Causes: Salvaging Neighborhood Shopping Districts," in *Shaping the Local Economy,* ed. Farr (Washington, DC: ICMA, 1984).
37. *Economic & Industrial Development News* 5, no. 13 (June 30, 1986): 9.

38. *Economic & Industrial Development News* 5, no. 7 (April 7, 1986): 7.
39. Douglas Yates, *The Ungovernable City: The Politics of Urban Problems and Policy Making* (Cambridge: MIT Press, 1977).
40. Michael Lipsky, *Street-Level Bureaucracy.*
41. International City Management Association, "Facilitating Economic Development: Local Government Activities and Organizational Structures," *Baseline Data Reports* 16 (November/December 1984): 3.
42. John P. Blair and Barton Wechsler, "A Tale of Two Cities: A Case Study of Urban Competition for Jobs," in *Urban Economic Development,* ed. Richard D. Bingham and John P. Blair (Beverly Hills: Sage, 1984), pp. 269–282.
43. Paul Peterson, *City Limits* (Chicago: University of Chicago Press, 1981), p. 20.
44. Ann O'M. Bowman, "Competition for Economic Development Among Southeastern Cities," *Urban Affairs Quarterly* 23 (June 1988): 511–527.

PART I
Urban Services

CHAPTER 2

Government Employees: The Agents of Service Delivery

Much of the writing about urban politics focuses on the characteristics and activities of top government officials, such as mayors, council members, and city managers, as well as the activities and interests of private sector elites such as corporate leaders. However, an equally important and interesting group of actors on the urban scene are the lower-level government employees who are responsible for everyday implementation of programs and routine delivery of urban services. As this chapter shows, these government workers are significant and interesting from at least two vantage points: (1) Particularly when represented by public sector unions, government workers may constitute a substantial political interest group in city politics, and (2) in their exercise of street-level and case-processing discretion, government employees are the most direct face of government that many citizens ever see. Government employees play an important liaison role between policymakers in city hall and the public.

MUNICIPAL EMPLOYEES: INTEREST GROUP OR STREET-LEVEL BUREAUCRATS?

With respect to their role as a significant political interest group, it is important to acknowledge that there is substantial variation across cities in the political power and organized activity of municipal employees. State law governing public sector labor negotiations at the municipal level is particularly diverse and constantly evolving. In general, however, local laws and policies involve one of two basic types of arrangements: (1) binding collective negotiations and (2) meet-and-confer arrangements that are not binding:

The binding collective negotiations process assumes roughly equal power of the parties, with the resultant being a legal, mutually binding contract. The meet-and-confer arrangement permits the parties to discuss issues of employment and, if agreement is reached, a memorandum of understanding is produced. But there is no legal obligation on the part of the employer either to enter into such discussions or to comply with any resulting understanding.[1]

The two arrangements are not mutually exclusive, however. Governments can have one arrangement with respect to some groups of employees and the other arrangement for the rest of their employees. As of 1982, 84 percent of the municipal governments reporting a labor relations policy to the Census Bureau had collective negotiations with respect to at least some of their employees, and 54 percent had meet-and-confer discussions, figures which suggest that substantial numbers of municipal governments use both arrangements.[2]

There is also variation in the extent to which organized public sector employees can legally strike. Unlike private sector unions, which are rarely constrained from using this weapon, the right to strike is very limited for public sector unions. However, eight states have given public employees a limited right to strike, with the limitation typically meaning that police and fire personnel cannot legally strike.[3] Strikes sometimes occur even in settings where they have not been legalized, however, although the nature of the job action is sometimes claimed to be a massive "sick-out," or in the case of police employees, the "blue flu."

Labor negotiations and associated activities are only one facet of the role of government employees as an organized interest group. Government employees have important stakes in many local government policies and decisions, and in many cities, they are numerous and organized enough to be viewed as a key player in local electoral politics. Theories of "bureau voting" have been developed that attribute growth of government budgets in part to the voting power of government workers:

There is evidence to support the contention that government employees are more likely to vote and that their voting strength is significant. It is estimated from available data that public employees, who represent a sixth of the workforce, cast more than a quarter of the votes. . . . The conventional wisdom in New York City is that municipal employees, each of whom can influence the votes of three relatives or friends, control a million votes, a number that greatly exceeds the margin of victory in any mayoral election.[4]

In short, one important perspective from which to examine government employees is that which treats them as an important political interest group represented by powerful public sector unions that serve as key players in the local electoral process and the local policymaking process.

Municipal employees are significant and interesting from yet another perspective, however. To appreciate this perspective, we must switch from a group-centered, political focus to an individualistic, management focus. Drawing on the insights of Lipsky and others, this alternative perspective emphasizes an important feature of municipal government employment: In many cases, the lowest-level employees exercise important levels of discretion and are thereby empowered to "represent" government in a very direct way to citizens. Through the many discretionary decisions that they make, often on matters of considerable importance to citizens, these lower-level employees can be said to make policy, even though they have traditionally been viewed as merely policy implementers.

> Unlike lower-level workers in most organizations, street-level bureaucrats have considerable discretion in determining the nature, amount, and quality of benefits and sanctions provided by their agencies. Policemen decide who[m] to arrest and whose behavior to overlook. . . . Teachers decide who will be suspended and who will remain in school, and they make subtle determinations of who is teachable.[5]

The discretion of lower-level employees is not unlimited or perhaps even universal. It is, however, very real for those employees who work in the field where direct supervision is less possible, for employees whose work involves case processing with complex decision rules requiring judgment calls, for employees who have attained at least paraprofessional status and the expectations of professional judgment that this entails, and for any government employees who "work in situations too complicated to reduce to programmatic formats."[6]

The discretion of lower-level employees, although quite real, is often quite problematic as well. It can be used to the advantage or the detriment of citizen-clients who interact with these employees, it can be used consistent with top leadership's policy orientations or in a way that undermines those policies, and it can be used in a way that exacerbates or eases conflict between citizens and the municipal government agents that they encounter. Many interesting developments in public sector management can be viewed as part of an ongoing tension between management efforts to control lower-level employees' discretion and employees' efforts to sustain a viable sphere of autonomy.

Municipal employees are, therefore, important because they constitute a significant political interest group in many cities; they are also important because, as individuals, many of them have discretionary power that can be problematic for management. These two different and important perspectives provide an organizing framework for exploring contemporary issues concerning municipal government employment. Before proceeding to that discussion, we must acknowledge a set of historical perspectives that should also be part of the organizing framework for discussion of municipal employees.

MUNICIPAL EMPLOYEES UNDER SIEGE

Government workers have been the focal point of two important waves of public resentment and criticism—one corresponding to the disruptive period of urban politics in the latter 1960s and the other corresponding to the "tax revolt" era of the latter 1970s. In the first of these periods of ferment, lower-level government workers were the focus of intense scrutiny because of their alleged nonresponsiveness or outright hostility to disadvantaged populations. Rather than serving as helpful, sympathetic agents, those lower-level employees who interacted most directly with poor and minority citizens were charged with insensitivity and prejudice. In studies conducted for the National Advisory Commission on Civil Disorders, for example, researchers concluded that the police "see themselves as outsiders in the ghetto, surrounded by an indifferent and hostile population. They tend to deny the legitimacy of Negro demands for equality, believing that equality has been mainly achieved."[7] Teachers were found to be more sympathetic but nevertheless to blame the problems of ghetto schools on culturally "deprived" students, and welfare workers were found to hold paternalistic attitudes toward their clients.[8] The beliefs and actions of these municipal workers came to be widely viewed as helping to ignite the urban disorders that occurred in many cities. More generally, tensions between lower-level government workers and the publics they were to serve led to serious consideration of the nature of the street-level bureaucrat's role, and to scholarly acknowledgment of their discretionary power.

In addition, this period of street-level convulsions led to various reform proposals designed to foster empathy between city workers and the inner-city publics they serve and to replace hostility and tensions with responsiveness. These reform proposals ranged from human relations training to the institution of citizen oversight bodies like civilian review boards for police.[9] An important reform idea that gained power from this convulsive period is the enhanced recruitment of minority citizens for street-level bureaucratic jobs. The notion that a more "representative bureaucracy" would yield gains in responsiveness and minimize tensions in ghetto areas is only one of the reasons for enhanced minority recruitment. Government jobs constitute important economic benefits for those who can get them, and minorities have not necessarily been fairly treated in the competition for such jobs. Hence, the drive for enhanced recruitment of minority citizens has also been propelled by the principle of equal opportunity. One of the key issues that we consider later in this chapter is the extent to which equal opportunity principles and a commitment to a more representative bureaucracy have in fact led to greater minority representation in the municipal labor force.

The second wave of public resentment of local government employees was part of the broader assault on government growth and taxes in the latter 1970s. As we will see in Chapter 7, many important proposals for fiscal limitation were enacted in this period, including California's well-known Proposition 13 and Massachusetts's property-tax-slashing Proposition 2½. These enactments, coupled with a pervasive mood of disaffection with government, constitute the tax revolt. Public sector employees became an important *symbolic* target of these sentiments, constituting an important focus for antigovernment rhetoric. In addition, government employees became a *substantive* target in the wake of tax revolt, as governments had to retrench and cut back.

> According to one state survey, Proposition 13 fallout has contributed to 17,000–18,000 dismissals, 2,000 early retirements, and 92,000 job vacancies left unfilled as a result of hiring freezes. . . . In Massachusetts, "Proposition 2½" may result in layoffs of as many as 20,000 local government workers. . . . During 1979 and 1980 . . . Newark dismissed 355 workers; Toledo, 135; Philadelphia, 135; Detroit, almost 2,000. . . . In New York City . . . over 45,000 workers—15 percent of the city's labor force—were laid off in 1975.[10]

Thus, whereas city workers were under siege in the 1960s because they epitomized the alien, nonresponsive face of government to many poor and black residents, they were under siege in the late 1970s because they epitomized wasteful, overgrown government to many tax-conscious citizens. The accumulated effects of these two waves of hostility toward government workers are of concern to many observers. Although the emphasis is perhaps more on trends at the federal level, this concern is exemplified by Larry Lane's observation that "the last 20 years . . . have brought a crumbling of the career system, a disappearance of civil service values . . . and the denigration and harassment of the people who attempt to work for public organizations."[11]

But is this highly pessimistic diagnosis warranted? This chapter explores a variety of contemporary trends and issues affecting city government workers. Some are manifestations of municipal employees' status as a significant political interest group, and some are manifestations of city workers' special role as direct bearers of government policy to citizen-clients. Most have roots in one or the other of the recent periods in which government employees were the focus of public criticism and hostility.

Weaving through all these organizing perspectives, however, is a powerful theme of recurring significance for city government workers—the reform principle of *merit* in employee selection, promotion, and retention. This principle, which has formed the basis for civil service systems and public personnel practices, stipulates that public sector employment should be based on ability; "political" considerations should be removed from decision making about public sector personnel. As a result, contemporary civil service systems formally keep elected officials at a distance from personnel decisionmaking, and use devices such as written tests to bring merit considerations to the forefront.[12]

The merit principle enjoys widespread acceptance, but adherence to this principle has not been free of conflict. Removing political considerations from decisions about public personnel seems straightforward as long as "political" is taken to mean "partisan." But other sorts of considerations, which are political but not partisan, are not as easily squared with principles of pure merit. Conflicts have emerged over affirmative action goals, which were designed to open the door to broader representation of minorities in the public sector workforce. Retrenchment and layoffs based on seniority, with the last in also the first out, do not square easily with merit principles either. In addition, there have been conflicts over how merit can in fact be assessed. Various testing devices have been alleged to discriminate more on the basis of race than on the basis of relevant abilities. These tensions over the meaning and relative importance of the merit principle in governing employment in the public sector percolate through many of the issues and trends discussed in the next section.

TRENDS AND ISSUES
IN PUBLIC SECTOR UNIONIZATION

In recent years, unionization has become much more successful in the public sector than in the private sector. Membership in unions representing government workers grew sharply in the 1968 to 1978 period especially, while private sector unions were losing members.[13] By 1985, the Census Bureau reported that 35.8 percent of government employees were union members, compared to 24.8 percent of private sector workers employed in manufacturing and 18 percent of workers overall.[14] In 1985, the American Federation of State, County, and Municipal Employees (AFSCME) had the largest membership of any of the AFL-CIO affiliated unions, with 997,000 members. Other unions relevant to public sector employment had substantial membership as well, such as the American Federation of Teachers (470,000) and the American Federation of Government Employees (199,000).[15] Fully 43 percent of the nearly 10 million full- or part-time government employees in 1985 were represented by a bargaining unit of some kind.[16]

There is mixed evidence concerning the impact that public sector unions have had on wage levels, employment levels, and municipal expenditures. In a review of twenty large-sample studies, Methe and Perry conclude that some types of municipal employees, most notably fire fighters and transit employees, have realized comparatively large wage gains through unionization. The unionized-nonunionized wage differential for transit workers, for example, has been estimated at 9 to 12 percent. On the other hand, other municipal employees, such as parks and recreation workers, sanitation workers, and library workers, do not seem to have realized particularly large wage gains through unionization.[17] Similarly, unionization has been linked to reductions in employment levels in large cities, an expected response to higher labor costs, but this does not hold true of uniformed employees. Finally, unionization and collective bargaining have been found to inflate municipal expenditures, especially in smaller cities where only core services are provided and where higher labor costs are not as easily offset with cutbacks in noncore programs.[18]

What is of particular concern to many observers are indications of growing militance on the part of public sector unions—militance that may in part be a reaction to the symbolic and substantive assaults on government workers in the tax revolt era. Kearney documents a variety of incidents that illustrate this apparent trend toward greater conflict.[19] For example, there have been retaliatory actions such as public referenda authorizing the firing of public safety workers who strike and eliminating cost-of-living raises and other wage formulas and court judgments requiring the payment of strike damages. In a number of cities, government officials have taken a get-tough approach when unions have not been able to control discontented workers who have engaged in activities such as wildcat strikes (see Box 2.1). On their side, public sector

---

BOX 2.1   Municipal Labor Conflict in Houston

A recent dispute in Houston illustrates the tensions between public sector workers and city government in situations of fiscal stress and shows that such tensions can lead to conflict among elected officials as well. In August 1986, city sanitation workers engaged in a wildcat walkout, despite the fact that public employee strikes are illegal under Texas law and even though the walkout was not sanctioned by the American Federation of State, County, and Municipal Employees, which represents many of the sanitation workers. The dispute was reportedly tied to increased workloads, layoffs of 159 workers, and 3 percent salary cuts, all made necessary as the city tried to cope with budgetary pressures following oil price slumps that hit the Texas economy hard. Leaders of the sanitation workers met with Mayor Kathy Whitmire to try to work out new route structures that would not increase workloads as much. The ninety-one employees who remained out despite their leaders' efforts to settle the dispute were dismissed by Mayor Whitmire, who claimed that they had broken a promise to return to their jobs and keep the garbage from piling up in the 100-degree heat while the dispute was negotiated.

The dismissals raised a new set of conflicts. One council member was quoted as saying: "I think she's just doing some image building. . . . Some consultant told her she needed to look tough, and she decided to get tough on these guys. The fact is everyone at City Hall knows the working conditions for these people weren't bad—they were horrible, atrocious." Other council members offered assistance to the workers should the mayor stand by her dismissal decision. On her part, Mayor Whitmire argued that the workers "needed and deserved to be fired" and stated: "I think it's important that we demonstrate illegal activity will not be tolerated."

Source: Peter Applebome, 1986. "Houston Mayor's Dismissals over Walkout Stir Ill Feelings," *New York Times,* August 24, 1986, p. 13.

unions have shown evidence of grouping for battle as well, and a number of analysts have predicted an increased use of the strike weapon along with other aggressive tactics.

On the other hand, the aftermath of an important recent court case suggests that public sector unions can play helpful, collaborative roles with local government leaders as well as more contentious, oppositional roles. The case also illustrates the role of the courts in protecting the interests of government workers, even in the face of hostilities like those involved in the tax revolt.

The case in question is *Garcia* v. *San Antonio Metropolitan Transit Authority,* decided by the Supreme Court in 1985.[20] Before 1985, state and local personnel practice had been guided by the Supreme Court's decision in the 1976 case *National League of Cities (NLC)* v. *Usery.* In the *Usery* case, the court had determined that the federal Fair Labor Standards Act (FLSA), as amended in 1974, did not apply to traditional state and local government employees. As a result, state and local government employees were not covered by the minimum wage, overtime pay, and other provisions of FLSA that provide substantial protection for private sector employees. When the Department of Labor moved to include nontraditional state and local government employees (e.g., transit workers, liquor store employees, and utility workers) under FLSA provisions, a suit was filed challenging that inclusion. In the case of *Garcia* v. *San Antonio Metropolitan Transit Authority,* the Supreme Court held that the provisions of FLSA should apply to all state and local employees, traditional and nontraditional alike, thus effectively overturning the *NLC* v. *Usery* opinion.

The *Garcia* case sent shock waves through state and local government. Straightforward and immediate application of FLSA to all employees would have imposed enormous costs. For example, watch operations like police and fire frequently involve scheduling patterns other than a standard, 40-hour work week. Imposing standard, overtime pay provisions on such operations would be enormously expensive. Consequently, the *Garcia* decision was immediately followed by a flurry of attempts to get Congress to provide relief in the form of amendments to the Fair Labor Standards Act. Initially, organized labor resisted these efforts, arguing that the *Garcia* decision was "a long overdue recognition of the rights of state and local employees."[21] However, in a substantial negotiating effort involving organized labor and state and local government associations, Congress devised a series of amendments to the Fair Labor Standards Act that mitigate the financial crisis that threatened as a result of the *Garcia* decision. For example, the amendments provide for the giving of "compensation time" rather than overtime pay under certain circumstances. Nevertheless, application of the Fair Labor Standards Act to all state and local government employees means that employees can file suit against these government employers if any provisions of the FLSA are seen as being violated. To the extent that public sector unions can be expected to serve as monitors of government compliance with FLSA and support groups for individual members claiming violations, the *Garcia* case functionally provides yet another vehicle for periodic conflicts between local government and public sector unions.

MINORITY REPRESENTATION
IN THE LOCAL LABOR FORCE

Considerable research has been generated in recent years concerning the extent of minority representation among municipal employees. A look at the numbers suggests that there have been notable achievements in enhancing minority representation but that affirmative action goals have been by no means fully realized.

For example, the International City Management Association's recent survey of cities and counties shows that in the largest cities (250,000 or more population) 4.9 percent of clerical jobs are held by blacks and 2.2 percent are held by Hispanics; 6.2 percent of city jobs in the "trades/field" category are held by blacks, and 1.8 percent are held by Hispanics. Blacks hold 4.5 percent and Hispanics hold 1.7 percent of the jobs in the "professional/technical" category. Minority representation in these city jobs is correspondingly smaller in smaller jurisdictions.[22] As a point for comparison, the 1980 census showed that blacks constitute 11.7 percent of the total U.S. population and 13 percent of the population within the nation's metropolitan areas; Hispanics constitute 6.4 percent of the nation's population and 8 percent of metropolitan area population.[23]

Stein's research on minority representation in city employment provides a better opportunity to compare minority job representation with minority population on a city-by-city basis, at least for a sample of 134 cities.[24] Table 2.1, adapted from her research, focuses on the ratio of percentage of the municipal work force that is minority to percentage of the city population that is minority. For example, a community that has exactly the same level of minority representation in its local government labor force as it does in its population will score 1.0. A community that has proportionately fewer minority city government employees than minority population will have a ratio of less than 1.0, and a community where the percentage of minorities in city government employment actually exceeds the percentage of the population that is minority will have a ratio of greater than 1.0.

Table 2.1 suggests that despite impressive levels of minority representation on some city workforces cities are overall still more likely to underrepresent than to overrepresent minorities. Nearly two-thirds (65 percent) of the sample communities show ratios of less than 1.0 and in one-quarter of the cities, minorities' share of local government jobs is less than three-fourths of the level minorities constitute in the city's population.

Furthermore, the progress that has been made with respect to minority

TABLE 2.1. MINORITY REPRESENTATION IN THE LOCAL GOVERNMENT LABOR FORCE FOR A SAMPLE OF U.S. CITIES

Ratio of Minority Share of City Jobs to Minority Share of the City's Population	Number of Cities	Percentage
1.5 or Higher	8	6
1.25 to 1.49	15	11
1.00 to 1.24	24	18
0.75 to 0.99	53	40
0.50 to 0.74	26	19
Under 0.50	8	6

Source: Adapted from Lana Stein, "Representative Local Government: Minorities in the Municipal Work Force," Journal of Politics 48 (1986): 694–713.

representation in the local government labor force appears to be very uneven across categories of employment. Despite affirmative action efforts, there is evidence that "the percentages of women, blacks, and Hispanics at the executive and professional levels in local governments are extremely low."[25] A 1984 survey of cities and counties shows that only 4 percent of employees in the professional category are black and only 2 percent are Hispanic; with respect to executive jobs, 0.3 percent are held by blacks and 0.1 percent are held by Hispanics.[26]

Table 2.1 also shows the tremendous variation in the extent to which city governments have minority representation in municipal employment. What factors might account for this variation? Most research on the subject has found, not surprisingly, that minority employment is primarily a function of size of minority population.[27] There has been less agreement, however, on the extent to which more overtly political factors, such as the existence of black mayors or minority city council members, might affect the allocation of city jobs to minorities. One study using a national sample finds that the presence of a minority mayor is not significantly related to black municipal employment overall and that the presence of a black mayor has only modest effects on minority employment in the more important administrative and professional positions.[28] Similarly, a study of Hispanic rather than black representation finds that the election of Hispanic mayors and council members does not seem to translate into increases in Hispanic public employment.[29] A comparative case study of ten California cities, on the other hand, concludes that black incorporation into the dominant coalition on the city council is a key factor in explaining increases in black employment in city jobs.[30] Another study finds that the presence of a minority mayor (in a mayor-council form of government) is a substantial factor favoring employment of racial minorities in city government.[31]

Minority representation on the local labor force is significant for two reasons. First, city jobs constitute important economic benefits and potential sources of economic advancement for minorities holding them. This perspective has inspired much of the research on the extent to which minorities have achieved gains in municipal employment opportunities. However, minority representation is significant for another reason as well. Having minority group members in city government positions, especially sensitive, street-level ones, has been viewed as one method for easing hostilities between street-level bureaucrats and those they serve. To what extent have gains in minority representation yielded this hoped-for benefit?

It is difficult to answer such a question for a variety of reasons. For one thing, comparable, nationwide data on the extent of hostile incidents between city government employees and citizens are not available. Second, as we have just seen, the extent to which there *is* substantial minority representation on the municipal workforce varies widely across American cities, making generalization difficult. In addition, gains in minority representation on the workforce have not necessarily been in those types of positions that best fit the model of the street-level bureaucrat who interacts directly with citizens on matters of great sensitivity. Police, for example, epitomize the role of the street-level bureaucrat, yet it is often noted that police unions have been particularly resistant to recruitment innovations that would open the ranks more quickly to minorities.[32] Throughout the country, police departments are dealing with charges that entrance examinations for the police are biased against minorities, which suggests that the struggle to achieve minority representation is not complete.[33] Nevertheless, there has been substantial improvement in representation, at least in the nation's largest cities, even for more resistant areas like policing. "The number of black police officers nationwide has more than doubled since 1972, to 42,000 from 20,000. There are 12 black police chiefs in cities including New York, Chicago, Washington and Houston."[34]

There is some evidence of decline in the worst and most visible form of hostility between street-level bureaucrats and citizens: police shootings of civilians. Such incidents were heavily implicated in the urban violence of the mid- to late 1960s, particularly when shootings or beatings involved white police officers and black civilians. Similar incidents still have the potential for sparking urban violence, as was the case in the riot that erupted in the Liberty City section of Miami in 1983 after a trial that exonerated four police officers of the beating death of a black resident. A recent Crime Control Institute study, however, shows that there has been a major decline since 1971 in police killings of civilians, at least in the nation's largest cities. In 1971 there were 353 such killings; in 1984 172 were killed. A 50 percent decline in the number of *black* civilians killed constitutes a substantial portion of the overall decline.[35] It is difficult to determine the extent to which minority representation on police forces has led to this decrease in shootings of minority citizens, although the result is consistent with the hopes of those promoting a representative bureaucracy. As Box 2.2 suggests, however, street-level tensions remain.

THE RIGHTS OF PUBLIC SECTOR WORKERS

If there have been substantial litigation and policy ferment concerning equal opportunity and the procedures by which individuals attempt to obtain government jobs, there have also been important developments concerning the rights

---

**BOX 2.2   Representative Bureaucracy and
Street-level Tensions: Controversy in Dallas**

In the early months of 1988, a series of street-level incidents involving the police and citizens led to broader conflict in Dallas, Texas, in a manner reminiscent of the 1960s scenarios that inspired calls for minority representation on police forces. Black and Hispanic leaders had for some time been criticizing the police department for being too quick to shoot when dealing with minority suspects. Indeed, a series of such shootings had led to congressional subcommittee hearings in May 1987. In January 1988, however, Officer Chase, a white patrolman, stopped a motorist for a traffic violation. Carl Williams, a homeless black man with a history of mental problems, was in the vicinity of the stop. After arguing with the officer, Williams took the patrolman's gun, knocking him down in the process, and then shot him to death where he lay. There were reports that one or more individuals in the crowd that had gathered around behind Williams had called out, urging him to shoot. Backup officers arriving on the scene shot and killed Williams.

Since this incident, the community and its leadership have been torn with conflict and countercharges. Police officers and supporters have wondered, sometimes aloud, whether the intense criticism of police use of deadly force might have caused Officer Chase to delay too long in drawing his own weapon and perhaps even created a climate for violence against the police. Others, like John Wiley Price, a black member of the Dallas County Commission, argued that ". . . to say that this happened as a result of comments in the past about police conduct was totally irrelevant and showed the height of irresponsibility." Many citizens argued that the shooting was not a race-related incident at all.

By February, in response to this incident and another slaying of a police officer, the city instituted two-person patrols. Meanwhile, various shows of citizen support for the police had been staged. However, the crowds at such pro-police rallies were mostly white, and racial tensions in the city continued to simmer.

Sources: "Dallas Citizens Side with Police," *Kansas City Times,* February 20, 1988, p. A-8; Peter Applebome, "Killing of Officer Stirs Anger in Dallas," *New York Times,* January 29, 1988, p. 9.

and responsibilities of individuals once they have a government job. On the one hand, it is important to recognize that government employment is *not* precisely like private sector employment. In some respects, rights that individuals take for granted are at least partially restricted whenever they take on the status of a public employee.

One example of these restrictions is residency requirements. It would be virtually unthinkable for private sector employers to formally require their employees to reside in a stipulated jurisdiction, but such requirements do exist for some public sector workers. Eisinger has in fact documented a strong resurgence of residency requirements in the 1970s, a development that he attributes largely to fiscal stress. That is, cities are interested in residency requirements as a way of discouraging the loss of tax base through suburban flight, as a way to ensure that the city's jobs serve as a source of employment for city residents, and because employment of residents is expected to enhance the circulation of salaries within the internal economy of the city.[36]

Residency requirements have also been justified on other grounds. For example, it is often claimed that it is important for emergency service personnel to live in the jurisdiction so that they can respond quickly if called in from their off-duty time. For this reason, residency requirements for police and fire personnel are particularly common. A 1982 survey of cities over 10,000 population sponsored by the International City Management Association (ICMA) finds that 30 percent of responding cities have residency requirements for police, compared to 21 percent in 1976. Sometimes this requirement applies to new appointments only (33 percent), and sometimes the requirement applies to sworn personnel only (45 percent). Thirty-six percent of cities responding to the ICMA survey had a residency requirement for fire personnel, up from 26 percent in 1976. However, the requirement applies across the board to all fire personnel in less than half (42 percent) of the communities.[37]

The key point about residency requirements is that they are an important constraint on city workers—a constraint that usually does not exist for private sector workers. Where city housing costs are enormously high compared to housing costs in outlying areas, residency requirements may be an important financial hardship for municipal employees.

Municipal workers' rights are also restricted in a special way by the federal Hatch Act and similar state laws that limit public employees from engaging in partisan political activity. Although not passed until 1939, the Hatch Act has origins in the reform movement at the turn of the century and was a reaction to the use of government employees for political campaigning. Without such provisions, government workers could be marshalled into a veritable army in support of a partisan spoils system, and parties could extract portions of workers' salaries as not-so-voluntary contributions to the campaign. The Hatch Act, recreated in modified form in 1940, allows public employees expression of political opinions but not as an organized part of a political campaign. Thus, for example, public employees are not permitted to serve as delegates to party conventions, to address political meetings, or to solicit campaign contributions. The 1940 act applied these regulations to personnel in state or local government employment if their activities are financed at all by federal grants or loans.[38] State laws emulating the federal act, or Little Hatch Acts, have also extended the restrictions to state and local government employees.

Hatch Act–style regulations can be seen in one sense as protecting government employees for these provisions insulate employees from forced contributions and pressures to engage in campaign activity in support of the party in power. On the other hand, the model of a politically neutral workforce can interfere with some of the political goals of public sector unions because their members are constrained from engaging in electioneering activities.[39] Furthermore, some individual government employees may find Hatch Act provisions to be more a restriction on their rights of free speech and free association than a protection from coercion to participate politically. Despite some discontent over these and other matters, the Hatch Act has weathered legal challenges and seems to have attained the status of settled law. The significant legal challenges to it were decided at least by the mid-1970s, and those court cases have "as a group, definitively resolved the constitutional issues raised by the enactment of a statutory bar on government workers engaging in partisan political activity."[40]

Residency requirements and restrictions on partisan political activity exemplify the ways in which public sector employment has been held to legitimately involve special obligations and unique limitations. But to what extent can public sector workers be subject to special limitations and regulation? Controversy over the rights of employees has emerged in cases in which such employees were fired for nonpolitical statements or activities that presumably would not be subject to penalty if they did not hold public jobs. These "expressive conduct" cases have tended to uphold the First Amendment rights of public sector workers.

For example, in a 1968 decision, *Pickering* v. *Board of Education,* the Supreme Court was faced with a case in which a school teacher had been fired for publishing a letter in the community newspaper that criticized the school board's budgeting.[41] In deciding to overturn this dismissal on grounds that it violated the teacher's First Amendment rights, the court instituted the principle of a balance between the interests of government in maintaining the unimpeded operation of organizational activities and the rights of the government employee, like any citizen, to freely express views on matters of public interest.[42]

Follow-up cases strongly reaffirmed the idea that government workers cannot be viewed as having ceded First Amendment rights simply by virtue of becoming public sector employees. For example, in *Givhan* v. *Western Line Consolidated School District* the court overturned the firing of a public school teacher, despite the fact that her expressive conduct consisted of aggressive and direct criticism of her employer. In *Connick* v. *Myers,* it became clear that the balancing test used by the Supreme Court does not always come down on the side of the aggrieved employee. In that case, an assistant district attorney had been fired for circulating a questionnaire to co-workers concerning various work policies and issues. The court upheld the firing on grounds that most of the questionnaire did not involve matters of broad public interest and that the manner in which the questionnaire was developed and circulated did significantly affect operations.[43]

The important point, however, is that in these expressive conduct cases, the court has developed and applied a standard that protects the free speech rights of government employees from easy abrogation. If Hatch Act limitations and residency requirements exemplify the ways in which public employees can be subject to special restrictions, the developing case law on expressive conduct exemplifies an area in which special restrictions are much more difficult to justify. In some respects, special restrictions like residency requirements are reminiscent of a philosophy of public sector employment that has been called the *doctrine of privilege*. Under this philosophy, which prevailed up until the 1950s:

> [i]t was generally accepted that since there was no constitutional right to public employment, it was a privilege to hold a government job. Moreover, because such employment was voluntary rather than compulsory, public employees had few rights which could not be legitimately abridged by the government in its role as employer. . . . public personnel administration was free to place virtually any conditions it saw fit upon public employment and the judiciary played almost no role in this policy area.[44]

By contrast, treatment of government workers' First Amendment rights in the expressive conduct cases is illustrative of the individual rights philosophy of public sector employment, which gradually supplanted the doctrine of privilege beginning in the 1950s. The individual rights approach stipulates that ". . . an individual cannot be required to sacrifice his or her constitutional rights as a condition of becoming a public employee. Public employees, like other citizens, had constitutional rights which were inviolable—even in the context of the employment relationship."[45]

Despite the emergence of an individual rights approach, elements of the doctrine of privilege can still be found in government employment matters, and the tension between these two philosophies concerning public employee rights and restrictions is unlikely to be definitely settled in the immediate future. Rather, new developments are likely to reinvigorate tensions and litigation.

A key example here is the contemporary debate over mandatory drug testing of employees. At the federal level, there have been a number of initiatives instituting such testing for certain classes of public employees, particularly where safety or law enforcement is involved, and some state and local governments have begun to institute drug testing programs as well. Following the logic of the doctrine of privilege, one might argue that if an individual wishes to be a customs officer, local police officer, or the like, the person should have no objections to submitting to a drug testing program. From this point of view, drug testing, like psychological tests and polygraph tests, are important devices for sustaining the legitimate and effective operation of the service in question, and any individual unwilling to comply should simply go elsewhere for employment. Interestingly enough, requirements for psychological tests, which arguably invade the individual's privacy at least as much as drug testing, seem to have elicited relatively little resistance. Some type of psychological examination is used in police employment decisionmaking by over two-thirds (68 percent) of cities reporting to ICMA's 1982 survey.[46]

From the point of view of individual rights, however, mandatory drug testing can be and has been challenged on constitutional grounds. In a court case (*National Treasury Employee Union* v. *Von Raab*) challenging the mandatory drug testing program instituted during the Reagan administration for Customs Service employees, the National Treasury Employees Union argued that the drug testing program is "demeaning, humiliating and offensive" and constitutes a violation of Fourth Amendment rights to protection against unreasonable searches and seizures.[47] However, the Supreme Court's decision in this case, rendered in March 1989 upheld the drug testing program. Writing for the majority, Justice Kennedy argued, "Unlike most private citizens or Government employees in general . . . employees involved in drug interdiction reasonably should expect effective inquiry into their fitness and probity . . . the same 'diminished expectation of privacy' applied to those who carry firearms because successful performance of their duties depends uniquely on their judgment and dexterity."[48] The Court's reasoning is widely expected to set a precedent for drug testing of law enforcement personnel at the state and local government levels.[49]

Even as the logic of the individual rights model of government employment continues to unfold, however, an even newer way of thinking about government employees may be emerging. This approach focuses on employment-related *needs* of government employees in a much more broad-ranging fashion than has traditionally been the case. Government agencies are now expected to deal with child care and other family needs through a variety of innovative programs and policies. As examples, new laws in Oregon and Tennessee require that employers provide unpaid parental or maternity leave, and the Internal Revenue Service is setting up child-care facilities for government workers.[50] In addition, a focus on employee needs is evident in the growth of new programs to assist government employees with various personal problems such as alcoholism, emotional and mental illness, and problems of drug abuse. These programs exist in thirty-nine states and a growing number of local governments.[51]

Programs focusing on the needs of public sector personnel can be viewed as special incentive programs. A 1984 International City Management Association survey of municipalities above 10,000 population finds that a variety of incentives beyond the traditional pay-bonus incentive are in use. For example, over one-quarter (27.2 percent) of the responding municipalities report that they provide for either a four-day work week or flexible work hours.[52] A variety of job enrichment strategies are also being used to help "employees increase their self-esteem and self-actualize their needs."[53]

Such developments may seem unusual in the wake of the tax revolt with its attack on wastefulness and undue expense in the government employment sector. On the other hand, much of what government does is heavily labor-intensive. Under these conditions, efficiency gains can perhaps best be realized through investments in the productivity of human resources. Programs focusing on employee needs are consistent with this recognition. Similarly, government, like private employers, is faced with some significant shifts in the nature of employment in postindustrial society, not the least of which is the dramatic movement of females into the full-time labor force. Traditional family situations, with one wage earner and the spouse at home providing child care, have been increasingly supplanted by situations with two wage earners, with resulting pressures for arrangements for alternative child care. Likewise, the increasing professionalization and technical specialization of work means that government, like private sector employers, has a substantial level of investment in employees in the form of training programs, recruitment efforts, and the like. Under these circumstances, government has a distinct interest in serving as a model employer dedicated to solving employee problems, because replacement of troubled employees is a more costly proposition.

TRENDS IN MERIT SYSTEM PRACTICES

Throughout this chapter, brief references have been made to the merit principle that is a key part of a reformist approach to public sector employment. But to what extent is the merit principle being realized in actual personnel practices? This section examines some important developments that are relevant to the issue of realizing merit ideals.

In the most straightforward terms, the merit principle holds that recruitment, advancement, and retention in government jobs should be based on job-related qualifications and performance rather than favoritism, particularly in the form of political patronage. How might we assess the extent to which this principle is being realized in practice?

One obvious response would be to examine the number of cities with civil service systems, or the proportion of government jobs that are covered by civil service requirements. Such an examination would be unlikely to reveal real differences in merit employment practices across cities. In fact, most cities have civil service systems. Nearly 90 percent of cities over 50,000 population have such systems.[54] But loopholes and special exemptions can readily be used to inject large amounts of patronage hiring into an ostensible merit system. For example, Chicago, which is traditionally viewed as the epitome of patronage practices, has actually had a civil service system since 1895. However, "temporary" appointments are exempt from civil service requirements, and numerous Chicago mayors have been able to use this loophole to maintain patronage hiring. Roughly 35 percent of the city's nearly 40,000 workers in 1980 were in such temporary appointments.[55]

More generally, however, local governments have been wrestling with the backlash from a period in which the merit principle was entrenched in politically isolated civil service commissions and exceedingly technical and rigid testing procedures for employee recruitment and evaluation. This technocratic period, running roughly from the mid-1940s to the 1960s, has been aptly described by Jean Couturier and Richard Schick:

> It was not unusual for civil service examiners, in ranking applicants to determine "the best qualified" to carry out their test scores to the third decimal place, as though the test instruments had been proved capable of making such reliable, valid distinctions among prospective clerks, manual laborers, or trained professionals. As a consequence, our civil services have been too far removed from the people that they are supposed to serve.[56]

Reactions to this technocratic period emerged in the tumultous decades of the 1960s and 1970s. Challenges to scientific testing for employee selection were brought, particularly by minorities who saw such tests as unfair obstacles to their job opportunities. A notable court case, *Griggs* v. *Duke Power Company* (1971), brought much of this to a head, for the court in that case insisted that if employee selection methods such as a particular test have a disparate effect on persons according to their sex, religion, race or ethnicity, the relevance of the test to the job must be proved; otherwise, there is unlawful discrimination.[57]

The *Griggs* case also provided a vehicle for a broader assault on the technocratic model of personnel administration. Although testing procedures had been the case in point, other requirements used in selection of personnel for government jobs could also be challenged on grounds that discriminatory purposes were hidden behind their ostensibly neutral front. Questions have been raised about physical requirements (e.g., height and weight minimums) and even about educational prerequisites. These challenges have ushered in a new era in which "the name of the game . . . has been to determine what are really BFOQs, or bona fide occupational qualifications."[58] Those requirements, testing procedures, and other devices that cannot be demonstrated to be important and necessary to ensure appropriate job performance cannot be sustained.

In the aftermath of the *Griggs* ruling and other challenges, city government testing and recruitment practices now are more likely to involve direct job performance skills and knowledge and less likely to involve general characteristics that are less demonstrably linked to job performance. A 1984/85 survey of large cities and counties conducted by the International City Management Association shows that nearly all (92 percent) of the responding local governments tested job performance skills and 80 percent did preemployment tests on job-related knowledge. By contrast, only 42 percent of the local governments used general aptitude tests, and only 20 percent used intelligence tests. In place of height and weight requirements, local governments are now much more likely to use tests of job-related physical agility as part of their preemployment testing practices for positions such as police and fire personnel.[59] In a 1986 survey of personnel directors in large cities, Stein finds that more than one-third (35.4 percent) report using fewer written tests for employee selection now than they did in 1972, a finding that reflects the delegitimization of the technocratic approach in general and written tests in particular.[60]

In short, the meaning of the merit principle is not so simple as once it might have seemed. Pressures to remove favoritism and political considerations from the recruitment and promotion processes for government workers led to excesses involving an overreliance on technocratic testing processes and potentially discriminatory job requirements. Reactions to these excesses have caused a reexamination of the meaning of "merit" with respect to government jobs, a reexamination that appears to have forced local officials to consider more carefully what the real basis for meritorious performance might be.

SUMMARY

This chapter has focused on local government employees below the supervisory level—that is, the streets and sanitation workers, police officers, fire fighters, health department case handlers, and other individuals who operate at the point where city services are delivered. These government workers are important in several ways. Individually, they may make crucial decisions affecting the lives of citizens who depend on them; collectively, they are often a powerful political bloc.

These government employees are also a focal point for conflict. The jobs that they hold are considered to be significant material benefits, and consequently there is conflict over who should hold them. Changing conceptions of merit swirl through government personnel systems, directly and indirectly affecting the processes by which these jobs are filled. Personnel administration has come to have an increasingly litigious flavor. Meanwhile, especially when they interact directly with citizen-clients in the service delivery process, there is also conflict over the way in which these government employees use their discretionary powers. As yet another aspect of conflict, we have seen that in times of fiscal stress, government employees become a focal point for critics of government growth and inefficiencies.

Along with these many conflicts, it is important to acknowledge that the way in which government employees are perceived is in considerable flux. This chapter notes the change from a doctrine of privilege, in which the individual was expected to give up certain rights in exchange for the privilege of holding a government job, to a doctrine reemphasizing the individual rights of government employees. Elements of both doctrines percolate through the public consciousness and through personnel practices, even as a newer doctrine emerges. This latter doctrine, emphasizing the needs of government employees, puts pressure on local governments to serve as model employers and to offer a variety of special programs and services that make up an investment in employees as human resources.

DISCUSSION QUESTIONS

1. Do you think that government workers should be subject to certain restrictions and requirements that do not necessarily apply to private sector workers? What sorts of restrictions and requirements do you think are justifiable? Is your assessment based on something like a doctrine of privilege, or are there other reasons for your conclusions?

2. Do you think that greater minority representation is needed in the local government labor force? If so, why? For what types of positions? What are the implications if greater minority representation is not achieved?

NOTES

1. Farouk F. Umar, and Roy V. Kirk, "Legal Context of Public-Sector Labor Relations," in *Handbook on Public Personnel Administration and Labor Relations,* ed. Jack Rabin, Thomas Vocino, W. Bartley Hildreth, and Gerald Miller (New York: Dekker, 1983), p. 314.
2. U.S. Department of Commerce, Bureau of the Census, *Labor-Management Relations in State and Local Governments,* vol. 3, no. 3, 1982 Census of Governments (Washington, DC: U.S. Government Printing Office, 1982), p. 1.
3. Umar and Kirk, "Legal Context of Public-Sector Relations," p. 315.
4. E.S. Savas, *Privatization* (Chatham, NJ: Chatham House, 1987), p. 26.
5. Michael Lipsky, *Street-Level Bureaucracy* (New York: Russell Sage, 1980), pp. 13–14.
6. Ibid., p. 15.
7. Peter Rossi, Richard Berk, David Boesel, Bettye Eidson, and W. Eugue Groves, "Between White and Black: The Faces of American Institutions in the Ghetto," *Supplemental Studies for the National Advisory Commission on Civil Disorders* (Washington, DC: U.S. Government Printing Office, 1968), p. 74.
8. Ibid., pp. 74–75.
9. Michael Lipsky, "Street-Level Bureaucracy and the Analysis of Urban Reform," in *Urban Politics: Past, Present and Future,* 2nd ed., ed. Harlan Hahn and Charles Levine (White Plains, NY: Longman, 1984), p. 216.
10. Richard C. Kearney, "Public Employment and Public Employee Unions in a Time of Taxpayer Revolt," in *Public Personnel Administration,* ed. Steven Hays and Richard Kearney (Englewood Cliffs, NJ: Prentice-Hall, 1983), p. 192.

11. Larry Lane, "Individualism, Civic Virtue, and Public Administration," *Administration & Society* 20 (May 1988): 34.
12. John Clayton Thomas and W. Donald Heisel, "The Modernization of Recruitment and Selection in Local Governments," in *Public Personnel Administration*, ed. Steven Hays and Richard Kearney (Englewood Cliffs, NJ: Prentice-Hall, 1983), p. 84.
13. Kearney, "Public Employment and Public Employee Unions," p. 195.
14. Bureau of the Census, *Statistical Abstract of the United States*, 107th ed. (Washington, DC: U.S. Government Printing Office, 1987), Table 693, p. 409.
15. Ibid., Table 691, p. 408.
16. Ibid., Table 694, p. 410.
17. David T. Methe and James L. Perry, "The Impacts of Collective Bargaining on Local Government Services: A Review of Research," *Public Administration Review* 40 (July/August 1980): 366.
18. Ibid., pp. 366–368.
19. Kearney, "Public Employment and Public Employee Unions," pp. 196–197.
20. The summary of the Garcia case relies heavily on the excellent description provided in Cynthia M. Pols, "The Fair Labor Standards Act: New Implications for Public Employers," *Municipal Yearbook 1986* (Washington, DC: ICMA, 1986), pp. 80–89.
21. Pols, "Fair Labor Standards Act," p. 82.
22. Evelina Mouldner, "Affirmative Action: The Role Local Governments Are Playing," *Municipal Yearbook 1986* (Washington, DC: ICMA, 1986), p. 27.
23. U.S. Bureau of the Census, *General Population Characteristics, U.S. Summary*, 1980 Census of Population (Washington, DC: U.S. Government Printing Office, 1983), pp. 1–19, 1–53, 1–55.
24. Lana Stein, "Representative Local Government: Minorities in the Municipal Work Force," *Journal of Politics* 48 (August 1986): 694–713.
25. Mouldner, "Affirmative Action," p. 26.
26. Ibid.
27. Peter Eisinger, "Black Employment in Municipal Jobs: The Impact of Black Political Power," *American Political Science Review* 76(1982):380–392; see also Stein, "Representative Local Government."
28. Eisinger, "Black Employment in Municipal Jobs," p. 388.
29. Susan Welch, Albert Karnig, and Richard Eribes, "Changes in Hispanic Local Public Employment in the Southwest," *Western Political Quarterly* 36 (1983): 670.
30. Rufus Browning, Dale Rogers Marshall, and David Tabb, *Protest Is Not Enough* (Berkeley: University of California Press, 1984), pp. 171–204.
31. Stein, "Representative Local Government," p. 708.
32. Ibid., p. 698.
33. Lisa Belkin, "Entrance Exams for Police Are Assailed as Biased," *New York Times*, January 31, 1988, p. 11.
34. Lena Williams, "Police Officers Tell of Strains of Living as a 'Black in Blue,' " *New York Times*, February 14, 1988, pp. 1, 14.
35. Ibid., p. 14.
36. Peter Eisinger, "Municipal Residency Requirements and the Local Economy," *Social Science Quarterly* 64 (March 1983): 88.
37. Ross Hoff, "Personnel Practices in the Municipal Police and Fire Services," in *Municipal Yearbook 1983*. (Washington, DC: ICMA, 1983), pp. 171, 173.
38. Jay Shafritz, Albert Hyde, and David Rosenbloom, *Personnel Management in Government* (New York: Dekker, 1986), pp. 241–244.

39. Stephen L. Hayford, "First Amendment Rights of Government Employees: A Primer for Public Officials," *Public Administration Review* 45 (January/February 1985): 242.

40. Shafritz, Hyde, and Rosenbloom, *Personnel Management,* pp. 244-245.

41. *Pickering* v. *Board of Education,* 392 U.S. 563 (1968).

42. Hayford, "First Amendment Rights of Government Employees," pp. 243-244.

43. Ibid., p. 244. The case citations are *Givhan* v. *Western Line Consolidated School District,* 439 U.S. 409 (1978), and *Connick* v. *Myers,* 103 S. Ct. 1684 (1983).

44. Shafritz, Hyde, and Rosenbloom, *Personnel Management,* p. 231.

45. Ibid., p. 234.

46. Hoff, "Personnel Practices," p. 169.

47. Stuart Taylor, Jr., "Justices to Rule on Drug-Testing Plan," *New York Times,* March 1, 1988, p. 7.

48. Linda Greenhouse, "Court Backs Tests of Some Workers to Deter Drug Use," *New York Times,* March 22, 1989, p. 11.

49. Ibid., p. 1.

50. "Employers Respond to Demand for Child Care," *PA Times,* January 15, 1988, p. 1.

51. Donna R. Kemp, "State Employee Assistance Programs: Organization and Services," *Public Administration Review* 45 (May/June 1985): 378.

52. Amy Cohen Paul, "Motivating Local Government Employees with Incentives," *Municipal Yearbook 1985* (Washington, DC: ICMA, 1985), p. 217.

53. Ibid., p. 218.

54. Frank Thompson, "The Politics of Public Personnel Administration," in *Public Personnel Administration,* ed. Steven Hays and Richard Kearney (Englewood Cliffs, NJ: Prentice-Hall, 1983), p. 6.

55. Anne Freedman, "Doing Battle with the Patronage Army: Politics, Courts, and Personnel Administration in Chicago," *Public Administration Review* 48 (September/October 1988): 848.

56. Jean Couturier and Richard Schick, "The Second Century of Civil Service Reform: An Agenda for the 1980s," in *Public Personnel Administration,* ed. Hays and Kearney (Englewood Cliffs, NJ: Prentice-Hall, 1983), p. 312.

57. Richard A. Loverd and Thomas J. Pavlak, "The Historical Development of the American Civil Service," in *Handbook on Public Personnel Administration and Labor Relations,* ed. Jack Rabin, Thomas Vocino, W. Bartley Hildreth, and Gerald Miller (New York: Dekker, 1983), p. 17.

58. Debra Stewart, "Assuring Equal Employment Opportunity in the Organization," in *Handbook on Public Personnel Administration,* ed. Rabin, p. 28.

59. "Local Government Recruitment and Selection Practices," in *Municipal Yearbook 1986* (Washington, DC: ICMA, 1986), p. 47.

60. Lana Stein, "Merit Systems and Political Influence: The Case of Local Government," *Public Administration Review* 47 (May/June 1987): 267.

CHAPTER 3

Improving Service Delivery: Innovation and Productivity Improvement

This chapter focuses on a pair of interrelated concepts that are important in the study of urban service delivery: productivity and innovation. Productivity has to do with management efficiency. It is typically defined in a way that relates the volume of production outputs to the volume of resource inputs used.[1] In some formulations, an effectiveness dimension is added to the definition of productivity. That is, some would argue that not all outputs should be counted equally, that some attention to the quality dimension should be included.[2] This could be done, for example, by defining productivity in terms of the relationship between volume of output *of an acceptable level of quality* (or at an adequate problem-solving level) and input resources used.

Unlike productivity, which has generated a family of technical definitions, the concept of innovation is more often used loosely to refer to any *new* product or process, regardless of the contribution of those novelties to efficiency goals. In the context of public management and urban service delivery, however, the concept of innovation is typically used to denote the adoption (and presumably the implementation) of new products or processes that are intended to improve performance or to cut costs. As some close observers of the topic argue, "Municipal governments have developed an interest in innovations as part of their concern with improving productivity."[3]

THE PUBLIC SECTOR PRODUCTIVITY PROBLEM

Productivity and the innovations that may yield productivity gains are not exclusively *public* management concerns. Kanter notes:

> In my travels around corporate America, in settings as distant geographically and culturally as a Los Angeles bank's high-rise headquarters, a snow-bordered Minneapolis electronics factory, a dingy Detroit engine plant, a Seattle instrumentation lab sitting among fishing boats, and a New York garment district sportswear showroom, I have been struck by an ever-louder echo of the same question: how to stimulate more innovation, enterprise, and initiative from their people.[4]

Kanter finds private sector companies in which innovation flourishes and in which productivity gains are impressive. She also finds many private sector companies with structures and practices that stifle innovation and interfere with productivity. Recent calls for public policies to reinvigorate the American economy and to bring back American competitiveness are also evidence that issues of innovation and productivity are by no means the exclusive preserve of the public sector.

Yet there are several important senses in which these interrelated themes have become especially critical with regard to service delivery in the public sector. On the one hand, public services have certain characteristics that in principle make them problematic on the productivity front. For one thing, services in general are typically thought to be less subject to productivity gains than goods manufacturing, primarily because the former are so labor intensive. Ammons, for example, suggests that long-term productivity information for the private services industry may be a revealing proxy for overall public sector performance. He notes that the private service industry productivity growth rate between 1948 and 1969 was 1.8 percent, compared with an overall growth rate of 2.3 percent.[5] Perhaps more important than this is the fact that public services are not subject to the discipline of market pricing. Therefore, both incentives for improving productivity and mechanisms for determining the worth of output are missing. User fees (see Chapter 7) are popular in part because they allow the public sector to approximate market pricing. But user fees, although growing in importance at the municipal level, are nevertheless applied to only a few selected services or aspects of service.

If there are reasons in principle to expect that productivity may be especially problematic for public services, there is also some suggestive evidence of a productivity gap between the private and the public sector. Growth in public sector employment or compensation relative to some private sector standard is sometimes presented as evidence of the lagging productivity of the public sector. For example, Ammons cites the following:

> From 1957 to 1976, compensation costs for state and local personnel rose 204 percent, compared with a Consumer Price Index increase of 102 percent during the same period. . . . From 1953 to 1973, state and local government compensation increased 188 percent, while wages in wholesale and retail, manufacturing, mining, contract construction, private nonagricultural, and the service industries rose 132%, 141%, 163%, 154%, 141%, and 171% respectively.[6]

Figures like these easily give the impression that the state and local public sector is using relatively greater and greater resources. Without corresponding increases in output, this would mean productivity losses relative to the private sector. There are obvious problems with the use of wage and compensation data to determine productivity patterns, not the least of which is the fact that such information provides only a partial estimate of resource inputs and tells us nothing about the output side. Nevertheless, for lack of better information, such figures are often used in discussions of private and public sector productivity.

Updated wage and salary compensation data show a somewhat different picture from that of the comparatively large public sector wage increases cited in the previous paragraph. Table 3.1, for example, shows trends in levels of both

TABLE 3.1. ANNUAL WAGE AND SALARY AND TOTAL COMPENSATION INFORMATION FOR GOVERNMENT AND PRIVATE SECTOR EMPLOYEES, 1975 TO 1983

	Average Annual Wages and Salaries			**Percentage Change**
	1975	*1980*	*1983*	*1975–1983*
Manufacturing	$11,903	$17,966	$22,170	86
Communications	13,726	21,388	27,647	101
Services	9,066	13,470	17,220	90
Real Estate[a]	10,618	15,864	20,725	95
Government[b]	11,451	15,939	20,263	77
All Domestic	10,836	15,785	19,460	80
Ratio of Government to All Domestic Industries	1.06	1.01	1.04	

	Average Total Compensation			**Percentage Change**
	1975	*1980*	*1983*	*1975–1983*
Manufacturing	$14,234	$22,055	$27,582	94
Communications	17,698	27,607	36,933	109
Services	10,108	15,246	19,843	96
Real Estate[a]	12,504	18,831	25,027	100
Government[b]	13,071	18,762	24,216	85
All Domestic	12,516	18,612	23,287	86
Ratio of Government to All Domestic Industries	1.04	1.01	1.04	

[a]This category includes finance and insurance as well as real estate workers.

[b]This category includes "government enterprise" activity as well as traditional government agency employees.

Source: Adapted from Table No. 697, *Statistical Abstract of the United States, 1986,* U.S. Bureau of the Census (Washington, DC: U.S. Government Printing Office, 1985), p. 416.

annual wage and salary and total compensation for government employees, for employees of all domestic industries, and for employees of several specific components of the private sector. The average wage or salary of a government employee increased less during this period than that of domestic industry employees as a whole, and less than any of the specific categories of private sector workers shown. In terms of total compensation, which includes various fringe benefits as well as wages and salary, growth in this period was relatively modest for government employees by comparison with some components of the private sector and about equal to the pace of change in domestic industry overall. If the period from 1950 to the mid-1970s was one of comparatively rapid growth of public sector compensation, as some data suggest, Table 3.1 suggests that such growth is no longer taking place. Table 3.1 hints at a residue of the period of comparatively steep rises in public sector wages, salaries, and total compensation, as shown by the bottom row of the table, which reports salary and compensation ratios of government sector to overall domestic industry.

Growth in the size of the government workforce relative to growth in the size of the private sector is sometimes taken as a revealing indicator in discussions of lagging public sector productivity. Table 3.2, however, reveals two important points about the growth of government employment since 1975. First, private sector employment has grown considerably more than has government employment—26 percent compared to 9 percent for 1975 to 1984. Second, what growth there has been in government employment has been concentrated at the state and local levels, and more especially the state government level.

There are obvious problems with any of these methods of assessing public sector productivity relative to that of the private sector. The most important is the lack of available information on government output and its worth.

TABLE 3.2. NONAGRICULTURAL INDUSTRY EMPLOYMENT, 1975 TO 1984

	Number of full-time-equivalent employees (in thousands)			Percentage Change
	1975	1980	1984	
Private Sector	62,259	74,166	78,477	26
Government	14,686	16,241	15,984	9
Federal	2,748	2,866	2,807	2
State	3,179	3,610	3,712	17
Local	8,758	9,765	9,465	8
Total	76,945	90,406	94,461	23
Percentage Government Workers	19%	18%	17%	

Source: Adapted from Table 694, Statistical Abstract of the United States, 1986, U.S. Bureau of the Census (Washington, DC: U.S. Government Printing Office, 1985), pp. 412–414.

Without such information, it is impossible to determine whether particular rates of growth in government employment, compensation, or overall spending constitute productivity losses or productivity gains.

In another sense, however, the lack of hard evidence on whether government productivity lags behind private productivity is beside the point. Widespread perceptions that government is less productive than private industry are important, regardless of the lack of adequate productivity indicators; and the *image* of unproductive public service bureaucrats is an enduring and powerful one. In other words, productivity is a *political* problem as well as an objective problem of management efficiency.

Municipal service delivery is perhaps especially susceptible to the creation of negative images because local public services are "direct, daily, and locality specific."[7] Lapses in performance are immediately noted by citizens. The visibility of local government workers sometimes suggests lapses even if the interpretation may not be justified. Many people, for example, have observed a street repair crew lounging beside the road with coffee and soft drinks. The crew may be on a legitimate rest break, but the ready response is that the workers are taking advantage of the taxpayers. Thus, by observation and anecdote, some justified and some not, the negative image of public sector performance is reinforced and extended.

The productivity problem is especially pressing for the public sector because of prevailing intellectual currents that associate efficiency with private sector practices and productivity lags with those government units that resist the wholesale importation of those private sector practices. As Downs and Larkey argue:

> Our picture of the private sector and those who control it is as unjustifiably romantic as our picture of the public sector is unjustifiably cynical. This idealized vision continually leads us to overestimate the potential contribution of private-sector techniques and sets the stage for frustration and disappointment.[8]

INNOVATION FOR PRODUCTIVITY IMPROVEMENT

One important response to the productivity issue has been the rush of attention to privatization strategies, a matter that will be considered in Chapter 5. This chapter focuses on initiatives for improving public services short of contracting them out or otherwise turning them over for private sector production. These efforts to improve public sector performance involve innovations.

Bingham and colleagues explain that there are three basic types of innovations that local governments adopt for productivity purposes: product innovations, process innovations, and service innovations. "Product innovations require adoption of physical change, process innovations require a change in method, while service innovations require the utilization of an agency or business to provide a new service to the organization."[9] The third of these—service innovations—have to do primarily with privatization strategies that will be covered in Chapter 5. This chapter focuses on the process and product innovations.

An Overview of Process and Product Innovations

Process innovations encompass various management methods or tools that have been extolled as productivity enhancers, such as zero-based budgeting, management by objectives, management information systems, and productivity bargaining. The extent of the use of these and other process innovations has been tracked by the International City Management Association,[10] the Urban Institute,[11] and more recently by Poister and McGowan.[12] We will turn to the results of this tracking shortly.

In addition to the management methods given in the previous paragraph, various changes in operational method may also constitute process innovations. That is, although innovations such as zero-based budgeting are often in the hands of management, other process innovations must ultimately be used by service delivery workers. Greiner and colleagues examine a host of job enrichment strategies, for example, that are intended to increase productivity by changing the nature of the job itself:

> This can be done in a variety of ways, including increasing the employee's autonomy (self-direction), increasing the variety of skills used or activities performed, giving the employee the opportunity to perform all aspects of a particular task rather than just part of it, allowing the employee to participate in management decisions, or increasing the direct feedback that employees receive on their job performance.[13]

Szanton has provided case analyses of two important process innovations involving policing operations.[14] One is a staffing arrangement called the "fourth platoon," which was instituted in New York City in 1969:

> For half a century, patrolmen had been divided into three platoons of equal size which manned the three daily eight-hour shifts, rotating shifts each week. But almost half of all crimes occurred during one eight-hour period (6:00 P.M.–2:00 A.M.). The obvious response was to arrange matters so that half the force was on duty during those hours. The method favored by the mayor's staff was the division of the patrolmen into four platoons, rotating their hours as before, but with two platoons always on duty during the high-crime hours.[15]

As obvious as this solution seems, it took decades of policing before it was "discovered," and it has not been adopted by all police departments yet. Similarly, with the help of a criminal justice research institute, New York City adopted another policing process innovation that in retrospect seems obvious:

In New York City, as in virtually all other American jurisdictions in the middle 1960s, the standard procedure when a person accused of a crime was apprehended by the police was that he was placed under arrest, and then shepherded by the arresting officer through the frequently slow processes of "booking," issuance of a "complaint," and then arraignment in court. . . . In 1964 . . . Vera undertook development of a procedure to substitute the use of summons for arrests . . . the key problem was that the arresting officers wanted . . . considerable knowledge about the accused before relinquishing physical control. Vera therefore supplied to the police precinct houses staff trained to acquire such information quickly . . . [and] the Vera representatives then "scored" each accused on a system designed to estimate his likelihood to actually appear in response to the summons.[16]

In contrast with process innovations, which involve new methods or procedures, product innovations involve the adoption and use of new equipment, devices, or other physical technologies. In various studies of municipal innovations, analysts have typically included at least some examples of product innovations, such as the following.

1. *Infrared heat detection devices* are "thermal imaging devices used by fire fighters in dense smoke to locate victims and the seat of a fire. The Probeye unit manufactured by Hughes Aircraft is one such device specifically engineered for fire service use. Through the eyepiece of the Probeye unit, the user sees a 4-inch-square picture of the area scanned, gradated from black (cold) to red (hot)."[17]

2. *Energy recovery from solid waste* disposal involves special incinerators for burning solid waste, either alone to produce steam for electricity generation or in combination with other fuels.[18] Closely related is the technology for resource recovery from solid waste, an innovation that attracted the interest of the federal government's Office of Technology Assessment (OTA) in the late 1970s and early 1980s. According to OTA:

The United States generates over 135 million tons of municipal solid waste (MSW) each year, and its disposal is a rapidly growing problem in many areas. Conventional methods, such as open dumping, landfill, incineration, and ocean burial, are either too expensive or environmentally unacceptable. Interest is also growing in methods of recovering valuable resources of MSW, which contains two-thirds of the national consumption of paper and glass, one-fifth of the aluminum, and over one-eighth of the iron and steel.[19]

Despite the reference to "methods" in OTA's description, special equipment is necessary to recover resources from solid waste. Hence, this is an important example of a municipal product innovation.

3. *Mechanized refuse collection vehicles* are another product innovation. These vehicles were developed through a collaborative effort by city officials in Scottsdale, Arizona, and industrial engineers, with funding support from the

Environmental Protection Agency. The vehicles "differed from the standard refuse collection vehicle in that one man could operate the truck, which mechanically lifted trash from a location near the curb into the body of the truck."[20]

4. *Mini-pumpers* "are short-wheel-based attack pumpers used by fire departments to respond to small fires and to supplement their standard pumpers. Generally equipped with a 250–300 gallons per minute pump and having a water tank capacity of 250–275 gallons, a mini-pumper has a far smaller pumping and water tank capacity than a full-sized pumper truck. Minis cost about one-third as much as standard pumpers."[21]

5. *OPTICOM* is a hardware system that is meant to deal with the problem of fire trucks (or other emergency equipment) being slowed down by traffic lights.[22] Once installed, it causes traffic lights to change automatically to green for oncoming emergency vehicles.

Many innovations are actually combination process-and-product innovations. This is perhaps most evident with respect to the use of computers in government. Danziger and Kraemer explain that in addition to large scale, repetitive, clerical uses, considerable attention has been given to "managerial utilization of computing, where its more 'brainy' capabilities are employed in management information systems and decision support systems."[23] An example is the use of computers by detectives. In this case, it is especially clear that the introduction of new hardware (i.e., computers) must be combined with both software products (management information systems, data banks, and the means to access them) and *changes in the methods by which detectives process cases.*

The same can be said of many innovations that involve physical technologies. Bingham and colleagues, for example, refer to an important innovation in municipal solid waste collection: the use of one-man, mechanized systems.[24] In this arrangement, "one man handles a collection route, remaining in the cab of his vehicle while performing all collection operations. Special vehicles such as the Barrel Snatcher make it possible for the operator to collect solid wastes without leaving the cab."[25] Clearly, this is an arrangement involving both product innovation (i.e., the special mechanized vehicle) and process innovation (the substitution of one-person crews with mechanized equipment-handling skills for several-person crews with division of labor).

At the extreme, it might be claimed that all product innovations are actually combination product-and-process innovations in practice, in that the introduction of new product technologies usually involves at least some change in operating procedures. Stated another way, even when the most well-developed, clearly defined, physical technologies are at issue, cities typically cannot simply innovate by fiat, as for example by deciding to purchase the equipment. Physical technologies often have very important implications for their users, and major reorganization of work methods is often needed to get product innovations successfully integrated into an ongoing service delivery system.

Similarly, the relationship between technical and administrative innovations has been studied. That distinction is not quite the same as the product-process distinction, but there is some connection. Damanpour and Evan define *technical innovations* as those "that occur in the technical system of an organization and are directly related to the primary work activity of the organization" and *administrative innovations* as "those that occur in the social system of an organization. The social system here refers to the relationships among people who interact to accomplish a particular goal or task."[26] Although this distinction is based on a concept different from that of the product-process distinction, the two overlap in practice. Damanpour and Evan's examples of technical innovations in their study of library services are primarily product innovations, such as various automation systems, the Kurzweil reader or the Optacon for the blind, electronic detection systems, and the like. Their list of administrative innovations is dominated by what we have been calling process innovations—formalized strategic planning, management by objectives, zero-based budgeting, job rotation, flex-time, incentive systems, and the like.

The technical-administrative distinction is an important addition to our discussion of types of innovation because it suggests something about the *relationship among types of innovation* and the consequences for organizations if there is an imbalance among types. Specifically, Damanpour and Evan argue that a balance between technical and administrative innovation is needed for organizational effectiveness. However, they also argue that in practice there tends to be an imbalance, or organization lag, with technical innovations being adopted at a greater rate than are administrative innovations. Using data from public libraries in six northeastern states, they demonstrate empirically that (1) in each of four periods between 1970 and 1982, the extent of technical innovation adoption was greater than the extent of administrative innovation adoption, and (2) the greater the degree of discrepancy between technical and administrative innovation, the lower the library's performance on standard efficiency measures.[27]

In short, there is evidence that the various types of innovations are not just categories useful for illustrating the broad range of innovation phenomena. Rather, product innovation implies the need for some corresponding level of process innovation because work methods must be adapted to accommodate new physical products. Similarly, an imbalance between attention to technical innovation and attention to administrative innovation can impair organizational performance.

The Track Record for Municipal Innovation

Local governments clearly do innovate, many times introducing new methods and products that can greatly improve service delivery. But do local governments innovate enough? This is a difficult question to answer, partly because communities differ from one another in innovativeness and also because there is no obvious standard for what is "enough" innovation. There is evidence of disappointing levels of local government innovation, however.

For example, one study reports on the extent of municipal use of a set of motivational methods intended to enhance productivity. The methods, which may be viewed as process innovations, are all specific forms of either monetary incentives, performance targeting, performance appraisal, or job enrichment. Some, such as performance bonuses or merit wage increase systems, are surely not even on the cutting edge of managerial innovation; they are methods that have been touted and used in at least some settings for a considerable time. The study is based on an Urban Institute–International City Management Association–National Governors Conference survey conducted in 1973, supplemented by two surveys done in 1976, with some follow-up done by the authors.[28]

With respect to monetary incentives for productivity enhancement, 42 percent of the reporting local governments in 1973 used performance-based wage increases, only 25 percent used suggestion award programs, and a miniscule 6 percent used performance bonus systems; as of 1976, only 10 percent of local governments used productivity bargaining, and only 16 percent were using management incentives for productivity improvement.[29] Various job enrichment innovations were also studied, with results suggesting some diffusion of these innovations since 1973. In 1973, only 15 percent of local government respondents reported using job enrichment techniques, but by 1978, Greiner and colleagues report, the number of local government users of this innovation had increased noticeably. Still, less than one-third of local governments were reportedly using this form of process innovation.[30]

More recent research suggests that the relatively low levels of local government use of these and similar process innovations in the mid-1970s simply meant that the take-off point for diffusion of the innovations had not yet occurred. A more recent study compares results of a 1982 survey of municipal use of several innovations with 1976 ICMA survey results on those same items. The comparison suggests a rather dramatic upswing in municipal use of a variety of innovative management tools in this six-year period. Over three-quarters of reporting cities (77 percent) claimed to use program, zero-based, or target-based, budgeting in 1982, compared with half in 1976, for example. Use of performance monitoring rose from 28 percent of surveyed cities in 1976 to 68 percent in 1982, and management incentive programs went from 16 percent of reporting cities in 1976 to nearly half (48 percent) in 1982.[31] Similarly, a study of use of computers by detectives in a sample of municipal governments shows that this innovation is rather broadly and deeply enmeshed in investigative operations.[32]

Although these results suggest a more recent upswing in municipal use of significant innovations, there are still reasons for concern about the adequacy of municipal innovation. For one thing, innovation usage appears to be very unevenly distributed across American municipalities. For example, while nearly two-thirds (60 percent) of cities over 500,000 report using zero-based or target-based budgeting in a 1982 survey, only about one-third (32 percent) of the cities under 50,000 population use this management tool; and while 70 percent of the largest cities report using management incentives, only 44 percent of the smallest cities use them.[33]

Another sign that there have been problems on the municipal innovations front consists of case studies and other evidence showing struggles over municipal initiatives, with full implementation of some innovations never being achieved for one reason or another. Sometimes, the struggle arises because goals are ambiguous and internal leadership is lacking, as was the case with an in-jail "redirection center" for pretrial inmates in New Haven.[34] An attempt to introduce a new electronic data processing arrangement in Oakland was unsuccessful partly because the initial advocate of the new hardware left before the equipment even arrived. In addition, there were oversights and misjudgments on the part of some participants and an organizational situation that stifled critical commentary.[35]

Municipal unions are sometimes obstacles to successful implementation of productivity innovations initiated by management. Police union resistance to New York City's attempt to experiment with one-person police cars in some areas is a frequently cited example.[36] But it can also be the case that innovations fail to be successfully implemented, despite the best efforts of line workers, because the vendor of the technology fails to come through adequately. This was the case with Fort Collins, Colorado's efforts to make use of a partially automated fire engine that would permit two-person rather than three-person teams. After a promising test period, Grumman, the maker of the system, recalled it because the automated hose and reel system did not work reliably and safely. Grumman, perhaps because of liability worries, refused to work further on the system and returned the money invested by the city. No other vendor could be found. Top city officials believe that the fire fighters did their best to make the new system work; inadequate development by the vendor was the problem.[37]

Efforts to understand difficulties in the municipal innovation process need not amount to placing blame on management, or unions, or vendors, or any other particular set of participants. It is apparent, instead, that a host of factors are important in the innovation process and that the fit between the innovation and the context in which it is to be used is a key consideration. We will return to this subject shortly. Before doing so, it is useful to consider one final indicator that levels of municipal innovation have been problematic.

External Agents in the Municipal Innovation Process

In principle, innovation can occur from the bottom up with little external influence and little visibility. Such would be the case if line workers themselves, or perhaps first-level operations managers, suggest novel ways of handling service delivery operations or tinker with equipment to effectively generate new technologies that might improve operations. In general, however, innovation requires investment of resources beyond the extra efforts of individual workers. Productivity-enhancing products and processes are invented and improved through processes of research and development that can be very costly. Individual local governments are unlikely to devote resources to research and development, partly because of the resource pressures of day-to-day service delivery and partly because investment in research and development is a classic collective good. That is, all local governments benefit from innovative processes and products for municipal applications, but it is not rational for any single local government to bear the substantial costs of research and development that will bring about these benefits for all.

As a result, municipal innovation is heavily influenced by external agents, most notably the federal government and various professional associations. In response to perceptions of productivity problems and lagging innovation, these external agencies have initiated a broad variety of programs and policies designed to collectively enhance local government innovation. The result is a mode of innovation from the ouside in that has gotten considerably more attention than the ongoing, smaller scale, and less visible form of innovation that occurs from the bottom up.

Either alone or in combination with various professional associations, the federal government has devoted considerable resources and attention to the issue of municipal innovation for productivity, which sometimes has come in the form of direct federal subsidies of technological innovations in one or a few cities that presumably could serve as demonstration sites. For example, the St. Louis police department's introduction of an advanced squad car tracking system built by the Boeing Corporation was made possible by federal grant support. In its heyday, funding from the Law Enforcement Assistance Administration underwrote a variety of municipal innovations in policing, often involving sophisticated equipment and leading to some criticism of the federal government's priorities in this area.

At least as important are the many federal government initiatives undertaken in conjunction with professional associations, foundations, universities, or research institutes. For example, the National Science Foundation created an Intergovernmental Science and Research Utilization (ISRU) program:

> ISRU has worked successfully with a number of communities in developing and testing technological solutions to municipal problems. While the pattern varies from city to city, the programs all involve the placement of an experienced engineer on the chief executive's staff, or the designation of an engineer from industry or academia as a technology advisor. The advisor is backed up by a nearby industry, university research lab, or some combination of technical resources.[38]

A better known example of this form of joint assistance is the Rand Corporation's efforts in New York City, especially during the Lindsay administration and immediately thereafter. The Rand Corporation had been established by the U.S. Air Force in the late 1940s in California as a think tank. In 1967, then-Mayor Lindsay invited Rand to help city departments, and in response, some Rand researchers did move to New York and begin work with city operations. Eventually, Rand's New York site was officially established as a separate think tank, the New York City-Rand Institute, which received funding support from both the federal government and the city. Several innovations, including the use of computerized modeling for water quality planning and "slippery water" (with polymers added to reduce friction and increase flow for fire fighting) were adopted and used by New York City with the help of the Rand Institute.[39]

More recently, the federal government has supported information dissemination networks to encourage municipal innovation. In the period 1983 to 1986, for example, the National Science Foundation, with supplementary funds from the U.S. Department of Transportation, contracted with the International City Management Association (ICMA) for a project called "Targeted Innovations Dissemination: An Approach to Maintaining and Expanding the State and Local Government Network." This project called for ICMA, together with the Council of State Governments and the Council for International Urban Liaison, to find and disseminate information about useful state or local government innovations. Ironically, this project spawned a side program—ICMA's "Fabulous Flops" program—which provides information about unsuccessful innovations. The idea is that failures are quite common and managers must learn to tolerate multiple failures yet still remain willing to make innovative efforts.[40]

In addition to joint projects for information dissemination by the federal government and professional associations, city officials are targeted for many other forms of information about techniques for productivity enhancement and service delivery or management innovations. Information is channeled through associations of line officials, such as the American Public Works Association, the International Association of Chiefs of Police, the American Water Works Association, and many others. It also comes from combination entitites like Public Technology, Inc. (PTI), a research and development organization formed by ICMA, the National League of Cities, the U.S. Conference of Mayors, the Council of State Governments, the National Association of Counties, and the National Governor's Conference.[41]

The existence of these many efforts to enhance municipal productivity and innovation suggests that the federal government and professional associations are responding to perceived productivity problems and less than adequate levels of municipal innovation. Although there have been many success stories along the way, there is also evidence of some disappointment at the results of these efforts. One close observer of the situation explains:

> [M]ost students of technology transfer are persuaded that federal efforts to date have been less than successful in accomplishing their goals. Many hardware and managerial innovations that could be helpful in mitigating urban problems are lying fallow. Either they are not adopted by their intended users, or if adopted, they are not implemented and placed into routine service.

They are often abandoned or so diluted that they cease to be innovative in any sense.[42]

More recently, a pair of researchers surveyed chief administrators of local government concerning their familiarity with productivity enhancement literature emanating from the American Society for Public Administration, ICMA, Public Technology, Inc., and many other prominent institutions and individuals involved in information dissemination. The results are disappointing, for they "expose a general lack of familiarity with serious productivity improvement literature directed toward the public sector."[43]

In their analysis of the role of professional associations in encouraging municipal innovation, researchers have found some mismatch between municipal officials' views of the key stumbling blocks to innovation and professional associations' efforts. Problems such as "availability of local funds" and "attitudes of local elected officials" or other higher-ups are highest on the list of factors that local officials see as important in adopting innovations. "Creating a climate for local acceptance" is the major remaining challenge from their point of view. Yet professional associations are geared more toward needs assessment and transmitting relevant information about innovations. Professional associations get high marks for their efforts along these lines, but they do not address the key remaining obstacle of creating a climate for local acceptance.[44]

In short, despite federal support, professional association projects, and other initiatives to encourage municipal innovation from the outside in, there is disappointment and an uneven track record of success. Perhaps for this reason, there has been a scaling back of federal efforts in recent years. These federally funded efforts have in part been replaced by locally devised, collaborative efforts to enhance municipal innovation. For example, in 1987 a network of 165 local governments in several states was being reorganized into a clearinghouse for innovative products, relying on dues of member communities for financial support. The Innovation Group had previously been supported with federal funds that were lost during the Reagan administration. This and similar networks in Florida, the Carolinas, Virginia, California, Colorado, Arizona, and Nevada show that, despite the disappointments of some federal efforts, there is municipal interest in productivity-enhancing innovations.[45]

Why do some organizations appear to be more innovative than others? What are the facilitators of innovation and what are the inhibitors? The following section takes up these questions.

THE DETERMINANTS OF MUNICIPAL INNOVATION

Research on innovation is often criticized for the proliferation of contrasting results that has been generated and the lack of cumulation, or synthesis. Part of the confusion arises from the fact that various questions have been asked and correspondingly various research approaches have been used. For example, a substantial body of work focuses on the question: Why do some cities or organizations innovate more (or earlier) than do others? To answer this, attention quite naturally focuses on characteristics of the organization and community setting, and comparative cross-sectional analysis is employed to account for different rates of adoption of innovations. An early but important codification of this approach and application to the municipal situation was provided by Bingham, who investigated several broad categories of community and organizational characteristics that are summarized in Table 3.3.[46]

One important category of determinants of innovation not included in Table 3.3 is the set of characteristics of new technologies that may have a bearing on the likelihood of the adoption of those technologies. Seven significant attributes of technological innovations themselves are likely to be relevant determinants of the likelihood of adoption and use: degree to which the new technologies require change in existing operating patterns, cost, reversibility, susceptibility to partial or prototype implementation, complexity, operability (which is to say confidence in the feasibility of the innovation based on testing in other settings), and breadth of impact.[47] Not surprisingly, it is expected that innovation is less likely to the extent that the new technologies at issue demand high levels of change in operating routines, are costly, are difficult to abandon if unsatisfactory and unsuitable for local trial implementation, are of unknown trustworthiness, involve sophisticated equipment or procedures that go beyond the normal range of expertise available, and have wide-ranging and significant consequences for the organization.

Research that focuses on the determinants of innovation generates impor-

TABLE 3.3. SOME HYPOTHESIZED DETERMINANTS OF MUNICIPAL INNOVATION

Determinants	Hypothesized Relationship to Innovation
Community Environment	
City Size	+
Dominance of conservative values	−
Organizational Environment	
Level of federal or state aid	+
Proximity to other innovating cities	+
Professionalism of local government	+
Existence of slack resources	+
Vendor activity	+
Organizational Characteristics	
Reformed government structure	+
Appointed decisionmaking body	+
Formal decisionmaking structure	−
Centralized decision structure	−
Organizational size	+
Level of funding	+
Presence of employee unions	−

Source: Adapted from Richard Bingham, *The Adoption of Innovation by Local Government* (Lexington, MA: Heath, 1976). Reprinted with permission.

tant insights about community and organizational contexts that are more and less conducive to innovation. It can, in a sense, be used as a menu for diagnosing the potential for the success of innovation in particular settings.

However, this approach is limited as well. For one thing, it has not yielded stable, generalizable information about the relative importance of various determinants of innovation. For example, the existence of slack resources (i.e., currently unused or underused resources, ranging from budget to personnel flexibility) is an interesting and problematic candidate as a determinant of innovation because it encaptures a key dilemma. If slack resources are needed for innovation, then fiscally stressed cities that are in dire need of innovation to rescue themselves from declining quality of service will actually be less capable of innovation than more fiscally advantaged cities. An interesting pattern of well-off cities getting better and problem settings getting worse is implied by the specification of slack resources as a determinant. But there is not, in fact, consistent empirical evidence that slack resources constitute an important determinant of innovation, nor for that matter is there consistent evidence on the importance of centralization of decision structure and other organization characteristics cited in Table 3.3 as determinants of innovation. The contradictions in existing studies have led some researchers to conclude, "A thorough understanding of the effects of resource scarcity on innovation in public organizations will require considerably more research."[48]

In short, there is much uncertainty still about the generalizability of various alleged determinants of innovation, and we do not know much about relative magnitude of importance and interaction effects. For example, if slack resources are important in the innovation game, can cities suffering fiscal strain nevertheless innovate if they have a combination of high levels of professionalism and dominant progressive values in the community? Can close proximity to other innovating cities effectively compensate for a lack of vendor activity in the community? Just how damaging to innovation efforts relative to other considerations are factors such as strong employee unions?

Apart from these unanswered questions, research based on the determinants of innovation is limited in that many of the explanatory variables are not readily controlled by local policymakers. Public officials cannot typically change proximity to other innovating cities, city size, or dominant community values. Such variables may enhance *understanding* of innovation conditions, but they provide little guidance to decisionmakers about useful strategies for maximizing the chances of successful innovation or about key pitfalls to be avoided in innovation campaigns.

A PROCESS UNDERSTANDING OF INNOVATION

There is an alternate strand of scholarship in innovation that has greater potential for providing insights to decisionmakers about aspects of innovation that they can control. In contrast with the multicity, quantitative studies that constitute the determinants approach, this alternate approach (which we will designate the *process* approach) relies more heavily on individual case studies that trace processes of innovation in particular settings over time, leading ultimately to diagnoses and prescriptions about innovation that draw from the literature of broader implementation and organizational change.

Perhaps the most important initial contributions to the process approach are those that offer conceptualizations of innovation as involving distinctive stages. Everett Rogers, for example, emphasizes that even after technological innovations are adopted, successful innovation requires a series of reinvention stages in which the innovation and preexisting organizational practices and structures are modified to fit each other. Specifically Rogers specifies (1) a redefining stage, in which end-users and others tinker with the innovation to get it to fit the organization's needs better, (2) a structuring stage in which the organization's structure is altered to accommodate the innovation, and (3) a relating stage in which actual, day-to-day behaviors of organization members are changed to accommodate the innovation.[49]

Others have developed similar typologies of stages of innovation or levels of use of innovation. For example, in an influential piece, Hall and Loucks identify eight levels of use of an innovation, ranging from total nonuse (in which the focal individual has little knowledge of or interest in the innovation) through orientation and preparation stages (in which the individual gathers information about the innovation, decides to use it, and prepares for its use) through mechanical and routine use stages to refinement, integration, and renewal stages in which the individual might change usage of the innovation, find ways to link usage with the efforts of others, and seek modifications in the innovation.[50]

Unlike the Hall and Loucks typology, which emphasizes various levels of actual use, the outcome of Rogers's reinvention stages can be either success or failure. Success comes in the form of the institutionalization of the innovation so that it becomes part of routine behavior and is no longer innovative. Failure involves either active rejection or passive nonuse because organization members cannot manage to adapt the innovation to local circumstances and they conclude that the innovation is inappropriate. Most important, stage theories of innovation make clear that an authoritative decision to adopt an innovative technology by no means translates into successful innovation.

A good example is provided in Starling's case study of the adoption of new electronic data processing (EDP) equipment in the city of Oakland, California. An expensive new system was installed, but it failed to function as expected. On-site personnel were not able to modify it so that it would work. The new system was not really rejected, nor was the initial adoption decision reversed. Rather, because the organization had such a large financial stake in the system, there was a long period of frustrating attempts to fix the system. This is a case of innovation failure because implementation was stymied despite the fact that official commitment to the innovation was sustained over a long time.[51]

The process approach to innovation provides several emphases that are missing from the determinants approach. It highlights the extent to which innovation is a process of mutual adaptation, so that new technologies can be fitted to existing organizational practices by tinkering with both. It also underscores the tremendous potential for the innovation process to derail, even though higher-level authorities have officially ordered the adoption of the innovation. In so doing, this approach also emphasizes the importance of what happens after the adoption phase, and it draws attention to the activities of lower-level employees whose activities can either make or break the innovation effort. Not surprisingly, then, the study of innovation converges with much of the conceptual work on implementation more generally and with larger concerns about organizational change and employee motivation. Rogers's reinvention stages become the setting for all the challenges that have been observed as organizations attempt to implement new policies.

The result is renewed attention to prescriptive aspects of innovation research and a focus on the things that are subject to manipulation, if not control, by managers. Loveless and Bozeman, for example, argue that ". . . some determinants of innovation are more likely than others to provide the public manager with 'leverage points.' "[52] With respect to organizational design features, they note that although some structural characteristics are not under the immediate control of the innovation-minded manager, others are: "Managers seeking to apply the lessons of innovation research in the design of organizations are well advised to encourage more organic organization structures . . . 'flatter' organizations (with lesser degrees of vertical differentiation) and organizations with greater horizontal complexity are often more innovative."[53]

These prescriptions are consistent with an emerging consensus on the nature of the innovative organization. This consensus, derived primarily from study of private sector organizations, emphasizes the need for flexible, nonhierarchical, participative organizational settings if innovation is to be expected. For example, Kanter concludes that to be innovative, organizations must be structured in an integrative rather than a segmented fashion.[54] Integrative structures are those that emphasize horizontal interdependencies rather than vertical dependencies and that facilitate communication through overlapping tasks, loose job definitions, and a lack of rigid subspecialty structures.

Reich makes parallel arguments concerning the nature of innovation in contemporary work settings. According to Reich, it is no longer possible to conceive of sharp distinctions between creative, top-level entrepreneurs and the drones who simply carry out their ideas in a traditional production process. Rather, contemporary society is characterized by products and services produced in environments in which innovation is piecemeal, ongoing, and linked to the many small ideas of lower-level employees. Information and ability are widely dispersed in the organization, and top management is not expected to be the primary source of new ideas and applications. This form of collective entrepreneurialism requires integrated work groupings and a minimum of rigid, hierarchical barriers to communication.[55]

Individual skills are integrated into a group whose collective capacity to innovate becomes something more than the simple sum of its parts. . . . Each participant appreciates what the others are trying to do; he is constantly on the lookout for small adjustments that will speed and smooth the evolution of the whole.[56]

Unfortunately, one cannot assume that the motivation to engage in such collective innovation is always present. When innovation is imposed from the top rather than derived from collective entrepreneurialism, the potential for difficulty is even greater. The process approach, with its focus on the dynamics by which individual members of organizations grapple with the demands of innovation, suggests diagnostic tools and prescriptive messages concerning the problematic behaviors of lower-level employees and middle managers. Sorg, for example, shows that street-level bureaucrats may engage in a variety of behaviors other than straightforward compliance with what a new policy or technology entails. They may *unintentionally* fail to conform either through excessive behavior (adding elements that were not originally intended) or deficient behavior (leaving out elements that are supposed to be a part of the new policy or other innovation). They may also *intentionally* resist conforming through strategies ranging from replacement of the official innovation with some other innovation, ritualistic activity that gives the appearance of conforming without the substance, delay, bluffing, and various forms of voice behavior (such as complaints and threats to quit) intended to get authorities to modify the new policy or technology.[57]

Although primarily useful as a diagnostic tool, Sorg's typology suggests prescriptive approaches as well. Street-level bureaucrats engaging in unintentional noncompliance through either excessive or deficient behavior may be engaging in the very sorts of adaptation that are part and parcel of Rogers's reinvention stages. Reinvention may be necessary to fit the new policy or technology to actual circumstances. This being the case, managers would do well to learn why street-level employees are adding to or subtracting from the originally envisioned innovation, rather than to clamp down with harsh control mechanisms designed to force compliance. Similarly, employees engaging in voice behavior may be communicating useful information about unforeseen contingencies and needed adaptations. Ritualism and delay do nothing to facilitate innovation, however. They do not constitute efforts to fit a new policy or technology to existing routines through mutual adaptation, and they do not provide managers with feedback about adaptations that are perceived as important.

For middle managers, the process approach to innovation studies offers a variety of prescriptions. Innovation-minded managers must foster external communication and the development of collaborative relationships with other organizations.[58] Other commentators emphasize the importance of encouraging initiative and using incentives in the form of prior investments rather than after-the-fact material rewards.[59]

THE FEASIBILITY OF PUBLIC SECTOR INNOVATION

The process approach generates numerous prescriptions designed to facilitate innovation, but it is one thing to offer prescriptions and quite another to see them realized. It could be argued that much of what has been written about innovation has a certain infinite regressive quality when applied to public sector organizations. First, we ask what it would take for the public sector to be more innovative. We discover that public sector decisionmakers must develop more horizontally complex organizations, greater incentives for individual creativity, and other hallmarks of a culture of innovation. But then, we may ask, what are the obstacles to the creation of these structures and practices that are alleged to facilitate innovation?

This concluding section offers some observations about the feasibility of greater public sector innovativeness in the political culture that characterizes the United States. As we have seen, research on productivity enhancement and innovation in the public sector focuses on community and organizational characteristics that are determinants of innovation and individual behaviors and on processes that show how technological innovations can be either successfully implemented or derailed in specific settings. Much of this literature yields optimistic conclusions concerning the capacity of public managers to facilitate innovation.

We would be less than realistic, however, if we did not acknowledge some key aspects of the American political culture that are not congenial to this drive for greater innovation in the public sector. Our political culture includes a strong strand of distrust of government and beliefs about the importance of limiting government. Accountability is, as it were, a more basic and pervasive value with respect to government than is efficiency. Many of the stultifying aspects of public sector bureaucratic organization that are commonly accepted as interfering with innovation endure because they are meant to ensure accountability. Multiple checkpoints, management controls, reporting requirements, and clear job definitions are not useful in encouraging creativity and innovation but nevertheless remain in place. The trade-off between accountability and innovativeness is not necessarily made clear, however. The opportunity costs of accountability controls typically go unstated. They exist, nonetheless, and their acceptance suggests the relative importance of accountability.

Stated another way, our political culture exhibits more concern with overactive government than with what Hirschman calls "flabby monopoly."[60] It is for this reason that innovation research drawing from private sector concepts leaves an odd residue of discomfort when applied to the public sector. For example, the concept of entrepreneurship has been taken from its private sector context and used to highlight the significant roles that some individuals play in mobilizing public sector organizations for innovation.[61] Useful as this application may be, it fails to confront the fact that the American public is at best ambivalent about entrepreneurship in the public sector. Entrepreneurship smacks of bureaucratic "empire building"—certainly not a positive symbol; nor is it demonstrable that risk-taking on the part of government is desired. One might more easily conclude that local government in America is expected, above all else, to be *reliable*. Uninterrupted service and stable taxes and predictable patterns of action seem much more valued than risk-taking, creativity, and innovation, even with the intent to promote efficiency.

Unlike many of the innovations discussed by analysts of private sector organizations, large areas of creativity are circumscribed for public sector officials who are not generally expected to derive whole new products and markets. Rather, public sector creativity tends to be restricted to cost-cutting methods for meeting an existing service responsibility. Public service professionals sometimes define new "markets" in the sense that increasingly broader client groups are captured by the professionals' definition of what is problematic and who needs their attention. Critiques of such professional dominance abound. The very existence of these critiques suggests the ambivalence that both American intellectuals and the American public have about an activist public sector.

In short, it is not clear that the American political culture provides a clear and compelling basis for governmental innovation in the broad, entrepreneurial, risk-taking, and new-product sense. Rather, the ideal of public sector innovativeness is narrower and efficiency-oriented. Without having them violate a variety of constraints, standards, rules, and procedures, we wish that local government officials could nevertheless find new and cheaper ways of solving established problems. In this sense, public sector innovation involves a constant search for ways to do as much or more with less. Innovation as creative penny-pinching may seem more trivial than entrepreneurial innovation, but it has at least the advantage of being consistent with important values of our political culture.

Recent publications by the International City Management Association show the importance of management action for enhancing such creative penny-pinching. For example, Raudsepp offers 101 different ways for management to facilitate employees' creative potential. Some of the more interesting include the following:

- Concentrate efforts on those aspects of organizational culture . . . that inhibit and stifle innovation.
- Dramatize particularly those problems to which creative solutions are now known to be needed.
- Match as much as possible project tasks and objectives with the true interests of each of the individuals involved.
- Encourage and motivate subordinates to come back again and again to the same problem until there is a creative breakthrough.
- Make sure that the most promising people are not bogged down with specific tasks every moment of the day.

- Creative people need time to think, without having their thoughts tied exclusively to a particular activity or task.
- Encourage calculated risk taking because it is an important ingredient in growth and innovation.
- Use creativity-related performance dimensions in your performance appraisals.[62]

In a related vein, McClure suggests important pitfalls to be avoided in any productivity-improvement initiative.[63] These include weak, top-level commitment to the effort, mindless fascination with fashionable productivity techniques, lack of clarity about the reasons for a productivity improvement initiative, and failure to assess in advance whether the organization is prepared for the initiative. Specifically, McClure suggests six important questions that should be asked as part of an assessment of the organization's readiness for an innovation and productivity enhancement program:

1. Are management-employee-union relations such that employees would support management's desire to tackle productivity improvement?
2. Does the company have a positive rating among its employees on such issues as working conditions, pay levels, company policy and administration, and job security?
3. Is top management willing to share with employees at all levels the economic benefits that will accrue from improvements in productivity?
4. Is the company's accounting system healthy and flexible enough to accept changes required to portray productivity effectively?
5. Is top management willing to listen to the employees?
6. Does top management believe the company's performance depends substantially on employee efforts?[64]

If the answers to many of these questions are "no," the implication is that the organization is not really ready to push for innovation and productivity improvement.

DISCUSSION QUESTIONS AND EXERCISES

1. To what extent are process and product innovations intertwined? To answer this question with a specific analysis, choose a product innovation—either one of those mentioned in this chapter or some other one with which you are familiar. Discuss the various changes in service delivery operations, work arrangements, or procedures that might need to take place if the product innovation were adopted.
2. Choose some public sector organization with which you are familiar or about which you can do some preliminary research. Do a diagnosis of the organization's potential for innovation, using the determinants of innovation in this chapter as guideposts (see Table 3.3). For example, does the organization have slack resources? Does it have a high level of professionalism? Is the decisionmaking structure decentralized or

centralized? Be prepared to explain what indicators you used to assess such factors as level of professionalism and degree of centralization of the decisionmaking structure. Should the various factors be weighted equally to derive an overall diagnosis? Explain.

3. Using the same organization that you identified for question No. 2, continue your diagnosis of potential for innovation by addressing the six assessment questions suggested by John McClure (see concluding section of this chapter). If you do not have information at hand to answer the questions, consider the following: How might a management assistant in the organization go about obtaining information to answer the six questions?

NOTES

1. George W. Downs and Patrick D. Larkey, *The Search for Government Efficiency* (New York: Random House, 1986), p. 8.
2. David Ammons, *Municipal Productivity* (New York: Praeger, 1984), p. 7.
3. Richard Bingham, Brett Hawkins, John Frendreis, and Mary LeBlanc, *Professional Associations and Municipal Innovation* (Madison: University of Wisconsin Press, 1981), p. 5.
4. Rosabeth Moss Kanter, *The Change Masters* (New York: Simon and Schuster, 1983), p. 17.
5. Ammons, *Municipal Productivity,* p. 14.
6. Ibid.
7. Douglas Yates, *The Ungovernable City* (Cambridge, MA: MIT Press, 1977), p. 18.
8. Downs and Larkey, *Search for Government Efficiency,* p. 23.
9. Bingham et al., *Professional Associations and Municipal Innovation,* p. 10.
10. Rackham Fukuhara, "Productivity Improvement in Cities," *Municipal Year Book 1977* (Washington, DC: ICMA, 1977), pp. 193-200.
11. John Greiner, Harry Hatry, Margo Koss, Annie Millar, and Jane Woodward, *Productivity and Motivation* (Washington, DC: Urban Institute Press, 1981).
12. Theodore Poister and Robert McGowan, "The Use of Management Tools in Municipal Government," *Public Administration Review* 44 (1984): 215-223.
13. Greiner et al., *Productivity and Motivation,* p. 8.
14. Peter Szanton, "Urban Public Services? Ten Case Studies," in *Innovation and Implementation in Public Organizations,* ed. Richard Nelson and Douglas Yates (Lexington, MA: Heath, 1978), pp. 117-142.
15. Ibid., p. 121.
16. Ibid., p. 128.
17. Bingham et al., *Professional Associations and Municipal Innovation,* p. 32.
18. Ibid., p. 33.
19. Office of Technology Assessment, *An Assessment of Technology for Local Development* Undated. (Washington, DC: U.S. Government Printing Office), pp. 7-8.
20. Robert Yin, Karen Heald, and Mary Vogel, *Tinkering with the System* (Lexington, MA: Heath, 1977), p. 45.
21. Bingham et al., *Professional Associations and Municipal Innovation,* p. 33.
22. W. Henry Lambright, *Technology Transfer to Cities: Processes of Choice at the Local Level* (Boulder, CO: Westview Press, 1979), p. 98.

23. James Danziger and Kenneth Kraemer, "Computerized Data-Based Systems and Productivity Among Professional Workers: The Case of Detectives," *Public Administration Review* 45 (January/February 1985): 196.
24. Bingham et al., *Professional Associations and Municipal Innovation*, p. 32.
25. Ibid.
26. Fariborz Damanpour and William Evan, "Organizational Innovation and Performance: The Problem of 'Organizational Lag,'" *Administrative Science Quarterly* 29 (September 1984): 394.
27. Ibid., pp. 402–405.
28. Greiner et al., *Productivity and Motivation*, p. 11.
29. Ibid., p. 31.
30. Ibid., p. 239.
31. Poister and McGowan, "Use of Management Tools," p. 218.
32. Danziger and Kraemer, "Computerized Data-Based Systems: Detectives," p. 198.
33. Poister and McGowan, "Use of Management Tools," p. 220.
34. Malcolm Feeley, "The New Haven Redirection Center," in *Innovation and Implementation in Public Organizations*, ed. Richard Nelson and Douglas Yates (Lexington, MA: Heath, 1978), pp. 39–68.
35. Jay Starling, *Municipal Coping Strategies* (Beverly Hills: Sage, 1986).
36. Bingham et al., *Professional Associations and Municipal Innovation*, p. 11.
37. John Arnold, Wendy Williams, and Linda Hopkins, "Three Fabulous Flops," *Public Management* 66 (December 1984): 7.
38. Bingham et al., *Professional Associations and Municipal Innovation*, pp. 17–18.
39. Szanton, "Urban Public Services?" p. 125.
40. William Hansell, "The Fabulous Flops Award or 'In Search of the Perfect Failure,'" *Public Management* 66 (December 1984): 3–4.
41. Bingham et al., *Professional Associations and Municipal Innovation*, p. 54.
42. Lambright, *Technology Transfer to Cities*, p. 2.
43. David Ammons and Joseph King, "Productivity Improvement in Local Government: Its Place Among Competing Priorities," *Public Administration Review* 43 (March/April 1983): 117.
44. Bingham et al., *Professional Associations and Municipal Innovation*, p. 104.
45. Elizabeth Voisin, "Innovators Breathe New Life Into Their Calling," *City & State* (May 1987): 33.
46. Richard Bingham, *The Adoption of Innovation by Local Government* (Lexington, MA: Heath, 1976).
47. Lambright et al., *Technology Transfer to Cities*, pp. 73–80.
48. Stephen Loveless and Barry Bozeman, "Innovation and the Public Manager," in *Handbook of Organization Management*, ed. William B. Eddy (New York: Dekker, 1983), p. 399.
49. Everett Rogers, "Reinvention During the Innovation Process," in *The Diffusion of Innovations: An Assessment*, ed. M. Radner et al. (Evanston, IL: Northwestern University, 1978).
50. Gene Hall and Susan Loucks, "A Developmental Model for Determining Whether the Treatment Is Actually Implemented," *American Educational Research Journal* 14 (Summer): 263–276.
51. Starling, *Municipal Coping Strategies*, pp. 235–264.
52. Loveless and Bozeman, "Innovation and the Public Manager," p. 406.

53. Ibid.
54. Kanter, *Change Masters,* pp. 180–181.
55. Robert B. Reich, *Tales of a New America* (New York: Vintage Books, 1987), pp. 123–124.
56. Ibid., p. 124.
57. James D. Sorg, "A Typology of Implementation Behaviors of Street-Level Bureaucrats," *Policy Studies Review* 2 (1983): 391–406.
58. Loveless and Bozeman, "Innovation and the Public Manager," p. 407.
59. Kanter, *Change Masters,* pp. 129–155.
60. Albert Hirschman, *Exit, Voice, and Loyalty* (Cambridge, MA: Harvard University Press, 1970).
61. Dennis Palumbo, Michael Musheno, and Steven Maynard-Moody, "Public Sector Entrepreneurs: The Shakers and Doers of Program Innovation," in *Performance and Credibility,* ed. Joseph S. Wholey, Mark A. Abramson and Christopher Bellavita (Lexington, MA: Heath, 1986), pp. 69–82.
62. Eugene Raudsepp, "101 Ways to Spark Your Employees' Creative Potential," in *Productivity Improvement Techniques,* ed. John Matzer, Jr. (Washington, DC: ICMA, 1986), pp. 121–131.
63. John McClure, "What to Avoid in a Productivity Improvement Effort," in *Productivity Improvement Techniques,* ed. Matzer (Washington, DC: ICMA, 1986), pp. 24–28.
64. Ibid., p. 26.

CHAPTER 4

The Citizen's Role
in Local Public Affairs

What participatory role does the citizen play in public affairs? If the question were about participation in *national* public affairs, the response would focus primarily on voting and related forms of electoral involvement. In the context of *local* public affairs, however, voting is only one, and perhaps one of the less significant, forms of citizen participation. This chapter considers four areas of citizen participation other than electoral involvement:

1. Open government policies like public hearings requirements and open meetings laws that pave the way for direct monitoring, oversight, and input into public decisionmaking by citizens.
2. Information-gleaning devices such as citizen surveys and government units for handling citizen complaints about individual concerns.
3. Neighborhood organization activity.
4. Coproduction strategies that bring the citizen into collaborative operations for service delivery alongside public service professionals.

The local electoral process provides a setting for other kinds of citizen participation as well as the four just listed. Voting in local elections is limited, however, even by comparison with the disappointing turnouts in national elections. Only about half the eligible population votes in presidential elections—the most visible of all American elections; typically, local elections draw only about 25 to 30 percent of eligible voters to the polls.[1] Voting in local elections is particularly diminished where there are institutions of reform government. That is, adoption of nonpartisanship and the council-manager plan have had a negative impact on local voter turnout.[2] In more specialized local elections, such as school board elections or referenda on local bond issues, the turnout is likely to be even more dismal.

In addition, research on urban voting is also quite limited.[3] The research that is available suggests an "ethnocultural interpretation of urban electoral politics"—that is, that local elections are contests between coalitions based on racial and ethnic group identification and partisan affiliation.[4] Furthermore, this interpretation holds for elections on issues (i.e., referenda) as well as candidate elections.[5] It holds even in ostensibly reformed, nonpartisan settings as well as nonreformed settings, providing there is racial and ethnic heterogeneity. The importance of endorsement by newspapers, community organizations, and partisan groups is substantial, whether or not parties are officially on the ballot.

Minuscule turnouts in many local elections, coupled with the limited research interpreting local voting patterns and the lack of a distinctive theory of *urban* voting, suggest that electoral involvement cannot be a key focus in a discussion of citizen participation in local affairs. Other forms of participation, however, have been the focal point of more visible activity and scholarly interest.

In large and small cities across America, citizens are participating in local governments' affairs in ways other than electoral politics. On the cooperative side, they are serving on various municipal boards and commissions, participating in goal setting and planning exercises with city officials, working on cleanup campaigns, crime prevention programs, and other collaborative projects of their neighborhood organization and city hall, attending city hearings on matters of interest to them, responding to municipal surveys designed to find out about neighborhood needs and citizens' evaluations of city service delivery, and engaging in many other collaborative or cooperative activities with city hall. As this chapter shows, however, citizen participation may be adversarial and confrontational rather than collaborative and cooperative. In fact, some of the most notable case studies of citizen participation involve heated conflicts between community groups and city officials over matters such as redevelopment projects.[6]

Several themes weave through the discussion of citizen participation in this chapter. One is the ongoing tension between professional city government and populist impulses. Much of the drive for new avenues for citizen participation derives from this tension. There are contradictions between our expectations of citizen involvement in a democracy and actual levels of citizen involvement in complex, technical decisions or in heavily bureaucratized and strongly professionalized service delivery operations. These contradictions become especially acute under historical conditions that underscore the distance between city hall and the community, as when proposed redevelopment projects threaten a neighborhood or when racial minorities perceive hostility or nonresponsiveness from city officials. Those were the characteristics precipitating incidents of city-community conflict in the 1950s and 1960s, respectively. More recently, tensions between city hall and the public are also highlighted whenever citizens perceive that city officials are attempting to insulate themselves from public input on issues that are highly technical but that have important and controversial effects on the community.

Whatever the source, when the contradictions between populist notions of citizen involvement and actual patterns of local practice are highlighted, calls for new forms of citizen participation typically follow. Innovative citizen participation programs are sometimes adopted like other innovations, as locals try out programs that have been successful elsewhere. For example, many programs that involve citizens in large-scale community planning exercises have been modeled on the successful and well-known Goals for Dallas program.[7]

Historically, the call for new forms of citizen participation in urban governance has often come from federal funding agencies or state government, thus giving citizen participation an unwholesome, mandated flavor from the viewpoint of local officials. For example, federal funding programs, such as the Community Development Block Grant and General Revenue Sharing, typically included requirements for public hearings or other forms of citizen input. These externally imposed programs for citizen participation do not always endure in their original, full-blown form. They are often revised by the "feds" and can disappear along with the grant funding program to which they are attached.

Although external mandates fade, federal grant programs disappear, and citizens lose interest in once-innovative citizen participation efforts, a legacy of citizen participation policies and programs often remains. However, this legacy differs across cities because of local experiences with various citizen participation innovations. In some cities—Dayton, Ohio, for example—efforts to get neighborhood residents involved in the federal Model Cities program have blossomed into an enduring and substantial role for neighborhood organizations in municipal affairs.[8] In other cities, experiments with neighborhood involvement have been less successful, or for other reasons a durable structure of neighborhood organizations has not been created to sustain this avenue for citizen involvement. In some settings, the use of municipal surveys to gather citizen input has been successful and useful enough that an ongoing citizen survey effort has been institutionalized. In many other settings, the whole concept of citizen surveys has been discredited, and the device is not used.

Yet another key theme to be emphasized is the expectations-disappointment dynamic that so often seems to accompany citizen participation initiatives. As we will see, the disappointment frequently results because of conflicting expectations about the degree of citizen control or power sharing that will occur. City officials usually do not turn over resource control to neighborhood organizations or allow decisions to be dictated by the citizen input they have solicited. Some analysts have concluded that citizen participation efforts are therefore often limited and trivial.[9] This chapter considers whether such a conclusion is truly warranted.

WHY CITIZEN PARTICIPATION PROGRAMS?

In a representative democracy, why should there be a need for additional channels for citizen participation in governmental affairs—citizen boards, neighborhood councils, and the like? This section considers three perspectives, each
offering a reason for greater citizen participation:

1. A perspective on the importance of intensive citizen participation for
   authentic democracy.
2. A perspective that assigns citizen participation programs the role of
   compensating for the inadequacies and biases of our institutions of
   representative democracy.
3. A perspective that emphasizes the capacity of citizen participation
   programs to assist government officials with planning, policymaking,
   and implementation.

With respect to the importance of citizen participation for authentic
democracy, there is an important intellectual current in American political life
that rejects the idea that citizenship in a representative democracy primarily
consists of periodic involvement in the selection of officials through electoral
processes. From this point of view, occasional opportunities to cast a ballot in
favor of one or another candidate make a pale imitation of full participation in
politics. Rather, real democracy demands much more intense involvement on
the part of citizens, so that they truly learn about public affairs, contribute to the
community, and in the process become more authentic democratic individuals.

From this viewpoint, greater political participation is at least as important
for the development of the individual's character as it is significant for the
conduct of public affairs. One of the strongest spokespersons for this view is
Pateman, who has argued:

> Finally, the justification for a democratic system in the participatory theory
> of democracy rests primarily on the human results that accrue from the
> participatory process. One might characterise the participatory model as one
> where maximum input (participation) is required and where output includes
> not just policies (decisions) but also the development of the social and political
> capacities of each individual, so that there is "feedback" from output to
> input.[10]

The field of public administration has more recently generated a parallel
argument concerning the responsibility of public sector managers to enhance
citizen interest in government. In a democratic setting, authentic public administration is said to require such responsibility for the nurturing of civic involvement. To those who believe that bureaucrats should be insulated from interaction with the public, with elected officials playing the public relations role,

these arguments will come as a shock. Nevertheless, proponents such as Louis Gawthrop insist that "To be sure, the established electoral process provides one avenue for the expression of citizenship; but, on an ongoing, day-to-day basis involving the intricacies of the public policy process, the art of government must be and can only be revitalized by the craft of management."[11]

A second set of arguments for citizen participation programs is based on the observation that city government institutions do not represent all citizen interests equally well. Given the lack of vigor in many local electoral processes, this is perhaps not surprising. Noting the decline in voter participation and the increase in citizen alienation that has been studied by many political analysts, one commentator concludes:

> This discovery does not mean that municipal government has ceased to function, nor that political contests have no importance. What it does suggest is that due to its weaknesses, political culture no longer provides enough inputs for democratic processes to function.[12]

This alleged decline in the political culture that would support meaningful choices in vigorous municipal election contests is not always and everywhere the case. In Denver's June, 1987, mayoral election there was a record turnout of 54 percent of registered voters.[13] Voter registration drives, mobilization of minority voting blocs, and other evidence of intense electoral competition can be found in other cities. However, as noted at the outset of this chapter, there is generally a low level of interest in local electoral processes. Under these conditions, it is difficult to expect that the governing coalitions that result will necessarily represent all interests equally well.

City government is often characterized as being more attuned to upper-class and business interests than to the interests of lower-income residents. In his influential treatment of the subject, Paul Peterson suggests that, because cities are at the mercy of mobile residents and investors, they must restrain redistributive spending and emphasize policies that keep the city attractive to investors.[14] Clarence Stone outlines a theory of systemic power, which shows how city officials are inevitably drawn to be more responsive to the upper class.[15] In Stone's analysis, upper-class individuals have substantial economic resources, control of important private organizations, and a lifestyle that accords them high levels of esteem, status, and expectations of civic responsibility. City officials are therefore predisposed to work with upper-class individuals in order to accomplish tasks. The structure of the situation leads to underresponsiveness to groups that do not have the attractive resources of the upper class.

In a related vein, city bureaucracies are often claimed to be too insulated and unresponsive to the average citizen's concerns. The unresponsiveness of city bureaucracies is sometimes attributed to the increasing size and complexity of the bureaucracy and sometimes to the growing professionalization of service delivery agencies. Urban service bureaucracies are said to conduct their operations according to bureaucratic decision rules based on professional, technical criteria, which can make city hall seem unresponsive to citizen concerns.[16] The classic example is the street department that seems unsympathetic to citizens who are demanding a traffic signal at a particular corner in their neighborhood where several school children have had close calls with vehicles. The department has criteria for determining which intersections warrant traffic signals, such as traffic volume, number of recorded accidents, character of the street (major arterial, tertiary residential), and distance to the nearest existing traffic signal. These rational and technical criteria are compelling from a specialist's perspective, but they may not be at all convincing to worried parents. Many citizen participation programs (e.g., those creating special forums in which citizens can have input on planning decisions and those creating liaison devices between city bureaucracies and neighborhood organizations) are efforts to insert ordinary citizens' concerns into the professional and technical world of urban bureaucracy.

Sometimes the alleged nonresponsiveness of urban bureaucracies is linked to more invidious biases than technical and professional concerns. Such was the case in the 1960s, when urban conflict erupted, often out of confrontations between police officers and black citizens, and the black community charged police departments and other urban institutions with insensitivity and outright brutality (see Chapter 2). These concerns are not necessarily a matter of historic interest only, with no relevance to the present. In August, 1987, the city council in Wichita, Kansas, was beset with complaints that police were not responsive to calls about black victims of crime. As was the case in many American communities in the 1960s, the Wichita city council turned to a citizen participation mechanism to deal with the problem. It convened a community relations task force to consider the complaints.[17]

A third perspective on citizen participation suggests that additional, innovative avenues for citizen involvement are helpful devices *for government officials.* Citizens can provide invaluable assistance in planning, decisionmaking, and the administration of municipal programs, thus providing a resource for public officials.

John Clayton Thomas argues that there are clear advantages for municipal officials in increased citizen participation through neighborhood organization activity.[18] Participation can head off the conflict and harassment that groups could otherwise use to stymie programs in which they have no stake. The collaboration of neighborhood organizations may help to lower the cost of service delivery—a matter that is taken up at greater length later in this chapter. Finally, many a local politician has discovered that neighborhood organizations can be mobilized in support of city programs and that they can be powerful allies.

Still other valuable contributions of citizen participation to government have been noted. Some researchers have argued that citizen input can be an important component of policy analysis techniques (e.g., cost-benefit analysis).

The major limitation of those analytic techniques is lack of comprehensive information—information about all aspects of a problem, about alternative solutions, and most especially about the impacts of alternative solutions on peoples' lives and their valuation of those impacts. These are subjects on which citizens can provide essential information if devices can be structured to get their input.[19]

In a related vein, Alvin Toffler argues: "The less democratic feedback . . . the more decisions become divorced from reality, and the greater the danger that errors will go uncorrected until they escalate into crisis. Democracy, in this sense, is not just theoretically "nice"—it is highly "efficient."[20]

TYPES OF CITIZEN PARTICIPATION

Four major types of citizen participation initiatives are considered here:

1. Open government policies like public hearings requirements, open meetings laws, and other descendants of the Administrative Procedures Act of 1946.
2. Information-gleaning strategies like citizen surveys and complaint-handling centers that are designed to facilitate the flow of information from citizens to government.
3. Neighborhood empowerment strategies like formal neighborhood council systems and other descendants of the Community Action Program.
4. Coproduction arrangements that involve joint citizen–city employee collaborations in service delivery or program administration.

The choice of these four major subtypes of citizen participation activity is based on several considerations. For one thing, they encompass much of the activity that has evolved under the banner of citizen participation. Second, they differ from one another in ways that are interesting to students of citizen participation. For example, Stuart Langton draws an important distinction between citizen-initiated and government-initiated citizen participation.[21] The distinction is important because it has much to do with who defines the role for citizens and who controls the effort. Strategies for gathering information from citizens are virtually always initiated by government. By contrast, some neighborhood empowerment formats and some coproduction arrangements are initiated by citizens, or are a product of joint development. Open government policies are an odd hybrid, involving policies that government must follow (e.g., public hearings), or even optional arrangements that may be initiated by city officials (e.g., cablecasting of city council meetings). Once in place, however, much of the initiative for use of the arrangements is in the hands of individual citizens or citizen groups.

Another important difference is the point in the policy process at which citizen participation occurs. Citizen participation can involve citizen input into agenda setting and policy decisionmaking. Or citizen participation can have a much more heavily bureaucratic flavor as citizens become involved in program implementation and service delivery. The conflicts that citizen participation creates may be different in legislative settings (where the key question is representativeness) from what they are in administrative settings (where the key question is interference with professional expertise). Open government arrangements like public hearings and neighborhood empowerment arrangements like neighborhood council systems tend to involve citizen participation at the policymaking stage, although such arrangements are not limited to this. By contrast, coproduction and information-gleaning strategies tend to involve citizen-bureaucrat interactions in the administrative stage.

Open Government Policies

Perhaps the broadest federal aid program of all, General Revenue Sharing affairs are requirements for public hearings and open meetings that provide opportunities for citizen oversight and input. Substantial numbers of the most important federal grant programs promulgated in the 1960s and 1970s included provision for such citizen participation. The Housing and Community Development Act of 1974, for example, required that citizens be informed and specifically stipulated that public hearings be held to obtain citizen input.[22] Perhaps the broadest federal aid program of all, General Revenue Sharing vastly extended the number of municipal governments subject to requirements for published information and public hearings.[23] These are only two of the fifty-five federal grant programs that, as of 1978, mandated that local government recipients hold public hearings to ensure citizen participation in deciding on the uses of the funds.[24]

Meanwhile, a variety of related mechanisms for ensuring citizen participation through open government arrangements have developed, frequently as a result of state mandates rather than federal grant-in-aid requirements. For example, many states now have laws applicable to local governments on open meetings. The laws typically require the posting of notices and agendas, the admission of the general public to meetings, and the restriction of private, executive sessions to only a few categories of business (e.g., individual personnel matters).[25] Many localities also have special times during regular council meetings that are reserved for public comment. The Freedom of Information Act of 1966 is perhaps better known, but virtually all states have laws on open records designed to make it easier for citizens to gain access to public documents.[26]

The movement toward open government has also been furthered by recent advances in telecommunications that have permitted an imaginative wave of experiments in "teledemocracy". In Reading, Pennsylvania, for example, Berks Community Television (BCTV) provides local public affairs programming over a cable television channel. Most municipal public hearings are cablecast, and during the coverage citizens can telephone in testimony as though they were personally in attendance at the hearing. Berks Community TV also produces regular local government shows such as *Inside City Hall,* which has one of the city council members appearing each week, with an open telephone line so that citizens can call in questions during the show.[27] Less elaborate arrangements that simply bring public meetings and hearings to the living rooms of citizens through telecast or cablecast technologies are springing up in a variety of communities.[28]

Judgments about the effectiveness of open government citizen participation vary somewhat according to the particular mechanism at issue. But more often than not, they emphasize the negative. Consider, for example, prevailing views about public hearings. Analysts observe that these, the most common of citizen participation forms, are "more often the most wasteful and useless."[29] Kweit and Kweit summarize some of the other counts against public meetings or hearings as devices for gaining citizen involvement:

> Public meetings are often plagued by low attendance. They also may become a forum for a few dissidents who do not represent the community. Questions, problems, and priorities are often fuzzy. While many groups may be represented, each is usually playing an advocacy role, and trade-offs between groups are usually not considered.[30]

Similarly, Van Valey and Petersen argue:

> When opportunities for citizen participation have been provided, the normal mechanism for this input has been the public hearing. Unfortunately, such hearings generally occur too late in the decisionmaking process, are often inconvenient and inhibiting in format, and frequently pit citizens against paid expert witnesses.[31]

Although the case in point concerns a hearings process at the state level (the California Energy Commission) rather than a municipal setting, Reagan and Fedor-Thurman are very cynical about levels of citizen interest and the representativeness and value of the citizen input that is received at hearings. They report that, even though a special public advisor position was created to enhance public involvement in the proceedings of the California Energy Commission, a total of only twenty-one citizens participated at any of the fifty-four sets of hearings held in one period. What little public involvement hearings did generate was often interest-group representation rather than input from individual citizens: "The mythical disinterested citizen contributing his or her thoughts for the common good was not in evidence."[32]

Still others are concerned about lack of substantive impact that citizens have when they do participate. If citizens appearing at hearings and providing input make no difference to the outcome of the decisionmaking body's deliberations, there are only tenuous grounds for citizens to sustain such involvement.

Unfortunately, systematic study of the impact of citizen participation on policy outcomes is surprisingly rare. One recent exception is a study of whether a neighborhood planning system in Atlanta increased the impact of citizen activism at zoning hearings on the zoning decision. The study finds that, after the institution of the neighborhood-oriented planning system, community support for zoning proposals was more often associated with official passage of the proposal; however, community opposition to zoning proposals was less likely to be successful, particularly in poorer and minority areas of the city.[33]

Other citizen participation mechanisms of the open government type also come in for their share of criticism. The research on provisions for open records has largely been confined to the Freedom of Information Act, but it shows serious problems in the form of unintended consequences that may be applicable to local experiences with open records as well. For example, the Freedom of Information Act has been used for corporate espionage and has created problems for law enforcement agencies. Furthermore, the act has been said to benefit organized interest groups and professional newsgatherers. The image of the ordinary citizen using an open records law to wrest otherwise unavailable information from the bureaucracy is largely unrealistic.[34]

Even the telecasting or cablecasting of city council meetings has been found to have some subtle negative consequences that proponents of open government would not have foreseen. The enhanced visibility of governance under such arrangements may stultify discussion of controversial issues, thus ironically leaving citizens less well informed. City council members may have difficulty controlling the agenda because free television time is available to those who would choose to grandstand or to insert irrelevant issues from the floor. Finally, the televising may discourage some sorts of citizens from pursuing local elected office.[35] Although these drawbacks do not necessarily outweigh the benefits, the point is that even so innocuous an arrangement for enhanced citizen involved as the televising of city council meetings can have consequences that do not fit the ideal model of participatory democracy.

With all these criticisms and apparent problems, why then do citizen participation mechanisms of the open government type remain so common? Are the criticisms warranted?

On the one hand, it is important to recognize that mechanisms like public hearings come in both plain and fancy versions. Public hearings can be held with or without detailed agendas being published in advance. They can be held at a central location only or held at decentralized locations. They can be held during workday hours or at more convenient times for the public. They can be held early or late in a decisionmaking process. They can be organized in a way that pits the lone voice of the amateur citizen against intimidating experts, or they can be organized to facilitate informed citizen input. In some cities, for example, city staff members have been assigned to supply neighborhoods with necessary technical information and background so that residents are better equipped to present their viewpoint at hearings. "Intervenor funding" to support appearances at public hearings by those who might otherwise be financially unable to attend was a goal of the citizen participation movement in its heydey. All these additional features can make a great difference in the effectiveness of public hearings as means for citizen input.

Although open government procedures like public hearings are often ineffective and irrelevant, they occasionally make a difference, and this potential for significance is what keeps them from becoming relics in the museum of citizen participation experiments. Robert Wagner, Jr., president of the Board of Education in New York, recalls how the testimony of the father of a handicapped boy led the board to reverse itself on the application of new state rules to the boy's case; New York's Mayor Koch recalls being so impressed with street vendors' arguments at a public hearing that he sent a statute back to City Council for revision.[36] Many a public official would have similar recollections of situations in which citizen input expressed at public hearings made a difference. The literature on urban politics includes numerous cases in which citizens were able to block offensive developments or otherwise change the course of public decisionmaking, partly through the use of public hearings.

Thus, although public hearings may often be ineffective in terms of policy impact, there are just enough exceptions to make them a tool worth keeping in the repertoire of citizen participation formats. As one New York citizen commented after giving testimony at a public hearing concerning a proposed shelter for the homeless: "I think they've made up their minds. I remain convinced, however, that someone has to go through this exercise just in case."[37]

Citizen participation mechanisms like public hearings, open meetings, open records and the like may be viewed as constituting minimum necessary requirements for citizen participation. They may not, in and of themselves, insure that citizens *are* more involved in local affairs. But without such devices, it would be very difficult to imagine effective citizen participation under any circumstances. In the hands of motivated individuals and mobilized groups, these devices have been very effectively used. They have transformed the local level into a much more open and accessible context than are state and federal government processes for the typical citizen.

Information-Gleaning Strategies

Information-gleaning strategies enable city officials to increase the information they receive concerning citizen preferences, issue positions, needs, and evaluations of services. Information gleaning can in principle be initiated by either citizens or government. In practice, however, information-gleaning strategies are predominantly initiated by government. They include devices like citizen surveys, which are typically designed, administered, and evaluated by city staff or by researchers collaborating with city staff. Partly at the urging of professionally oriented organizations like the Urban Institute, municipal governments have been encouraged to use citizen surveys regularly as a means of gathering systematic data on citizen ratings of city services for use in evaluation and planning.[38] Surveys have taken hold and are regularly used in many cities, particularly as a way to "balance the often unrepresentative element of participation found in public hearings."[39] City officials may not be sure that neighborhood organization leaders truly represent neighborhood residents or that those citizens appearing at hearings represent a cross section of the community. Through the technology of random sampling and survey research, however, they can ensure that feedback is gathered from a representative set of citizens.

Nevertheless, citizen surveys have a number of important problems and limitations. For one, it is not clear that citizen survey responses can be used in any straightforward way to objectively assess service conditions or validly determine preferences. For example, because survey responses showing a desire for more services do not truly obligate citizens to pay for them, the surveys do not genuinely show preferences for more services in the economist's technical sense of showing "willingness to pay."[40] Considerable research on citizen evaluations of services calls into question the legitimacy of using the evaluations as straightforward measures of service quality. Instead, "dominant findings in this research suggest that service evaluations are influenced more by general and symbolic attitudes than by concrete, objective experiences."[41]

Much of the criticism of citizen surveys is based on questions about the lack of correspondence between citizen evaluations and objective service delivery activities. It is important to note, however, that this leads to criticism of the relative weakness of survey-based indicators at pointing up economic problems with service delivery. Objective indicators of service inputs and outputs are understandably better than subjective indicators for determining more effective and efficient mixes of inputs. Acknowledging this, Jeffrey Brudney and Robert England argue that citizen surveys are nevertheless important for pointing out the more political problems with service delivery, such as perceptions of a lack of responsiveness and perceived inequities.[42]

Because citizens are typically not involved in either the design or use of surveys that assess service delivery performance, many commentators would not even include them in a menu of citizen participation formats. However, much more elaborate citizen participation exercises, using a combination of surveys and other information-gleaning tools, are notable experiments in citizen participation. Goals programs, often modeled after the mid-1960s "Goals for Dallas" effort are a prime example. Under these arrangements, a combination of task forces, questionnaires, neighborhood meetings, and the like are used to involve as broad a cross section of the community as possible in planning exercises. By the mid-1970s, a variety of cities from Hartford to Kansas City and from Seattle to Austin had undertaken long-range planning exercises such as these.[43]

Just as new telecommunications technology has sometimes been used to enhance open government strategies for citizen participation, so also has this technology been used for innovative, information-gleaning programs. Perhaps the best known of these is the "electronic town meeting" held in Upper Arlington, Ohio, using the interactive cable QUBE system.[44] The city's planning commission was concerned that their elaborate study of alternative futures for the community had resulted in little citizen interest. Consequently, they arranged an elaborate experiment in which an informational program on planning issues was aired over the cable system. Questions were posed during the show, and viewers who had subscribed to the interactive feature of the cable system were able to use push-button responses to register their answers. They were also able to push buttons to indicate when they thought the discussion had bogged down or seemed no longer useful.

Much of what is written about these citizen-oriented planning exercises is laudatory, although sometimes it is difficult to determine what has been accomplished. The sheer scope of the effort, sometimes taking months or years, including thousands of citizens, and resulting in elaborate final reports, is itself ambitious enough to leave many participants with a great sense of accomplishment. However, many commentators have argued that this sort of "anticipatory democracy" is an important advance over previous modes, which involve after-the-fact complaints about programs or policies.[45]

At a minimum, one can acknowledge that citizen participation in this format is immensely time consuming and expensive. It can generate considerable citizen enthusiasm, build a sense of community, and presumably yield creative and appropriate ideas for long-range planning, but it is too ambitious for everyday use. Hence, it is most likely to be a successful experiment on those relatively rare occasions when the community faces a need for major rethinking of policy goals.

Other citizen participation plans of the information-gleaning type are more appropriate for routine municipal administration rather than large-scale policy change. These plans include various ombudsman arrangements by which citizen complaints about city services are fielded, responded to, and used as feedback.

Whether or not there are special arrangements for handling their complaints, citizens do complain—about missed trash pickups, flooding problems, potholes that need to be filled, vandalism in neighborhood parks, and many, many other matters. There has been considerable debate about whether these citizen-initiated contacts with public officials constitute a form of political participation, or whether they are too particularistic and limited in importance to qualify. Similarly, there has been conflicting research on which types of individuals and which types of settings generate the most contacts with public officials.[46] There is considerable evidence that *need* for help, or at least perceived need, is an important factor in generating citizen contacts with officials; there is also evidence that, like other forms of political participation, citizen complaint-making requires minimum levels of political knowledge and confidence.[47] The importance of need tends to diminish the usual pattern by which better-educated and higher-income individuals are more participative. Furthermore, institutional arrangements can affect patterns of citizen-initiated complaints. Neighborhood organizations can mobilize residents for complaint-making, although not all neighborhood organizations adopt such a strategy; and the existence of centralized complaints units or ombudsman offices like those described following can reduce the significance of political sophistication as a prerequisite for individual complaint-making.[48]

From the viewpoint of citizens, the lack of special institutions for handling complaints may mean that complaints are ignored or that responses are slow. Where representation of neighborhood concerns is strong, such as cities with council members elected from wards, citizens may be well served by council members who act as individual ombudsmen. But this approach is inadequate in cities that have reformed structures, including at-large, nonpartisan elections. Reformism does not totally kill the council members' constituency service role, but it does insulate council members from particularistic neighborhood concerns and removes some of the motivation for running interference with the bureaucracy on the citizen's behalf.

Even where at-large, nonpartisan structures have not been adopted, council members have limited capabilities as ombudsmen for citizen complaints. For one thing, some bureaucrats may not take kindly to what they view as "interference" on the part of elected officials.[49] The growing professionalization of urban service bureaucracies can make them more resistant to complaints referred to them by politicians. At the same time, the growing scope and complexity of municipal functions have probably outpaced the constituency service ability of the typical council member, especially in cities where members of the local legislature are part-time, amateur politicians.

From the viewpoint of urban managers as well, there are important advantages in developing special ombudsman-like institutions for handling citizen complaints. The creation of such units can have some public relations value, of course, but there is more to it than this. In the process of fielding, referring, and following up on citizen complaints, these units generate important information on needs and problems in the community—information that can be useful in planning and in budget justification. Furthermore, information on how quickly and how well individual departments respond to complaints can be used as a management tool for evaluating the performance and ensuring the accountability of those department heads to the city manager, mayor, or other chief administrative office.

For all these reasons, many cities have created central complaints units, or administrative ombudsman offices. The Action Center in Kansas City, Missouri, is a typical example. Created in 1974 after exploration of similar structures in St. Petersburg and Dallas, it is organizationally housed in the office of the city manager. The unit handles complaints and requests concerning virtually any city service except for policing, for which there is a separate complaints process. When a complaint or request is received, the Action Center opens a case file on it and refers the problem to the appropriate city department, thus providing a clearinghouse function for citizens who do not know their way through the city bureaucracy. The Action Center also keeps track of departmental response to each problem, and keeps citizens informed of the status of their requests. When a department reports completion of response to a problem, the Action Center sends the citizen a postcard requesting an evaluation of the department's response. The Action Center follows up on any case in which the evaluation card is returned with a poor rating. Finally, the Action Center maintains a data base on citizen complaints and department responses that is used, among other things, in evaluation of department heads.

Like most information-gleaning strategies, however, centralized complaints units have an important limitation as a means for enhancing citizen involvement in local public affairs. They ask for a very limited amount of citizen involvement, and they are too structured and controlled by government itself to allow for genuine dialogue between concerned citizens and public officials. This very limitation is simultaneously an advantage of central complaints units, citizen surveys, and the like. They do not demand an unrealistic commitment of citizen time and energy. By the same token, with the exception of the multifaceted goal-setting exercises, information-gleaning strategies must be viewed as weak citizen participation devices on grounds that citizens are not truly immersed in learning about key issues or likely to have much impact on decisionmaking.

Neighborhood Empowerment

In stark contrast with most of the open government and information-gleaning forms of citizen participation, strategies for bringing neighborhood interest groups into local governmental affairs have had so much success that they have become a new layer of governance in many cities. Consider, for example, the following developments.

Many citizens have neighborhood council systems designed to ensure that residents of the city's neighborhoods have a say in matters affecting the neighborhoods. St. Paul, Minnesota, is one example. It has a system of seventeen district councils that have a role in reviewing zoning, housing, and development matters. Each council hires and fires its own staff and has a small budget provided by city government. A system of budgeting for capital improvements involves representatives from the neighborhoods in rating projects and proposing final allocations.[50] Similarly, Portland, Oregon, has an Office of Neighborhood Associations with five district offices that allocate more than $1.2 million and provide technical assistance to neighborhood groups. "A board of representatives from the neighborhood organizations hires and fires staff for the district offices and selects priority issues. An annual 'neighborhood needs' process allows each neighborhood to communicate its priorities to every city department."[51]

These arrangements for the formal involvement of neighborhood organizations in planning and budgetary processes are replicated in more or less sophisticated versions in many American cities. But neighborhood organization activity is by no means restricted to these formal roles, as granted in innovative arrangements approved by city government. Neighborhood organizations often play more contentious roles. They periodically mobilize residents to attempt to block city projects that are perceived as threatening to neighborhood interests. The literature of urban politics is filled with many examples of neighborhood organizations mobilized to protect neighborhood interests against perceived intrusions of highway projects, urban renewal projects, undesirable facilities such as landfills, and many other development efforts.[52]

Given these many visible roles, it should not be surprising that city officials see neighborhood organizations as one of, if not the most important of, the various urban interest groups. On the basis of results of a random sample survey of heads of police, fire, and public works departments in cities of more than 50,000 population, Abney and Lauth report that nearly three-quarters of the respondents (73 percent) say that neighborhood groups are among those with the most influence; by comparison, half of the respondents say that business associations like the chambers of commerce are among the most influential, and 26 percent say that "good government" groups like the League of Women Voters are among the most influential.[53] Many elected officials acknowledge the significance of neighborhood groups in another way—by incorporating them into the political coalitions that form their power base. Although it ultimately backfired, such was the strategy of Mayor Dennis Kucinich in Cleveland.[54]

Meanwhile, academic commentators indirectly acknowledge the power of neighborhood organizations by complaining about their contribution to the fragmented, hyperpluralist nature of urban governance. Yates, for example, argues that the American city is "ungovernable" and characterized by "street fighting pluralism" partly because of the plethora of citizen organizations that have emerged:

> These diverse, fragmented citizen interests have produced a bewildering array of street-level community organizations that seek to give voice to one neighborhood demand or another. Typically they represent highly segmented and crystallized political interests: any neighborhood is likely to have scores of these small, competing community organizations.[55]

Despite these many acknowledgements of the power of neighborhood organizations, many commentators emphasize the limitations and weaknesses of this kind of citizen participation. For example, the neighborhood organization approach to citizen participation is supposed to compensate for existing governing institutions' inability to adequately represent these subareal residential interests. Yet the neighborhood organizations themselves are frequently criticized on representational grounds. City officials claim that they cannot be sure that organizational leaders truly speak for the neighborhood. This is not surprising because in many cases only a tiny minority of citizens are involved. In his study of Cincinnati's elaborate system of neighborhood representation via community councils Thomas finds that between 3.3 and 12.6 percent of eligible citizens are members—figures that fall far below the already dismal voting turnout figures of 25 to 30 percent for Cincinnati.[56]

The representation function of neighborhood-oriented citizen participation mechanisms is often threatened by systematic biases in the extent of citizen involvement. Social scientists have found that communal participation like neighborhood organization activity is much more common among individuals of higher socioeconomic status than among those of lower status.[57] In particular settings, this generalization may or may not be supported. In his Cincinnati study, for example, Thomas finds "that community council membership is not broadly representative of the full Cincinnati population. Some people, such as homeowners and those of higher socioeconomic status, are more involved than others."[58] By contrast, a study of the system of elaborate neighborhood associations in Birmingham, Alabama, finds that participation is not accounted for by socioeconomic indicators; rather, neighborhoods with older houses seem best able to maximize citizen involvement.[59] Still, the overall point remains: The neighborhood movement is often criticized for reinforcing class biases in political participation because middle- and upper-class neighborhoods can often take better advantage of this tool than can disadvantaged areas.

In a related vein, neighborhood organizations are sometimes criticized for losing their open, participatory, grass-roots character when they attempt to become established as successful negotiators with government agencies. Community organizations are said to become more professionalized and bureaucratized—that is, more like the public organizations with which they must deal—as they develop from their initial populist roots.[60] Other research has suggested that this evolution is not inevitable, that community organizations can be successful while avoiding the antipopulist tendencies just described if a conscious strategy is used to keep the organization's agenda attuned to residents' concerns.[61]

These criticisms of community organizations are linked to yet another enduring problem of neighborhood empowerment. From the outset, the neighborhood movement has grappled with tensions between two approaches: (1) a *collaborative approach,* in which community organizations accept government funds, implement joint projects with city agencies, and generally emphasize the administration of programs of importance to the area, and (2) an *advocacy approach,* in which community organizations attempt to maintain their autonomy from government agencies so that they are neither distracted nor co-opted from putting pressure on city officials on policy issues. The collaborative approach has been adopted by many community organizations. The result, according to many analysts, is a loss of power and independent purpose. Summarizing her study of school-related community organizations, Gittell concludes:

[F]ederal, state, and local policies . . . in recent years have mandated school organizations and provided funding to community organizations for the delivery of supplementary educational services. These policies have effectively diffused the energies of independently based organizations and have been replaced by service-delivery and mandated advisory organizations. . . . These new-style organizations have the most direct access to the system but the least influence on school policy.[62]

Comparison of the neighborhood movement in the United States with corresponding developments in Europe yields further insights into this criticism of neighborhood empowerment. In their comparison of the United States and Germany, for example, Peter Franz and Donald Warren find that in Germany neighborhood groups sustained a confrontational protest approach and eventually became part of a national-level political movement of substantial importance. By way of comparison:

In the U.S. case national policy linked to citizen participation goals became a basis for subsidizing grass-roots neighborhood organizations. The combined effects of cooptation and professionalization within the U.S. context have helped to transform a nascent social movement into an established fixture using a rhetoric of "empowerment" rather than a reality of autonomous power.[63]

Critics such as these would be still less impressed with the achievements of those neighborhood organizations and community councils that were not even grass-roots groups to begin with. In cases like Birmingham's community council system[64] or Wichita's Citizen Participation Organization,[65] a network of neighborhood-based organizations is created by city government on the basis of an artificial division of those cities. Such government-initiated arrangements may incorporate pre-existing citizen organizations where they can be found, but the overall picture is one of a government strategy for managing citizen input and a system that is dependent for its success on city government's continuing support.

By contrast, some neighborhood organizations are created through grass-roots organizing and maintain an approach that emphasizes community empowerment, self-help activities, a willingness to directly confront institutions that threaten neighborhood interests, and the building of coalitions among neighborhood organizations. The most notable of these organizations are founded on the model prescribed by Saul Alinsky, a well-known community organizer from 1939 to 1972. An example is Oakland Community Organizations (OCO), a politically influential coalition of over fifty neighborhoods in Oakland, California, that has successfully pressured the city to start an urban homesteading program to make vacant homes available at minimal cost to those needing them, has successfully lobbied for passage of an ordinance mandating that developers getting city subsidies hire Oakland residents, and has been instrumental in the campaign to restructure the at-large city council into a local district system.[66]

Despite such exceptions, arrangements for enhancing citizen participation through organized neighborhood representation are criticized primarily by those who would define success in terms of genuine empowerment. Such empowerment is probably not a realistic expectation in the U.S. context. In addition to all the limitations just outlined, there are "historical splits between the concerns of community and workplace, the continuing political and economic fragmentation of metropolitan areas, and racial hostility among neighborhood groups."[67]

On the other hand, there are accomplishments short of total power sharing that others may find important. Neighborhood organizations have become institutionalized channels for citizen input into policymaking and are often intimately involved in planning activities and in the allocation of such resources as Community Development Block Grant funds. Neighborhood organizations are important vehicles for getting citizens involved in activities that have been overlooked by those concerned exclusively with the policymaking side of local government. These activities, which are more in tune with a collaborative approach to citizen participation, can best be described as examples of coproduction.

Coproduction Strategies

In Tokyo, residents are expected to divide their garbage by type (such as burnable items and noncombustibles) and set out only the right type on the designated day. Getting 8.4 million residents to take the appropriate steps may seem to be no mean feat, and in fact not everyone responds correctly. Officials report that as much as 20 percent of collected garbage may be of the wrong type, but the arrangement is viewed by sanitation officials as a key device in enhancing the efficiency and effectiveness of garbage collection.[68]

The Tokyo example is a good one to introduce the concept of coproduction because innovations in garbage collection that require contributory effort on the part of citizens have come to be viewed as the epitome of coproduction. Most simply defined, *coproduction* is a system in which the ultimate consumers of a service contribute to its production or delivery rather than having professionals exclusively responsible for production and delivery.[69] If citizens take garbage to the curb or, as in the Tokyo case, sort by type, they are playing roles in the production process that would otherwise be performed by sanitation workers. The substitution of citizens' labor for the more expensive labor of professional sanitation workers might be expected to yield cost savings—one of, but by no means the only, rationale for coproduction.

The often-cited example of garbage collection gives discussions of coproduction a mundane tenor that is a marked step down from the lofty tone of other discussions of citizen participation. Certainly coproduction is a far cry from goals of empowerment in policymaking processes. Rather, the focus is on citizen involvement at the implementation stage. To the extent that there is direct interaction between citizens and public officials, the latter are typically agents of service delivery—that is, they are the street-level bureaucrats of whom Michael Lipsky speaks.[70]

The facts that coproduction involves citizens in implementation more than does policymaking and focuses on interactions with street-level bureaucrats rather than having citizen representation at the legislative stage should by no means trivialize this form of participation. Problems with interactions between citizens and bureaucrats have been the focus of many important urban conflicts in the past when various groups of citizens have reacted to the perceived nonresponsiveness of these street-level bureaucrats. And the potential for conflict always remains. Coproduction is in part an acknowledgment of the important positive roles that citizens can play in the implementation of urban programs and the successful delivery of urban services. Coproduction arrangements often assume that a minimal level of cooperation exists between urban service bureaucrats and citizens. Coproduction arrangements are also believed to enhance the responsiveness of urban service bureaucrats and citizens' appreciation of the difficulties and complexities that "professional producers" face.[71]

Apart from curbside trash collection and other examples of sanitation service, designs for coproduction have focused heavily on law enforcement. Block-watch programs, property marking drives, volunteer citizen patrols, and similar endeavors have been at the forefront of much of the discussion of coproduction.[72] There are other examples of coproduction in practice as well. In the face of fiscal stringency, some communities have created adopt-a-park programs through which residents take on much of the responsibility for maintaining the park in their area, thus substituting their volunteer labor for the more expensive or simply unavailable labor of workers in the parks and recreation department. A variety of volunteer programs, some of long standing, exemplify citizen participation as coproduction. As Robert Poole notes, "Even today the vast majority of American fire departments are manned by volunteers, costing the taxpayer not a penny. Some of the country's best emergency ambulance service is provided by a large volunteer rescue squad in the Bethesda/Chevy Chase area of Maryland adjoining Washington, DC. Volunteer groups can provide valuable services in schools, recreation, and social services as well."[73]

Some commentators define coproduction in such a way that quite subtle contributions of citizens are included as important coproduction activities. Whitaker, for example, argues that many services involve as their primary objective "the transformation of the consumer . . . [t]he terms 'raw material,' 'finished product,' and 'consumer' all refer to the same individual."[74] In education, students young or old cannot be educated against their will; they must participate, typically with professional teachers, in the process of creating their own education. Similarly in the health area, citizens collaborate with professional producers by modifying their own behavior. As the AIDS epidemic has made abundantly clear, citizen contributions in the form of behavior change are an absolute requirement for the containment of the disease.

A variety of problems, challenges, and limitations have been discussed as systematic information about coproduction programs begins to accumulate. There has been considerable debate about the extent to which coproduction actually yields greater effectiveness and efficiency. As Percy explains, "The conventional wisdom . . . is that many types of citizen action enhance the delivery of urban services, although researchers have yet to measure precisely the amount of service improvements associated with particular forms of coproduction."[75] It is indeed possible for coproduction strategies to detract from service provision, as some city police departments found when volunteer patrols became part of the problem rather than part of the solution.[76]

Even if coproduction leads to *effective* service delivery, it may not yield cost efficiencies. It is important to note that citizen labor, although cheaper than professional labor, is not cost-free.[77] It is worth something to the citizen contributing it. Furthermore, the introduction of substantial numbers of volunteers may create the need for supervisors, trainers, coordinators, or others, thus adding new costs to service delivery.[78]

Coproduction may mean that the level and quality of service delivery are increased, not that existing services are provided more cheaply. In education, for example, coproduction programs may be used to provide a variety of extras, enrichments of the educational program that are highly desired by citizens. This does not, of course, save the school district a cent. There is some empirical evidence indirectly suggesting that coproduction strategies are widely used for enrichment of service beyond base levels. In his examination of ICMA survey data on alternative methods of service delivery, James Ferris finds that service areas like the arts, health and human services, and recreation are especially notable for coproduction. These are areas "where there is less agreement as to the appropriate level and, hence, a greater likelihood for an excess demand potential to exist for certain individuals."[79]

In short, although coproduction may sometimes save the city some money, as perhaps in the case of adopt-a-park programs where citizens virtually take over a function for a subset of parks, management efficiency is by no means a guaranteed outcome of coproduction strategies. But citizen participation in the form of coproduction has other very important advantages, at least in principle. As Levine explains:

> . . . coproduction lays the foundation for a positive relationship between gov-
> ernment and citizens by making citizens an integral part of the service deliv-
> ery process. Through these experiences citizens may build both competence
> and a broader perspective, a vision of the community and of what it can and
> should become.[80]

This may seem a lot to expect from a format that involves citizens in local governance primarily by having them contribute, sometimes in relatively small ways, to the production of everyday city services. The idea, however, is that such involvement "increases citizen knowledge of service production technology and constraints."[81] Such knowledge can counteract citizen tendencies to expect more than is possible from city agencies. Furthermore, to the extent that coproduction involves direct interaction between citizens and street-level bureaucrats, an improvement in city-community relations is expected. Direct interaction is expected to increase the information that street-level bureaucrats have about citizen needs and to make those needs more legitimate, compelling, and likely to generate responsive action.[82]

There is little systematic evidence about the extent to which coproduction yields these educative outcomes for citizens or enhanced relations between citizens and city bureaucracies. However, especially since the efficiency gains of coproduction have been called into question, these alternative visions of what coproduction can accomplish have received increasing emphasis.

Like the other strategies for enhancing citizen participation, coproduction is subject to some important problems. In particular, equity questions have been raised about coproduction. Just as neighborhood empowerment strategies are sometimes said to reinforce social class inequities in political organization and participation, so has it been argued that the more affluent individuals and neighborhoods are in a much better position to take advantage of coproduction arrangements.[83] When there are two parents and only one has to work to support the family, there are possibilities for the nonworking spouse to engage in volunteer action that enhances education services, recreation possibilities and the like. Opportunities for such volunteerism are much more restricted for families with two wage earners and for families headed by a single parent. Similarly, higher-status individuals have a variety of resources, ranging from flexible time to organizational ties to monetary resources that make their contributions to coproduction arrangements readily possible, whereas similar contributions from lower-status individuals might be more difficult to generate.

Coproduction strategies are also problematic in a variety of other ways. Hostility and resistance from city workers and public sector unions may need to be overcome. Potential liability problems may have a chilling effect on efforts to involve citizens in service delivery operations. Apart from these practical problems, critics may claim that coproduction diverts citizens from larger policy issues and reinforces their preoccupation with narrow, particularistic, consumption-oriented matters.

Despite these problems and criticisms, coproduction programs have taken root in many communities. A 1982 ICMA survey of 1,780 local governments found that 19 percent use volunteers for recreational services, 9 percent use volunteers in crime prevention programs, 17 percent in fire prevention programs, 9 percent in programs for the elderly, and 15 percent in emergency medical service.[84] Volunteerism and coproduction are not majority strategies, but they are important in many communities despite the lack of clear evidence of gains in efficiency and despite the many practical problems and evaluative challenges discussed earlier.

SUMMARY

The preceding sections have explored four distinctive modes of citizen participation that encompass many of the participatory innovations of importance that have evolved in recent years. Having made this exploration, are there any overall, summative judgments that we can make about the adequacy or quality of citizen participation in urban public affairs? For three reasons, the answer is probably "no."

First, overall judgments are complicated by the very different goals of various forms of citizen participation. As the preceding sections suggest, different outcomes are expected from different formats. Or, stated another way, different approaches to citizen participation reflect different understandings of what participatory democracy is all about.

Early in this chapter, three viewpoints on the purposes and value of citizen participation were discussed: (1) a viewpoint that stresses the educative value of political participation for citizens, (2) a viewpoint that emphasizes the capacity of citizen participation programs to force greater governmental responsiveness and accountability to citizen interests, and (3) a viewpoint that expects citizen participation to be a helpful tool for government officials—that is, a means for gaining citizen cooperation and support. The four forms of citizen participation that have been examined in this chapter can be arrayed against these three perspectives. Table 4.1 provides such a cross-classification, with rough, summary judgments about the extent to which each citizen participation format contributes to each goal or perspective.

The summary judgments in Table 4.1 are open to debate. They are judgment calls based on a consideration of both the logic of the citizen participation format (i.e., what it seems designed to do) and existing evidence on the results of these modes of citizen participation. For example, coproduction is rated weak as a method for improving government responsiveness to citizen interests, in part because the logic of this method is only tangentially related to this goal and in part because of a lack of empirical evidence demonstrating responsiveness outcomes. By contrast, both coproduction and information-gleaning strategies are rated as moderate on assistance to government. Both are designed to achieve

TABLE 4.1. SUMMARY OF EFFECTIVENESS RESULTS FOR FOUR TYPES OF CITIZEN PARTICIPATION

	Citizen Learning	Pressure for Responsiveness	Assistance to Government
Open Government	Mixed	Mixed	Weak
Information Gathering	Weak	Weak	Moderate
Neighborhood Empowerment	Mixed	Mixed	Mixed
Coproduction	Moderate	Weak	Moderate

this aim, and there is at least some evidence that the goal is achieved—that is, the sustained popularity of both formats, promotion of both through relevant professional community networks, and occasional scholarly reports of success in use.

Table 4.1 includes yet another type of rating. The "mixed" rating was given in those situations where there seems to be notable variation in cities' experiences with the citizen participation program. This suggests yet another reason why overall, summary judgments about the success of citizen participation efforts are difficult to develop. The same strategy for citizen participation may yield very different results in different settings or under different circumstances.

This is particularly the case with strategies for getting citizens more involved in neighborhood organization activity. In some cities, this approach has been a potent one, perhaps because socially distinctive neighborhoods with their own grass-roots organizations existed before there were governmental initiatives targeted toward neighborhoods. In other cities, neighborhood organization strategies have been a major disappointment as fledgling organizations failed to sustain citizen interest. Similarly, open government strategies have sometimes yielded dramatic successes for citizen groups fighting for their interests, and some of the more elaborate experiments using telecommunications have been an important educational function for citizens in particular settings. However, hand in hand with these reports of success are other reports of the problems, limitations, and disappointments with open government devices. So, then, summary judgments about citizen participation innovations are inhibited by both the different goals of different efforts and substantial variation in experiences with some of the formats.

One final matter complicates any effort to come to a summary judgment about the quality of citizen participation in urban America: differing expectations about the extent of necessary change. Some analysts are incrementalists, willing to applaud citizen participation experiments that yield improvements short of radical system change. Proponents of teledemocracy experiments that improve citizen access to ongoing government proceedings exemplify these remedial expectations. Unlike those who expect "a significant transformation of our political system," these individuals "seek to modify incrementally the existing political system and institutions; that is, they set out to use communication technologies to improve, rather than transform, the functioning of existing institutions."[85]

In stark contrast, other analysts see the need for much more dramatic and radical change. Gottdiener, for example, argues that incremental improvements in citizen participation simply buttress a system that prevents the emergence of true participatory democracy:

> Within the present milieu, the question of citizen participation cannot be addressed seriously. Mindless advocacy of mass democracy moves us away from

confronting the real issues of local politics. The system has a powerful means of coopting struggles that seek to enter into the game of politics as it is currently structured. . . . Expansion of involvement for formerly disenfranchised groups and mobilizations targeted toward new political demands merely make the present system stronger precisely because of greater participation in it.[86]

In short, there is an apparently unbridgable gap in analysts' visions of how much change there must be before citizen participation programs can be called a success.

DISCUSSION QUESTIONS AND EXERCISES

1. Do you think that neighborhood organizations enhance the representativeness of local governance or detract from it? Explain. Perhaps there is no single answer to this question. Perhaps the answer varies depending on the play of a number of factors. What factors might be important in this regard? Explain.

2. Imagine that you are the assistant city manager in a community of about 100,000 population. The city manager has given you the task of designing a citizen survey to be administered annually for purposes of obtaining feedback on the effectiveness of city service operations. In your preliminary meetings with them, department heads react negatively to the proposal. They argue that citizens don't really know the facts about service delivery and that a survey is likely to generate mostly misinformation and emotional reaction. What would you do in this situation? How might you convince the department heads of the usefulness of the survey instrument? What types of survey questions would you recommend? What uses for the survey would you recommend? What pitfalls need to be avoided, and how would you propose to avoid them?

3. Coproduction strategies can presumably be used in a number of areas of service delivery beyond the usual example of curbside trash collection. Make a list of additional coproduction possibilities. Try to be as imaginative as possible. Now consider what might be involved in successfully implementing each coproduction possibility. Do some types of services have special promise for coproduction? Do some confront substantial obstacles? Explain.

NOTES

1. Robert S. Lorch, *State & Local Politics: The Great Entanglement,* 3rd ed. (Englewood Cliffs, NJ: Prentice-Hall, 1989), p. 55.
2. Albert Karnig and B. Oliver Walters, "Decline in Municipal Turnout: A Function of Changing Structure," *American Politics Quarterly* 11 (October 1983): 491–505.
3. Joel Lieske, "The Political Dynamics of Urban Voting Behavior," *American Journal of Political Science* 33 (February 1989): 150–174.
4. Ibid., p. 169.
5. Elaine B. Sharp, "Voting on Citywide Propositions: Further Tests of Competing Explanations," *Urban Affairs Quarterly* 23 (December 1987): 233–248.

6. Bryan D. Jones and Lynn W. Bachelor. *The Sustaining Hand* (Lawrence, KS: University Press of Kansas, 1986). See also Martin Meyerson and Edward C. Banfield, *Politics, Planning, and the Public Interest* (New York: Free Press, 1955).

7. Elaine DiSerio, "Goals-Setting Programs," *Citizen Participation* 4, no. 5 (Summer 1983): 17.

8. *Citizen Participation* 4, no. 4 (Spring 1983): 13.

9. Sherry Arnstein, "A Ladder of Citizen Participation", in *Citizen Participation Certification for Community Development*, ed. Patricia Marshall (Washington, DC: National Association of Housing and Redevelopment Officials, 1977) pp. 40-50; Marilyn Gittell, *Limits to Citizen Participation* (Beverly Hills: Sage, 1980).

10. Carol Pateman, *Participation and Democratic Theory* (New York: Cambridge University Press, 1970), p. 43.

11. Louis Gawthrop, "Civis, Civitas, and Civilitas: A New Focus for the Year 2000," *Public Administration Review* 44 (March 1984): 104.

12. M. Gottdiener, *The Decline of Urban Politics* (Newbury Park, CA: Sage, 1987), p. 50.

13. Thomas J. Knudson, "Victory Leaves Denver Mayor in Search of a Broad Alliance," *New York Times,* June 18, 1987, p. A-28.

14. Paul Peterson, *City Limits* (Chicago: University of Chicago Press, 1981).

15. Clarence Stone, "Systemic Power in Community Decision Making: A Restatement of Stratification Theory," *American Political Science Review* 74 (December 1980): 978-990.

16. Bryan Jones, *Service Delivery in the City* (New York: Longman, 1980), pp. 80-82.

17. "Inquiry Ordered on Wichita Police," *Kansas City Star,* August 12, 1987, p. 4a.

18. John Clayton Thomas, *Between Citizen and City* (Lawrence: University Press of Kansas, 1986), pp. 16-17.

19. Mary G. Kweit and Robert W. Kweit. "The Politics of Policy Analysis: The Role of Citizen Participation in Analytic Decision Making," in *Citizen Participation in Public Decision Making,* ed. Jack DeSario and Stuart Langton (New York: Greenwood Press, 1987), pp. 19-37.

20. Alvin Toffler, "Introduction On Future-Conscious Politics," in *Anticipatory Democracy,* ed. Clement Bezold (New York: Random House, 1978), p. xviii.

21. Stuart Langton, "What Is Citizen Participation?" in *Citizen Participation in America,* ed. Stuart Langton (Lexington, MA: Heath, 1978), p. 21.

22. Patricia Marshall, "Citizen Participation: A Requirement in the Community Development Block Grant Program," in *Citizen Participation Certification for Community Development* (Washington, DC: NAHRO), p. 3.

23. Advisory Commission on Intergovernmental Relations, *Citizen Participation in the American Federal System* (Washington, DC: U.S. Government Printing Office, 1979), p. 4.

24. Ibid., p. 113.

25. Elaine Sharp, "Consequences of Local Government Under the Klieg Lights," *Communication Research* 11 (October 1984): 497.

26. Advisory Commission on Intergovernmental Relations, *Citizen Participation in Federal System,* p. 270.

27. F. Christopher Arterton, *Teledemocracy: Can Technology Protect Democracy?* (Newbury Park, CA: Sage, 1987), pp. 97-99.

28. Sharp, "Consequences of Local Government," pp. 498-499.

29. Jack DeSario and Stuart Langton, "Citizen Participation and Technocracy," in *Citizen Participation in Public Decision Making*, ed. DeSario and Langton (New York: Greenwood Press, 1987), p. 14.
30. Kweit and Kweit, "Politics of Policy Analysis" p. 30.
31. Thomas Van Valey and James Peterson, "Public Service Science Centers: The Michigan Experience," in *Citizen Participation in Public Decision Making*, ed. DeSario and Langton (New York: Greenwood Press, 1987), pp. 39-40.
32. Michael Reagan and Victoria Fedor-Thurman, "Public Participation: Reflections on the California Energy Policy Experience," in *Citizen Participation in Public Decision Making*, ed. DeSario and Langton (New York: Greenwood Press, 1987), p. 94.
33. John D. Hutcheson, Jr., and James E. Prather, "Community Mobilization and Participation in the Zoning Process," *Urban Affairs Quarterly* 23 (March 1988): 364.
34. Lotte Feinberg and Harold Relyea, "The Freedom of Information Act: A Collage"; Lotte Feinberg, "Managing the Freedom of Information Act and Federal Information Policy"; and Priscilla Rega, "Privacy, Government Information, and Technology," all in a symposium in *Public Administration Review* 46 (November/December 1986): 603-639.
35. Allan Cigler and Elaine B. Sharp. "The Impact of Television Coverage of City Council," *Journal of Urban Affairs* 7 (Spring 1985): 65-74.
36. Sam Roberts, "Hearings Let Public Speak; Who Hears," *New York Times*, August 17, 1987, p. 17.
37. Ibid.
38. Harry Hatry, Louis Blair, Donald Fisk, John Greiner, John Hall, Jr., and Philip Schaenman, *How Effective Are Your Community Services?* (Washington, DC: Urban Institute and ICMA, 1977).
39. Advisory Commission on Intergovernmental Relations, *Citizen Participation in Federal System*, p. 276.
40. For a treatment of this problem and possible survey-based strategies to address it, see John P. McIver and Elinor Ostrom, "Using Budget Pies to Reveal Preferences: Validation of a Survey Instrument," in *Citizen Preferences and Urban Public Policy*, ed. Terry Nichols Clark (Beverly Hills: Sage, 1976), pp. 87-110.
41. Paul Allen Beck, Hal Rainey, Keith Nicholls, and Carol Traut, "Citizen Views of Taxes and Services: A Tale of Three Cities," *Social Science Quarterly* 68 (June 1987): 229.
42. Jeffrey L. Brudney and Robert E. England. "Urban Policymaking and Subjective Service Evaluation: Are They Compatible?" *Public Administration Review* 42 (March/April 1982): 130-131.
43. David E. Baker, "State, Regional, and Local Experiments in Anticipatory Democracy: An Overview," in *Anticipatory Democracy*, ed. Clement Bezold (New York: Random House, 1978), pp. 5-35.
44. This summary description is based on Arterton, *Teledemocracy*, pp. 138-141.
45. Clement Bezold, "Beyond Technocracy: Anticipatory Democracy in Government and the Marketplace," in *Citizen Participation in Public Decision Making*, ed. DeSario and Langton (New York: Greenwood Press, 1987), p. 66.
46. Philip B. Coulter, *Political Voice: Citizen Demand for Urban Public Services* (Tuscaloosa: University of Alabama Press 1988); see also Elaine B. Sharp, *Citizen Demand-Making in the Urban Context* (Tuscaloosa: University of Alabama Press, 1986), pp. 8-19, 37-56.

47. Bryan Jones, Saadia Greenberg, Clifford Kaufman, and Joseph Drew, "Bureaucratic Response to Citizen Initiated Contacts: Environmental Enforcement in Detroit," *American Political Science Review* 72 (1977): 148–165; John Thomas, "Citizen Initiated Contacts with Government Agencies; A Test of Three Theories," *American Journal of Political Science* 26 (1982): 504–522; Elaine B. Sharp, "Citizen Demand-Making in the Urban Context," *American Journal of Political Science* 28 (November 1984): 654–670.
48. Sharp, *Citizen Demand Making*, pp. 81–99.
49. Kenneth Greene, "Administrators' Reactions to Elected Officials' Contacts: Avoidance or Cooperation," paper presented at the Annual Meeting of the Southwestern Political Science Association, San Antonio, Texas, March 17–20, 1982.
50. Ken Thomson, "Directions for Democracy," *National Civic Review* 76 (May–June 1987): 203.
51. Ibid., p. 204.
52. Geno Baroni, "The Neighborhood Movement in the United States: From the 1960s to the Present," in *Neighborhood Policy and Planning*, ed. Phillip Clay and Robert Hollister (Lexington, MA: Heath, 1983), pp. 177–192; Jay D. Starling, *Municipal Coping Strategies* (Beverly Hills: Sage, 1986), pp. 99–138.
53. Glenn Abney and Thomas Lauth. "Interest Group Influence in City Policymaking: The Views of Administrators," *Western Political Quarterly* 38 (March 1985): 151.
54. Pierre Clavel, *The Progressive City* (New Brunswick, NJ: Rutgers University Press, 1986), Chap. 3.
55. Douglas Yates, *The Ungovernable City* (Cambridge, MA: MIT Press, 1977), p. 25.
56. Thomas, *Between Citizen and City*, p. 45.
57. Sidney Verba and Norman Nie, *Participation in America* (New York: Harper & Row, 1972).
58. Thomas, *Between Citizen and City*, p. 46.
59. Steven Haeberle, "Neighborhood Identity and Citizen Participation," *Administration & Society* 19 (August 1987): 178–196.
60. Terry Cooper, "Bureaucracy and Community Organization: The Metamorphosis of a Relationship," *Administration & Society* 11 (February 1980): 411–444.
61. Curtis Ventriss and Robert Pecorella, "Community Participation and Modernization: A Reexamination of Political Choices," *Public Administration Review* 44 (May/June 1984): 224–231.
62. Gittell, *Limits to Citizen Participation*, p. 242.
63. Peter Franz and Donald Warren, "Neighborhood Action as a Social Movement," *Comparative Political Studies* 20 (July 1987): 237.
64. Haeberle, "Neighborhood Identity and Citizen Participation," pp. 178–180.
65. Elaine B. Sharp, "Citizen Participation and Urban Capacity Building: Representation and Conflict," *Urban Affairs Papers* 3 (Winter 1981): 33–45.
66. Donald Rietzes and Dietrich Rietzes, *The Alinsky Legacy: Alive and Kicking* (Greenwich, CT: JAI Press, 1987), pp. 190–191.
67. Susan Clarke, "More Autonomous Policy Orientations: An Analytic Framework," in *The Politics of Urban Development*, ed. Clarence Stone and Heywood Sanders (Lawrence, KS: University Press of Kansas, 1987), p. 113.
68. Clyde Haberman, "In Tokyo Sorting for the Curbside Piles," *New York Times*, June 29, 1987, p. B8.
69. Stephen Percy, "Citizen Participation in the Coproduction of Urban Services," *Urban Affairs Quarterly* 19 (June 1984): 433.

70. Michael Lipsky, *Street-Level Bureaucracy* (New York: Russell Sage, 1980).
71. Elaine B. Sharp, "Toward a New Understanding of Urban Services and Participation: The Coproduction Concept," *Midwest Review of Public Administration* 14 (1980): 105–118.
72. Paul Lavrakas, "Citizen Self-Help and Neighborhood Crime Prevention Policy," in *American Violence and Public Policy,* ed. Lynn A. Curtis (New Haven, CT: Yale University Press, 1985), pp. 87–116.
73. Robert Poole, *Cutting Back City Hall* (New York: Universe Books, 1980), p. 27.
74. Gordon Whitaker, "Coproduction: Citizen Participation in Service Delivery," *Public Administration Review* 40 (1980):240.
75. Percy, "Citizen Participation in Coproduction," p. 436.
76. Ibid., p. 435.
77. Ibid., p. 437.
78. James M. Ferris, "Coprovision: Citizen Time and Money Donations in Public Service Provision," *Public Administration Review* 44 (July/August 1984): 329.
79. Ibid., p. 330.
80. Charles Levine, "Citizenship and Service Delivery: The Promise of Coproduction" *Public Administration Review* 44 (March 1984): 181.
81. Percy, "Citizen Participation in Coproduction," p. 438.
82. Ibid.
83. Mark S. Rosentraub and Elaine B. Sharp. "Consumers as Producers of Social Services: Coproduction and the Level of Social Services," *Southern Review of Public Administration* 4 (March 1981): 516–528.
84. Ferris, "Coprovision," p. 330.
85. Arterton, *Teledemocracy,* p. 133.
86. Gottdiener, *Decline of Urban Politics,* pp. 283–284.

CHAPTER 5

Improving Service Delivery: Privatization

City governments interested in improving the cost effectiveness of their service delivery operations can strive for improved productivity through technological innovations (see Chapter 3); they can also make use of citizen participation programs, such as coproduction schemes, that can improve service delivery (see Chapter 4). In recent years, however, perhaps most attention has been paid to a third way to achieve cost savings: privatization of city services. Privatization can involve the use of either the profit or the nonprofit sectors to provide services that municipal governments have been providing. To the extent that nonprofit organizations are involved, privatization begins to overlap with the ideas of coproduction and citizen volunteerism discussed in Chapter 4. However, the fervor behind the privatization concept derives more from the role of the private, for-profit sector in municipal service delivery.

At its core, the privatization claim is based on notions that competition, the profit motive, and other key features of the private, for-profit sector can yield efficiencies that are lost when municipal government is a monopoly provider of a service. Privatization, therefore, goes to the heart of major debates about the proper role of government in a capitalist state and the advantages and weaknesses of the market mechanism for allocation of resources. Not surprisingly, discussions of privatization are often heated and ideological. Strong partisans of privatization portray government as a bloated and nonresponsive monopoly provider, subject to problems of red tape, civil service rigidities, and patronage abuses. Dedicated opponents of privatization portray it as a device for allowing greedy firms to debase the public interest in quality service delivery by cutting corners for a profit and undermining the professionalization that has been achieved in governmental provision of services.

This chapter considers the many alleged advantages and disadvantages of privatization and provides an overview of the evidence concerning the results of privatization efforts, particularly in the form of contracting out to private firms. The chapter concludes with an argument for a contingent approach to privatization. That is, debates about whether or not privatization is appropriate are unlikely to yield useful conclusions. Rather, we should be considering the *circumstances* under which privatization is more appropriate and those under which it is less appropriate, and the *service characteristics* that tell us whether privatization is a feasible strategy.

PRIVATIZATION: A RANGE OF APPROACHES

Local governments have long had many important relationships with private firms. These of necessity will continue regardless of the current debate over the wisdom of privatization. Consider, for example, the private sector's role as a *supplier* of materials to city hall. Even if snow removal is a completely municipal operation, the city must still rely on private sector vendors as a source of supply of everything from major pieces of snow-removal equipment to smaller items like tools for its maintenance garage to supplies like gasoline, salt, and sand. Private sector vendors also supply municipal governments with software packages for fleet maintenance or routing programs, as well as other supplies or services that may be important in the management or support function for snow removal or other traditional city services.

The role of supplier for the private sector is not what is at issue. Privatization refers, instead, to one of several roles that the private sector can take on in the actual process of service delivery itself. At the extreme, privatization can mean that city government simply abandons a function, leaving the field open for firms in the private sector. This simple withdrawal of governmental responsibility for certain functions is sometimes referred to as "load shedding."[1]

Simple withdrawal of governmental responsibility may not be at all that simple, however. Problems of political feasibility make this a relatively rare form of privatization. For this reason, load shedding is not one of the key forms of privatization discussed in this chapter.

Other forms of privatization maintain a role for government as overseer and procurer of service delivery, with the private sector (either for-profit or nonprofit) taking on the responsibilities for actual service delivery operations. In fact, recognition of the distinction between these two key roles and of the possibility that different organizations can be involved in each is an essential element in the privatization movement. Different authors sometimes use different terminology; for the sake of consistency this book adopts the language suggested by Kolderie. The role of *production* in his terms includes the "operating, delivering, running, doing, selling, and administering that goes into actual service delivery." Government can turn this *production* role over to the private sector, yet still maintain its responsibilities to the public through its role in *providing* for service. Providing includes the financial decisionmaking, regulation, standard setting, requirements, and other policymaking matters through which government can exert control over what services are delivered and by whom.[2]

The privatization concept requires recognition that government need not necessarily be involved in the production of many of the services that are now exclusive government operations. Savas provides a typology that helps to illustrate the point.[3] The typology is replicated here (see Figure 5.1) because it can also be used as a diagnostic tool for assessing privatization possibilities in various situations.

The typology is based on two dimensions. One identifies whether the good or service in question can be jointly consumed. That is, can multiple individuals simultaneously enjoy it without using it up? The second dimension focuses on excludability: Can those persons who have not contributed to the production of the good or service realistically be excluded from enjoying it?

As Figure 5.1 shows, these two dimensions suggest four kinds of goods or services. *Private goods* are those that cannot be jointly consumed and that have high excludability. They can therefore be produced and sold in the private market. Furthermore, through the interaction of supply and demand in the competitive market, we can expect the production of appropriate amounts of these goods at appropriate prices.

At the other extreme are *collective goods,* those that can be jointly consumed and that have low excludability. A classic case can be made for government provision of collective goods and services because the competitive

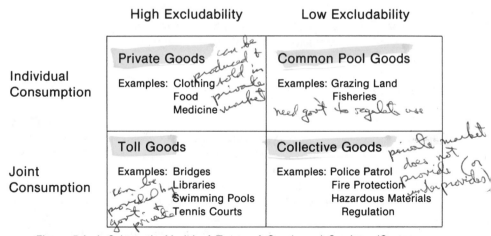

Figure 5.1. A Schematic Model of Types of Goods and Services (*Source:* Adapted from E. S. Savas, *Privatization: The Key to Better Government* [Chatham House Publishers, 1987], pp. 56, 38–41.) Reprinted with permission.

market either will not provide them at all or will underprovide them. That is, it would be irrational for any one individual or firm to produce a pure, public good because the firm could not then prevent everyone from enjoying the good, whether or not they help to defray the cost. Government provision avoids this problem in that taxation coerces all to contribute to the public goods that government provides. Even where public goods are concerned, however, it is not necessary for government actually to produce the good or service in question so long as it takes the provider role of arranging for tax revenues that can then be used to defray the costs incurred by a private producer.

The third type of good in Figure 5.1 is the *toll good,* which is characterized by jointness of consumption and high excludability. For example, within the limits set by problems of congestion, many individuals can simultaneously use a library. Yet it is possible to exclude noncontributors from enjoying the library. The library could restrict checkout privileges and entry to the library itself to those individuals who have a library card, which is obtainable by paying a fee, or "toll." Many governmentally produced services, like libraries, swimming pools, and boat docking facilities, are toll goods. From a privatization point of view, these toll goods could be produced by private firms. In fact, many of them are provided both by government and by the private sector.

The fourth type of good in Figure 5.1 is the *common pool good,* which does not have joint consumption properties but does have low excludability. As Savas argues, many common pool goods, such as aquifers, are naturally occurring phenomena. The key problem with respect to these goods is that they become destroyed through overuse that is brought on by the fact that individuals who do not contribute to the maintenance of the good can freely make use of it. As with collective goods, a strong case can be made for government involvement to provide the common pool good or to institute regulations designed to prevent destruction of naturally occurring common pool goods.

Savas's typology identifies those situations in which government action may be needed to compensate for failure of the private market to adequately provide the good. However, government action need not necessarily mean government production of the good. The privatization approach incorporates an array of strategies by which government acts as a service arranger while making use of the private sector for service production.

One form of privatization that is based on this division of labor is *franchising.* Under a franchising arrangement, government awards to one or more firms the rights to provide some service within its jurisdiction, and citizens pay the service provider directly, just as they would any private firm that they patronize. Franchising frequently carries with it certain obligations on the firm or firms that are awarded the franchise—obligations in the form of standards, requirements, or regulations set by government.[4] In this sense, private firms operating under franchise are not totally free agents, and government's "provider" role can involve extensive intervention and control over the quality and quantity of what is provided.

Although not always the case, franchises are often used for utility kinds of functions, such as electric power, cable television, and bus transportation. A franchise operation allows the city to have a regulatory role in overseeing something that has the attributes of a natural monopoly, as many utilities do. More generally, franchises are used for services that can be viewed as toll goods.[5] The franchising arrangement respects the fact that private firms can capably provide the service; yet government, in its arranger role, can set minimum standards of quality, prevent monopoly pricing, and otherwise insist on standards of service in the public interest.

A 1982 ICMA national survey of cities and counties shows that franchising is used by these local governments for a number of services or functions. Most notably, 15 percent of the reporting governments have franchises for residential solid waste collection, 14 percent for streetlight operation, 10 percent for reading utility meters, and 9 percent for airport operation.[6]

Other ways of splitting service delivery into a production role for the private sector and a provision role for government are also considered by analysts of privatization. For example, grants or subsidies can be provided to private organizations to encourage them to provide a service that the city might otherwise have to produce.[7] Although funding by grant is typically associated with the federal government, local governments have long played a role in subsidizing certain activities. A closer look at subsidies for economic development, in the form of tax abatements and related incentives, will be considered further in Chapter 10. For the moment, it is important to note that grants and subsidies often are used to encourage provision of cultural or recreational services and health and human services.[8] For example, the 1982 ICMA survey of cities and counties shows that the most frequent uses of subsidies are for operation of day-care facilities (in 15 percent of the jurisdictions), operation of mental health and retardation facilities or programs (in 15 percent of the jurisdictions), operation of cultural or arts programs (in 17 percent of the jurisdictions), and operation of museums (in 16 percent of the jurisdictions).[9]

Local government is sometimes an important mediating party in subsidizing various human services by allocating funds they have initially received from the federal government to nonprofit organizations in the community. For example, many local, nonprofit organizations that receive funding from the United Way and various other sources also receive some support from city or county government in the form of grants of General Revenue Sharing or Community Development Block Grant monies.[10] Many communities have faced pressure from local nonprofit organizations to enhance these subsidies as General Revenue Sharing has been phased out.

Vouchers are another mechanism by which government can sustain a provider role while the private sector takes on a service production role. The key aspect of voucher systems is that citizen-consumers also take on part of the provider role by selecting the firms or agencies they will go to for service. Under a voucher system, consumers (typically members of a group whose consumption is being subsidized) are given authorization slips that can be used to purchase service from any one of several possible vendors. The set of vendors can include some combination of nonprofit, for-profit, and governmental entities. Competition among potential vendors, along with the element of consumer choice, are hallmarks of the voucher system.[11] The 1982 ICMA survey of cities and counties shows that, although vouchers may seem an attractive idea in principle, they are rarely used in practice. Less than 4 percent of cities and counties report using vouchers for any individual service asked about. To the extent that vouchers are used, they are used for programs for the elderly, paratransit programs, day care, and a few other human service or recreational programs.[12]

CONTRACTING OUT FOR LOCAL SERVICES

Of all the forms of privatization that might be considered, the one that is most widely used and heatedly debated is contracting with a private, or nonprofit, organization for production of a service. Under a contracting arrangement, various firms submit bids indicating their price for providing a particular service in a particular way to a particular population. These particulars concerning what the service must involve are provided by local government in a process of defining bid specifications. In its provider role, local government selects the organization that will get the contract to produce the service. Typically, by law the selection is based on the lowest bid. Other laws governing the selection process are common. One, for example, requires the use of sealed bids to prevent favoritism in the selection of a contracting firm.

Contracting is one form of privatization that has very much taken hold at the local government level and has had especially strong growth since the 1970s.

> Over the period 1973–1982, the number of cities contracting out legal services increased from 187 to 788. The number of cities contracting out data processing rose from 9 to 337. Only 5 cities contracted out park maintenance in 1973; by 1982, 142 cities did. Meanwhile the dollar amount of service contracts joining municipal governments with private firms tripled, from $22 billion in 1972 to $66 billion in 1980.[13]

A recent survey of 1,086 local governments, conducted by Touche Ross and Company, The Privatization Council, and the International City Management Association (ICMA) also shows the significance of contracting in urban management. Almost 80 percent of the cities either used or planned to use private contractors in some way for local service delivery, and about 40 percent either had or were planning to use private contractors for a combination of facility construction and operation.[14] A 1982 ICMA survey focusing on residential solid waste collection shows that only about one-third (34.1 percent) of the reporting cities rely exclusively on municipally produced service. About one-fifth of the cities (21.6 percent) used private haulers under contract to local government, 11.8 percent had a system of private haulers contracting directly with citizens, and another 17 percent had some combination of these arrangements.[15]

The same survey also reveals that there are substantial differences in levels of use of privatization for solid waste collection, depending on region and city status. Contracting arrangements for solid waste collection are noticeably less common in the South than in other regions of the country. Suburban cities are about twice as likely as either metropolitan center cities or nonmetropolitan cities to use contracting.[16]

A more comprehensive look at contracting in municipal service delivery is provided by the 1982 ICMA survey of cities and counties. Table 5.1 shows some of the results of this survey.[17]

Close inspection of Table 5.1 suggests that local governments tend to contract with for-profit firms for physical services, like many of those in public works and transportation, and for support services. Nonprofit firms by contrast are more predominant in health and human services. One could conclude from Table 5.1 that regulatory functions of many kinds are less attractive for privatization than are distributive services. For example, regulatory functions like animal control, inspection and code enforcement activities of the public works department, and traffic control or parking enforcement show negligible levels of contract activity. This may be because these regulatory functions are more sensitive and potentially controversial than services that distribute benefits; consequently, government officials may be unwilling to lose direct control over them. Furthermore, regulatory functions involve the exercise of coercive authority, an exercise that is traditionally reserved for government.

This does not mean that cities have been unwilling to use some private contracting in the regulatory area. In fact, there has even been some use of contracting in law enforcement, which many would argue is a core government function involving society's delegation of the legitimate use of force. As Poole notes:

> The most common pattern has been for a city to hire a security firm to perform some particular task which requires a higher level of service than can be provided with expensive city police officers. Thus, Lexington, Kentucky, hired one such company to patrol its high-crime housing projects. St. Petersburg, Florida, hired a guard service to patrol its parks. Houston has a private firm guarding its city hall area. Most cities have hired private security firms to provide the security inspections at their airports.[18]

More recent reports suggest further expansion in the use of private contractors for law enforcement service. Public facilities ranging from schools and other

TABLE 5.1. USES OF CONTRACTING IN A NATIONAL SAMPLE OF CITIES
AND COUNTIES

	Percentage Contracting with:	
	For-Profit Firm	Nonprofit Firm
Public Works/Transportation		
Residential solid waste collection	34	0
Street repair	26	1
Street/parking lot cleaning	9	0
Tree trimming/planting	30	1
Inspection/code enforcement	6	1
Public Safety		
Ambulance service	23	9
Traffic control/parking enforcement	1	1
Vehicle towing and storage	78	0
Health and Human Services		
Animal control	6	8
Day-care facility operation	33	34
Programs for elderly	4	28
Drug/alcohol treatment programs	6	38
Parks and Recreation		
Parks landscape/maintenance	9	2
Recreation services	4	12
Support Functions		
Building/ground maintenance	19	1
Data processing	22	2
Legal services	48	2
Tax bill processing	22	2

Source: Adapted from Table 3/2 in Harry Hatry and Carl Valente, "Alternative Service Delivery Approaches Involving Increased Use of the Private Sector," 1983 Municipal Yearbook (Washington, DC: ICMA), p. 203. Reprinted with permission.

government buildings to public parks and public housing are patrolled by private firms in communities such as Denver, Houston, Los Angeles County, New York, San Francisco, and Seattle, and 44 percent of law enforcement officials surveyed recently say that governments in their area contract out for security services.[19]

The Pros and Cons of Contracting: Evidence and Arguments

Given that a substantial number of cities have some experience in contracting with the private sector for some type of service delivery, one would think that there must be substantial evidence about the results of contracting. Indeed, there is some, but the evidence varies from unsystematic case studies to anecdotal success reports to more systematic assessments. In general, the findings are supportive of proponents' claims that contracting out yields gains in cost effectiveness.

For example, the 1987 ICMA survey of 1,086 cities that was referred to earlier finds average savings of 20 percent from privatization.[20] Robert Poole cites a variety of success stories involving contracting. In emergency ambulance and paramedic services, he notes that (1) an Illinois Department of Transportation study concluded that private service costs about half what public service does, (2) Glendale, California's choice of a pair of private ambulance firms resulted in a $146,085 cost as compared with a $519,180 public provision cost; and (3) Medevac, Inc. has been able to provide paramedic services under contracts with the city of El Monte and San Mateo County at a cost of $562,000, as compared with the fire department paramedic program's $1,875,000.[21]

Sanitation service has received a fair amount of attention with respect to the results of private contracting. Summarizing the research, E. S. Savas concludes:

> The evidence is overwhelming and clear: Contract collection is more efficient than municipal collection. . . . Municipal collection is 29 to 37 percent more costly than contract collection, while no more effective or equitable. The reasons are attributed to (1) the use of more men to do the same amount of work, (2) more absences by workers, and (3) the use of less productive vehicles.[22]

More recent evidence further corroborates this evidence. From research on Knoxville, Tennessee's sanitation service contract experience with Browning Ferris Industries (BFI), Michael Fitzgerald reports that the city had first-year savings of $400,000 over what the status quo would have been, and he projects savings of $950,000 for the 1986 to 1987 period and at least $1 million for the following year.[23]

Other municipalities report impressive cost savings from contracting out. For example, Phoenix claims $5.3 million in annual savings due to contracting out seventeen city services, and Los Angeles claims yearly savings of $200 million (out of a $7 billion budget) as the result of its extensive contracting program.[24]

Systematic, cross-city analysis of cost savings from contracting was commissioned by the Department of Housing and Urban Development. The research examined eight services in twenty cities in the metropolitan Los Angeles area. The study found that when scale of service, level of service, service conditions, and quality of service are held constant, municipal service delivery is noticeably more expensive than service produced by private contractors. The percentage difference between municipal and private production costs ranged from 28 percent for residential refuse collection to about 40 percent for street cleaning, street tree maintenance, and turf maintenance, to 73 percent for janitorial service to 96 percent for asphalt overlay construction of streets. Only for payroll processing was there no difference between public and private service delivery.[25]

How do private firms achieve these comparative cost efficiencies? Efficiencies can be, and sometimes are, based on economies of scale or on use of the most technologically advanced equipment. For example, in the twenty-city study described in the foregoing paragraph, researchers found that private contractors used wider, heavier pavers for asphalt overlay operations than did municipal departments, and private contractors also were more likely to have computerized or other state-of-the-art traffic signal systems than were municipal providers.[26]

Particularly for those many services that are labor intensive, however, differences in cost effectiveness between the public and private sectors are probably attributable to the different personnel practices of the two sectors. James Ferris and Elizabeth Graddy note that private contractors tend to ". . . require more work from employees (less liberal vacation and leave for equivalent salaries); use the least qualified personnel able to perform each task; use part-time labor wherever appropriate; require that managers be responsible for equipment availability as well as labor availability; allow first line supervisors hiring and firing authority; and use less labor intensive means of producing the services."[27]

Arguments about the advantages and disadvantages of contracting go well beyond the simple issue of whether private firms provide the service on a more cost-effective basis. Proponents of contracting argue that, in addition to the cost-effectiveness advantage, contracting out is a desirable strategy because it can stimulate improvements in the production of municipal agency service.[28] This could occur if a city used a combination of municipal and private provision for a particular type of service, or if it insisted that government agencies compete along with private providers to determine which got to provide service in a given year. These methods create a competitive situation for the municipal agencies and are believed to enhance their performance. For example, the city of Phoenix has both private firms and its own sanitation department bidding for garbage collection service. At the beginning of the 1980s, the private sector was the low bidder, but by 1988 the city department was outbidding the reigning private sector contractor—Waste Management Inc.[29] One might also conclude that contracting out a particular service makes agencies responsible for other services more aware of the possibility, thereby motivating improved performance.

For cities with strong municipal unions, contracting may be viewed as an attractive alternative because of its reliability. Interruption of service can occur if labor negotiations result in strikes, slowdowns, or sick-outs. To the extent that private sector providers rely on nonunionized workers and generally have greater control of their personnel, contracting out provides more reliable service.[30]

Furthermore, the differences in personnel practices between the public and the private sectors that have been noted can give greater flexibility for cutbacks in times of retrenchment. Private vendors can more easily lay off their workers than can local governments; in the latter case, civil service rules and powerful municipal labor unions can be obstacles to change (or protectors of workers, depending on your point of view).[31]

Finally, contracting can be a desirable alternative from the viewpoint of minimizing liability. Other things being equal, local governments may perceive that their trash collection service is as efficient and effective as could be had with private firms under contract. Yet, should a single sanitation worker be injured and create considerable financial exposure for the community in a lawsuit, the city's perspective on privatizing trash collection service would be likely to change dramatically.

Just as proponents of contracting out claim numerous advantages, so do opponents have a long list of disadvantages. Unlike the cost savings advantage, which is empirically quite well documented for proponents, many of the disadvantages listed by opponents are in the form of potential problems rather than systematically documented trends. For example, opponents of contracting often argue that it results in "creaming"—that is, contractors focus on the easiest or otherwise most desirable clients and consumers, while avoiding more problematic clients.[32]

Another argument against contracting is that because it taps the profit motive of suppliers it provides incentives for cutting corners and generally providing shoddy service to maximize profits. The problem with both this claim and arguments about creaming is that they ignore the oversight and monitoring role that local government is supposed to maintain under a contracting arrangement. Contract specifications can be written with clear requirements about who must receive service and about quality levels. Responsible contracting should involve monitoring to determine whether the requirements are met in practice.[33]

Fixler and Poole describe a variety of innovative efforts that communities are using to maximize contractor accountability:

> Cypress, California, for instance, has the right to ask its custodial-services contractor to remove unsatisfactory employees and to deduct the cost of doing incomplete work from the contractor's fee. Gainesville, Florida, built incentives and penalities into its vehicle-maintenance contract. Hall County, Georgia, requires its contract fire chief to report to the city manager to discuss and resolve management problems and issues. . . . Loma Linda, California, can adjust the contract price downward if its landscape maintenance contractor fails to perform the specified work.[34]

A more difficult matter is raised by those who allege that increased contracting yields greater opportunities for graft and corruption. Whenever substantial sums of money are at issue, as is the case with many city contracts, the potential for corruption is present. Charges of corruption involving cities' contracting operations are all too common. For example, several supervisors in New York City's Department of Housing Preservation and Development were officially charged in 1988 with taking bribes from private firms interested in gaining contracts to repair housing for the city.[35]

The weakness of the corruption argument is that it is not uniquely applicable to the privatization situation. Opportunities for corruption occur whenever government either does business with private firms or generally makes decisions with significant financial ramifications for private firms. Hence, the decision not to contract out for private service production does not really minimize opportunities for corruption. It simply means that the potential for corruption is focused in different areas—most notably, local government's procurement of materials and supplies from private vendors, and local government regulation of the private sector. For example, in August, 1987, public officials in forty towns in New York State were charged as a result of an FBI sting operation in which an FBI agent had posed as a "vendor of snowplow blades, street signs, nuts and bolts, chains, fencing, and other street products sought by municipalities."[36] Bribes were accepted by public officials who were engaged in procurement of materials to be used in regular city-provided services. There is a potential for corruption whether public services are privately or publicly produced.

Besides concerns with creaming, slipshod work to maximize profits, and possible potential for corruption, opponents of contracting out have raised concerns about the costs of regaining in-house capacity if privatization of service delivery fails. Failure can occur either because the private firm or firms involved lose interest in renewing the contract, go bankrupt, or provide service that is not of acceptable quality. If a different, private supplier is unavailable, or if contracting is discredited because of the failure, local government will be expected to revert to traditional municipal provision of the service, but the personnel, equipment, and organizational capacity to do so may have been lost in the wake of the initial decision to privatize. The start-up costs of recapturing lost in-house capacity can be considerable.[37]

Perhaps the most powerful arguments offered by opponents of contracting out focus on issues of appropriateness and accountability. One important line of argument suggests that the decision to privatize a service through contracting is *not* simply a decision to provide the same service in a more cost-effective fashion. Rather, because there are important legal differences between the public and the private sectors, the decision to privatize has additional nonfiscal implications. For example, whereas public organizations are subject to a variety of open records and open meetings laws, the proceedings and records of private organizations are protected by privacy laws and the Fourth Amendment.[38]

More generally, critics argue, "When a public function is assigned to a private entity, usually through a contract, there is an inevitable weakening in the lines of political accountability."[39] The distinction between "provision" and "production" noted at the outset of this chapter would seem to weaken this critical claim. After all, even if public officials contract with a private firm to produce a service, are they not ultimately responsible for the quality of its production? Is this not what monitoring and contract compliance activities are all about? While this is in part true, critics have an interesting point in their claim that contracting weakens lines of political accountability. Blame is harder to place when the public and private sectors are jointly involved in service delivery (one as producer and one as provider), and government's capacity to oversee its many contracting agents may not be equal to the task.

Furthermore, critics of privatization argue that increasing use of this approach can threaten constitutional rights. Reviewing an important series of cases, Harold Sullivan concludes:

> Even when government remains responsible through both funding and regulation for provision of a service, if production is in private hands, an employee can be dismissed, and a citizen can be denied service without the minimal constitutional safeguards that would apply if production had been in public hands. Constitutional restraints only apply when government compels a specific decision affecting an individual employee or client or when a public employee or official participates directly in a specific action.[40]

Thus, for example, citizens who believe that they have been arbitrarily denied benefits under a contracted out local program would not be able to successfully challenge the decision on grounds of violation of due process under the Fourteenth Amendment. There is some evidence that the courts treat certain functions, which have traditionally been governmental functions, as subject to constitutional restraints regardless of the entity performing them. But the courts have also been quite stingy in interpreting what is a traditional public function. Consequently, privatization through contracting out is viewed as providing large loopholes for the evasion of constitutional restrictions on government.[41]

A Contingent Approach to Contracting

Much of the argument about privatization in general and contracting in particular has a passionate pro or con tone, but perhaps the most useful approach is a contingent one. That is, the appropriateness of contracting may depend on particular circumstances and service characteristics. The question of whether or not to contract out should be approached from a diagnostic rather than an ideological posture. This section explores four important contingencies: service specificity, availability of private producers, potential for efficiency gains, and potential for conflict.

Service Specificity. Service specificity is the extent to which the details of what the service involves and the criteria for assessing service delivery can be clearly stipulated.[42] When service specificity is low, it becomes much more difficult to write a contract that stipulates what is wanted and holds the contracting parties to agreed-on standards. Specificity is a function of tangibleness and complexity.

For services with tangible outputs, it is much easier to write a contract specifying service output. The second is product complexity. If a product has many dimensions, some of which are difficult to delineate or define in a contract, it is likely to be difficult to monitor effectively.[43]

Human services, like health and education-related services, are frequently alleged to be more vulnerable to service specificity problems. By comparison with, say, physical services that are based on engineering standards, human services involve intangible, sometimes even undefinable, products.

The service specificity dimension may be more complex than this, however. Human services are not necessarily impossible to specify. It depends on the efforts and abilities of contracting agents to define standards and criteria that clearly establish the service at an acceptable level of quality. A good example of this is the series of moves made by the State of Illinois in 1984 to improve its contracting relationship with private vendors providing home-care services with matching funds from Title XX of the Social Security Act.

In FY84, responsibility for client intake and assessment of needs was removed from the providers and placed with local case management agencies. These agencies . . . were given responsibility for determining client eligibility, developing a care plan, referring the client to a contract provider for service, and monitoring the delivery of the service. . . . for FY86, Illinois developed service standards which established minimum supervisor-to-worker ratios, minimum pre- and in-service training requirements for workers, and the frequency and type of supervision activities required.[44]

In short, human service or not, it is possible to define with precision what standards of service are desired and to create contracting arrangements that provide government with a good deal of control in the contract-monitoring process. Granted, the specifications for human services may focus predominantly on *inputs* rather than *results*. But this is neither unique to human services nor necessarily an irrelevant way of specifying what is wanted. With respect to sanitation services, for example, good contracts involve input-oriented specifications. Knoxville's success story with sanitation service involved a contract that "contained specific provisions relating to spillage and litter, approved containers, and collection equipment, procedures and hours."[45] While spillage and litter are results-oriented specifications, the others are all inputs.

The general point is that service specificity depends at least as much on city officials' efforts and abilities to craft detailed contract specifications as it does on inherent qualities of various types of services. Some services, like human services, may be more challenging subjects for specification of standards, but this does not mean that usable standards and specifications cannot be developed. Furthermore, as more and more cities gain experience with contracting, it becomes possible for city officials to develop a stock of successful approaches to contract specification that can be shared through professional networks.

Availability of Producers. Another key contingency is the availability of private sector vendors for the service at issue.[46] Where there are no suitable vendors, contracting is obviously impossible. And where there is only one, the argument that contracting improves efficiencies through competition loses its merit.

This contingency translates generally into a stronger case for contracting in larger settings than in smaller ones because a greater array of potential private vendors is likely to exist in the more developed local economies of large cities.[47] By contrast, smaller cities that are not in metropolitan areas will not have a pool of private sector vendors simply because of their small size.

We must be cautious about overgeneralization. Smaller cities are not necessarily limited in their contracting capacity on grounds of vendor availability. Many of the key private sector vendors engaging in government contract work are large national corporations that contract with many cities, large and small, across the country. Examples include Browning Ferris Industries (BFI) and Waste Management Inc. in sanitation services and Guardsmark, Inc., Wackenhut, and Pinkerton's in security services. Thus, for some services at least, cities need not have their own local pool of vendors but can draw on larger, multisite vendors.

Second, it is also important to note that although contracting opportunities are a function of vendor availability, the opposite can also be the case: Vendor availability is affected by contracting opportunities. This was very much apparent in the field of home health care, where the number of for-profit firms mushroomed when state agencies began contracting for services using federal Title XX matching grant monies.[48] Similarly, the growing need for corrections facilities has fostered a dramatic private sector entrance into this field. As Dennis Palumbo explains:

> Private industry has suddenly become interested in the possible profits that may be available in this growth; at a price of about $47,000 per bed, the 106,000 beds will cost approximately $5 billion, so there are substantial monies and possible profit involved in this growth industry. Companies such as Merrill Lynch, E.F. Hutton, and Shearson Lehman/American Express look upon this as a straightforward marketing opportunity for them.[49]

The volume of potential government business in smaller communities would obviously not generate the scale of vendor interest shown in this statewide and national issue. But the point remains: Where contracts are to be had, new vendors often emerge. Even smaller cities may see the growth of a competitive group of local haulers in response to the city's willingness to contract out refuse collection.

Potential for Efficiency Gains. From the outset, it has been clear that the primary arguments for contracting out concern cost savings. Much of the debate over the value of contracting has to do with whether these cost savings actually result. More recently, some analysts have suggested that the potential for cost savings varies across different types of services and therefore is an important element in deciding whether contracting out is warranted in particular circumstances.

For example, scale economies are one key source of cost savings. Scale economies occur either where savings on input price can be had from large-scale purchase of equipment and materials, or when problems with peak load capacity can be smoothed out by contracting with a supplier with a larger geographic scope.[50] Thus, for example, smaller communities should find contracting compelling for services that have substantial purchase needs for materials and equipment because a large contract firm can get better buys on large orders of such inputs than the smaller city itself can. Smaller cities should find contracting to be a good option for things like ambulance service. To have enough personnel and equipment available for a crisis or peak load situation, the individual small city would have personnel and equipment sitting idle much of the time. A larger producer of such a service can get fuller use of personnel and equipment because a lull period in one portion of its jurisdiction will be offset by calls in some other portion.

By contrast, large cities may find no economy of scale in contracting out if their own scale of operations matches or exceeds that of potential contracting firms. For example, it has been argued that contracting with private vendors means a *loss* of economies of scale for New York City:

> As the largest purchaser of sanitation trucks in the country, New York City can negotiate bulk sales with lower per unit costs. Moreover, the purchase is so attractive to manufacturers that they will cooperate with city officials in designing equipment particularly beneficial to New York. This allowed productivity managers to move from three-person to two-person trucks in the Department of Sanitation, thus saving millions of dollars in labor costs and enhancing services.[51]

New York City may be an extreme case, but it amply illustrates the point that larger cities may not find any scale economy advantages in contracting. These larger cities may be more interested in the efficiency gains that contracting may provide due to the labor practices of the private sector. As noted earlier in the chapter, private firms use more part-time labor, have less generous policies for time off, and generally pursue more cost-effective labor policies. For this reason, large cities may be more likely to entertain prospects for contracting when labor-intensive services are at issue.[52]

Potential for Conflict. The very labor practices that can make contracting for labor-intensive service seem attractive can also make privatization anathema to some groups—most notably organized labor in the public sector, which has fought long and hard for generous pay, fringe benefit packages, and job

BOX 5.1   A Case Study of Reversing Privatization

Decisions about whether to use municipal service or private, contract service are not necessarily simple matters of dollars and cents. In October 1987, city council members in Kansas City, Missouri, voted (9 to 4) to change back to municipal provision of crash, fire, and rescue service at the Kansas City International Airport (KCI), after seven years of contracting with a private firm. Contracting out for airport fire services began in 1980 in the context of conflictual labor relations between city management and the local fire fighters' union. The fire fighters had gone out on strike in 1975, and had engaged in a work slowdown in December 1979 after negotiations over wages and benefits broke down. In January 1980, the city contracted with J.J. Security, Inc. for provision of airport fire services for one year. Shortly after, the city's fire fighters went out on strike. In ensuing years, the city contracted with Wackenhut Services, Inc. for the airport fire service.

The city's decision to switch back to municipal provision took many observers by surprise and generated heated controversy. Some civic leaders raised questions about the problem of service disruption, which had precipitated private contracting in the first place. For example, Irving Hockaday, Jr., an influential business leader, noted, "In the event of a firefighters strike, the spectacle of calling in the National Guard to keep the airport open does not enhance the community's reputation for progressiveness." Others claimed that the switch back to municipal provision would be costly. Whereas private service through Wackenhut cost $466,551 in 1987, the cost of service when the municipal fire department had last provided it (1978/79) was $638,434. The city manager's office estimated that municipal service could cost as much as $900,000 in 1988 if 22 senior-level fire fighters were transferred to provide the service. Meanwhile, leaders of Local 42 of the International Association of Fire Fighters had been lobbying the city with figures suggesting that the switch would cost only $30,000 more each year. Their claim was made on the premise that airport provision could be handled with eighteen new junior-level fire fighters and the assumption that the city's new contract with Wackenhut would have been more than the 1987 contract figure.

The reasons for the city council's choice to reinstate public provision after a period of satisfactory contracting are not totally clear. But some clues can be gleaned from comments made by various participants. A lawyer representing the fire fighters' union, for example, argued that labor relations with the union should be returned to a more positive footing. "At some point," he observes, "we reach the point where bygones should be bygones." One city council member argued that the leadership of the fire fighters' union was now different and better to work with. In response to those resisting the reinstatement, he noted: "There seems to be a feeling in the business community that we have to continue punishing the fire fighters. I think public safety is the issue here."

Source: Jeff Taylor, "Firefighters Union Wins KCI Contract," *Kansas City Times,* October 9, 1987, pp. 1, 14; Jeff Taylor, "Reassigning KCI Rescues to Fire Department Stirs Protest," *Kansas City Times,* September 26, 1987, pp. 1, 16; James C. Fitzpatrick, "Using Firefighters at KCI Could Be Costly, Official Says," *Kansas City Times,* September 29, 1987, pp. 1, 12.

security. In communities with strong public sector labor unions, there is likely to be strong resistance if city government attempts to privatize services, because the labor practices of private sector providers may seem like reversals of the gains that organized labor has toiled for over the years. The power of municipal labor unions is directly threatened by contracting.

Strong proponents of privatization view this resistance from organized labor as an obstacle to be overcome rather than a valid consideration in the decision about whether to contract out a particular service. However, cities that have strong municipal labor unions have good reason to value harmonious relationships with those unions. Labor contracts periodically have to be renegotiated, and an environment of good will can be important in arriving at reasonable contract settlements in a timely fashion without work stoppages or slowdowns. Efficiency gains from contracting out a few services to private firms may thus be outweighed by the costs associated with loss of good labor relations more generally. In sum, unless a city plans to bypass municipal unions altogether with a program of across-the-board privatization, there are strong grounds for treating the anticipated reaction of municipal unions as an important contingency (see Box 5.1 on page 117).

SUMMARY

Just as deinstitutionalization was a powerful idea shaping public policy in the 1970s, so privatization has been a powerful policy idea for the 1980s. Privatization was a centerpiece of the Reagan administration. More important here, however, privatization has been put into practice in numerous local governments across the country.

From this experience, it is clear that privatization, at least in the form of contracting out, can and typically does generate cost savings. Despite this, debate about the wisdom and utility of contracting out continues to rage because cost effectiveness is not the only value that must be pursued in public sector decisionmaking. Service quality, equity, and impacts of individual choices on the overall labor relations climate of the public sector are also relevant considerations. This chapter has documented the cost effectiveness results that seem to be realized from contracting with the private sector, but also it has suggested a variety of contingencies that should be taken into account in deciding whether to pursue this strategy in particular cases. Proposals to contract out or adopt other forms of privatization often engender intense emotional debate. This is because they touch on deep and cross-cutting ideological currents, such as the virtues of private enterprise and the limitations of the profit motive. The thesis of this chapter, however, is that privatization cannot be characterized as a beneficial or detrimental move *in the abstract.* Choices about privatization can be better made if they are based on evaluation of relevant local circumstances and contingencies, ranging from the structure of the local market to the significance of client equity concerns for the particular service.

DISCUSSION QUESTIONS

1. Consider the list of specific services that were outlined in Figure 1.1 of Chapter 1. Which of these might be appropriate candidates for private sector production through a contracting arrangement? Which of these are less appropriate, or perhaps even problematic candidates for contracting? Why? Which service characteristics are relevant in your decisionmaking about each of the specific services? (Examples: service specificity, potential for economies of scale through purchasing, potential for scale economies through other means, appropriateness of private sector personnel practices, likely availability of private vendors.) Was either tradition or the likely political sensitivity of any of the services a factor in your decisionmaking?

2. Discuss the case outlined in Box 5.1 of this chapter. Why do you think Kansas City governmental leaders decided to abandon a contracting arrangement in favor of a return to municipal provision of the service in that case? If your speculation is correct, are the reasons adequate and defensible? Why or why not? In a scenario like the one in Box 5.1, what do you think the most important considerations in decisionmaking should be?

NOTES

1. E. S. Savas, *Privatizing the Public Sector: How to Shrink Government* (Chatham, NJ: Chatham House, 1982), p. 118.
2. Ted Kolderie, "The Two Different Concepts of Privatization," *Public Administration Review* 46 (July/August 1986): 286.
3. The typology and the following section describing it is based on E.S. Savas, *Privatization: The Key to Better Government* (Chatham, NJ: Chatham House, 1987), pp. 35–47.
4. Harry P. Hatry and Carl F. Valente, "Alternative Service Delivery Approaches Involving Increased Use of the Private Sector," *Municipal Yearbook 1983* (Washington, DC: ICMA, 1983), p. 204.
5. Savas, *Privatizing the Public Sector,* p. 66.
6. Hatry and Valente, "Alternative Service Delivery Approaches," p. 204.
7. Ibid., p. 205.
8. Savas, *Privatizing the Public Sector,* p. 67; Hatry and Valente, "Alternative Service Delivery Approaches" p. 206.
9. Hatry and Valente, "Alternative Service Delivery Approaches," p. 206.
10. Elaine B. Sharp, "Local Government and General Revenue Sharing Allocations to Nonprofit Organizations: Getting a Handle on the 'Twilight Zone'," in *Policy Evaluation for Local Government,* ed. Terry Busson and Philip Coulter (Westport, CN: Greenwood Press 1987), pp. 81–98.
11. Savas, *Privatizing the Public Sector,* p. 68.
12. Hatry and Valente, "Alternative Service Delivery Approaches, p. 205.

13. Stephen Moore, "Contracting Out: A Painless Alternative to the Budget Cutter's Knife," in *Prospects for Privatization*, ed. Steve Hanke (New York: Academy of Political Science, 1987), p. 62.
14. Elizabeth Voisin, "Surveyed Cities Would Privatize," *City & State* (October, 1987): 33.
15. Annie Millar, "Residential Solid Waste Collection," *Municipal Yearbook 1983* (Washington, DC: ICMA, 1983), p. 193.
16. Ibid., p. 193.
17. Hatry and Valente, "Alternative Service Delivery Approaches," p. 203.
18. Robert Poole, Jr., *Cutting Back City Hall* (New York: Universe Books, 1980), p. 40.
19. Philip Fixler, Jr., and Robert Poole, Jr. "Status of State and Local Privatization," in *Prospects for Privatization*, ed. Steve Hanke (New York: Academy of Political Science, 1987), p. 172.
20. Voisin, "Surveyed Cities Would Privatize," p. 33.
21. Poole, *Cutting Back City Hall*, pp. 85-86.
22. Savas, *Privatizing the Public Sector*, p. 93.
23. Michael R. Fitzgerald, "The Promise and Performance of Privatization: The Knoxville Experience," *Policy Studies Review* 5 (February 1987): 609.
24. Moore, "Contracting Out," p. 63.
25. Eileen B. Berenyi and Barbara J. Stevens, "Does Privatization Work: A Study of the Delivery of Eight Local Services," *State and Local Government Review* (Winter 1988): 14.
26. Ibid., p. 18.
27. James Ferris and Elizabeth Graddy, "Contracting Out: For What? With Whom?" *Public Administration Review* 46 (July/August 1986): 332-344.
28. Kolderie, "Two Different Concepts of Privatization," p. 287.
29. Louis Uchitele, "Public Services Found Better If Private Agencies Compete," *New York Times*, April 26, 1988, pp. 1, 34.
30. Savas, *Privatizing the Public Sector*, p. 90.
31. Ibid.
32. Kolderie, "Two Different Concepts of Privatization," p. 287.
33. Ibid.
34. Fixler and Poole, "Status of State and Local Privatization," p. 173.
35. M.A. Farber, "New York Housing Aides Accused of Taking Bribes," *New York Times*, February 18, 1988, p. 16.
36. Ralph Blumenthal, "F.B.I. Says Public Officials Accepted 105 of 106 Bribes Offered in 2-Year Operation," *New York Times*, August 12, 1987, pp. 1, 15.
37. Robert Bailey, "Uses and Misuses of Privatization," in *Prospects for Privatization*, ed. Hanke (New York: Academy Press of Political Science, 1987), p. 150.
38. Ronald Moe, "Exploring the Limits of Privatization," *Public Administration Review* 47 (November/December 1987): 453-460.
39. Ibid., p. 457.
40. Harold Sullivan, "Privatization of Public Services: A Growing Threat to Constitutional Rights," *Public Administration Review* 47 (November/December 1987): 464.
41. Ibid., pp. 464-466.
42. Savas, *Privatizing the Public Sector*, p. 78.
43. Ferris and Graddy, "Contracting Out," p. 333.
44. Bette Hill, C. Jean Blaser, and Pamela Balmer, "Oversight and Competition in Profit

vs. Nonprofit Contracts for Home Care," *Policy Studies Review* 5 (February 1987): 592.

45. Fitzgerald, "The Promise and Performance of Privatization," p. 610.
46. Savas, *Privatizing the Public Sector,* p. 80.
47. Ferris and Graddy, "Contracting Out," p. 333.
48. Hill, Blaser, and Balmer, "Oversight and Competition," p. 589.
49. Dennis Palumbo, "Privatization and Corrections Policy," *Policy Studies Review* 5 (February 1987): 598.
50. Ferris and Graddy, "Contracting Out," pp. 332–333.
51. Bailey, "Uses and Misuses of Privatization," p. 149.
52. Ferris and Graddy, "Contracting Out," p. 333.

CHAPTER 6

The Equity Side of Urban Services

Much of the criticism of urban services and much of the activity designed to improve them are directed to efficiency and effectiveness. The preceding chapters have outlined these concerns and the initiatives for privatization, technological innovation, and other means for enhancement of productivity. But urban services can be judged by a quite different criterion as well. Questions of equity can also be raised about urban services. This chapter deals with the equity, or fairness, issues that have emerged both in the political sphere and among scholars of urban services.

At the outset, it is important to acknowledge two very different angles from which questions of equity can be explored. First, there are fairness issues surrounding the distribution of existing city services. In this sense, an equity-focused analysis considers questions such as the following: Are basic city services, like police patrol, street paving, snow removal, garbage collection, and recreational services, available in equal amounts and equal quality to all? If there are inequalities, are they patterned in a suspect way? That is, do some groups or neighborhoods consistently get more or better services than others? And is it the affluent, the politically well connected, or racial majorities who are the consistent winners in the distributional process? Or are there valid, technical reasons that some areas or groups are served differently than others—reasons that have nothing to do with racial discrimination, political payoffs, or class biases? The first section of this chapter deals with these and related questions involving the distributional aspects of equity.

As several commentators have noted, however, this first approach to equity-focused analysis ignores a potentially very important set of questions about *which services cities choose to provide* in the first place. If, for example, cities were to provide services that are more important to better-off groups than to the disadvantaged, while simultaneously refusing to provide particular services that are needed by the disadvantaged, a different sort of equity question might be raised. From this second perspective, equity is not just a matter of fair distribution of services; it is a matter of fairness in the mix of services available.

This second form of equity analysis focuses primarily on redistributional programs and services. Redistributional programs and services provide benefits that are targeted to the least-well-off segments of the community. To the extent that they are financed with the tax contributions from better-off segments, while providing benefits primarily to the poor, they can have the net effect of slightly changing the distribution of income in the community—hence, the term *redistributional*. However, such programs and services typically do not have a conscious goal of income redistribution. Rather, they are problem-solving, need-oriented types of programs, such as provision of shelter to the homeless, public health care services, and other forms of local "welfare."

In a persuasive analysis, Paul Peterson has argued that cities are constrained from doing much in the way of redistributional services.[1] The second section of this chapter examines Peterson's argument in greater detail and explores the nature and extent of redistributional service delivery in America's cities.

EQUITY IN THE DISTRIBUTION OF TRADITIONAL CITY SERVICES

In the 1970s, there was a flurry of attention to questions of equity in city service delivery that arose in part from an important focusing event—the case of *Hawkins* v. *Shaw* (1971), in which the U.S. Court of Appeals determined that the tiny community of Shaw, Mississippi, had engaged in racial discrimination in its provision of city services and that the municipal government would have to improve services on the black side of town to bring them up to the quality on the white side of town.[2]

This landmark case created great expectations that similar equalization cases would be successfully brought in many other locations, and it spurred a generation of scholars to examine existing distributions of services in American cities for evidence of discrimination. In retrospect, these high hopes and ambitious research agendas have resulted instead in considerable disappointment, for unexpected obstacles loomed on both the legal and the scholarly front.

On the legal front, it quickly became clear that *Hawkins* v. *Shaw* was a deceptively straightforward case. The differences in service quality in black and white areas were striking, and the court was willing to find discrimination simply based on the showing that white neighborhoods had better services than black neighborhoods.[3] In follow-up cases, court decisions have effectively added the requirement that discriminatory *intent* be proven. For example, in

Mount Healthy City Board of Education v. *Doyle* the court insisted that the plaintiffs must show that, in addition to having a discriminatory purpose, the government action in question must not be primarily based on an additional, legitimate public purpose. That is, it had to be shown that "but for" the discriminatory intent, the government's actions would have been different.[4]

In a parallel fashion, the U.S. Supreme Court has resisted a finding of discrimination in educational opportunity, despite the fact that reliance on the property tax for school financing has created huge disparities in the amount spent per student in different school districts. In the 1971 case *Serrano* v. *Priest,* a state court in California had ruled that the system of school financing based on local property taxes caused unacceptable inequities and invalidated the existing school finance system.[5] However, two years later, in *San Antonio Independent School District* v. *Rodriguez,* the U.S. Supreme Court "refused to concur with lower court decisions invalidating the use of property taxes to finance education."[6]

While these new difficulties were being added to the burden of those wishing to challenge the equity of service delivery arrangements, scholars of service delivery were encountering interesting difficulties in their efforts to evaluate service delivery patterns. These difficulties can be grouped into the following three categories: (1) measuring existing service distributions, (2) drawing inferences about the meaning of existing service distributions, and (3) settling on suitable equity standards for making judgments about service distributions. The following subsections describe each of these areas of difficulty.

Measuring Existing Service Distributions

At first, it might seem that there would be very little problem in finding out how existing city services are actually distributed, but there are a variety of challenges that confront the would-be analyst.

First, an appropriate *unit of analysis* needs to be determined. The unit of analysis is the individual, group, or spatial unit about which data will be collected and for which comparisons can later be made. Typically, researchers have used spatial units, such as neighborhoods, as their units of analysis, in part because city services are organized by such spatial units and city records are kept according to such spatial divisions.

However, spatial units are not typically the real interest of equity analysts. The questions prompting investigation normally have to do with whether the pattern of urban service distribution reveals racial or income-group biases or a tendency to reward those who support the dominant political party. Neighborhoods are of interest only to the extent that they can be characterized as being the special preserve of one or another income, racial, or partisan political group. In a case like *Hawkins* v. *Shaw,* there was a very clear "other side of the tracks" where black residents lived, while white residents lived elsewhere. Consequently, analysis of differences in service *by area* could meaningfully reflect differences in service *by race.* Because there is substantial racial segregation in many American cities, spatial units like neighborhoods can sometimes be meaningfully used to explore for racial differences in urban service treatment. In some places, however, neighborhoods are not so homogeneous by race, income, or political affiliation. In such circumstances, the use of spatial units to come to conclusions about racial or income groups is suspect.

There are other difficulties with spatial units as well. For one thing, city departments may not keep operational data by area. In addition, not all aspects of city services can be appropriately captured with a spatial unit of analysis. For example, although it is possible to compare "frequency of police patrol" from one neighborhood to another (e.g., Neighborhood A is patrolled by one squad car per shift, whereas Neighborhood B has two cars per shift), "courtesy of police treatment of citizens" may be more appropriately treated as an individual-level comparison (e.g., Citizen A rated the police as "somewhat rude" in their encounter, but Citizen B rated the police as "extremely polite" in their encounter). To the extent that racial or income-group differences are the focus of attention, the individual experiences can then be aggregated by race or income group (e.g., 60 percent of black residents rated police treatment as polite, whereas 72 percent of white residents rated police treatment as polite).

Finally, spatial units of analysis can be problematic simply because they are so diverse and inconsistent. The U.S. Bureau of the Census provides one mapping of a city that divides it into census tracts and even smaller block groupings. Census data on racial composition and income are then useful for characterizing these subareas. However, most cities would be sliced into very different subareas for purposes of police service delivery. The police districts and beats would not be aligned with census tracts. Furthermore, there would likely be yet other mappings of the city representing sanitation routes, fire protection subdistricts, parks and recreation department subareas, voting precincts, and the like. These conflicting mappings mean that researchers interested in racial and socioeconomic patterns in service delivery must creatively and laboriously bring data from several mappings of the city into conformity with the spatial definition of neighborhoods or census tracts that is the basis for the analysis.

In addition to the difficulties of finding an appropriate unit of analysis, there are problems with *what should be measured.* For any given service, there are both quantity and quality aspects that might be measured. Does one look at which neighborhoods have more parks or which neighborhoods have better parks? Furthermore, quality of service is multidimensional. Is quality of parks better reflected in park size, the level of maintenance, or the extensiveness of park facilities such as baseball diamonds?

The optimal response to these challenges is to use multiple indicators. The Urban Institute has long recommended that urban managers who are monitoring service quality should use multiple measures "to avoid excessive focus on one aspect of a service at the expense of others."[7] However, the expense and difficulty of obtaining information about city services means that in practice the researchers may not always be able to have multiple indicators of quality for any given service. In his study of urban service distribution in San Antonio, for example, Robert Lineberry was able to obtain multiple measures of parks and recreation service (park distance, developed acreage at closest park, general evaluation of closest park, distance to nearest pool, quality of pool, playground quality, sportsfield quality, playground use, sportsfield use, and pool use). However only single measures were used for police patrol (man-units of police patrol to census tract during calendar year), fire protection (distance to nearest fire station), and sewers (percentage of housing units with public sewers).[8]

Questions about what should be measured are closely tied to questions about *data sources*. To a large extent, persons investigating patterns of service delivery are at the mercy of municipal service agencies and must use the data that are kept by these agencies. These data sources range from excellent to haphazard to nonexistent. Quite apart from concerns about the reliability and validity of these data sources, there is the problem that examination is skewed toward those aspects of service for which there are agency data, while other important aspects of service go unexamined.[9] For example, data on reported crime are always available because police departments nationwide collect those data for the FBI's Uniform Crime Reports. Data on other aspects of policing, such as preventive patrol and service calls on noncriminal matters, may not be as systematically maintained. As a result, the crime-fighting role of police departments may be overemphasized relative to the order maintenance and noncriminal service aspects of policing.

There are methods by which information on city services can be collected, independent of existing bureaucratic records. Direct inspection of conditions and facilities, using trained observers, is one method that has been recommended by the Urban Institute. Obviously, this method is feasible only for those services or aspects of services that have obvious physical manifestations. For example, trained observers could be provided with a rating scheme for street litter, perhaps using pictures for comparison to anchor various points along the rating scale. They would then be dispatched to preselected locations where they would make a visual inspection and assign an appropriate rating.[10]

There is a more widely used method for independent collection of data on city services. Using the highly developed technology for random sample surveys, citizens can be asked directly about their experiences with city services and their evaluations of those services. There are several advantages to this approach. It allows for data collection on individuals rather than requiring inferences about individuals from neighborhood traits. Furthermore, it taps the citizens' own subjective assessments of service outcomes that matter to them, rather than relying on the researcher's judgments about which objective conditions and service inputs are important.[11] Finally, use of citizen survey data rather than agency records relieves concerns about reliability and validity problems caused by self-serving record-keeping practices.

However, there are some important problems with the use of citizen survey data as well. Some research has shown that objective indicators of urban service quality (like police response time or distance to nearest park) are unrelated to citizen evaluations of those services.[12] Such findings have raised questions about the grounds for citizens' subjective evaluations of city services. Others have argued that citizen evaluations of particular city services result from a two-step process, with *perceptions* of city government's activities preceding *evaluation* of those activities.[13] However, citizen perceptions about service delivery can be accurate or inaccurate, and they may be affected by expectations, beliefs about what other neighborhoods are receiving, and a potentially broad array of other political attitudes.[14] Given these many complicating factors, citizen survey data often become a controversial basis for drawing conclusions about "who gets what" in city services.

Inferences about the Meaning of Service Distributions

A second set of challenges facing the equity analyst involves interpretation of the data and measurements discussed in the previous section. For a number of reasons, apparently straightforward data about urban service distribution are not straightforward at all, at least when conclusions about equity are at issue.

First, there is the challenge of sorting out the impact of city actions and the impact of forces beyond the control of city government. The problem here is that most urban services deal with problems that are only partially affected by those services; underlying conditions and the actions of other parties are equally if not more important in determining the extent of problem abatement that is attained. For example, Robert Lineberry argues that the amount of fire protection that a given property attains is only partly determined by the fire protection services of city government. It is also affected by the basic condition of the property (how structurally sound, how flammable), the degree of carelessness of its occupants, the responses of owners to insurance industry policies, and many other factors.[15] Stated another way, if Neighborhood A suffers more fire loss than Neighborhood B, it may initially be difficult to determine whether this is because city fire services were poorer in Neighborhood A, because the conditions of properties and the practices of occupants in Neighborhood A were more conducive to fire, or both.

For reasons closely related to the problem just discussed, city government efforts to encourage citizen coproduction of services often raise equity concerns. Recall from Chapter 4 that coproduction means the combined efforts of citizens and service professionals to create desired levels of urban services. However, not all citizens are equally capable of responding to these invitations to coproduce services. Some citizens have less free time, less physical mobility, and less organizational skills than others. Surveys of citizens in Fort Worth and Sherman, Texas, show that, although there were no significant racial differences in the extent of citizen coproduction with the police department, households with higher incomes were more likely to be involved than those with lower incomes.[16] Urban service outcomes are always affected by underlying conditions and private actions as well as governmental efforts. But coproduction programs concern some equity analysts because they seem to further advantage those groups that have the resources to make investments in quality urban services while overlooking the problems of groups that do not have those resources.

The problem of inputs other than city government actions affecting service distribution is closely related to questions about the choice of an appropriate equity standard. One of the most thorny equity controversies concerns the debate about whether government is responsible for equality of inputs or equality of results. If underlying service conditions and the process by which inputs are converted to outputs were everywhere the same, there would be no difficulty. Equality of inputs could, in such a scenario, be the standard of fairness, and equal results would be expected from equal inputs. In fact, because city services are only one of many factors affecting results, equal inputs do not guarantee equal results. Fairness may require greater city efforts in some areas or for some populations than for others, in order for the results of service delivery to be anything close to equal. A striking example of this approach is Savannah, Georgia's Responsive Public Services program, initiated in 1973. Under that program, the city has established a set of indicators of need. Neighborhoods across the city are assessed using these problem-focused indicators, such as extent of flood hazard and fire incidence. The city then targets its service delivery inputs according to these indicators of need. The result is a compensatory pattern of resource allocation "primarily benefiting black, needy residents."[17]

A second key challenge for those wishing to draw conclusions about equity from observed service distributions is the matter of bureaucratic decision rules. Much research on urban services has shown that city services are distributed according to rational, technical, and professional criteria of the public sector bureaucracies responsible for them.[18] For example, many police departments allocate patrol cars and officers to beats on the basis of a formula that takes into account the number of crime calls in the area, perhaps the severity of the crime calls, and other such "objective" factors. Bryan Jones and his colleagues have found that sanitation service in Detroit is distributed on the basis of several bureaucratic decision rules designed to rationally allocate effort according to workload. These rules include one that allocates personnel and equipment to routes according to the weight of garbage to be collected and another that allocates extra attention to areas where there are special collection problems, such as the alleyway pickup that must be done in the central city area.[19]

Bureaucratic decision rules create an inferential problem for persons analyzing the equity of city services. Although not *ostensibly* distributing services on the basis of race, income, or the political attachments of residents, these rules may nevertheless functionally create such perverse patterns. For example, imagine a community in which the best-off areas are all in the hilly section of town, and the poorer neighborhoods are in the flatlands. If the street department has a decision rule to snowplow hilly areas first, the apparently rational, problem-related rule will have the effect of systematically providing priority attention to the "haves" and deferred attention to the "have-nots." Similarly, the Oakland library has a decision rule to allocate new book acquisition monies to branch libraries according to the volume of circulation of existing books at each branch and to order the same types of books for each branch—specifically, the classic works rather than vocational texts or popular fiction. These works do not fit the needs and tastes of lower-class residents, so circulation in branch libraries serving lower-class areas is typically lower than circulation in branch libraries serving higher-class areas. Because monies for new book acquisition are allocated on the basis of circulation rates, the result is systematically lower resource allocations to lower-class areas.[20]

Stated another way, bureaucratic decision rules can have important distributional consequences from a racial, social, or political perspective. But does fairness demand that rules based on rational, problem-solving criteria be jettisoned if they are shown to systematically disadvantage certain groups? In the court cases following *Hawkins* v. *Shaw* (see earlier discussion), the court seemed to be suggesting otherwise. From the court's perspective, local government rules that have a disproportionately unfavorable impact on racial minorities do not necessarily signify discrimination, and hence can stand. Discriminatory intent must be shown. Because racial classifications have been treated as particularly suspect by the court, this unwillingness to overturn decision rules with unintended racial consequences has suggested to many observers that challenges to service delivery rules benefiting certain income groups or political allies would be even less convincing to the court.

On the other hand, bureaucratic decision rules can well be deemed unfair by analysts, neighborhood activists, and others, even if the courts do not stand willing to find discrimination. Political conflict sometimes erupts over these rules and their perceived equity consequences (see Box 6.1). For these reasons, urban politicians and managers are well advised to temper the rational, technocratic impulses behind bureaucratic decision rules with sensitivity to their sometimes perverse distributional consequences.

There is yet a third reason that analysts have had difficulty in drawing defensible conclusions about the equity of urban service distribution: debate over the selection of services subjected to equity analysis. Many studies of urban service distribution have focused on a narrow range of services with particular characteristics that may have a bearing on patterns of distribution. Specifically, distributional studies have emphasized routine, repetitive, labor-intensive services like police patrol, fire protection, and garbage collection, rather than the exceptional, long-term decisionmaking of capital-intensive services like water

---

BOX 6.1   Conflict over a Bureaucratic Decision Rule in Los Angeles

In June 1987, voters in South Central Los Angeles rejected a proposal that would have increased property taxes in this poor, crime-prone, inner-city area of Los Angeles for the purpose of adding 300 more police officers to the area. A local council member had proposed the measure in response to the youth gang and drug problem that has plagued the neighborhood in recent years. Recent city-wide ballot measures to raise property taxes for more policing have been rejected. Opponents of the plan argued that it established a dangerous precedent of providing police protection on the basis of an area's willingness to pay taxes.

Opponents of the plan also argued that the area would not have been so desperate for additional police officers if the police department's deployment formula were fairer. They claimed that the deployment formula takes into consideration the dollar value of property crimes and thereby skews the police officer assignment toward wealthier neighborhoods. The police chief, meanwhile, denies that the deployment formula is unfair, claiming that South Central Los Angeles has 16 percent of the city's population but 29 percent of the existing police officers deployed to neighborhoods. An independent consulting company was retained to study this controversial, bureaucratic decision rule.

Source: Judith Cummings, "Voters Reject Los Angeles Police Plan," *New York Times,* June 4, 1987, p. 13.

---

and sewage treatment infrastructure construction, new highway construction, and the like. Since routine, labor-intensive services are those for which the actions of street-level bureaucrats and decisions of middle management are crucial, it should not be surprising that the literature has also emphasized these influences on urban service distribution.[21]

On the other hand, there has been some analysis of a more varied set of services. For example, Robert Lineberry's research on San Antonio includes attention to capital-intensive services (public sewers, public water, and certain aspects of parks and recreation service) as well as more labor-intensive, routine services such as police patrol.[22] Taking the whole body of urban service distribution research into account, a rather broad array of services has been examined in one city or another. But this itself has created a problem—the problem of aggregating diverse findings into broader conclusions about equity in city services. Within a particular city, results of distributional analysis across several services may lead to mixed results. For example, a classic study of street, school, and sewer services in Oakland, California, yielded findings that some service distributions favored the better-off while some favored the worse-off. Rather than a clear-cut answer to the question of whether urban services are distributed fairly, such mixed results leave us with the unsatisfying conclusion that there are "unpatterned inequalities" in service delivery.[23] Attempts to summarize such mixed results across various research sites also creates confusion and conflict. For example, although most analysts have adopted the broad conclusion of unpatterned inequalities in urban services, some have argued that "there seem to be more cases where an 'underclass' hypothesis is supportable than is generally stated."[24]

Determining an Appropriate Equity Standard

So far, we have seen that attempts to evaluate the equity of urban service distribution encounter a host of difficulties concerning measurement methods and interpretation of empirical findings. In addition, conclusions about equity are not easily made because there is no consensus about an appropriate evaluative standard for judging equity. For example, the preceding section referred to the debate over equality of inputs versus equality of results as competing equity standards. This section shows that there are yet other equity standards from which to choose and little agreement about which is preferable.

To appreciate the variety of equity criteria, or distributional standards of fairness, consider the following typology, which includes six different equity standards: strict equality, need, effort expended, money invested, results, and ascription.[25]

1. *Strict equality* means that everyone gets exactly the same amount of the desired good. Note that for this and many of the other standards a pair of substandards can be envisioned—one interpreting the definition as applying to inputs and one interpreting the definition as applying to results. For example, strict equality can mean that everyone should have all their garbage collected once a week (equality of results) or that everyone should get three bag's worth of garbage collected each week (equality of inputs).

2. In contrast with strict egalitarianism, a *need-based standard* for distribution argues that fairness means different shares for different individuals, because some individuals have greater need than others. To the extent that many urban services are oriented toward problem solving, they lend themselves to needs standards. Under a needs standard, resources are mobilized where problems are greatest, and individuals are eligible for special programs if they have a particular problem. Examples include the allocation of police patrol resources on the basis of the severity of crime in various areas and the provision of special recreational programs for disadvantaged youth.

3. The *effort expended standard* means that the desired good is distributed according to the work or activity contributed to it by various members of the community. As explained earlier, coproduction schemes implicitly follow this distributional standard. Citizens who participate in the police department's crime prevention programs are safer from crime than those who do not, parents who volunteer for parent-child school activities get a better education for their children, and neighborhoods where citizen organizations are willing to invest time in public park support activities end up with more satisfactory recreational services.

4. A closely related standard is one that would distribute desired goods on the basis of *money invested.* The money invested standard is much like

the economist's criterion of willingness to pay and approximates what is often called market equity. However, it can be interpreted in a variety of ways. For example, distributing services on the basis of who pays more in taxes is one version of the money invested standard. Although most city services are not overtly based on this standard, those financed by user fees are (see Chapter 7). If only those persons who are willing to pay a membership fee get to use the municipal swimming pool, these recreational services are based on money invested. Special assessment districts exemplify the money invested principle as well because particular goods or services, like new sidewalks, are provided to persons within a subarea that is subject to a specific tax to pay for those goods or services. Programs like urban homesteading also distribute on the basis of money invested, at least in part. The homesteading program makes abandoned homes available at a negligible price to those who are willing to invest money to rehabilitate them as residences.[26]

5. The *results standard* of equity distributes desired goods on the basis of where they are most likely to yield good quality of output. Stated more simply, a results standard argues that public sector resources should be used to back winners or to invest in likely successes. A study of city services in Oakland found one example of a results standard of distribution—a decision rule that allocates higher new-book acquisition budgets to branch libraries with higher circulation rates.[27] According to this rule, new-book ordering should be concentrated in locations where it will do the most good—that is, where the books will actually be used. Another example of the results standard in practice is the provision of employment and training assistance to only those individuals who are qualified for skill training.[28] Individuals who are illiterate or who have other severe problems that would get in the way of successful skill training for employment would be weeded out under a results-oriented standard of what is fair.

6. *Ascriptive standards* are those that base distribution on "genetic or socially defined characteristics such as sex, race, socioeconomic class, or age."[29] Suspicion that urban services were allocated on the basis of ascriptive standards such as race and class prompted much of the initial research on urban service distribution in the aftermath of the *Hawkins* v. *Shaw* case. From this perspective, ascription hardly seems a formula for fairness. On the other hand, ascription is a widely used and frequently accepted standard. For example, programs of transportation assistance for the elderly, such as Dial-a-Ride services, use an ascriptive standard (age) as a proxy for need. Age is also an important ascriptive standard in the distribution of educational services. Socioeconomic class is a distributional standard in housing rehabilitation programs that are targeted to low-income households.

This typology of different equity standards suggests one key reason for disagreement about the fairness of existing urban service distributions: lack of consensus about what fairness means. Different individuals, applying different standards to a given case, will draw different conclusions about fairness. The situation is further complicated by the fact that many urban services and government programs use multiple standards, either at different stages of program implementation or as a means of progressively narrowing the scope of who is eligible for a program. For example, Chicago's urban homesteading program is based in part on a need standard because only families with less than a specified income and with designated space needs (because of family size) are eligible. In addition, however, the program adds money invested and results standards by requiring a minimum income and an assessment that the applicant has the wherewithal to take on a rehabilitation and home ownership project.[30] Debate can arise then about the relative weight given to various distributional standards in programs using multiple standards. For example, should results-oriented considerations be relaxed somewhat for families that have very pressing needs?

There is very little in the way of definitive, noncontroversial conclusions about urban service equity, even when the focus is on the traditional services that cities provide. Rather, disparate research findings feed a continuing debate about the relative importance of race, class, politics, and professional service delivery rules in determining who gets what. This section has shown that the controversy and continuing debate can be traced to three sets of problems for equity analysts: how to adequately measure who gets what, how to differentiate unfair city government practices from adverse underlying conditions or professionally objective rules, and which equity standard to apply to any given case.

Despite these analytical difficulties, questions of fairness are an important aspect of urban service administration. Equity debates can flair up suddenly, can simmer beneath the surface of city politics, and can create occasions for acerbic community conflict, as earlier examples have illustrated (see Box 6.1). Claims that some neighborhoods receive better services than others are an important part of the "street-fighting pluralism" that is said to characterize city government.[31]

But are more substantial issues of fairness overlooked in this debate over how existing city services are distributed? Is it not possible that city governments "discriminate" against the underclass, not by giving poorer neighborhoods less snowplowing services than rich neighborhoods, but by emphasizing basic housekeeping services to the exclusion of helping services more specifically designed for the poor? The next section considers this second perspective on equity, with its focus on the mix of redistributive and distributive services.

EQUITY AND LOCAL GOVERNMENT'S ROLE IN REDISTRIBUTIONAL SERVICES

As noted at the outset of this chapter, questions about the pattern of distribution of city services get at only one version of the equity issue. Another perspective on equity has to do with the types of services that cities choose to provide in the first place. Some commentators have argued that the latter is the more significant question and that a narrow focus on distribution of traditional services overlooks crucial issues of fairness.[32] Stated another way, "it may matter little 'who gets what' when it already has been determined in earlier stages of the policy process that there will be little to get."[33]

An important contributor to urban analysis suggests that, given the nature of urban political systems, there will typically be little to get in the way of redistributional services, which is to say, services designed to aid the more disadvantaged segments of the community. In *City Limits,* Paul Peterson argues that in order to remain economically viable, cities must compete with each other to keep the higher-than-average taxpayers of the community. Since cities cannot erect legal barriers to prevent the loss of valued businesses and residents, they must design their taxing and spending policies so as not to alienate those valued institutions and residents, which means that redistributional activities must be held to a minimum. By logical derivation, it also means that the level of redistributional spending that a city does undertake is a function of its fiscal capacity rather than the extent of need for redistributional programs.[34] Ironically, those communities with the most poverty, unemployment, hunger, and homelessness will not, according to this theory, be among the highest spenders on programs to aid these disadvantaged groups; rather, the higher redistributive spenders will be cities with stronger tax bases because they can finance redistributive programs with minimal impact on tax rates.

Peterson's analysis provides an important theoretical perspective on redistributional policies in American cities. An alternative perspective, offered by Schneider, stipulates that redistributive spending and spending overall will typically be higher in local governments that are more homogeneous.[35] This is because heterogeneity, especially in terms of income, creates a situation of conflicting interests in which individuals with higher incomes are unwilling to bear higher tax rates to finance government services that benefit groups with lower incomes. In local governments with greater income homogeneity, however, it is much easier to develop a consensus for government spending on programs.

Finally, there is a third perspective on redistributional programs that is based on recognition that these programs can serve functions other than the overt, problem-solving functions of welfare and other social service programs. Specifically, redistributional programs have been interpreted as having a latent function of social control. Government's level of commitment to these programs can then be understood as a response to various conditions of social conflict or crisis that create the need to head off dangerous, violent responses on the part of the have-nots of society.

Perhaps the most articulate proponents of the social control perspective on redistributional programs are Piven and Cloward. They have argued that the explosive growth in the welfare rolls that we have witnessed in this country can be traced to the riots and other violence in many of the nation's cities in the 1960s. In response to pressures at the local level and national Democratic Party concerns, eligibility requirements for welfare were relaxed, according to this argument.[36] From the social control perspective, the level of need for redistributional programs is not an irrelevant factor, as it is in Peterson's theory, but the need that is relevant is the need to suppress disruptive behavior or the threat of disruptive activity on the part of disadvantaged groups.

Piven and Cloward's thesis was offered to account for change over time in the federal government's level of commitment to one specific redistributional program: Aid to Families with Dependent Children (AFDC). More recently, the social control thesis has been applied to local government as well in an effort to explain differences in city governments' commitments to locally funded welfare programs.[37] From this point of view, city governments increase their budgetary outlays for redistributional services like welfare whenever there are threats to the social order. Such threats to the social order can be in the form of mass insurgency, like the urban violence of the 1960s, or in the form of increased crime rates, or even dramatic income inequality, with its implications of unrest from the have-nots.

Peterson's thesis, Schneider's thesis, and the social control thesis provide sharply contrasting explanations for variation in local redistributional activity. Peterson argues that redistributional effort is a function of resources available, so that redistributional spending is actually dislocated from need. Schneider argues that redistributional effort is a function of the consensus-building capacity of the community, which depends on whether the population is homogeneous or heterogeneous. The social control thesis argues that redistributional effort is greater in places and at times in which there are conditions constituting a threat to the dominant social classes. Before evaluating these contrasting perspectives on why some cities engage in more redistributional spending than others, it is important to consider the overall size and scope of redistributional activity at the local level.

How Much Redistributional Activity?

How much redistributional activity do cities undertake? Casual observation suggests that Peterson's thesis cannot be correct. Everywhere, it seems, cities are involved in programs and services designed to assist the disadvantaged, including the poor, the homeless, the mentally ill, drug and alcohol abusers, and so forth. Local involvement with new social problems and innovative solutions to chronic problems is everyday fare in the media.

For example, in Philadelphia the homeless are being helped through an innovative program that combines housing rehabilitation, placement, and job training. The city has budgeted $11 million for this program, to purchase and renovate houses that the federal government has acquired through mortgage defaults.[38] In a much more controversial program directed at the mentally disturbed homeless, New York City launched a program to force 500 of the most severely mentally ill street people into hospital treatment—a program that eventually led to a showdown between Mayor Koch and Joyce Brown, one of the first homeless individuals taken up in the program. Meanwhile, nineteen cities have begun collaborating in a foundation-supported program to provide health care to the homeless—a program that had provided service to more than 85,000 individuals by the fall of 1987.[39]

Some cities are using their regulatory powers to force the private sector to take on additional social service responsibilities. Rather than limiting redistributional burdens, as Peterson suggests cities must do to compete for private investment, some cities are directly placing these burdens on the shoulders of developers. For example, Boston and San Francisco have insisted that developers pay fees of several dollars per square foot of new construction to subsidize low income housing.[40]

Despite these anecdotal reports of new city initiatives in social services, spending on redistributional programs is a relatively small portion of total spending by local government. U.S. Bureau of the Census data for fiscal year 1985/86 show that only 5.4 percent of municipal government spending was for public welfare, another 6.1 percent was for health and hospital spending, and another 4.8 percent was for housing and community development programming, for a total of 16.3 percent of general expenditures devoted to these redistributional program categories.[41] Cities are even less involved in redistributive activity *in the sense of budgeting locally raised revenues for such services.* A substantial share of cities' redistributional spending is derived from federal and state monies for specific social programs. Nevertheless, city governments are deeply involved in redistributive activity. They operate programs and services funded by federal and state monies, and they collaborate with private and nonprofit organizations to provide various human services.

Several of these points can be highlighted with a look at Kansas City, Missouri's budget, which also provided illustrative material in Chapter 1. For fiscal year 1986/87, Kansas City officials budgeted for nine programs that are clearly targeted for the disadvantaged. In addition, some portion of Truman Medical Center funding may be relevant to our analysis of redistributional spending because this urban health care facility is particularly important to the poor.

Table 6.1 shows the various programs, their purposes as stated in city budget documents, and the revenue sources used to pay for them. The table makes clear that the city does spend millions of dollars for redistributive programs and services, ranging from health care for disadvantaged populations to legal aid, special transportation assistance, recreation, and other services especially for have-not groups. On the other hand, as large as these dollar amounts may seem in the abstract, they are small by comparison with city operations in total. Even if all the operations of the city-subsidized Truman Medical Center are counted as redistributional services, Kansas City still devotes only 6.3 percent of its budget to redistributional services. If the Truman Medical Center is not included, the portion of Kansas City's total budget that is devoted to redistributional services is a minuscule 2.5 percent. To further put this in perspective,

TABLE 6.1. REDISTRIBUTIONAL SERVICES AND PROGRAMS IN KANSAS CITY, 1986-1987

Item	Estimated Spending	Percentage Nonlocal Funding Share
Health Department		
Refugee disease control	$ 218,644	40
Maternal and child health	2,574,432	62
Neighborhood health centers	511,575	93
Housing and Community Development		
Rehabilitation Programs	3,639,000	100
Law Department		
Legal aid for the indigent	301,778	73
Neighborhood Development Department		
Neighborhood services to "assist low-income families" (paint-up, weatherization, etc.)	1,338,678	3
Transportation Department Share-A-Ride for elderly and disabled; employment transit assistance for low income workers	1,405,525	21
Urban Community Services Department		
Youth services—child care, recreation, nutrition and summer employment for disadvantaged youth	987,021	0
Social services—casework, emergency assistance, literacy programs, and other services to the disadvantaged and the elderly	569,080	18
Truman Medical Center	17,080,000	n.a.
Grand Total	28,625,733	
Total Minus Truman Medical Center	11,545,733	
Total City Budget	451,494,597	
Redistributional Share		
Including Truman Medical Center	6.3%	
Excluding Truman Medical Center	2.5%	

Source: Budget, Fiscal Year 1986-1987, City of Kansas City, Missouri.

the roughly $11½ million budgeted by the city for redistributional services (not counting the Truman Medical Center) amounts to only 17 percent of what is budgeted for the police department alone.

Furthermore, a substantial portion of what the city spends for redistributional programs is actually revenue received from higher-level governments, sometimes in the form of grants specifically intended for particular uses and sometimes in the form of open-ended General Revenue Sharing (GRS) from the federal government. Table 6.1 shows that some programs, like the city's neighborhood health centers and its housing rehabilitation program, are almost totally funded by federal or state grants, and others, like legal aid for the indigent and the maternal and child health program, are predominantly funded from these intergovernmental grants.

If Kansas City is at all typical, Peterson and other commentators are quite correct in asserting that cities are broadly constrained from committing local revenues to redistributional programs. On the other hand, the Kansas City case highlights the fact that cities can be involved in redistributional programs in other ways, particularly when funds from the federal government or the state are available for use.

What the Kansas City budget data fail to show adequately is the variety of ways in which local governments are involved in redistributional programming. A better portrait of this is provided by the results of a survey of cities and counties conducted by the International City Management Association in 1984. That survey asks about a number of different roles that the local government might play, including (1) direct provision of a service using local government employees, (2) joint provision of a service in collaboration with another government, (3) contracting with another government or with a nongovernmental group to provide services, (4) provision of financial support to a nongovernmental group delivering the service, and (5) provision of in-kind support like facilities or staff assistance to a nongovernmental group engaged in service delivery.[42] Some of the results of this survey are presented in Figure 6.1, which focuses only on city governments.[43]

Figure 6.1 shows that no single method of city government involvement in social service provision is dominant. The types of city government involvement depend on the specific service at issue. For example, in-kind support of private or nonprofit organizations is the most typical method by which city governments help to provide nutrition centers for the elderly and food distribution to the general needy population. In addition, at least 10 percent of cities provide these services themselves, and substantial numbers of cities provide nutrition centers for the elderly through either subsidy to private or nonprofit organizations, contracts with other governments, or joint service with other governments. By contrast, the most common local government role in special transportation for the elderly has city government providing the service itself, using city employees and facilities. Comparatively few cities take on any role in emergency financial assistance to individuals. When city governments are involved, however, it is most typically with direct government administration of the service. Provision of crisis shelter, such as homes for victims of spouse abuse, is also comparatively rare; the most typical city government role is subsidizing a private or nonprofit organization that provides the shelter. Despite the emergence of homelessness on the political agenda of the 1980s, this survey shows that few cities play any role in emergency housing services. Among those that do, direct government provision, in-kind support to nongovernmental organizations, and subsidies to nongovernmental organizations are about equally prevalent.

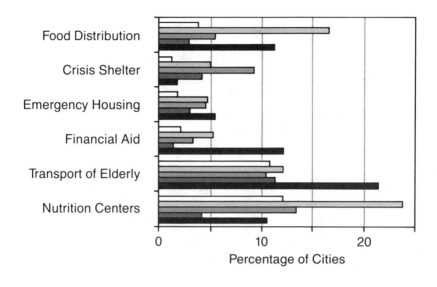

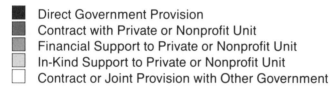

Figure 6.1. Types of City Government Involvement in Selected Social Services, 1984 (*Source:* Adapted from Robert Agranoff and Alex Pattakos, "Human Services in Local Government," *Municipal Yearbook 1985* [Washington, DC: International City Management Association, 1985], p. 207.)

Figure 6.1 shows that, if direct provision of service were the only role considered, city governments would appear to be quite uninvolved in the provision of redistributive social services. However, when all the possible roles were taken into account, city government involvement appears to be more substantial. Furthermore, county governments are even more likely to be involved in the delivery of redistributive social services. This is summarized in Figure 6.2, which shows the percentages of cities and the percentages of counties in the ICMA survey that are engaged in at least one of the methods for provision of each of the social services. Like the glass that can be described as either half empty or half full, Figure 6.2 can be interpreted as showing surprisingly widespread or disappointingly limited involvement of city governments in important social services. Setting aside the question of whether local governments are doing enough, Figure 6.2 clearly shows that city governments' role in providing for the needs of have-not citizens is not

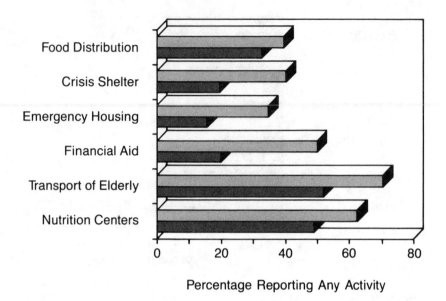

Percentage Reporting Any Activity

■ City Governments
□ County Governments

Figure 6.2. City and County Government Involvement in Selected Social Services, 1984 (*Source:* Adapted from Robert Agranoff and Alex Pattakos, "Human Services in Local Government," *Municipal Yearbook 1985* [Washington, DC: International City Management Association, 1985], p. 207.)

trivial. County governments' role is even more substantial. The majority of county governments surveyed are involved in the two social services intended for the elderly. At least one-third and as many as half of the counties are involved in the provision of the more general social services for the needy.

In sum, despite the constraint that Peterson emphasizes, local governments are involved in the expenditure of funds for redistributive social services, although substantial portions of such funds are likely to have been received from the federal or state government. More important, local governments interact with a variety of other local institutions concerned with redistributive social services. Officials may subsidize one or more nonprofit organizations, contract with others for the provision of particular services, share facilities and staff with nonprofit organizations for some services, and contract with other governmental units for other services. Local governments are therefore important players in a complicated, multiorganizational picture of social service delivery. They frequently are "the primary actor in putting together the disparate pieces on the local scene" and serve as a "partner, acting in concert with other governments and/or major private sector entities in planning and solving human service problems."[44]

Not all local governments are equally likely to take on these roles in the provision of redistributive services. Figure 6.2, for example, shows that many governments are *not* involved in the provision of nutrition programs for the elderly, emergency financial aid or shelter, and other forms of assistance to the disadvantaged. Especially dramatic differences have been observed in various cities' responses to the homelessness problem of the late 1980s. For example, some cities have attempted to eject the homeless from the jurisdiction, either with aggressively enforced prohibitions on overnight sleeping in public places or with "greyhound therapy"—giving bus tickets to mentally ill homeless individuals. Other communities have provided some emergency shelter, ranging from minimalist responses like space for tent cities to collaboration with nonprofit organizations to provide shelters equipped with social services. Still other communities have pursued a strategy of benign neglect, simply allowing the homeless essentially to take over certain public spaces.[45]

Why do some local governments devote more effort and resources than others to social problem solving for the disadvantaged? Three responses to this question were given earlier. The social control thesis suggests that spending will be greater in those places where threats to the established social order have been perceived by the dominant class. Peterson's thesis suggests that spending will be greater in those places where the local tax base provides greater resources to engage in social programming while maintaining a competitive tax rate. By implication, both theses suggest that redistributive spending will be greater in communities that are the beneficiaries of larger amounts of federal grant monies. Schneider's thesis suggests that spending will be greater in those places where the population is more homogeneous in terms of income.

There is no conclusive evidence about these theses. Peterson's initial work shows that fiscal capacity does seem to be an important predictor of combined state and local redistributive spending and that very rough indicators of demand and need for redistributional services are not consistently important predictors. Ironically, but consistent with Peterson's thesis, state and local spending for old age assistance, aid to dependent children, unemployment benefits, welfare, and health and hospitals are all higher in cities with higher incomes.[46]

The social control thesis has been tested largely with respect to changes in the federal government's response to urban turmoil, and the results have been mixed and inconclusive.[47] When the social control thesis is tested with respect to local government spending for a specific redistributional program (General Assistance), the results do not support the social control thesis. At the same time, the results raise a new challenge to Peterson's thesis by showing that poverty level is the most important predictor of welfare recipient rates for both whites and for blacks.[48] This suggests that welfare practices *are* sensitive to need, not just fiscal capacity.

Schneider's empirical evidence is restricted to an examination of a sample of suburban governments. However, that empirical analysis shows that greater levels of income homogeneity are linked to higher levels of redistributive spending. In addition, Schneider's analysis indirectly challenges Peterson's thesis by showing that redistributive spending declines as the median income of the jurisdiction increases.[49]

There is also evidence that the redistributive policies of local governments are sensitive to both political factors and professional control. Kenneth Wong cites various studies showing that black mayors spend more on social services and welfare than do white mayors, and he also argues that reform institutions and professional control provide a more supportive environment for redistributive programs:

> In short, where professional autonomy over resource allocation is greater, so is local responsiveness to the objectives of redistributional programs. Reform agencies are more likely to routinize their program operation, adapt to redistributive program missions, and in the end, develop a modus vivendi that supports the redistributive goals.[50]

If there is no consistent, conclusive evidence concerning the validity of competing explanations of variation in redistributive spending, there is also continuing controversy about the impact of federal grants on local redistributive activities. Part of the controversy stems from the fact that the intergovernmental aid system is so complex. Federal grants might be expected to stimulate local spending for redistributional services if the grants are earmarked for such services and perhaps especially if the grants require a local matching effort. However, only some federal grant programs have these features. Others, like General Revenue Sharing and some block grants, can be used at the discretion of local officials. The available evidence suggests that the sorts of redistributive social services at issue here have not been a very high priority when local governments have spent GRS money.[51]

Another reason for controversy about the impact of the federal role is the fact that this role is constantly changing. Debate about what federal grant programs have accomplished intertwines with debate about the consequences of federal aid cuts and debate about what the federal role should become.

From an equity perspective, the reasons for city variation in redistributive services are important. If cities with more substantial poverty, homelessness, hunger, and joblessness problems are providing less in the way of relevant social services than cities with less substantial problems, simply because their fiscal capacity is less, then the need-based equity standard is clearly violated. If the pattern of intergovernmental fiscal aid redistributes income geographically but without targeting assistance to disadvantaged individuals, again need-based equity standards remain unrealized.[52] If federal and local social service efforts are geared toward the heading off of overt social conflict, need-based equity standards may inadvertently be served, although the result depends on the processes by which have-not groups mobilize to challenge authority and the tendencies of elites to perceive relevant threats.

SUMMARY

In this chapter, two versions of the equity question have been examined. One asks about *distribution* of the basic traditional services that city governments virtually everywhere provide. In that version, equity concerns stem from the possibility that certain racial, economic, or political groups might be systematically deprived of their fair share of these services. The second version of the equity question asks about local government's role in *redistribution*. In this version, equity concerns stem from the possibility that cities are constrained from providing the social services that are of particular importance to the least advantaged segment of the community.

Neither version of the equity question has been well answered. As this chapter has shown, this is in part because of limitations on our ability to determine what local governments are actually doing with regard to distribution and redistribution, and why. It is also because normative debates about appropriate equity standards and about the amount of redistribution that is desirable have not been resolved.

Ultimately, it may be the continuing debate that is of importance even if no resolution of the question is at hand. Continuing debate at least signifies that these equity questions are on the public agenda. For each version of the equity question, however, there is a response that threatens to neutralize debate and make the equity question moot. With respect to city government's distribution of traditional services, it is the bureaucratic decision rule response, which argues that distribution is based on objective, technical, professional standards. With respect to city government's redistributional role, it is Peterson's argument of the inevitably limited capabilities of local government. In their most simplistic forms, each of these responses brings the equity discussion to a premature close.

On closer inspection, however, both the concept of the bureaucratic decision rule and Peterson's thesis suggest important matters that deserve further attention. Astute urban managers and politicians realize that the distributional consequences of supposedly neutral, service delivery rules can lead to damaging political conflict. Consequently, the fairness of distributional impacts must be a part of urban service decisionmaking, along with professional and technical standards and rules. Similarly, although Peterson's thesis has been very influential, it is perhaps most useful in reminding us that redistributional adequacy is an open question in the evolving federal system.

DISCUSSION QUESTIONS AND EXERCISES

1. Using some community with which you are familiar, imagine what would be involved in doing a fairness analysis of some particular city service of interest to you. How might you determine whether service delivery is biased against black citizens or other minorities? What data would you collect? Why? How? What fairness standard would you use to interptet the data? Why?

2. Find out how redistributive services such as those listed in Figure 6.2 are handled in your community. You might examine copies of city and county budgets, check newspaper articles, talk with public officials, and ask leaders of the United Way.

NOTES

1. Paul Peterson, *City Limits* (Chicago: University of Chicago Press, 1981).
2. Ralph Rossum, "The Rise and Fall of Equalization Litigation," *The Urban Interest* (Spring, 1980): 2–3. The full citation for the case is *Hawkins* v. *Shaw*, 437 F. 2d 1286, 1287 (5th Cir. 1971).
3. Robert L. Lineberry, *Equality and Urban Policy: The Distribution of Municipal Public Services* (Beverly Hills: Sage, 1977), p. 130.
4. Rossum, "The Rise and Fall of Equalization Litigation," pp. 3–5.
5. *Serrano* v. *Priest*, 5 Cal. 3d 584 (1971).
6. David R. Berman, *State and Local Politics* (Boston: Allyn & Bacon, 1987), p. 276; the full citation for the case is *San Antonio Independent School District* v. *Rodriguez*, 411 U.S. 1 (1973).
7. Harry Hatry, Louis Blair, Donald Fisk, John Greiner, John Hall, and Philip Schaenman, *How Effective Are Your Community Services?* (Washington, DC: Urban Institute and ICMA, 1977), p. 5.
8. Lineberry, *Equality and Urban Policy*, p. 81.
9. Rodney Hero, "The Urban Service Delivery Literature: Some Questions & Considerations," *Polity* 18 (1986): 659–677.
10. Hatry et al., *How Effective Are Your Community Services?* pp. 207–213.
11. Gerald S. McDougall and Harold Bunce, "Urban Service Distributions: Some Answers to Neglected Issues," *Urban Affairs Quarterly* 19 (March 1984): 355–372.
12. Brian Stipak, "Citizen Satisfaction with Urban Services: Potential Misuse as a Performance Indicator," *Public Administration Review* 39 (January/February 1979): 46–52; Karin Brown and Philip Coulter, "Subjective and Objective Measures of Police Service Delivery," *Public Administration Review* 43 (January/February 1983): 50–58.
13. Stephen Percy, "In Defense of Citizen Evaluations as Performance Measures," *Urban Affairs Quarterly* 22 (September 1986): 66–83.
14. Elaine B. Sharp, *Citizen Demand-Making in the Urban Context* (University, AL: University of Alabama Press, 1986), p. 75.
15. Lineberry, *Equality and Urban Policy*, p. 71.
16. Robert Warren, Mark Rosentraub, and Karen Harlow, "Coproduction, Equity, and the Distribution of Safety," *Urban Affairs Quarterly* 19 (June 1984): 447–464.
17. Llewellyn M. Toulmin, "Equity as a Decision Rule in Determining the Distribution of Urban Public Services," *Urban Affairs Quarterly* 23 (March 1988): 390.
18. Frank Levy, Arnold Meltsner, and Aaron Wildavsky, *Urban Outcomes: Schools, Streets, and Libraries* (Berkeley: University of California Press, 1974); Ken Mladenka, "The Urban Bureaucracy and the Chicago Political Machine: Who Gets What and the Limits of Political Control," *American Political Science Review* 74 (December 1980): 991–998.
19. Bryan Jones, Saadia Greenberg, and Joseph Drew, *Service Delivery in the City* (New York: Longman, 1980), pp. 120–128.

20. Levy, Meltsner, and Wildavsky, *Urban Outcomes,* p. 195.
21. William C. Baer, "Just What Is an Urban Service, Anyway?" *Journal of Politics* 47 (August 1985): 890.
22. Lineberry, *Equality and Urban Policy,* p. 81.
23. Ibid., p. 142.
24. Hero, "Urban Service Delivery Literature," pp. 666–667.
25. This listing of fairness standards is based on Jennifer Hochschild, *What's Fair: American Beliefs About Distributive Justice* (Cambridge, MA: Harvard University Press, 1981), as modified by William Blanchard, "Evaluating Social Equity: What Does Fairness Mean and Can We Measure It?" *Policy Studies Journal* 15 (September 1986): 33–38.
26. Blanchard, "Evaluating Social Equity," pp. 43–47.
27. Levy, Meltsner, and Wildavsky, *Urban Outcomes,* p. 195.
28. Blanchard, "Evaluating Social Equity," p. 40.
29. Ibid., p. 33.
30. Ibid., p. 46.
31. Douglas Yates, *The Ungovernable City* (Cambridge, MA: MIT Press, 1977).
32. Richard Rich, "The Political Economy of Urban-Service Distribution," in *The Politics of Urban Public Services,* ed. R. Rich (Lexington, MA: Heath, 1982), p. 7.
33. Hero, "Urban Service Delivery Literature," p. 661.
34. Peterson, *City Limits,* pp. 41–50.
35. Mark Schneider, "Income Homogeneity and the Size of Suburban Government," *Journal of Politics* 49 (February 1987): 36–53.
36. Frances Fox Piven and Richard A. Cloward, *Regulating the Poor: The Functioning of Public Welfare* (New York: Vintage, 1971).
37. Mitchell Chamlin, "General Assistance Among Cities: An Examination of the Need, Economic Threat, and Benign Neglect Hypotheses," *Social Science Quarterly* 68 (December 1987): 834–846.
38. William K. Stevens, "Homeless, Not Helpless in Philadelphia," *New York Times,* May 3, 1988, p. 9.
39. Charles Moore, David Sink, and Patricia Hoban-Moore, "The Politics of Homelessness," *PS* 21 (Winter 1988): p. 57.
40. William K. Stevens, "Developers Expanding Role in Social Services," *New York Times,* November 28, 1987, p. 28.
41. U.S. Bureau of the Census, *City Government Finances, 1985–1986* (Washington, DC: U.S. Government Printing Office, 1988), p. ix.
42. All municipalities with populations over 10,000 were contacted for the survey, and 29.3 percent responded. Counties with populations of 50,000 or more were contacted for the survey, and 14.5 percent responded.
43. ICMA asked about a much broader array of social services than those highlighted for analysis here. The selection of services for this analysis was based on two considerations: (1) to ensure faithfulness to the theme of redistribution, services that are more clearly targeted for the economically disadvantaged were of greater interest; (2) to ensure variety, some services for the elderly were included along with those for the general needy population. Services targeted for children and youth posed some problems on the first criterion and are therefore not included in this analysis.
44. Robert Agranoff and Alex Pattakos, "Human Services in Local Government: Pat-

terns of Service at Metropolitan Levels," *Municipal Yearbook 1985* (Washington, DC: ICMA, 1985), p. 203.

45. Moore, Sink, and Hoban-Moore, "Politics of Homelessness," pp. 57–59; Josh Barbanel, "Societies and Their Homeless," *New York Times,* November 29, 1987, pp. 1, 8, sec. 4.

46. Peterson, *City Limits,* p. 56.

47. Edward T. Jennings, Jr., "Racial Insurgency, the State, and Welfare Expansion: A Critical Comment and Reanalysis," *American Journal of Sociology* 88 (May 1983): 1220–1236.

48. Chamlin, "General Assistance Among Cities," pp. 842–843.

49. Schneider, "Income Homogeneity," pp. 46–48.

50. Kenneth Wong, "Economic Constraint and Political Choice in Urban Policy-Making," *American Journal of Political Science* 32 (February 1988): 9.

51. Michael D. Reagan and John Sanzone, *The New Federalism,* 2nd ed. (New York: Oxford University Press, 1981), p. 119.

52. Paul Peterson, Barry Rabe, and Kenneth Wong, *When Federalism Works* (Washington, DC: Brookings Institution, 1986), p. 23.

PART II
Bricks and Mortar and Money

CHAPTER 7

Financing Local Government

Whether we are more interested in the quality and quantity of basic residential public services that local government provides or local government's capacity to invest in activities and facilities to enhance economic development, questions about financing are never very far below the surface. This chapter examines issues of local government finance, including an overview of basic finance concepts and trends, an examination of the fiscal health of American cities, and a discussion of the causes and consequences of fiscal trouble. Most particularly, we consider erosions in local popular control that accompany many recent trends in urban finance.

AN OVERVIEW OF TRENDS
IN URBAN GOVERNMENT FINANCE

This treatment of trends in urban finance differs from others in two important respects. First, many analyses of urban finance focus heavily on city spending patterns. However, for a variety of reasons (not least of which is the ultimate concern with the fiscal stress question), this chapter is concerned primarily with city revenues. In addition, analyses of trends and current conditions in urban finance typically focus on aggregate data, such as the total volume of property taxes collected by all city governments in particular years. Some information of this type will be used, but it is important to recognize that variation across the nation's cities is at least as interesting and relevant to our description as are aggregate trends that lump all cities together or at best differentiate them by broad groupings according to region or size. Consequently, this chapter relies heavily on U.S. Bureau of the Census finance data for fiscal years 1977 and 1983 for a systematic random sample of 208 cities with more than 50,000 population—that is, every other city in this size range. Having information on individual cities enables us to examine interesting patterns of differences across cities.

In addition, having finance information for the two time points—1977 and 1983—is important because the period between these two time points includes a significant and tumultuous set of policy developments in local finance. In addition to the recession of 1981 to 1982, this period encapsulates what is commonly called the tax revolt—a period in which various tax rollbacks and other constraints on state and local government finance were instituted, either through direct popular initiative or by legislatures under pressure. The tax revolt is described more fully later in this chapter. For the moment, we must consider some basic concepts and definitions that we use.

The following sections describe each of the four basic sources of city revenue: (1) intergovernmental revenues, (2) ownsource tax revenues, (3) own-source nontax revenues, and (4) borrowing. The sections discuss trends and the current status of cities with respect to each of these revenue sources.

Intergovernmental Revenues

Intergovernmental revenues are transfers of revenue from other governments, such as grants from the federal government, grants or sharing of revenues from the state government, and various revenues from other local governments. Revenues from other local governments are typically payments for services rendered, as when one city contracts with another or with a county government for some service. These interlocal transfers are not included in our later discussion of intergovernmental revenue because they are different from the state and federal grants and revenue sharing that most people mean when they refer to intergovernmental revenue.

One of the key trends in urban finance since the 1960s has been the change from a period of growing dependence on intergovernmental aid, especially federal aid, that lasted through most of the 1970s, to an era of declining federal revenues. As Roy Bahl notes:

> For every 1 percent increase in GNP between 1954 and 1976, federal general revenues . . . grew by about 1 percent, state and local government revenues from own sources by about 2 percent, and federal aid by about 5 percent. With this trend came a growing reliance by state and local governments on federal aid. By 1978, federal aid accounted for 22 percent of total state and local government revenue and was a more important financing source than any of the [local tax revenues].[2]

But this dependence on federal aid reached its highpoint in 1978 and has been declining since—first gradually, then more noticeably and with more vocal cries of dismay as the popular and broad-based General Revenue Sharing Program joined other, less visible federal aid programs on the chopping block.

A look at our 208-city sample shows what has happened to intergovernmental aid flows in these communities—a look that verifies the general notion of a downward trend since 1978. It also shows how different America's cities are in their relative dependence on intergovernmental aid and losses of that aid. Table 7.1 shows that on average cities got 17 percent of all their revenues in 1977 from state government and another 16 percent from the federal government; by 1983 dependence on the state for funds was on average about the same as it had been in 1977, but the percentage of all revenue accounted for by federal funds had declined from 16 percent to 10 percent. These figures depict the "average" city. Table 7.1 also shows great variation across cities. Even in 1977, for example, one-quarter of all cities got more than 24 percent of their revenues from the state and more than 22 percent of their revenues from the federal government. One or more cities got upward of half of all their revenues from the federal government, and some cities were virtually as dependent on state government. By contrast, 10 percent of the cities in our 208-city sample got less than 5 percent of their revenues from either federal or state government, and 25 percent of the cities got less than 9 percent from either source. These marked differences remain in 1983, although as Table 7.1 shows, the "intergovernmental" cities at the higher levels of dependence are receiving at least 14 percent of revenues from the federal government, not 22 percent as in 1977.

There have also been dramatic differences in cities' experiences with the federal aid slowdown in the 1977 to 1983 period. Table 7.2 shows that 10 percent of our sample cities experienced a loss of 16 percentage points or

TABLE 7.1. DEPENDENCE ON INTERGOVERNMENTAL REVENUE, 1977 AND 1983

	Percentage of 1977 Revenue		Percentage of 1983 Revenue	
	State Government	*Federal Government*	*State Government*	*Federal Government*
10th Percentile	4	5	3	3
25th Percentile	9	8	6	5
50th Percentile	16	15	12	9
75th Precentile	24	22	22	14
Mean for All Cities	17	16	16	10
Highest Value	49	53	57	34

Source: U.S. Department of Commerce, Bureau of the Census, *City Government Finances in 1983–1984; City Government Finances in 1977–1978* (Washington, DC: U.S. Government Printing Office, 1986, 1980).

more in the extent to which their revenues are gleaned from "the feds" and a loss of at least 11 percentage points in their reliance on state aid. In general, however, Table 7.2 portrays substantial stability between 1977 and 1983 in the extent to which cities rely on revenues from state government. On average, cities declined only 1 percentage point on that score. By contrast, the decline in dependence on federal aid is more notable, with the average city declining 6 percentage points and fully one-quarter of the cities declining at least 11 percentage points.

Ownsource Tax Revenues

Cities derive substantial funds from locally imposed taxes of various kinds. The most important of these historically has been the property tax, which is levied at a governmentally determined rate against the assessed value of property. The property tax has become one of the least popular and most controversial of all local taxes and therefore the focus of both local tax revolts and state policy changes to soften its impact.

One important policy change is the narrowing of the definition of what is taxable property. Personal and household property, business inventories, and intangible property (such as stocks and bonds) traditionally were included as property to be taxed. However, personal property is totally exempt in at least six states; at least twenty-one states and the District of Columbia exempt business inventories from taxation; at least twenty-eight states exempt household property; and all but about sixteen states fully or partially exempt motor vehicles. Intangibles are taxed in only eighteen states.[3] In addition to these trends away from taxation of certain categories of property, state governments have mandated additional property tax exemptions in order to further various policy

TABLE 7.2. CHANGE IN DEPENDENCE ON INTERGOVERNMENTAL REVENUE, 1977–1983

	Percentage Increase or Decrease in Total Revenue	
	State Government	*Federal Government*
10th Percentile	−11	−16
25th Percentile	− 6	−11
50th Percentile	− 1	− 5
75th Percentile	2	1
Mean for All Cities	− 1	− 6
Highest Value	44	18
Lowest Value	−40	−44

Source: U.S. Department of Commerce, Bureau of the Census, *City Government Finances in 1983–1984; City Government Finances in 1977–1978.* (Washington, DC: U.S. Government Printing Office, 1986, 1980).

goals. For example, a number of states exempt property "used exclusively for publicly encouraged activities, such as pollution control and abatement," and most states exempt property "used for 'publicly beneficial' purposes, such as that owned by religious, charitable, or educational institutions."[4]

Another substantial development concerning the property tax is the trend toward classification of property into categories, which are then subject to different assessment rates. For example, the state of Kansas has established categories that distinguish commercial property from residential property; commercial property is to be assessed at 30 percent of full market value whereas residential property is to be assessed at 12 percent of full market value. Only five states had classification systems for property taxation before the 1970s; in that decade, nine more states and the District of Columbia adopted such systems.[5]

The trend toward property classification is in large part a response to developments that have made the property tax an explosive issue for homeowners and farmers. For years, regular and timely reassessment of property was honored more in the breach than in practice in many localities. Substantial discrepancies in property valuation resulted. For example, homes that had been elaborately renovated would still carry the same assessment as they had before improvement, whereas newly built homes would have relatively high assessments. Furthermore, assessment practices could be used to informally ensure lower property taxes for some groups. Older homes or downtown business properties, for example, might be assessed at a relatively small proportion of their true market value. In short, de facto classification systems existed in many areas.

However, beginning in the late 1960s, court decisions and state legislative decisions in a number of states mandated equalization of property valuation, often through required, statewide reassessment of property. At the same time, training and professional standards for assessors were improving, and computerized techniques enhanced the capacity for timely reassessment. As a result of these developments, de facto classification systems were dismantled, and the property tax burden shifted in politically volatile ways toward groups that had previously been protected. In some areas, most notably California, rapidly rising property values made the effects of timely and uniform property reassessment even more volatile. The trend toward final classification systems for property taxation is a response to these developments.[6]

In addition to the property tax, many cities levy a local sales tax, either on all items purchased (general sales tax) or on particular items only (selective sales tax). Not all states have authorized local sales taxes. As of December 1985, municipalities in twenty-four states were authorized to have a local sales tax; in another eight states, counties or transit districts were authorized to have local sales taxes although municipalities were not.[7] A comparatively small number of cities have a local income or wage tax. Municipalities are authorized to levy such taxes in only eleven states (Alabama, Arkansas, Delaware, Georgia, Iowa,

Kentucky, Michigan, Missouri, New York, Ohio, and Pennsylvania). In all these states except Ohio, Pennsylvania and Kentucky, a handful of municipalities at most are actually using a local income or wage tax.[8] Finally, there are a variety of other, minor taxes that some localities levy, such as license taxes and franchise taxes on utilities.

Ownsource Nontax Revenues

Apart from the tax revenues discussed in the previous section, cities raise revenues locally from charges or fees for service and from a set of miscellaneous, smaller nontax sources. Charges are sometimes referred to as "fees for service" because that is what they are—"amounts received from the public for performance of specific services benefitting the person charged and from sales of commodities and services except by city utilities."[9] Typical user fees or charges are swimming pool entrance fees, charges for library use, and tolls for parking lots, bridges, and tunnels. The exclusion of payments for city utilities from the "user fee" category is a Census Bureau convention, presumably based on the fact that although some cities have municipally run utilities and others do not, the volume of payments for such services in places that do would overwhelm our view of user fees that are more generalizable across cities.

User fees have been touted as significant tools for urban finance that cities *should* rely on more heavily. There are a variety of reasons for this enthusiasm for user fees. Robert Poole, for example, provides an excellent summary of the alleged advantages of user fees:

1. User fees are like prices of private goods and allow citizens to act more like consumers, thus expressing their preferences and discouraging cities from providing services at levels that citizens don't want.

2. Unlike tax-supported services, services based on user fees do not give the appearance of being "free" goods. Thus, citizens are encouraged to economize on their use of city-provided services and to invest in risk-minimizing gestures that may keep them from having to call on city services like fire-fighting services.

3. User fees can reduce crowding and congestion. If a facility like a municipal swimming pool is being heavily used at peak hours, citizens may be encouraged to go to off-peak hours of use if peak fees are high and off-peak fees are a bargain.

4. User fees have the potential to be more fair than other financing methods because nonusers do not subsidize users as is the case with tax-supported services that are freely available but used only by certain groups. To the extent that there are concerns about lower-income groups losing access because of fees, a targeted subsidy can be provided in the form of free passes or the like.

5. User fees are even touted as a partial solution to the problem of suburban use of central city service, without corresponding contributions

to the central city tax base. User fees can be assessed against all users, whether they are residents, commuters, or tourists.[10]

There has been increased attention to user fees, but there is little evidence that cities in the aggregate have changed much in terms of reliance on them. Census data for all city governments show that in 1973 to 1974 charges made up 18 percent of all locally raised revenue; in 1984 to 1985, charges constituted 21 percent of locally raised revenue, a very modest increase.[11]

Finally, cities obtain funds from a variety of miscellaneous revenues that include, for example, interest earned on city funds, money from the sale of property, fines, and the like. Although apparently trivial, the miscellaneous revenue category is nontrivial in terms of volume of funds. Throughout most of the 1970s, the miscellaneous category constituted no more than 10 or 11 percent of all locally raised revenue, but by 1983 to 1984 miscellaneous revenues were 18 percent of the total—nearly as important a revenue source as charges and fees, which constituted 21 percent of the total that year.[12]

A look at our 208-city sample for 1983 tells us something about the diversity of cities with respect to the various ownsource revenues we have discussed. Table 7.3 shows, for example, that whereas cities on average get 37 percent of ownsource revenue from the property tax, 25 percent of the cities get more than half of their local funds from this one source. And a few cities, like Brockton, Massachusetts, and West Haven, Connecticut, get 90 percent or more of their revenues from the property tax—an explosive situation indeed given the political volatility of the property tax. All but one of the ten top cities in property tax dependency in 1983 are in Connecticut, Massachusetts, or New Hampshire.

TABLE 7.3. DEPENDENCE ON VARIOUS SOURCES OF LOCAL GENERATED REVENUE, 1983

	Percentage of Locally Raised Revenue					
	Property Tax	*Sales Tax*	*Income Tax*	*Other Taxes*	*Charges or Fees*	*Miscellaneous*
10th Percentile[a]	11	0	0	1	6	6
25th Percentile	17	0	0	1	13	11
50th Percentile	30	13	0	3	21	16
75th Percentile	53	29	0	6	27	23
Mean for All Cities	37	16	3	5	21	18
Highest Value	93	74	58	42	68	58

[a] The 10th percentile is the figure below which 10 percent of the cities fall, the 25th percentile is the figure below which 25 percent of the cities fall, and so forth.

Source: U.S. Department of Commerce, Bureau of the Census, *City Government Finances in 1983-1984.* (Washington, DC: U.S. Government Printing Office, 1986).

The sales tax is an important revenue source in a number of the 208 cities. One-quarter of the cities receive 29 percent or more of their revenue from this source, and on average cities obtain 16 percent of their revenue from it. However, many cities are not authorized to levy a local sales tax. Hence, in another quarter of the cities the sales tax is nonexistent.

Table 7.3 also shows the rarity of the local income tax. At least three-quarters of the 208 cities do not have the income tax. Yet in Kettering, Ohio, it yields 58 percent of all locally raised revenue. Other forms of local taxation are also relatively rarely used and quite typically modest in revenue production. Yet in Charleston, West Virginia, these other taxes account for over two-fifths of local revenues.

Charges and fees are more important. In the average city, they yield about one-fifth of local revenue, and another quarter of the cities get between 21 percent and 27 percent of their revenue from user fees and charges. In one city—Flint, Michigan—two-thirds of all local revenues are derived from user fees.

Finally, Table 7.3 shows that cities' reliance on miscellaneous revenues is much similar to their reliance on charges and fees. On average, a little less than one-fifth of local revenues are derived from miscellaneous sources such as fines, interest, and money from the sale or rental of city property. But one-quarter of the cities get between 16 percent and 23 percent of their revenues and another quarter of the cities get more than 23 percent of their revenues from this source.

Borrowing and Municipal Debt

A final source of revenue for cities, and one that is particularly important for financing the construction or renovation of physical facilities, is borrowing. There is a bewildering array of debt instruments, and the technicalities of local government borrowing intimidate many observers. However, on closer inspection, the basics of local debt practices are easily understood.

We must begin by distinguishing municipal bonds, which generate long-term borrowed funds for the community, from municipal notes, which are used to get short-term funds. Short-term debt here means less than one year before being due for repayment; long-term debt is borrowed money that can be owed for longer than one year and sometimes for periods as long as 20 years. A comparatively small volume of city borrowing is in the short-term debt category. Consequently, most of our discussion focuses on long-term debt, although, as we will see later in the chapter, short-term debt may be revealing as an indicator of fiscal stress.

There are two types of long-term debt. The more traditional type is the general obligation bond, which is guaranteed by local government's pledge to use its "full faith and credit" to pay off the bonds. Typically, voter approval is required before local governments can issue general obligation bonds. By contrast, revenue bonds constitute nonguaranteed debt. The issuing government's full taxing powers are not pledged to pay off the bonds. Rather, the bonds are paid off by the income expected from the project being constructed. For example, revenue bonds might be used to build a parking garage; the parking fees collected once the facility is built would then be used to pay off the revenue bonds. Because they are riskier, revenue bonds typically offer somewhat higher interest rates to the investor than do general obligation bonds. However, revenue bonds do not necessarily require voter approval as general obligation bonds typically do.[13]

To obtain borrowed funds, cities must be able to find investors willing to buy their bonds. A key attraction of municipal bonds generally is the fact that they are tax exempt—that is, the interest that is paid to the bondholder is not taxed by the federal government. In most states, the interest on local bonds is not taxed by state government either. However, at different times and in different cities, bonds can represent various levels of risk to the potential investor. For example, it would have been very risky to buy bonds issued by the city of Cleveland as it tottered on the brink of fiscal collapse in 1978. Cleveland in fact defaulted in December of that year. Buying the bonds of economically sound cities that have careful and professional budgetary practices would not be so risky, however. Judgments about the relative riskiness of various municipal bonds are made by private investment rating firms, most notably Moody's Investors Service and Standard & Poor's Corporation. Their judgments are summarized in the bond ratings that they give to cities. Moody's ratings, for example, range from Aaa (best quality) through a number of intervening ratings like Baa (medium grade) and Ba (speculative) to Ca (speculative in the highest degree) and C (lowest rated). Somewhat different factors are considered by the different organizations offering municipal bond ratings:

> Although they both analyze a locality's economic base and the quality of management practiced by the borrower, Moody's counts prior debt most heavily and places very high priority on the borrower's general debt history. Standard & Poor's, on the other hand, has become particularly concerned with a borrower's economic base, and therefore weighs heavily such indicators as per capita income levels, employment mix, population dynamics, and building activity.[14]

Bond ratings are obviously of enormous importance to cities. Because cities with riskier bonds must pay more interest to attract investors, the city's bond rating can have an enormous impact on the cost of borrowing for the city. In the extreme, poor ratings may make it impossible for the city's bonds to attract investors.

The key trend in local government borrowing in the past decade has been the rise in importance of nonguaranteed debt relative to the more traditional full-faith-and-credit debt. In the late 1960s and most of the 1970s, general obligation debt accounted for about 60 percent of all long-term municipal debt outstanding, but by 1982 nonguaranteed debt had taken over as the main form of outstanding debt, constituting 59 percent of the total.[15]

There are many reasons for the revenue bond explosion. It has been claimed that nonguaranteed debt provides a handy escape from debt limitations, voter approval requirements, and other accountability controls that apply to general obligation debt.[16] In addition, use of revenue bonds increased as cities began to use Industrial Revenue Bonds (IRBs), a form of nonguaranteed debt, for economic development purposes.

Table 7.4 shows how these general trends are played out in our 208-city sample. The numbers in the table show volumes of the different forms of outstanding debt as percentages of total revenues (locally raised and intergovernmental). This puts the volume of debt in perspective, in a sense showing how much debt the city has compared to its resources. In 1977, half of the cities had at least half (52 percent) as much general obligation (GO) debt as total revenues; the upper quarter of the cities had at least 75 percent as much GO debt as total revenues—seemingly substantial volumes. Some cities were already heavy users of revenue bonds in 1977. The top quarter of cities on this score had at least 72 percent as much nonguaranteed debt as total revenue.

By 1983, we see increasing reliance on revenue bonds compared to GO debt. The top quarter of cities with respect to nonguaranteed debt had at least 1.2 times as much of that debt outstanding as total revenues. By comparison, a city had to have GO debt exceeding only 56 percent of total revenues to be in the top quarter of GO debt users.

TABLE 7.4. OUTSTANDING DEBT, BY TYPE, AS A PERCENTAGE OF TOTAL REVENUES, 1977 AND 1983

	1977		1983	
	General Obligation	Revenue Bonds	General Obligation	Revenue Bonds
10th Percentile	4	0	4	0
25th Percentile	26	1	12	3
50th Percentile	52	25	35	32
75th Percentile	75	72	56	120
Mean for All Cities	55	60	41	94
Highest Value	206	559	202	3264

Source: U.S. Department of Commerce, Bureau of the Census, City Government Finances in 1983-1984; City Government Finances in 1977-1978 (Washington, DC: U.S. Government Printing Office, 1986, 1980).

FISCAL TROUBLE: THE KEY THEME
IN URBAN FINANCE

The overwhelming preoccupation in the urban finance field is the issue of cities not having adequate resources to carry on routine functions and meet demands for new services and activities. Indeed, this preoccupation has generated a family of labels to describe the phenomenon, ranging from "fiscal stress"[17] to "fiscal strain"[18] to "fiscal crisis."[19] Cities are said to be "running in the red",[20] engaging in "cutback management"[21] or "retrenchment," and generally struggling with the problem of inadequate resources. Various key events serve as benchmarks and continuing reminders of the problem: New York City's financial near-collapse in the mid-1970s; Proposition 13 in California, which dramatically rolled back property taxes and focused public attention on local governments' fiscal challenges; and the cutbacks in federal aid under the Reagan administration that led to cries of doom from urban mayors.

But what is fiscal stress, or whatever we choose to call the fiscal trouble that allegedly has caused American cities to stumble? Is it as widespread as these focusing events might lead us to believe? Is it significant and enduring enough to warrant the popular and scholarly attention that it has attracted?

Answering such questions is difficult, in large part because, as Rubin notes, "There are nearly as many definitions [of fiscal stress] as authors, and, not surprisingly, there is little consensus on how widespread fiscal stress is."[22] It is difficult to assess the extent of a problem if there is no agreement on what the problem is.

As we will see more clearly in the next section, different conceptualizations of what the fiscal problem is are intimately bound up with different theories concerning the causes of the phenomenon. For the moment, we can focus on a useful distinction made by David Stanley.[23] Stanley argues that the broad, amorphous phenomenon of urban fiscal trouble can initially be divided into two major categories: fiscal crisis and long-term decline. Fiscal crisis is the dramatic, immediate problem that occurs when "a city has neither cash nor credit to meet near-term expenses such as payroll and supplies." Fiscal crisis is the extreme condition of near-bankruptcy. By contrast, long-term decline is that situation "in which the city's economy, social conditions, and general enjoyment of life are slowly deteriorating." A third category suggested by Stanley is fiscal distress, which is the everyday struggle of even the most affluent of communities to "balance the budget without raising taxes or cutting services."[24]

Notice that these categories of fiscal trouble can provide us with a model of the depth of fiscal trouble, as shown in Figure 7.1. Long-term decline (Level 1) involves broad economic and social trends within the city—trends heavily influenced by regional and national trends over which city hall may have little or no control. Problematic changes in this economic and social environment have implications for the city's tax base, its economic development capacities,

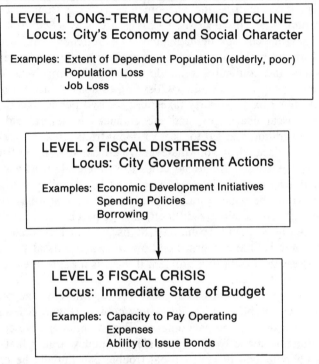

ECONOMIC AND SOCIAL ENVIRONMENT
Locus: Regional, National, and International Trends

Examples: Job Shifts from Frostbelt to Sunbelt
Private Sector Disinvestment in Center Cities
Change from Industrial to Post-Industrial U.S. Economy

LEVEL 1 LONG-TERM ECONOMIC DECLINE
Locus: City's Economy and Social Character

Examples: Extent of Dependent Population (elderly, poor)
Population Loss
Job Loss

LEVEL 2 FISCAL DISTRESS
Locus: City Government Actions

Examples: Economic Development Initiatives
Spending Policies
Borrowing

LEVEL 3 FISCAL CRISIS
Locus: Immediate State of Budget

Examples: Capacity to Pay Operating
Expenses
Ability to Issue Bonds

Figure 7.1. A Schematic Model of Urban Fiscal Trouble

and the service demands it faces. Coping with these implications is the stuff of fiscal distress (Level 2). Depending on how successful the city is in managing the challenges of fiscal distress, fiscal crisis (Level 3) may never be reached. By implication, however, if the dislocations at Level 1 are too severe for city government to handle, or if city government is inadequately responding to the challenges of the fiscal distress, the ultimate consequence is direct threat to the creditworthiness, solvency, and fiscal legitimacy of city government itself, or fiscal crisis.

This conceptualization is admittedly simplistic, but it does provide us with a framework for organizing the various indicators of fiscal trouble that can and have been used. Furthermore, it is a framework that nicely parallels the various indications of fiscal strain offered by analysts such as Clark and Ferguson:

One is that a city suffers fiscal strain if it has a weak or declining economic base, especially characterized by population loss. . . . A second conception stresses the municipal bond market which summarizes the judgment of informed investors. . . . Our conception leads us to focus on how it [the city] obtains resources from its "environment." . . . As the socioeconomic base changes, municipal officials must formulate new policies to maintain balance between resources and expenditures. Cities that do not adapt rapidly enough suffer fiscal strain.[25]

In other words, long-term decline is reflected in Clark and Ferguson's notion of declining economic base, which shows up in population loss. Fiscal crisis fits with Clark and Ferguson's suggestion of summary judgments of the investment community, judgments reflected in bond ratings. Finally, the middle stage between the challenge of long-term decline and the ultimate failure of fiscal crisis is the adaptation stage, which we have characterized as fiscal distress. Various indicators of how city officials are adapting (or failing to adapt) at this stage can be suggested. Two that we use are the following:

1. *Per capita taxes.* A high tax burden presumably shows that a city has not found ways to discipline expenditure demands or found alternative revenue sources to keep tax burdens from becoming oppressive and counterproductive to economic development;

2. *Volume of short-term debt as a percentage of total revenues.* Heavy use of short-term debt presumably suggests that a city is having difficulty meeting its immediate obligations, or at a minimum that it has some short-term cash-flow problem.

We can examine how the cities in our 208-city sample are doing with respect to the indicators of long-term decline, fiscal distress, and crisis that have been suggested. Relatively few cities came close enough to fiscal crisis in 1983 to suffer the loss of one of the top bond ratings. Figure 7.2 shows that 35 percent of the 208 cities got the next to the best rating and another 4 percent got the best bond rating in 1983. Few cities got less than an A rating, and none got less than Baa in 1983. Things were much the same in 1977, with 44 percent of the cities getting one of the top two bond ratings and few getting less than an A rating.

Table 7.5 shows that there is considerable variation across our 208 cities with respect to the other possible indicators of fiscal trouble that have been suggested. The average city grew 5 percent between 1977 and 1983, but some cities experienced dramatic population gain while others lost population—as much as a 19 percent loss in St. Louis, Missouri, and a 26 percent loss in San Bernardino, California. Notice that the former easily fits the stereotype of a declining, industrial-belt city but that the latter does not. Notice also that rapid population growth could be said to create its own special forms of fiscal challenge because cities must expand facilities and services and cope with new problems of congestion. Hence, a city like Fullerton, California, with its 183

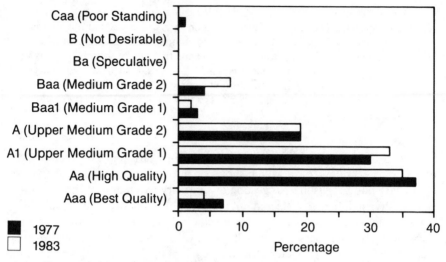

Figure 7.2. Moody's Bond Ratings for a Sample of Cities, 1977 and 1983

percent increase in population in five years, may be confronting some fiscal pressures as well but clearly of a different sort than those associated with long-term decline.

While the average city levies $178 per person in property taxes, some cities, like Enid, Oklahoma, do not use the property tax at all; at the other extreme, Stamford, Connecticut, collects $1,116.36 in property taxes per person, and Newton, Massachusetts, collects $949.29 per person in property taxes. If we consider the combined burden of all city-levied taxes, the average city gets $285 per capita, but some cities have extremely low tax burdens—for example, Florissant, Missouri, at $47.92 per capita and Fort Smith, Arkansas, at $57.49. By contrast, total taxes in New York City are $1,359.20 per person and in Alexandria, Virginia, $1,112.25.

Finally, Table 7.5 shows that, although at least half of the cities have no short-term debt outstanding and the average city has short-term debt representing only about 5 percent of total revenues, some cities are heavy users of short-term debt. These include Jacksonville, Florida, with 79 percent as much short-term debt outstanding as total revenues, and Hamilton Township, New Jersey, with about two-thirds as much in short-term debt obligations as total revenues.

It is important to realize that these various indicators point to somewhat different aspects of fiscal trouble. Consider, for example, the eighteen cities that received less than an A bond rating from Moody's in 1983 (see Table 7.6). These cities may not be teetering on the edge of fiscal collapse, but the investment community did not have full confidence in them in 1983. Some of these, like Philadelphia and Erie, Pennsylvania, and St. Louis, Missouri,

TABLE 7.5. INDICATORS OF FISCAL TROUBLE, 1983

	Mean	Median	Minimum	Maximum
Percentage Change in Population, 1977–1983	+5%	+2%	−26%	+183%
Property Taxes Per Capita	$178	$119	0	$1,116
Total Local Taxes Per Capita	$285	$228	$48	$1,359
Short-Term Debt as a Percentage of Total Revenue	5%	0	0	79%

Source: U.S. Department of Commerce, Bureau of the Census, *City Government Finances in 1983-1984; City Government Finances in 1977-1978* (Washington, DC: U.S. Government Printing Office, 1986, 1980).

appear to be victims of long-term economic decline. Even though none of the other three indicators show trouble signs for them, investment in them is deemed risky. Meanwhile, other communities, like Las Vegas, Nevada, and Laredo, Texas, are clearly not suffering long-term decline—if anything, they

TABLE 7.6. FISCAL TROUBLE INDICATORS FOR EIGHTEEN CITIES WITH POOR BOND RATINGS, 1983

City	Per Capita Taxes	Property Taxes Per Capita	Percentage Population Change 1977–1983	Short-Term Debt/Revenue
Laredo, TX	$103.00	$ 41.30	+29%	0%
Galveston, TX	246.82	127.13	5	0
Providence, RI	630.72	622.90	−4	13
Philadelphia, PA	661.29	144.74	−8	1
Erie, PA	173.59	132.66	−6	0
Utica, NY	222.14	140.13	−10	59
Passaic, NJ	248.08	242.50	+7	0
Newark, NJ	193.63	139.41	−1	0
Las Vegas, NV	129.59	48.96	+14	0
Lynn, MA	257.73	251.29	+3	25
Lawrence, MA	299.26	294.16	+1	0
Fall River, MA	237.87	233.26	−7	2
Cambridge, MA	815.84	784.60	−7	12
Brockton, MA	379.48	375.21	+3	11
Jersey City, NJ	382.79	372.23	−5	5
St. Louis, MO	529.26	77.24	−19	0
Monroe, LA	374.48	86.27	−12	0
Waterbury, CT	532.64	522.31	−2	27

Source: U.S. Department of Commerce, Bureau of the Census, *City Government Finances in 1983-1984* (Washington, DC: U.S. Government Printing Office, 1986).

are growing dramatically. At the same time, they show no trouble signs in the form of short-term debt or heavy tax loads. In fact, what distinguishes these two is an unusually *low* volume of total taxes per capita. Although other factors not considered here could be responsible for their low bond ratings, one suspects that the investment community finds them risky because they have such minimal public revenues to cope with their dramatically rising population. Still other communities on the list show signs of fiscal trouble either in the form of substantial short-term debt, substantial population loss, inordinately high tax burdens, especially in the form of property taxes, or some combination of these.

CAUSES OF FISCAL STRESS

There is great diversity in theories about the sources of cities' fiscal troubles. In this section, we consider the most important of these, along with the perspectives on urban politics implied by each theory.

The Tax Revolt and Fiscal Stress

It is often stated that the tax revolt of the late 1970s is a key contributor to urban fiscal stress.[26] California's Proposition 13 in 1978, which rolled back property taxes dramatically, is viewed as the most visible and dramatic opening salvo of this movement, which saw various fiscal limitations passed in many other states. By 1983, twenty states had some new form of fiscal limitation that applied either to state governments, municipal governments, or both.[27]

This is obviously a simplistic explanation and one that does not achieve the level of theoretical sophistication that many other explanations do. It also fails to account for the fiscal trouble that cities experienced before the tax revolt era, such as New York City's financial crisis in 1975 and Cleveland's default in 1978. But if we broaden our conception of tax revolt to include the various forms of populist fiscal limits imposed on cities over a longer period, the tax revolt explanation becomes more interesting and less narrowly bound to the most recent burst of limitations enacted in the Proposition 13 era. In short, various limits and accountability controls could be said to contribute to fiscal distress by making urban fiscal decisionmaking less flexible and therefore making it more difficult for cities to adapt to economic challenges and shocks to existing revenue sources.

A number of fiscal constraints have emerged in the last fifteen years as direct populist reactions to local taxes or as part of a broader drive to keep local fiscal practices accountable to popular control. Property taxation, for example, is heavily encrusted with various fiscal constraints that have emerged as a result of hostility to the property tax. In eleven states there are legal limits on the aggregate local government property tax rate (i.e., municipal, county, school district, and special district combined); in eight of these eleven states, these legal limits were enacted *prior* to what we now view as the tax revolt era of about 1978 to 1980. An even larger number of states (twenty-six) have specific limits on the tax rate that municipalities may impose. In all but two of these states, such limits were enacted before 1978.[28]

From the tax cutter's perspective, the problem with these early forms of property tax limitation is that they could be, and were, easily evaded. A city can increase its levy dramatically even while staying within the rate limit if it increases assessments. Consequently, a more recent wave of legal limits on the property tax involves limits on the total property tax levy or limits on assessment increases. In twenty states, there are now limits on property tax levies; more than half of these states enacted the levy limit in 1978 or later. Seven states have limits on assessment increases, and in six of these the limits are of 1978 or later vintage.[29]

Thus, California's Proposition 13 and a correspondingly dramatic property tax rollback in Massachusetts in 1980 (Proposition 2½) must be viewed in perspective. They are both episodes in an ongoing tug of war between populist impulses toward tax minimization and local governments' needs to protect their revenue base. What is perhaps most notable about the tax revolt era of 1978 to about 1980 is not that tax revolt sentiments were new but that tax-limiting efforts were either more severe, in the sense that levies were actually rolled back, or that more sophisticated and broad-ranging limitation devices were adopted.

Proposition 13, for example, was much more than a simple rate limit. It limited property taxes to 1 percent of full value of the property, but it also rolled back assessments to their 1975–1976 levels and limited assessment increases to 2 percent per year. The first year of tax reduction under Proposition 13 yielded a property tax revenue loss in California estimated at $7 billion.[30] Massachusetts' Proposition 2½, approved by voters in 1980, limits property taxes to 2.5 percent of fair market value or to the 1979 rate, whichever is less. Local governments in Massachusetts were required to reduce their levies by 15 percent per year until this limit was reached.[31] As a result of this measure, property taxes declined 75 percent in Boston and by more than a third in many other areas of the state.[32]

Meanwhile, fiscal limits were being extended by means other than limits on property tax. A 1976 New Jersey law instituted one of the earliest overall expenditure limits on municipal government. Under this law, growth in expenditures from locally raised revenues were limited to 5 percent per year, exclusive of new construction spending.[33] Only two other states (Arizona and California) have followed suit with such expenditure limits applicable to local government. In Missouri, the Hancock Amendment, passed in 1980, subjects local government revenue decisions to the discipline of a required voter referendum. All new or increased taxes, licenses, or fees must be approved by voters. Only four states have similar general revenue limits.[34]

The recent tax revolt era has added a variety of newer, more complex, and sometimes severe fiscal limits with respect to city government revenues or expenditures, but the limits and accountability devices that apply to city government indebtedness are much older. Indebtedness has not been subject to a recent convulsion of new and expanded legal controls. However, the controls that apply to general obligation (i.e., full faith and credit) debt are substantial. For example, issuance of general obligation bonds requires voter approval in most states, and in many states there are also debt ceilings that limit the total volume of debt.[35] It is important to note, however, that such limitations and controls typically do *not* apply to revenue bonds (i.e., nonguaranteed debt).[36]

Finally, there are fiscal limits on cities in the form of limits on the legal authorization that they have to use various revenue sources. For example, as we saw earlier in the chapter, twenty-four states have authorized municipalities to levy a local sales tax. Even in these states, there are limits on the use of the sales tax. A number of states that authorize a municipal sales tax cap the rate of the tax, most typically at one cent on the dollar; voter approval of the local sales tax is required in many states, and in some locations there are earmarking requirements for the revenue generated. Rochester, Minnesota, for example, must use its sales tax revenue for flood control.[37]

There is considerable debate about whether the various fiscal limitations just described genuinely contribute to fiscal stress. It is often argued that these fiscal limits do not have real teeth and that local officials have a variety of strategies at their disposal for replacing lost revenues. Limits on general obligation debt have been particularly weak. They can be evaded either by (1) the creation of separate, special-purpose authorities, so that several entities within a given area can each run up debt to the legal limit or by (2) greater use of revenue bonds, which are not subject to the same requirements as general obligation bonds.

Furthermore, many of the revenue-oriented limits focus exclusively on the property tax, but this does not prevent cities from replacing lost property tax revenue with alternative taxes or user fees. In fact, most empirical studies of the impact of recent fiscal limits have found that strategies for revenue replacement through reliance on alternative, uncapped local sources are heavily used.[38] As MacManus argues:

> States that have imposed the heaviest restrictions on municipal property taxing powers have, perhaps unintentionally, contributed to the fiscal health of their cities. By imposing heavy restrictions on the property tax they have in effect mandated diversification of their municipalities' revenues.[39]

However, change from traditional revenue sources to newer sources does not always come easily. Without state authorization, some alternative revenue sources such as local sales or income taxes are not available, and the adoption of new revenue sources must be done with an eye to local political feasibility. A new sales tax is not necessarily politically palatable simply because property tax increases have become politically insupportable.

To the extent that the tax revolt-inspired limits and other legal constraints on city revenues caused fiscal trouble, it is perhaps best understood as fiscal trouble in David Stanley's sense of fiscal distress.[40] That is, legal constraints and fiscal limits precipitate new challenges for urban fiscal managers and make the task of budget balancing that much more complicated. Were there no legal limits at all on cities' revenue-raising powers, there still would be fiscal trouble for some cities in the sense of disruptions or decay in the local economy. At worst, fiscal controls constrain the adaptive responses that city officials may wish to make to larger problems of economic decline. Similarly, communities blessed with a prospering local economy can, as many well-off California communities found, taste a bit of the challenge of fiscal distress as a result of fiscal controls inspired by the tax revolt.

In short, fiscal distress is experienced by many cities. It encompasses the everyday stuff of difficult spending choices, struggles to find new revenue sources, attempts to balance the pressures of operating expenses with the need for capital investments, and battles over budget priorities and strategies. Both the most recent era of tax revolt and the longer history of accumulating fiscal constraints on local government make more difficult the adaptive struggles that are a part of fiscal distress. But the existence of such constraints does not necessarily dictate whether officials will be successful in managing city finances through inevitable periods of fiscal distress.

Other Explanations of Fiscal Stress: External and Internal

The adaptations that local officials make or fail to make in the context of fiscal distress are obviously of central importance. If appropriate adaptations are made, fiscal distress need not become fiscal crisis; if adaptations are either not attempted or not successful, genuine fiscal crisis is surely the result. As we move on from the more limited tax revolt explanation of fiscal trouble, we see that other explanations differ from one another primarily in terms of the reasons given for adaptive failure. Specifically, there is a school of thought that attributes failure to external forces and a quite different school of thought that attributes failures to political dynamics internal to the city.

The school that blames external forces includes a variety of explanations that focus on trends and developments that are beyond the control of local officials. It portrays city officials as ultimately helpless, despite their best adaptive efforts, in the face of social, economic, and structural dynamics that are regional, national, or even international in character. The most straightforward of these explanations are those that focus on population migration and resultant erosion of the tax base[41] or the private sector disinvestment trends that underlie regional long-term economic decline.[42] These explanations make up a litany of the economic shocks that can overwhelm a city and lead to strained city budgets: the movement of industry and jobs, plant closings that drastically affect cities that are heavily reliant on a single large employer, the movement of people and jobs from central cities to suburbs, and more recently, the activities of footloose multinational industries that can "move investment and operations in and out of areas with a minimization of incurred losses."[43]

These demongraphic and economic trends are sometimes portrayed in a rather bloodless way that makes them seem inevitable, yet unintentional. The best examples of this are incorporated in "Wagner's Law"-style explanations of the growth of government.[44] Explanations based on the growth of government relate to the fiscal crisis issue because population, job, and loss of tax base translate into fiscal stress only to the extent that local officials do not simultaneously downscale government budgets to create a "balance between fiscal policy and the social and economic base."[45] If local government spending commitments constantly mushroom despite a drop in private sector wealth to support them, then we have the scenario for fiscal crisis. But under what circumstances does public sector spending spiral upward? Wagner's Law of Rising Public Expenditures posits that industrialization leads to growth of the public sector because:

1. Greater economic affluence creates greater expectations for public services.
2. The complex interdependencies of industrial society place demands on government for problem solving.
3. There are "growing investment demands of an industrialized economy."[46]

As we will see in a moment, the last of these has been given a great deal of attention by other theorists.

Wagner's Law is a rather depersonalized explanation of government growth, and hence of fiscal pressures, that focuses on key economic and demographic trends in industrial society. A more pointed version of the external forces school of thought is provided by the radical urban planner Robert Goodman, who offers a theory of regional rotation. According to this theory, "By either threatening to, or actually moving from city to rural area or suburb, or from one state to another, business is attempting to create more hospitable conditions for itself in all regions of the country."[47] In areas that lose jobs, particularly higher-paid, unionized, industrial jobs, the work force is quickly disciplined as unions are undercut and support is quickly made available for policies to make the area once again attractive to industry, such as "public subsidies, tax abatements, no-strike pledges, and lower wages."[48] Although this at first appears to be an argument that local officials *can* control their fate through appropriate adaptive policies, Goodman's theory is ultimately more cynical, for he argues that regional rotation is an ongoing cycle. Areas that are winners quickly become losers again as wages increase and as industry moves on to other loser communities where wages and land values are depressed enough to make location attractive.

Among the various "external forces"-types of explanations of fiscal crisis, perhaps the best known and most comprehensive is that offered by James O'Connor in *The Fiscal Crisis of the State*.[49] O'Connor argues that the role of the state in capitalist society is to contribute to capital accumulation in the private sector and to maintain the legitimacy of the capitalist system. Both roles drive the state toward fiscal crisis. The necessary investments for private sector productivity are increasingly being socialized through state spending while resulting profits are, of course, not socialized. Furthermore, there are many contradictions of advanced capitalism (like neighborhood disruption resulting from development efforts, pollution, unemployment, and the like) that exacerbate the legitimacy problem of the capitalist system. The state is left holding the bag with respect to these problems as well and can deal with them only through greater outlays on welfare and policing. The inevitable result of all this is fiscal crisis for the local state.

O'Connor's formulation seems to imply that all cities in advanced capitalist settings will inevitably share in the fate he describes. Yet, as we have seen, the fiscal health of cities varies enormously. One could argue in response that different cities occupy different positions in the economic structure of capitalist society, and that some will therefore experience fiscal crisis sooner than others. However, like all the explanations of the external forces type that emphasize the helplessness of the local state in the face of this inevitable crisis, O'Connor's theory is weakened by the successful weathering of fiscal crisis in New York and other urban settings.[50]

Although the various explanations that we have summarized differ from one another in important points, they are similar in one respect: Each presumes that fiscal crisis is more or less inevitable for those cities subject to the external forces at issue. Neither the city's role in a capitalist society, nor the demographic trends that wash over it, nor the fallout from economic decisions of multinational firms are in any real sense under the policy control of city officials. These trends are of such magnitude that the adaptive responses open to city officials, such as a scramble for new revenue sources to keep the local fisc healthy, seem trivial and unlikely to stem the tide of long-term economic decline.

By contrast, other explanations of urban fiscal crisis focus more on political dynamics within the city. From this perspective, cities are not helpless in the face of external social and economic trends. However, responses to these trends are influenced by political factors internal to the city.

For example, there are various excessive government explanations that presume that government officials have important stakes in "expanding government's share of the economy beyond the size demanded by the public."[51] By implication, this budgetary growth is also damaging to the long-term fiscal health of the polity. Similarly, other analysts speak of various "state-centered" theories of government action:

> The components of the State do not simply spring into motion in order to sat-
> isfy the demands of society. Historically, the State has always manifested an

interest of its own, one that can be identified as seeking to preserve its conditions of existence relative to private needs. This separate and autonomous interest defines a State-centeredness in the relation between society and the State.[52]

One of the most common explanations in the excessive government style is that of bureau voting, which is aptly summarized by Irene Rubin:

> Bureaucrats' ends will always be served by a larger bureaucracy, which typically provides higher salaries. Because bureaucrats have the power and the interest to vote, they always vote in favor of expansion. The larger the bureaucracy, the more votes it has, and the more power it has to expand itself. In this model, government employment should constantly increase.[53]

The theory of bureau voting is not very well supported with empirical evidence, but the conceptual power of this model, with its imagery of empire-building bureaucrats and growth-oriented union leaders in the public sector, endures.[54] Commentary on New York City's fiscal crisis, for example, inevitably included attributions of blame to bureau leaders and public sector unions.

Still other excessive government, or state-centered, explanations begin with the presumption that elected officials as well as bureaucrats have interests in expanding government spending. These explanations focus on the institutional mechanisms that are available for officials to expand government activities beyond citizen preferences. Such explanations are a particular hallmark of public choice theorists. In particular, public choice theorists point to certain "fiscal illusions," like debt financing and complex or indirect or otherwise difficult-to-comprehend tax systems, that cause citizens to misunderstand the true costs of government and therefore to demand more services than they otherwise would.[55]

Unlike these excessive government explanations of urban fiscal stress, other explanations characterize urban governments as *reacting* to escalating demands for services and spending, rather than instigating government growth out of bureaucratic self-interest. Irene Rubin calls this the "political vulnerability" theory of fiscal stress.[56] This theory emphasizes demand overload in postindustrial society. Escalating consumer demand for goods and services, in the public as well as the private sector, leads to unreasonable expectations and overburdened governments.[57] Furthermore, proliferation of interest groups is viewed as exacerbating demand overload in that interest groups provide a mechanism for aggregating varied citizen preferences and articulating them in decisionmaking settings.

Cascading demands would not be as problematic were government institutions strong enough to resist unreasonable demands. Central to the political vulnerability model, however, is the idea that various structural characteristics of city government make it less capable of resisting. In particular, cities with unreformed government institutions are characterized as being less capable of insulating themselves from demands than those cities with reformed institutions. By the same token, demographic changes can break down the coalitions that mayors of unreformed cities have been able to use to sustain electoral support without excessive spending.[58]

Perhaps one of the most thorough and compelling treatments of fiscal stress via the political vulnerability theory is that of Martin Shefter, who uses New York City as a case example of the cyclical character of fiscal crisis.[59] Shefter's argument begins with the acknowledgment that budgetary imbalances can result from either external economic and demographic trends or from change in the structure of local political coalitions, or both. New York City, for example, has experienced influxes of Irish, Jewish, and southern black populations at various times in its history, and each influx had implications with respect to city service demands, competition for jobs, the management of public order, and political necessities for successful electoral coalitions.[60] Under these circumstances, a city is vulnerable to a withdrawal of support from the investment community, which may begin to lack confidence in the city's capacity to repay its debts. This precipitates immediate fiscal crisis.

> Fiscal crises characteristically discredit the city's top elected officials and lead to their defeat. The shock of defeat often convinces local politicians that they must acquiesce to changes in the political practices and public policies that enabled their opponents to triumph. The political alliances local politicians engineer, and the fiscal policies they pursue to regain and retain control over the city government, can then endure until further changes in the national or international economic and political systems again tempt them to increase municipal spending more rapidly than municipal revenues, which will spark yet another fiscal crisis.[61]

Shefter's theory of fiscal strain is a cyclical one, in which responses to fiscal trouble yield reforms and new political coalitions, which in turn are undone by new fiscal incidents brought on by the vulnerability of political coalitions.

A Synthesis of the Various Theories of Fiscal Trouble?

The preceding sections have outlined a variety of explanations of urban fiscal trouble. Responsibility has been attributed to the tax revolt, to sweeping economic and demographic trends so dramatic that they overwhelm local adaptive policies, to the inevitable contradictions of advanced capitalist society and the state's fated role in that structure, to the self-interested, expansionist tendencies of bureaucrats and labor unions, to complex taxing arrangements and other public finance practices that make it possible for expansion-minded officials to dupe the public, and to fragile urban political structures that tempt local politicians to buy electoral support with expenditures that cannot be supported by the existing revenue base. Is there some way in which we might sort through this smorgasbord of theories of fiscal stress to separate the more worthy from the less, or perhaps even to synthesize seemingly conflictual explanations into broader, more comprehensive theories?

As different as the various explanatory approaches are, some synthesis is surely possible. The political vulnerability school of thought, for example, offers an important vehicle for recognizing the importance of both external forces and internal political dynamics. Were there no external shocks in the form of economic dislocations, demographic change, and the like, city revenue bases would be relatively stable, and there would not be the sorts of challenges that tempt city officials to spend their way to a new political consensus.

Accepting that some external shocks are inevitable, we need not accept that their occurrence inevitably pushes cities into fiscal crisis, as some explanations seem to imply. For one thing, there are distinct differences in the character, magnitude, and consequences of various external shocks confronting different cities, or the same city over time. The waves of new immigrant populations that have descended on New York at various times in its history are quantitatively and qualitatively different from each other and from the substantial influx of illegal migrants that many southwestern cities have been experiencing. Different still are the influxes of new populations that many small cities have faced as industry has spread from metropolitan cores to exurban peripheries.

Furthermore, as various analyses of internal forces remind us, responses to external shocks differ in different settings. In cities where political institutions insulate officials from spiraling demands, there is less danger than in other settings of a spending response that is fiscally irresponsible. The nature of the dominant political coalition is also likely to affect responses to external shocks. For example, where business elites are a key to the dominant political coalition, there may be effective pressure to keep taxing and spending low to sustain a good business climate. For all these reasons, external shocks may or may not precipitate fiscal crisis. It all depends—on the severity of the shock and the responses of local leaders.

The insights of both public choice theorists and tax revolt analysts are relevant here as well. Spiraling spending in excess of revenue growth is more likely to be the response to external shocks where institutional arrangements and political subcultures allow fiscal illusion strategies that hide the true scope of government's activities and its cost to taxpayers. Furthermore, responses to budgetary challenges are sure to differ in different settings because of the legacies that various episodes of tax revolt have left across the American urban landscape. In some settings, local politicians will find it more difficult to deal with instability and external shocks by increasing the scope of government because legal constraints hem in their capacity to tax, borrow, or spend; in other settings, local politicians are subject to fewer or weaker constraints of this sort.

There seems to be nothing inevitable about urban fiscal crisis, although there will inevitably be fiscal pulling and hauling as city officials respond in varying ways to the economic and demographic forces that they do not directly control. Structural theories, like James O'Connor's analysis, provide important insights about the fiscal challenges facing cities, but they should be modified to take account of variations across urban settings.[62] This is, of course, what many neo-Marxist analysts have attempted to do—for example in treatments that differentiate cities by the stage of capitalism they have reached.[63] In short, many of the various theories of fiscal stress can be worked into a larger synthesis, providing that we adopt a contingent point of view, emphasizing differences in both the nature of external challenges facing cities and the factors shaping city leaders' responses to those challenges.

ADAPTATION TO FISCAL CHALLENGES: SOME IMPLICATIONS

Much of the preceding section emphasized adaptations and responses of city officials in the face of fiscal challenges. This section evaluates several adaptive strategies, including:

1. Increased reliance on intergovernmental aid, especially from state government.
2. The adoption of new revenue sources, particularly those that are less visible to the public.
3. The use of off-budget enterprises and public sector leasing arrangements to evade constraints on borrowing.
4. The spending down of funds that might normally be devoted to maintenance of the city's infrastructure.

These strategies can, and usually are, evaluated in terms of their success or failure in staving off fiscal crisis. But the various adaptive strategies that city officials have been using and the tools that have become important for coping with fiscal challenge have important consequences beyond their success or failure in budget management. Urban officials may very well have coped with the worst aspects of fiscal challenge through creative use of these strategies, but the strategies also carry important and problematic implications.

The most problematic implications fall into two, interrelated categories: (1) encroachments on local control of local financial matters, and (2) erosion of accountability to the public. The following section discusses various examples of each of these and the connections between the two.

As Peterson reminds us, city governments are not closed, autonomous jurisdictions but, rather, entities with permeable membranes.[64] Local political economies are very much affected by extralocal trends and actions, ranging from the macroeconomic policies of the federal government to the decisions of multinational firms. This is true regardless of city officials' preferences or actions.

Nevertheless, in important ways, the strategic financial practices and adaptive choices taken by urban officials have opened the door for still greater extralocal influence in urban affairs. This is nowhere more apparent than in local government borrowing. In the wake of recent fiscal crises in New York and elsewhere, the investment community has become much more sensitive to the potential riskiness of local government bonds and much more interested in scrutinizing potential borrowers. In an effort to ensure the confidence of the investment community, cities have ceded substantial decisionmaking power to financial advisors.[65]

Bond rating agencies have also come to assume considerable importance. Public officials make decisions with an eye to the reactions of these rating agencies. In her analysis of fiscal crisis in "Southside," Irene Rubin describes how Moody's bond rating service made the city's fiscal troubles very visible by downgrading its bonds and by simultaneously putting considerable pressure on the city to change its ways. The result was a series of major cutbacks and a reordering of local practices.[66]

The sum total of all these developments is enhanced influence for the investment community vis-à-vis local decisionmaking:

> Substantial power . . . is thus directly exercised by the financial community over cities in trouble and indirectly exercised over others wanting to stay out of trouble. Two features of such power make it extremely problematic for city governments. First, it is power exercised in such a way as to be unaccountable to voters. Voters cannot force lenders to lend to their city government, nor can they impose a lowering of the interest rate charged. The city is therefore subject to strong sanctions over which local voters have no control. . . . Second, it is power exercised in a way that is usually invisible or unintelligible to voters; even when its workings *are* seen, their effects are often unacceptable to significant elements of the population.[67]

As these comments show, there is strong connection between the two categories of problematic implications of local finance—encroachments on local control and erosion of accountability to the public. Developments that cause local officials to cede greater influence to the investment community simultaneously diminish local voters' capacity to influence or even to understand important financial decisions.

If cities have become more influenced by the investment community as a result of fiscal troubles and the effort to avoid them, they have also ceded additional influence to other levels of government. In some senses, this is not a new development. In the heyday of federal aid to state and local government, there was much concern that federal monies might distort local priorities or that the funding agencies' requirements would be intrusive. Some scholars have studied mandates—that is, responsibilities, procedures, or activities imposed on one level of government by another. An important class of mandates affecting local governments are those imposed by the federal government as required conditions for obtaining aid. They are the proverbial strings attached to grants. It has been shown that the 1960s and 1970s, which constitute the period of rapid growth in federal aid to local governments, also saw "substantial growth in direct local governmental regulation by the federal government. Civil rights policy, environmental policy, occupational health and safety, energy conservation, and consumer protection are examples of areas in which federal regulators increasingly came to deal directly with local governments."[68] In their inventory of mandates affecting selected local jurisdictions, Catherine Lovell and Charles Tobin found 1,260 federal mandates, 82 percent of which were imposed as conditions of aid.[69]

The era of increasing federal aid has come to a close. State aid has been more stable, and if anything, there has been an upsurge in the states' roles with respect to their local governments. Lovell and Tobin found 3,415 state mandates affecting local governments in their study, compared with the 1,260 federal mandates. Unlike the federal mandates, which are most typically conditions of aid, state mandates are almost always direct orders (specifically, 95 percent of the total are in this category) that must be obeyed independent of funding considerations.[70]

State mandates include fiscal planning, record keeping, and reporting requirements that states may have imposed to help keep cities out of financial trouble. Twelve percent of all state mandates studied by Lovell and Tobin were specifically in the category of fiscal procedures, and another 8.5 percent were fiscal constraints such as rate limits or expenditure caps.[71]

There is other evidence that states have assumed greater influence vis-à-vis cities as a result of episodes of fiscal crisis. It is symbolized by Big Mac, the state board appointed to oversee New York City's finances during its period of fiscal crisis. Nor is New York City simply an isolated case of state intervention in urban fiscal troubles. Since the adoption of Proposition 2½ in Massachusetts, a number of cities have turned to the Division of Local Services in the state's Department of Revenue. The ceding of local control that comes with this help is clear, as in the example of Chelsea, which obtained a $5 million interest-free loan from the state in 1986. "In return for the loan, the State division ordered some bitter medicine. A finance control board, comprising state and city officials, was set up to watch how Chelsea spends every penny. 'If they want us, they have to give up a lot,' said Kenneth Marchurs, director of accounts in the division of local services."[72]

It is important to note that this increased state influence does not necessarily involve more state revenue-raising effort than local effort. In a recent study comparing state and local revenue systems before and after the recent period of dramatic urban fiscal crisis and tax revolt (1977 to 1982), David Lowery shows that there has been virtually no fiscal centralization. That is, the states' share of total state and local revenue remained virtually unchanged.[73]

Recently, Gottdiener has argued:

> The fiscal crisis felt first in the cities of the frostbelt and most spectacularly played out by New York, changed the very basis of local finance. . . . During the period of fiscal restructuring that followed this crisis, control of city finances passed over into the hands of state, federal, and private financial interests and out of the grasp of local residents and their elected city officials. The last vestiges of local control of municipal resources were snatched from the voters by changed arrangements for city solvency.[74]

Some might object that this statement is too extreme. Yet the specifics we have discussed, ranging from state fiscal oversight to state and federal mandating to investment community influences, suggest why scholars of urban affairs might be drawn to such conclusions. Even if we allow that surely not *all* vestiges of local control of municipal resources have been lost, there has clearly been encroachment on the fiscal powers of urban officials.

The forms of encroachment are largely externally initiated, as we have seen. However, local borrowing practices also include an example of encroachment on the power of city government officials that is invited by city officials themselves in response to the fiscal challenge of legal constraints on borrowing. Recall that there are substantial restrictions on local borrowing practices, such as debt limits and voter approval requirements. An important strategic response to such limits has been the creation of special authorities—for example, hospital boards, airport construction boards, sewage treatment authorities, and park commissions. These authorities are supervised by semiautonomous boards of directors appointed by the city or state officials creating the authority, and they play a significant role in the construction of many capital facilities that are important components of the urban infrastructure.[75] For this reason, we will examine their role further in Chapter 8.

For the present, a key feature of these authorities is their financing. Authorities are sometimes referred to as off-budget enterprises (OBEs) because their revenue, spending, and debt are not part of the budget of the city or state government that set them in motion. They issue bonds, especially revenue bonds, and collect user fees and charges that provide the basis for paying off the bonds and sustaining operations. What is more, the creation of these entities enables general purpose governments like cities or counties to evade restrictions on public debt because such quasi-governmental corporate entitites often are not subject to legal restrictions on public debt that apply to general purpose governments.[76]

Although this may be a successful strategy for circumventing restrictive debt limits, there is a price to be paid in terms of loss of local control. Alberta Sbragia argues that the proliferation of these authorities has contributed to fragmented power and authority of urban governance:

> In short, city officialdom does not control much of the capital infrastructure on which the city's most basic functions depend, and it therefore exercises

much less control over the kinds of recreational, transportation, and even business opportunities that residents will have than most voters assume.[77]

The proliferation of off-budget enterprises to evade debt limits illustrates the other key consequence of local officials' adaptive responses: erosion of public sector accountability. Off-budget enterprises have been criticized on a variety of grounds, ranging from the fragmentation argument just noted to charges of proneness to corruption.[78] But the single most common criticism they evoke is that they short-circuit accountability. Their activities are not subject to the same oversight as departments of regular governmental agencies, they make legal constraints like debt limits functionally irrelevant, and they are argued to be insulated enough from popular accountability that arrogant, insensitive policies frequently emerge.[79]

Efforts to diversify revenue sources are another key strategy for local officials adapting to fiscal trouble. Revenue diversification is a desirable development on many grounds. It makes budgeting more flexible and less dependent on a single tax source. On the other hand, diversification tends to complicate the local revenue structure, and this means that the true tax burden can more easily be kept from the public.[80] Furthermore, many of the alternative revenue sources that cities have pursued are individually more characterized by possibilities for fiscal illusion than traditional revenue sources like the property tax. Sales taxes, for example, are paid in small bits as parts of private transactions. Taxpayers may therefore be much less conscious of the total amount of sales tax that they pay in a year than they are of their property tax burden.

Leasing is another adaptive strategy that can circumvent popular accountability. As a strategy for financing facilities or equipment, leasing is much like borrowing. Rather than issuing bonds, using the proceeds to build a facility or buy equipment, and paying back investors over time, local government under a leasing arrangement "borrows" an asset owned by a private party, while agreeing to a payment obligation over time.[81] Nevertheless, because leasing is not technically borrowing, it is not subject to volume ceilings, voter approval, and similar accountability controls that apply to traditional local government bonds. These attributes are acknowledged to be an important part of the appeal of public-sector leasing.[82]

Leasing can be more expensive than traditional borrowing.[83] Yet there has been a strong upsurge in public sector leasing, especially in places like California where constraints on traditional borrowing are especially stringent. Public sector leasing commitments in California jumped from $422 million in 1982 to $2 billion in 1984.[84]

Similar problems are associated with another adaptive response to financial challenge: deferred maintenance. The infrastructure of America's cities (i.e., its streets, bridges, sewers, water treatment plants, and the like) are crucial public assets (see Chapter 8). Maintenance of existing infrastructure is at least as important as investment in new or replacement infrastructure. However, deferring maintenance expenditures is a classic response in the face of fiscal troubles.[85] Those researchers who have interviewed public officials about their adaptive responses to fiscal difficulties emphasize that "among all mechanisms that hold down total spending, limiting infrastructural outlays usually has the least immediate repercussions: city employees seldom lose jobs, perceived necessary services are not cut back, officials aren't blamed for callousness towards the poor."[86]

From an accountability point of view, deferred maintenance is troublesome. Some infrastructure—streets, for example—is quite visible. Deferred maintenance quickly translates into potholes, and citizens quickly let public officials know that they feel the cost of using funds for purposes other than street maintenance. However, the quality of certain infrastructure cannot be judged because, like water mains, it is invisible until catastrophic failure occurs.

As Herman Leonard explains, the quality of public officials' caretaking of infrastructure assets is also invisible in another sense.[87] Local governments are not required to keep records of the actual value of public assets and their depreciation over time. The result is another adaptive strategy that passes costs on to future taxpayers and violates principles of accountability:

> Using up existing capital assets—permitting a deterioration of infrastructure through deferred maintenance—is a form of public spending that operates at the lowest level of accountability. . . . It takes place by default, without explicit authorization. Not only does it not need an appropriated spending program to happen; it even takes appropriated maintenance or reinvestment expenditures to keep it from happening. And, since it is the result of an ongoing physical process rather than of a direct government activity, information about it is rarely collected.[88]

Like the other strategies discussed, deferred maintenance may be practiced by well-meaning public officials, hard-pressed to cope with fiscal troubles and understandably grasping for every available strategy to manage the situation. The accountability consequences and other problematic aspects of this strategy are so great, however, that infrastructure maintenance has recently attained a prominent place on the political agenda.

SUMMARY

At times it may seem that public sector officials are wizards. Somehow, despite economic shocks, legal constraints, political sensitivities to tax increases, and federal aid cutbacks, municipal life goes on with much less in the way of painful budget cutting than one might have expected. Layoffs are relatively rare, few programs are cut, and many of the services to which citizens have become accustomed seem to operate much as usual. Furthermore, defaults or near-defaults are quite rare. Even in Cleveland and New York, which have experienced financial crises, the fiscal house has been put back in order without noticeable impact on the lives of ordinary citizens in those communities.

As this chapter has shown, however, these happy results have not come without some subtle but important costs in the form of encroachments on local control and erosion of accountability. Local fiscal decisionmaking is heavily influenced by investors and state overseers, and local officials are being forced to justify their actions to these extralocal actors, perhaps more than to the citizenry. Meanwhile, a variety of the strategies and sophisticated financial tools that urban managers have been using carry with them significant costs in the form of lessened accountability to voters and sometimes other problematic features as well. It is not clear that costs like these can necessarily be avoided. It is important, however, that students of urban public affairs be conscious of these costs as well as the adaptive successes that the costs purchased.

DISCUSSION QUESTIONS AND EXERCISES

1. Choose a city for study, preferably one with a population of at least 50,000. Use the *County and City Data Book 1988* as a source of information. How diversified is the city's revenue base? To answer this question, determine what percentage of the city's total general revenue comes from the property tax, how much from the sales tax, how much from intergovernmental revenues, and how much from other sources. Discuss your findings, and compare them with the 208-city sample results in this chapter. Is your study city heavily dependent on the property tax? If so, what are the possible implications, politically and fiscally? Is your study city heavily dependent on intergovernmental revenues? If so, what are the possible implications?

2. As a more elaborate exercise, you might conduct an analysis like the one in question No. 1 but over a series of years. To do this, you will need a source such as the *City Government Finances* series published by the Bureau of the Census. What trends in city financing do you detect for your study city? Is it becoming less or more reliant on the property tax? The sales tax? Intergovernmental revenues? Why?

3. Again using the *County and City Data Book 1988* as your source, make a preliminary diagnosis of the fiscal health of your study city. Has it lost population between 1980 and 1986? Are property taxes per capita relatively high? The data book does not provide specific information on short-term debt, but it does show total debt outstanding on a per capita basis. Does this figure seem high for your study city? You might also determine whether your study city is included in the listings of cities in the *Municipal Yearbook,* published annually by the International City Management Association. If so, find a yearbook that includes Moody's Bond Ratings for the individual cities listed. What is your study city's bond rating? Compare your findings with those reported for the 208-city sample in this chapter and with the findings of your classmates. Does your study city appear to be in fiscal trouble, relatively speaking? Explain.

4. Which of the various explanations for fiscal stress that have been presented in this chapter is most compelling from your point of view? Why?

NOTES

1. These are derived from U.S. Bureau of the Census, *City Government Finances in 1977-78* (Washington, DC: U.S. Government Printing Office, 1980), and the companion volume *City Government Finances in 1983-84,* published in 1986.
2. Roy Bahl, *Financing State and Local Government in the 1980s* (New York: Oxford University Press, 1984), p. 14.
3. John O. Behrens, "The General Nature of 'the' Property Tax Today," in *The Property Tax and Local Finance,* ed. C. Lowell Harriss (New York: Academy of Political Science, 1983), p. 20.
4. Susan MacManus, "State Government: The Overseer of Municipal Finance," in *The Municipal Money Chase,* ed. Alberta Sbragia (Boulder, CO: Westview Press, 1983), p. 153.
5. Arthur C. Roemer, "Classification of Property," in *The Property Tax and Local Finance,* ed. Harriss (New York: Academy of Political Science, 1983), p. 108.
6. Ibid., pp. 109-110.
7. Advisory Commission on Intergovernmental Relations (ACIR), *Significant Features of Fiscal Federalism,* 1985-86 ed. (Washington, DC: U.S. Government Printing Office, 1986), pp. 95-97.
8. Ibid., pp. 87-88.
9. U.S. Bureau of the Census, *City Government Finances in 1977-78* (Washington, DC: U.S. Government Printing Office, 1980), p. 107.
10. Robert W. Poole, Jr., *Cutting Back City Hall* (New York: Universe Books, 1980), pp. 32-34.
11. U.S. Bureau of the Census, *City Government Finances in 1984-85* (Washington, DC: U.S. Government Printing Office, 1986), p. 1, and the companion volume *City Government Finances in 1977-78* (1980), p. 7.
12. Ibid., 1986 and 1980, p. 1 and p. 8 respectively.
13. Alberta M. Sbragia, "Politics, Local Government, and the Municipal Bond Market," in *The Municipal Money Chase,* ed. A. Sbragia (Boulder, CO: Westview Press, 1983), p. 72.
14. Ibid., p. 76.
15. Elaine B. Sharp, "The Politics and Economics of the New City Debt," *American Political Science Review* 80 (December 1986): 1271-1288.
16. Kathryn Newcomer, Deborah Trent, and Natalie Flores-Kelly, "Municipal Debt and the Impact of Sound Fiscal Decision Making," *Municipal Yearbook 1983* (Washington, DC: ICMA, 1983), p. 219; Sbragia, "Politics, Local Government, and Municipal Bond Market," p. 72; Susan MacManus, "The Impact of Functional Responsibility and State Legal Constraints on the 'Revenue-Debt' Packages of U.S. Central Cities," *International Journal of Public Administration* 3 (1981): 67-111.
17. Charles Levine, "The New Crisis in the Public Sector," in *Managing Fiscal Stress,* ed. C. Levine (Chatham, NJ; Chatham House, 1980), pp. 3-12.
18. Terry Nichols Clark and Lorna Crowley Ferguson, *City Money* (New York: Columbia University Press, 1983).
19. Martin Shefter, *Political Crisis/Fiscal Crisis* (New York: Basic Books, 1985).
20. Irene S. Rubin, *Running in the Red* (Albany, NY: State University of New York Press, 1982).

21. Charles Levine, "Organizational Decline and Cutback Management," in *Managing Fiscal Stress,* ed. Levine (Chatham, NJ: Chatham House, 1980), pp. 13-32.
22. Ibid., p. 5.
23. David T. Stanley, "Cities in Trouble," in *Managing Fiscal Stress,* ed. Levine (Chatham, NJ: Chatham House, 1980), pp. 95-122.
24. Ibid., p. 95.
25. Clark and Ferguson, *City Money,* pp. 43-45.
26. James P. Pfiffner, "Inflexible Budgets, Fiscal Stress, and the Tax Revolt," in Sbragia *The Municipal Money Chase,* ed. Sbragia (Boulder, CO: Westview Press, 1983), pp. 37-66.
27. Jack Citrin, "Introduction: The Legacy of Proposition 13," in *California and the American Tax Revolt,* ed. Terry Schwadron (Berkeley: University of California Press, 1984), pp. 10-11.
28. ACIR, *Significant Features of Fiscal Federalism,* 1985-86 ed. p. 146.
29. Ibid.
30. Betsy Strauss, Marjorie Mikels, and Donald Hagman, "Description of Propositions 13 and 4," in *Tax and Expenditure Limitations: How to Implement and Live Within Them,* ed. Jerome G. Rose (Piscataway, NJ: Rutgers Center for Urban Policy Research, 1982), p. 19.
31. ACIR, *Significant Features of Fiscal Federalism,* 1980-81 ed. (Washington, DC: U.S. Government Printing Office, 1981).
32. Pfiffner, "Inflexible Budgets, Fiscal Stress, and the Tax Revolt," p. 47.
33. ACIR, *Significant Features of Fiscal Federalism,* 1981 ed., p. 158.
34. ACIR, *Significant Features of Fiscal Federalism,* 1986 ed., p. 146.
35. Richard Aronson and John L. H ley, *Financing State and Local Governments* (Washington, DC: Brookings Institution, 1986), p. 175.
36. MacManus, "State Government," p. 162; see also Sbragia, "Politics, Local Government, and Municipal Bond Market," p. 72.
37. ACIR, *Significant Features of Fiscal Federalism,* 1985-86 ed., pp. 95-97.
38. Elaine Sharp and David Elkins, "The Impact of Fiscal Limitation: A Tale of Seven Cities," *Public Administration Review* 47 (September/October 1987): 385-392.
39. MacManus, "Impact of Functional Responsibility and State Legal Constraints," p. 101.
40. Ibid., p. 95.
41. Rubin, *Running in the Red,* p. 5.
42. Barry Bluestone and Bennett Harrison, *The Deindustrialization of America* (New York: Basic Books, 1982).
43. M. Gottdiener, *The Decline of Urban Politics* (Newberry Park, CA: Sage, 1987), p. 78.
44. David Lowery and William D. Berry, "The Growth of Government in the United States: An Empirical Assessment of Competing Explanations," *American Journal of Political Science* 27 (November 1983): 667.
45. Clark and Ferguson, *City Money,* p. 45.
46. Lowery and Berry, "Growth of Government in the United States," pp. 668-669.
47. Robert Goodman, *The Last Entrepreneurs* (Boston: South End Press, 1979).
48. Ibid., p. 59.
49. James O'Connor, *The Fiscal Crisis of the State* (New York: St. Martin's Press, 1973).

50. Gottdiener, *Decline of Urban Politics,* pp. 124–125.
51. Lowery and Berry, "Growth of Government in United States," p. 673.
52. Gottdiener, *Decline of Urban Politics,* p. 105.
53. Rubin, *Running in the Red,* p. 8.
54. Lowery and Berry, "Growth of Government in United States," p. 674.
55. Ibid., p. 673.
56. Rubin, *Running in the Red,* p. 8.
57. Elaine B. Sharp, *Citizen Demand-Making in the Urban Context* (University, AL: University of Alabama Press, 1986).
58. Rubin, *Running in the Red,* p. 9.
59. Shefter, *Political Crisis/Fiscal Crisis.*
60. Ibid., p. 4.
61. Ibid.
62. Larry Sawers, "New Perspectives on the Urban Political Economy," in *Marxism and the Metropolis,* ed. William K. Tabb and Larry Sawers (New York: Oxford University Press, 1984), pp. 3–17; see also Andrew Kirby, "Nine Fallacies of Local Economic Change," *Urban Affairs Quarterly* 21 (December 1985): 207–220.
63. This is much the thrust of Irene Rubin's argument in "Structural Theories and Urban Fiscal Stress," *Urban Affairs Quarterly* 20 (June 1985): 479.
64. Paul Peterson, *City Limits* (Chicago: University of Chicago Press, 1981).
65. Sbragia, "Politics, Local Government, and Municipal Bond Market," pp. 77–79.
66. Rubin, *Running in the Red,* p. 101.
67. Sbragia, "Politics, Local Government, and Municipal Bond Market," p. 103.
68. Catherine Lovell and Charles Tobin, "Mandating—A Key Issue for Cities," *Municipal Yearbook 1980* (Washington, DC: ICMA, 1980), p. 75.
69. Lovell and Tobin, "Mandating," p. 74.
70. Ibid.
71. Ibid.
72. Georgina Fiordalis, "Dose of Fiscal Prevention Aids Massachusetts Towns," *City & State* (October 1986): 13.
73. David Lowery, "After the Tax Revolt: Some Positive, If Unintended Consequences," *Social Science Quarterly* 67 (December 1986): 743.
74. Gottdiener, *Decline of Urban Politics,* p. 15.
75. Annmarie H. Walsh, *The Public's Business* (Cambridge, MA: MIT Press, 1978).
76. James T. Bennett and Thomas J. DiLorenzo, *Underground Government: The Off-Budget Public Sector* (Washington, DC: Cato Institute, 1983), p. 34.
77. Sbragia, "Politics, Local Government, and Municipal Bond Market," p. 100.
78. Diana Henriques, *The Machinery of Greed* (Lexington, MA: Heath, 1986).
79. Jameson Doig, " 'If I See a Murderous Fellow Sharpening a Knife Cleverly' . . . The Wilsonian Dichotomy and the Public Authority Tradition," *Public Administration Review* 43 (March/April 1983): 292–304.
80. Lowery, "After the Tax Revolt," p. 739.
81. Herman Leonard, *Checks Unbalanced: The Quiet Side of Public Spending* (New York: Basic Books, 1986), p. 183.
82. Steve Hemmerick, "Broadside Report: Public Sector Leasing," *City & State* (January 1986): 11; Leonard, *Checks Unbalanced,* 183. Leonard also acknowledges (pp. 100–102) that increased costs of borrowing, fueled by investors' concerns about unexpectedly high interest rates, provided a motivation for leasing alternatives.

83. Hemmerick, "Broadside Report," p. 13.
84. Ibid., p. 11.
85. Leonard, *Checks Unbalanced,* p. 170.
86. Michael A. Pagano and Richard J. T. Moore, *Cities and Fiscal Choices: A New Model of Urban Public Investment* (Durham, NC: Duke University Press, 1985), p. 84.
87. Leonard, *Checks Unbalanced,* pp. 171–175.
88. Ibid., p. 177.

CHAPTER 8

The Urban Infrastructure: Problems and Prospects

Infrastructure, or the physical face of the city, consists of the public facilities and structures that are essential parts of any city, large or small. Extending the physical analogy, Joel Tarr defines urban infrastructure as the "sinews" of the city: ". . . its road, bridge, and transit networks; its water and sewer lines and waste disposal facilities; its power systems; its public buildings; and its parks and recreation areas."[1]

Like many other topics relating to American cities, the urban infrastructure has recently attracted crisis rhetoric. The task of this chapter is in part to explore the problems of urban public infrastructure and to consider just how critical these problems really are. Along the way, we will see that infrastructure questions have recently moved to a prominent position on the public agenda in reaction to perceptions that neglect has created a crumbling infrastructure. We will also examine the complex relationships among the federal, state, and local governments in the provision of infrastructure, the important political and financing questions that surround capital improvements projects, and the important role of quasi-governmental entities (i.e., authorities, commissions, public corporations) in the creation and operation of major capital facilities.

NATURE AND SIGNIFICANCE OF URBAN INFRASTRUCTURE

Throughout this analysis, it is important to bear in mind that urban infrastructure is associated with both economic development and with traditional urban service delivery. With respect to the latter, one need only point out that virtually all urban services have some infrastructure component. Stated another way, even the most labor-intensive forms of service delivery are based on and supported by capital facilities. Fire protection requires adequately designed and located fire stations, not to mention usable streets and a reliable system of water distribution. Similarly, although the typical householder may be more conscious of the sanitation worker who carts away the trash every week, the system that carries off the household waste water for treatment is equally important to public health and sanitation in the community. Finally, park and recreation services involve investments in swimming pools, tennis and basketball courts, public restrooms, and other physical facilities.

The relationship between urban infrastructure and economic development has recently received more attention than the basic service delivery aspects of infrastructure. Various commentators emphasize that, "Without the provision of adequate streets, water supply, and sewage treatment, it would be difficult indeed for directly productive activities to proceed, at least without tremendous cost to the producer."[2] Furthermore, failure to provide quality infrastructure is alleged to deter economic activity. "For example, U.S. Steel has claimed that it costs approximately $5 million per year in additional transportation costs because of a weight reduction on a poorly maintained bridge in the Pittsburgh area."[3] The connection between the quality of public facilities and economic activity is not always this direct or dramatic, but public transportation facilities, water systems, and the like are surely of substantial importance for business and industry. This was, in fact, the logic behind public support of railroads, canals, and other transportation-oriented infrastructure in the mid-nineteenth century.[4] The contemporary resurgence of interest in infrastructure is driven by concerns about economic development.

INFRASTRUCTURE IN CRISIS

Of late, Americans have been repeatedly reminded of infrastructure problems by failures, sometimes catastrophic, that seem to reveal that the infrastructure in this country is crumbling around us (see Box 8.1).

Examples include: the collapse of the Silver Bridge in West Virginia in 1968, leading to the creation of the National Bridge Inspection Program; the potential disaster of the weakened and near-collapse condition of New York City's Queensboro Bridge, which fortunately was discovered in time for "Band-Aid" repairs; the appearance of a dangerous crack in the Manhattan bridge . . . a rupture in Jersey City's major aqueduct, which left the city and surrounding user communities without drinking water for six days in the summer of 1982 . . . the bursting of an eighty-year-old dam in Colorado that resulted in a wall of water flooding the town of Estes Park in the summer of 1982."[5]

BOX 8.1   The Williamsburg Bridge and Infrastructure Crisis

In the spring of 1988, the Williamsburg Bridge, which normally carries 240,000 commuters between Brooklyn and Manhattan, had to be temporarily closed because of safety concerns. A Transportation Department engineer had heard an unexplained sound coming from the interior of the bridge—a squealing sound interrupted by an ominous bang. Officials acknowledged that the roadbed structure of the bridge was badly corroded due to "years of poor maintenance, incomplete inspections and ignorance about how quickly steel can rot away under the harsh conditions above the East River." They also acknowledged that the problems with the Williamsburg Bridge were becoming urgent for many of the city's other bridges. About half of the city's bridges are categorized as "structurally deficient" by state transportation officials.

Source: Kirk Johnson, "New Woes for Closed Bridge; 240,000 Face Traffic Crush," *New York Times,* April 14, 1988.

In the same vein, Leonard reminds us that "A pothole in Holyoke, Massachusetts, recently swallowed a 1979 Ford Mustang. The early-morning collapse of a section of the Mianus River bridge on the Connecticut Turnpike killed three people."[6]

If these seemingly everyday reports of egregious failure are not enough, analysts have compiled further evidence of problems. Drawing on a variety of government sources, Choate and Walter compile the following partial list of evidence for their theme of *America in Ruins:*

> One of every five bridges in the United States requires either major rehabilitation or reconstruction. . . . No reliable estimates exist of the investments required to modernize our ports, but numerous instances exist of harbor facilities unable to service efficiently world shipping coming to American docks. . . . The 756 urban areas with populations of over 50,000 will require between $75 billion and $110 billion to maintain their urban water systems over the next 20 years. Approximately one-fifth of these communities will face investment shortfalls. . . . Over one-half of the nation's 3,500 jails are over 30 years old. At least 1,300 and perhaps as many as 3,600 of these facilities must be either totally rebuilt or substantially rehabilitated in the 1980s.[7]

One of the difficulties in assessing the scope of the infrastructure crisis is that there are so many different ways of demonstrating infrastructure shortfalls. Recent commentators have given five indicators, many of which are illustrated in the foregoing examples.[8] First, there is direct observation, often based on anecdotal evidence or journalistic accounts of isolated but catastrophic infrastructure failures. Reports of bridge failures or potholes swallowing Mustangs clearly exemplify this basis for determining infrastructure problems.

Second, maintenance and replacement cycles are another basis for assessing the scope of the problem. Given the "explicit acknowledgment that capital stock wears out," estimates of infrastructure needs can be based on information about how old the existing facilities are.[9] Choate and Walter's observation that half the nation's jails are over 30 years old exemplifies this approach to problem definition. One of the difficulties with this approach is that "not enough is known about appropriate replacement cycles nor about the rate at which facilities wear out."[10] Although some infrastructure is quite old, it may not necessarily be inadequate. Drawing on some systematic observation of the condition of existing infrastructure, George Peterson concludes: "It seems probable that earlier generations bequeathed us a capital plant that was more durable and more resistant to temporary neglect than our standard accounts assume."[11]

Many assessments of the infrastructure problem rely on yet a third indicator—the dollar amount of capital investment needed to bring infrastructure to acceptable standards. An example from the Choate and Walter list previously quoted is the observation that between $75 billion and $110 billion will be needed for cities to maintain their water systems over the next 20 years. The difficulty here is in deriving appropriate standards. In many cases, assessments of this sort can amount to no more than aggregated wish lists. Many of the estimates of the infrastructure problem that are based on the needs approach have been criticized as inflated and unrealistic.

> While the standard or standards chosen often include physical condition and design criteria as well as level of service and demand-related criteria, most needs studies have been based on unstated assumptions about economic, social, and environmental objectives, performance standards, and growth trends. . . . The result of the traditional needs approach generally has been estimates of capital investment requirements far in excess of . . . even the most optimistic projections of new revenue sources. As a result, many needs studies have been viewed as self-serving and lacking any real credibility.[12]

The fourth method for assessing the scope of the infrastructure problem would have us focus on the "costs to the private sector due to the inadequate condition of the infrastructure."[13] U.S. Steel's claim that it costs an additional $5 million each year because of an inadequate bridge in the Pittsburgh area is one example of this way of thinking about the scope of the infrastructure problem. By comparison with the needs approach, which is criticized for often failing to distinguish *real* needs from nice ideas, this approach identifies infrastructure needs in terms of the dollars-and-cents costs that existing, poor-quality infrastructure can impose on the local economy. Unfortunately, "no systematic effort to estimate such monetary losses has been undertaken by local governments."[14] The monetary losses approach falters on the grounds of lack of available information.

Lack of available information is far less a problem with respect to the fifth and final method for assessing the scope of the infrastructure problem:

examination of trends in government expenditures for infrastructure, at least if investment in new or replacement infrastructure is the primary interest. It is common practice for governments to keep separate capital budgets, and the U.S. Census Bureau can therefore readily report information on capital outlays annually. Observation of trends in capital outlay form the basis for one important definition of the infrastructure crisis: "State and local capital spending in real terms has declined erratically but steeply since 1968."[15] Choate and Walter, for example, report that state and local investment in public works, in constant 1972 dollars, declined from $33.8 billion in 1970 to $26.1 billion in 1977; expressed as a share of Gross National Product (GNP), total government investment in public works (federal, state, and local) declined from 4.1 percent in 1965 to 2.3 percent in 1977.[16]

More recent information on state and local capital outlays shows that the problem is a continuing one. Figure 8.1 underscores the fact that state and local governments in the aggregate have not been cutting back on their expenditures for infrastructure, although there have been periods of stability rather than growth in such expenditures. However, stability in capital expenditures translates into a decline in real spending because inflation erodes purchasing

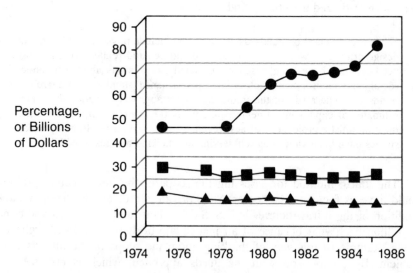

▲ As Percentage of Total Direct Spending
● In Billions of Dollars
■ In Billions of Constant (1967) Dollars

Figure 8.1. State and Local Capital Outlay, 1975–1985 (*Source: Statistical Abstract of the United States*, 108th ed. [1988] and 107th ed. [1987]. [Washington, DC.: U.S. Department of Commerce, Bureau of the Census], pp. 259 and 444 [1988]; pp. 254 and 463 [1987].)

power of budgeted dollars. Even the strong upsurge in state and local capital spending in the 1978 to 1981 period is largely negated by the effects of inflation. In real, inflation-adjusted dollars, state and local capital spending declined after 1975 and has not reached that level of real outlay again.

In addition, the importance of capital spending relative to other spending has declined since 1975. Figure 8.1 shows erosion in the percentage of total direct spending of state and local governments that is devoted to capital outlay. These subnational governments have been devoting less and less attention to capital outlay relative to operating expenditures, a pattern that is suggestive of underinvestment in infrastructure.

There are several difficulties with using capital spending trends as indicators of the scope of the infrastructure problem. One weakness of the approach is that it leads us to an overly narrow view of the problem and possible solutions because available data reflect investment in new or replacement capital facilities, *not maintenance* of existing structures. As Herman Leonard argues:

> [Proposals to enhance investment in new infrastructure] all manage to miss the central lesson of two decades of experience with infrastructure. . . . [They all] look at a set of crumbling infrastructure systems and assume that all we need to do is find enough money to build new ones. But this ignores the key question—why are the current systems crumbling?[17]

The answer, according to Leonard, is lack of attention to maintenance—a lack of attention fostered by accounting systems that provide incentives for public officials to scrimp on maintenance. Focusing attention on how much capital outlay there is for new infrastructure can divert us from the possibility that the infrastructure crisis is a crisis of undermaintenance of existing facilities.

A focus on capital expenditure trends has other limitations as well. One of the foremost experts on infrastructure finance, George Peterson, explains:

> The statistical argument for more infrastructure investment bears some resemblance to the statistical argument for greater defense spending. . . . Just as the sustained decline in real outlays for defense and the share of the federal budget devoted to defense through 1980 established a presumption in favor of greater defense spending, so does the decline in real infrastructure spending. . . . In neither case are spending trends alone the best evidence. The apparent lag in infrastructure investment needs to be checked against the condition and performance of public facilities.[18]

This critique of expenditure trends as an indicator of the scope of the infrastructure crisis brings us back to the other indicators discussed earlier, such as direct observation of the actual condition of various facilities. As we have seen, those indicators are beset with problems and limitations as well. Systematic and objective monitoring of the actual condition of urban infrastructure is all too rare. Anecdotal reports, based on catastrophic failures, are much more common.

The infrastructure problem is therefore in part an information problem. It is difficult to know how serious the problem is or where investments are most needed without solid, systematic, and comparable observations of the condition of facilities. As difficult as this problem may be for an individual community attempting to engage in capital planning, it is vastly compounded for the federal government, which makes large allocations of aid to state and local governments for infrastructure development. Not surprisingly, then, one of the key recommendations of a recent study commissioned by the Joint Economic Committee of the U.S. Congress is that "Congress mandate the coordinated development of an annual inventory and assessment of basic infrastructure and an evaluation of basic infrastructure conditions."[19]

CAUSES OF THE INFRASTRUCTURE PROBLEM

To the extent that there are inadequate capital facilities in urban America, what is the source of the problem? Several culprits have been identified, including urban fiscal stress and deferred maintenance responses, federal disengagement and other difficulties with the federal role, and limitations of government systems for managing capital projects efficiently. The following sections consider each of these possible sources of difficulty.

Urban Fiscal Stress and Deferred Maintenance

One of the most common arguments about the infrastructure crisis holds that it is in large part a reflection of the fiscal pressure gripping many of the nation's cities. Some cities tottered on the brink of financial collapse in the late 1970s, and a number of others were reeling under the shock of the tax revolt and other populist fiscal limits described in Chapter 7. Under these circumstances, various commentators argue, it is not surprising that capital investment and maintenance expenditures suffered.

It is often suggested that maintenance expenditures are especially vulnerable during times of fiscal stress because deferred maintenance is a relatively invisible and politically painless way for city officials to adapt to fiscal pressures. Rather than cutting back on services, officials can divert funds that would have gone for maintenance to regular operating expenses. Quoting the mayor of Lincoln, Nebraska, Herman Leonard illustrates the appeal of this response to fiscal pressure: "In the choice between laying off police and maintaining sewers, the sewers always lose."[20] At least in the short term, the consequences of this adaptive strategy are limited because citizens do not realize that the quality of the community's infrastructure has been placed at risk so that fewer hard choices need to be made about operating expenses.

Although fiscal stress and resulting deferred maintenance are surely very real phenomena, explanations of the infrastructure crisis that rely on these phenomena have several problems. Systematic study of capital outlay and maintenance expenditures for key categories of infrastructure in several major cities shows that there is no simple link between level of fiscal stress and either capital or maintenance spending. For example, a decline in maintenance spending for streets and bridges was observed among both fiscally stressed and better-off cities; water and sewer systems seem to have been better maintained, even in fiscally stressed cities; and idiosyncratic trends in capital outlays are observed, rather than consistent differences between fiscally stressed and better-off cities.[21] These findings lead to the conclusion that ". . . much of the writing on the crisis of urban infrastructure overplays the responsibility of fiscal stress in the neglect of maintenance activities."[22]

Similarly, logical consideration of the timing of infrastructure problems relative to the timing of fiscal crises leads to conclusions that challenge any simplistic connection between the two:

> The persistence of infrastructure needs over time in such communities as New York and Cleveland should also raise questions about the linkage between fiscal health and the condition of public facilities. The decay of these structures and systems cannot be attributed simply to a decline in urban capital spending following such crisis events as the collapse of capital spending in New York and Cleveland, the austerity faced by such older cities as Detroit and Boston, and the broad impact of Proposition 13 on California communities. While these events did undermine the abilities of cities to meet capital improvements needs, many of these same needs had gone unmet in the preceding few years.[23]

Even as local *fiscal* explanations of the infrastructure crisis are being qualified, local *political* explanations are being re-emphasized and highlighted. Infrastructure needs are one of a variety of competing needs. To the extent that infrastructure is either first on the chopping block in times of fiscal stress or systematically underemphasized during more normal times, the reasons have to do with the ways local politicians evaluate competing needs and with important features of infrastructure spending. Contrarily, where capital spending is sustained despite budgetary pressures, political dynamics often help to explain why.

These themes are amply demonstrated by Heywood Sanders, who suggests that some types of infrastructure spending, in some situations, are politically attractive.[24] In growing communities, infrastructure investment, even in relatively "invisible" items like sewer system expansion, is attractive and politically viable because it generates benefits for a broad array of interests, ranging from contractors and suppliers who will do the work to landowners and developers whose properties will be enhanced by the infrastructure that supports growth. The community at large also benefits because revenues from things like surplus water and sewer fees can be used to help the city's budget picture, as can new sales taxes and other revenues attributable to the new growth.

In communities that are not growing, infrastructure spending *of a particular type* can also be politically attractive. As Sanders explains:

> The real political value of urban infrastructure improvements is to be found in their specifics—projects that benefit and are visible to a specific ward, neighborhood, or city block. Specific projects provide a form of political currency, which can be exchanged and doled out, employed to reward and punish, to build political coalitions and win votes. The political value of rebuilding a sewer or resurfacing a street thus reflects some popular interest in this sort of project and the ability of an elected official to decide who gets what.[25]

We need not take this to mean that "pork barrel" in its most negative connotation is the type of capital spending that works in nongrowth settings. The point is that winning popular support for capital spending typically means attention to the *distributive* forms of infrastructure—that is, the neighborhood-based projects that are visible and responsive to area-specific needs.

The politics of gaining public support for infrastructure investment is well illustrated in a recent case example from Kansas City.[26] In March, 1988, both Kansas City, Missouri, and Jackson County, in which central Kansas City is located, placed a $1.5 billion package of capital improvements measures before the voters. The proposals ranged from relatively "flashy" redevelopment projects, like $17.5 million for the renovation of Union Station and $12.5 million for public improvements to a riverfront development site, to basic service facilities, like $30 million to construct and equip a police and fire communications center, $4 million for fire stations, $5.9 million for police stations, $66 million for sewage treatment and disposal facilities, and $330 million for improvements to the Kansas City International Airport. Distributive public works were represented in the form of proposals that part of a one-cent sales tax continuation and part of a new half-cent sales tax be used for neighborhood improvements. In addition, there was a proposed $5 million revenue bond issue for expansion of the museum. Jackson County officials had two items on the ballot—a proposed half-cent sales tax to be used for a wide variety of capital improvements purposes, including the county's share of the costs of renovating Union Station, and a proposed half-cent sales tax for design and construction of a horse-racing track.

These various ballot proposals obviously represented a range of substantially different purposes, some more citywide, some more localized, some readily understood as economic development projects, and some less so. In addition, the proposals differed in the type of financing involved. Some were proposals to issue general obligation bonds, a matter that requires a two-thirds majority in Missouri. Others were proposals to issue revenue bonds, which require only majority approval. Several major proposals were for new or renewed sales taxes, which require majority approval.

Public officials and civic leaders made substantial efforts to work together on a campaign to convince voters to adopt the package of proposals. Although city and county officials often go their separate ways, they agreed to work together in this case, especially with respect to a joint venture on the Union Station renovation. A campaign committee, the 21st Century Progress Committee, raised over $400,000 in contributions, primarily from corporations and the construction industry. Over $90,000 was spent for radio and TV campaign advertising alone. The television ads showed heavy construction equipment moving in a motorcade through the city, to a background track of dramatic music and either the mayor or the county executive declaiming about the need for the city to get moving. Meanwhile, however, a coalition of several small citizens' organizations had formed to oppose the capital improvements package, with arguments that the city was neither collecting nor spending existing taxes efficiently, that tax abatements were being given when they should not be, and that a no-frills approach to infrastructure improvement was needed. Additional difficulties emerged when city and county leaders could not seem to settle definitively on a specific renovation plan for Union Station.

When the dust had settled after the March 8, 1988 election, eleven of the fifteen ballot issues involved in the capital improvements package had failed. The only propositions to gain voter approval were the one-cent sales tax renewal (for schools and various capital improvements including the zoo and neighborhood improvements), a $110 million revenue bond issue for waterworks improvements, a $66 million revenue bond issue for sewer improvements, and a $5 million revenue bond issue for the museum. Some proposals gained majority support but not the extraordinary majority required for general obligation bonds. Consequently, many postelection analyses laid blame on this rule. Others argued that the package was simply too large, asking voters for too much at once. Still others argued that proposals like the Union Station redevelopment scheme were neither properly conceived nor adequately sold to the voters. Similarly, the poor showing of some redevelopment items like the riverfront improvement project suggests that even a community hungry for economic development will not necessarily approve proposals that are not compelling.

If relatively large capital projects like sewer extensions can be attractive in growing communities and smaller, distributive forms of capital spending can be attractive in communities of all sorts, some important forms of infrastructure investment cannot generate such political appeal. These include maintenance spending. As we have already noted, this does not generate the visible benefits that new neighborhood fire stations and similar distributive investments do. Also included in the politically problematic category are relatively large-scale facility repairs or enhancements, especially in settings that are not experiencing growth. An example cited by Sanders is the storm drainage system in Cincinnati, which has long been an acknowledged problem. Although the city has committed some funds every year to patchwork gestures, some observers conclude that a comprehensive response is unlikely.[27] There is not a political coalition to support the large-scale public works endeavor that would be needed for an overall solution.

In sum, the fiscal stress explanation for the nation's urban infrastructure problem has been found wanting. It is not that fiscal problems are totally irrelevant to cities' capital outlays. Rather, recent commentators have noted that fiscal stress is a very incomplete, even misleading explanation for infrastructure problems. According to this point of view, political considerations are at least as important as fiscal considerations, and political considerations vary across cities and across different types of capital spending.

Infrastructure Problems and the Federal Role

Yet another target of finger pointing in discussions of the infrastructure problem is the federal government. Specifically, cutbacks in federal aid have led to cries that federal retrenchment is creating important dislocations in state and local infrastructure investment.

It is certainly true that the federal government has historically played a major role in financing infrastructure through grant-in-aid programs to state and local governments. Such grants totaled $10.8 billion in 1975 and rose to a high point of $22.4 billion in 1980.[28] In the years following 1980, there have been declines from this all-time high—in particular, a 1.3 percent decline in 1981, followed by an 8.6 percent decline in 1982.[29] To the extent that General Revenue Sharing was being used for capital improvements, its recent demise can also be expected to affect infrastructure investment adversely, especially if localities had been spending federal aid on projects and facilities for which they would not have invested local funds—that is, avoiding what is called substitutive spending. Studies of General Revenue Sharing, the Community Development Block Grant, and the Comprehensive Employment and Training Act show that communities have been avoiding substitutive behavior and that there has been a low level of replacement of lost federal aid with local resources devoted to the same purposes. However, the replacement funding that has been detected "was highest in areas of traditional or longstanding state and local concern, for example health and infrastructure programs such as highways and mass transit."[30] In short, while the withdrawal of federal aid affects cities adversely, at least some forms of infrastructure spending are being sustained with locally derived revenues.

Just as the broader fiscal stress argument is weakened by timing considerations, so should we be cautious of attributing infrastructure problems primarily to federal retrenchment in the post 1980 period. Problems of underinvestment that are showing up as bridge failures and poor-quality street and sewage systems today have longer-term roots. Lack of adequate attention to these facilities must have been occurring even during years of relatively handsome federal aid. As one analyst comments:

> Whatever the cause of the slowdown in state and local capital spending, it seems unfair to pin responsibility on inadequate growth in total federal assistance. Over the period 1975–1980, federal capital aid was growing in real terms at the same time that state and local expenditures from their own resources were rapidly declining.[31]

Furthermore, it is important to note that the federal government's role is not restricted to direct grants-in-aid. The federal government also indirectly subsidizes local infrastructure investment through the tax-exempt status of municipal bonds. The fact that they are tax exempt means that local governments do not have to pay as high an interest rate when they issue them as would be the case if investors buying the bonds had to pay taxes on their bond earnings. Those lost tax payments, because of the tax-exempt status of local bonds, cost the federal treasury $3.8 billion in 1975, $5.4 billion in 1979, and $6.9 billion in 1982.[32] Estimates place the cost to the federal treasury in fiscal year 1989 at $12.9 billion.[33]

Furthermore, the federal government plays a nonfiscal role in infrastructure development as well. In particular, "it frequently sets the standards which define 'needs' and which guide type and method of construction."[34] To the extent that cities have invested in secondary wastewater treatment facilities, for example, it is because of federal laws mandating certain levels of water quality as well as federal aid to help pay for such facilities. Similarly, federal standards for road construction, bridges, and the like are important in dictating state and local practice.

But if the federal government plays a variety of positive roles in addition to the direct funding role, it has also been criticized for having various negative impacts on local infrastructure development. In particular, there have been criticisms that federal aid programs are too rigid, thus skewing local priorities and not allowing local governments to adapt federal aid programs to their most pressing infrastructure needs. This problem arises from the fact that much of the federal aid that is available for assisting with capital projects is in the form of separate, categorical grant programs—one for sewage treatment, another for hospital construction, another for airport construction, and so on. Over time, funding levels for the different categorical programs vary considerably—the result of agenda setting and priority setting at the national level. The needs of particular local governments at particular times may not fit the changing tides of federal funding, however. As Royce Hanson notes, "It is not of much value to a city if funds are available for bridge repair when its most pressing need is for a new water system."[35] As a result, one of the policy recommendations of the Joint Economic Committee examining the infrastructure crisis was that infrastructure assistance programs be made more flexible.[36]

The federal government has also been criticized for an overemphasis on construction of new facilities to the detriment of repair and maintenance spending. For example, until 1984 the federal government provided 75 percent of the capital costs of sewage treatment facilities (the local government providing the other 25 percent as match); after 1984, the ratio switched to 55 percent federal funds and 45 percent local match. But no funds are provided to subsidize maintenance of these sewage treatment facilities. As they age, there may well be underinvestment in maintenance because it is a 100 percent local responsibility.[37] Although there have been some policy changes with regard to eligibility of maintenance activities for federal support, this emphasis on funding new construction remains.[38]

From a larger perspective, however, both political and fiscal difficulties in finding available funds for infrastructure at the local level inevitably lead to calls for greater help from the federal government. Whether in the form of demands for greater federal grants-in-aid or in the form of proposals for a National Infrastructure Fund established with monies obtained through the taxable bond market, there are sure to be continuing pressures for an enhanced federal role in bankrolling local infrastructure investments.[39] As one commentator notes, however, to the extent that infrastructure investment is a form of economic development activity, this should be an area that is less in need of federal support than redistributive activity.[40]

Problems of Management: Waste and Delay

Yet a third target for blame concerning inadequate public infrastructure is that set of practices by which government manages (or fails to manage) capital project development and implementation. Stated most simply, even if adequate resources are initially available for public sector investment in infrastructure, the ultimate results will be disappointing if those resources are squandered through wasteful and inefficient implementation processes.

Policies and practices that permit accumulated delays in implementation of public works projects are important problems because the cost of delay itself is so important. For example, it has been estimated that compensating for increased costs due to delay is eating up about 20 percent of national public works appropriations.[41] The costs of delay can be seen even more dramatically on an individual project. For example, after the controversial Westway highway project in New York City was abandoned, costs of delay mounted rapidly as officials searched for an alternative. It has been estimated that $90,000 per day was the cost in lost purchasing power as the decisionmaking dragged on.[42]

Even when public officials choose to go ahead with an infrastructure project and obligate funds for the purpose, there are still a variety of important sources of delay that can create roadblocks to efficient implementation. Choate and Walter provide a comprehensive listing that shows the importance of preconstruction delays rather than delays in the construction process itself.

These include (1) delays in regulatory processes, ranging from land use regulations to building regulations to environmental regulations; (2) delays resulting from citizen involvement and its attendant controversies; and (3) delays resulting from the large number of intergovernmental clearances that exist, especially for projects receiving federal or state aid.[43]

Delays in the regulatory process often arise because those regulatory activities are not bound by any time limits. Many infrastructure projects require approvals and permits of various kinds from government agencies, and the process of obtaining them can drag on if there are no requirements that the approval or permit application be processed within a set period. Projects that involve multiple jurisdictions or agencies can easily be delayed because of a lack of coordination among the different jurisdictions and agencies, turf battles that tie up the project, and similar problems of jurisdictional fragmentation.[44]

Furthermore, public works projects can become mired in controversies that effectively stalemate action. Because major public works projects often involve spatial reallocations and disruptions, they are particularly susceptible to such controversy. Siting of facilities that would not be desirable neighbors—for example, airports, correctional facilities, and sewage treatment plants—involves the allocation of spatial costs and is often controversial. Urban managers and politicians quickly become familiar with the NIMBY syndrome—a popular acronym for the "not-in-my-back-yard" sentiment that greets so many facility siting proposals. Public works projects like urban highways that displace people and businesses are also intensely controversial. Hearings and other citizen participation requirements provide one avenue that those opposed to a project can use to delay progress. Lawsuits are another. In fact, legal appeals are a particularly potent weapon for opponents because the resulting delay means substantial, perhaps even crippling, added costs for the project.

Finally, public works projects are vulnerable to delay simply on grounds of the sheer number of mandatory procedures and clearances that they typically involve. This is especially true of local projects that receive federal funding and that must therefore comply with the full range of federal requirements as well as a host of local rules, procedures, and contingencies. Even an abbreviated listing of these would include condemnation proceedings for site acquisition, development of environmental impact statements, planning and design activities, often including open hearings or other citizen participation requirements, relocation processes for displaced homeowners and businesses, and many more.[45] To the extent that these must occur serially rather than simultaneously, the time of the preconstruction phase lengthens.

Some of the sources of delay are beyond the immediate control of local officials, or they result from attention to values other than efficiency in project implementation. For example, litigation and other forms of citizen resistance are substantial sources of delay, but these avenues for the protection of individual rights and the maintenance of popular control are not easily attacked. However, some sources of delay do not result from attention to important democratic values and are within local government's power to control. For example, public officials might consider time requirements, simplifications, a general streamlining of permitting and other regulatory procedures, and improved long-term planning.[46] These reforms are of particular importance when the public sector is relying on the private sector to build needed infrastructure, either under contract with the city or as part of a negotiated agreement with a private developer (see Chapter 10). A recent survey of cities and counties by the International City Management Association finds that substantial numbers of local governments have activated such reforms. For example, 27 percent of responding communities have a consolidated, one-stop unit for issuing permits, 29 percent negotiate directly with developers concerning regulatory requirements, and 16 percent have revamped their building regulations.[47]

ALTERNATIVE STRATEGIES: PRIVATIZING
FOR INFRASTRUCTURE DEVELOPMENT

The difficulties of providing infrastructure in traditional ways with traditional financing mechanisms has led to the proliferation of alternative strategies. As in the case of privatization to improve service delivery (see Chapter 5), many of these strategies involve new relationships between the public sector and the private sector, or redefinitions of responsibilities between the two sectors. Three of these strategies are considered here: (1) leasing arrangements, (2) public-private bargaining over the linkage between infrastructure provision and development authorization, and (3) the use of quasi-public authorities to undertake infrastructure development tasks that stymie traditional government agencies.

Public Sector Leasing

As discussed in Chapter 7, public sector leasing is one of the faster growing strategies at the local level. In that chapter, public sector leasing was described primarily as a financing alternative. That is, a lease is much like a debt in that it imposes a relatively long-term obligation on the user of an asset to pay the owner of the asset; meanwhile, the user of the asset is essentially 'borrowing" it during the period of the lease. Yet, unlike traditional borrowing, such leases are not subject to the various accountability controls that local government bond issues are. Hence, public sector leasing has been portrayed as a way of evading those debt limits, voter approval requirements, and the like.[48]

But the advantages of leasing go beyond these. The federal government places restrictions on the income (called *arbitrage income*) that local governments can earn from the investment of tax-exempt bonds. Leasing arrangements provide mechanisms for the local public sector to generate pools of funds that are not subject to these investment restrictions. These pools of funds are generated when local government sells an asset like a building to private sector

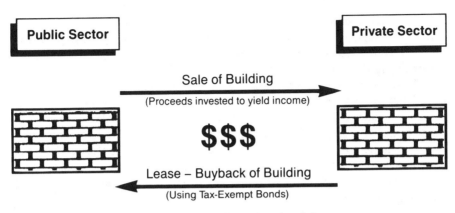

Figure 8.2. A Public Sector Leasing Scheme

investors. At the same time, the arrangement provides opportunities for private sector investors to enjoy the tax advantages of the property investment.

The logic of the arrangement is charted in Figure 8.2.[49] Using lease-to-buy-back arrangements, a local government can first sell a facility, generating a pool of funds that can be invested in high-yield securities. The local government also issues tax-exempt bonds, which are slated for use in buying back the facility. The first pool of funds is used to pay back the tax-exempt bonds. But because that pool of funds has also been yielding arbitrage income through investment, the whole arrangement nets the city additional monies that can be used for such things as rehabilitation or expansion of the facility. Meanwhile, the private investors who have been holding the facility as temporary "owners" during the period of this arrangement also benefit. Specifically, they might enjoy the tax advantages of depreciation of the facility.

Although much of the discussion of public sector leasing focuses on complex arrangements involving tax advantages, federal rules, and other such matters, public sector leasing can also be viewed more simply as a mechanism by which local governments can enjoy the use of capital facilities without taking on the direct responsibilities of construction and ownership. To the extent that the private sector can more cheaply and more expeditiously undertake capital projects than can government itself, it makes sense for cities to use leasing arrangements for long-term rental or for lease-purchase. Likewise, to the extent that government wishes to avoid liability problems or other headaches that may accompany facility ownership, a leasing arrangement may be useful.

Negotiated Private Sector Provision of Infrastructure

In some circumstances, cities can use their regulatory powers over land use to force developers to provide infrastructure that the city might otherwise have to provide. Consider, for example, the situation in which a developer wishes to build either a residential or a commercial project. If the project is in a particularly desirable location from the developer's perspective, the city is in a good position to extract commitments from the developer for provision of an array of infrastructure extensions or improvements beyond the typical responsibilities for provision of streets and sidewalks.

For example, in Orange County, California, which is an extremely high-growth area, county officials took an aggressive role in extracting infrastructure agreements during approval of the Aliso Viejo project—a large residential development in a very desirable area of the county. By the time the plan was approved, local government had extracted commitments from the developer to provide a 3,400-acre greenbelt, all internal highways, roads, and bike trails, plus library facilities, fire stations, and parks, and the financing of water and wastewater infrastructure.[50]

Other analysts have noted examples of this trend toward greater obligations being imposed on the private developer regarding the provision of infrastructure:

> In some cases, developers are granted construction or zoning permits on the condition that they implement programs to minimize the effect of increased traffic on surrounding roads. In other cases, private business is contributing directly to highway improvements. In Dallas, real estate developers are contributing to the construction of a new light rail system by donating most of the system's right of way.[51]

Private developers' contributions can come in the form of direct provision of infrastructure, design changes that minimize the extent of demand for new or expanded public works, and land dedications as in the Dallas light rail case. Alternatively, local governments may substantially increase the fees that they charge as part of the regulatory process preceding development, thus providing a larger revenue stream to pay for needed infrastructure. A number of different types of development fees can be considered in this regard:

> [Developers fees can include] . . . (1) planning fees, such as those assessed for rezoning, environmental studies, and map approval; (2) building department fees for building, plumbing, mechanical, and electrical permits, (3) "growth impact" fees such as those assessed for parks and schools; and (4) utility charges for storm drain, sewer, and water connections.[52]

A study of San Francisco Bay Area local governments shows that many of them have dramatically increased these fees since the passage of Proposition 13, which limits property taxes. "Some fees have been doubled, or even tripled, and new fees (such as 'bedroom taxes' and school impact fees) have been adopted. . . . Many cities have adopted some form of pay-as-you-go policy to cover the cost of development-related services."[53]

The feasibility of local government strategies to extract more from developers in the way of either fees or responsibility to provide infrastructure is dependent on the attractiveness and profitability of the development situation.

It is much easier to extract additional commitments from a developer in exchange for approval of a project that is potentially very lucrative than for a project that is less so. For this reason, these strategies are likely to be used more heavily in high-growth areas than in declining areas, and they are better suited to commercial or industrial projects than residential projects.[54] Declining areas, by contrast, may find it difficult to extract infrastructure commitments or impact fees from developers. Officials in declining areas may not even be willing to risk the attempt to extract such concessions. Instead, public officials in those circumstances are more often in the position of giving concessions to developers in the form of tax breaks, subsidized loans, and the like. In their study of Detroit's negotiations with General Motors, for example, Jones and Bachelor show that officials in this declining city were so desperate to keep GM from relocating its Cadillac/Fleetwood assembly plant elsewhere that concessions on the part of the city were inevitable.[55]

Even in high-growth areas these strategies can be controversial. Some observers of the California scene have argued that escalation in development fees there are a form of blackmail on developers, that they lead to undesirable increases in housing prices and can put a chill on development activity; others argue that higher development fees have minimal effects on development activity and that such fees are legitimate acknowledgments of the fact that new development brings demands for infrastructure improvements that should not be subsidized by existing residents.[56]

In general, local governments' ability to pursue negotiated commitments from private developers in exchange for approval of development regulations depends on several factors, including the extent of local government's land use powers and the legal powers that it has to enter into contracts with developers, as well as more subtle factors such as local traditions and expectations. An example is Fairfield, California, where development fees for residential building are very high and where industrial users are asked to bear the total cost of additions to sewerage and waste treatment facilities that their operations require. The city's long-term commitment to these policies makes each new negotiation with a developer "almost routine, whereas it would have been revolutionary in most jurisdictions."[57]

Public Authorities and Infrastructure Provision

In many ways, general purpose government is not well equipped to deal with large public works and infrastructure development projects. For one thing, it is hamstrung by a myriad of rules, regulations, and policies. Much of this red tape is important for maintaining democratic accountability, protecting individual rights, and preserving other values, but it can also detract from efficient, innovative, and creative action. For example, we have noted that delay imposes tremendous costs on public works projects. Many of the sources of delay are rules, regulations, and policies that apply to cities and counties.

For these and other reasons, general purpose governments like cities, counties, and states have often created special purpose entities to construct and operate various sorts of facilities. These special purpose entities go by a variety of names: boards, commissions, authorities, off-budget enterprises, and the like. For the sake of simplicity, we will consistently use the term *authority* in the discussion that follows.

Although there are some differences among authorities, especially from state to state, the important thing is their corporate form and their comparative freedom from the constraints faced by general purpose governments. Authorities are created by a state statute or local ordinance defining the scope of the authorities' activities. They are normally governed by boards of directors appointed by governors, mayors, or the like and are frequently composed of local business leaders. However, day-to-day operations are handled by an executive director, who may in many cases be given considerable latitude and receive little oversight from the board.[58]

The revenue sources of authorities clearly distinguish them from their close cousins—special districts—and from regular city agencies. Special districts, such as school districts, are like general purpose city government in that they have taxing powers, and tax revenues are not a trivial part of their budgets. Authorities, on the other hand, do not have taxing powers. Their revenues derive from user fees and charges that they assess, such as bridge and tunnel tolls, airport landing fees, utility payments, and the like. Many authorities also receive substantial amounts of revenue in the form of government grants. That is, they can be subsidized by the state or local governments that create them or by the federal government. The federal government has in fact been a key promoter of authorities during several historical periods. For example, programs like urban renewal and public housing stipulated that local governments should create authorities to receive federal funds.[59]

Authorities can also issue revenue bonds, which are retired by revenues from user fees. In fact, authorities are very heavy users of revenue bonds, so much so that some commentators have traced the explosive growth in revenue bonds in the 1970s to a wave of new authorities across the country.[60] Although data cannot be obtained on authorities alone, the U.S. Census Bureau reports data on special districts other than school districts. The Census Bureau's special districts category includes a wide variety of authorities as they have been defined here, as well as some special districts with taxing powers. These Census Bureau data show that the combination of authorities and special districts generated $16.4 billion worth of outstanding debt from revenue bonds in 1971 to 1972; by 1976 to 1977, the volume of this debt had nearly doubled, to $31.6 billion; and by 1981 to 1982, the volume of outstanding revenue bonds had roughly doubled again, to $61.3 billion.[61]

Authorities can be very large organizations, with a magnitude of operations rivaling general purpose, municipal government. This is especially the case with regional authorities, whose jurisdiction can cover multiple counties and even two-state areas. Figure 8.3 illustrates three of the country's major

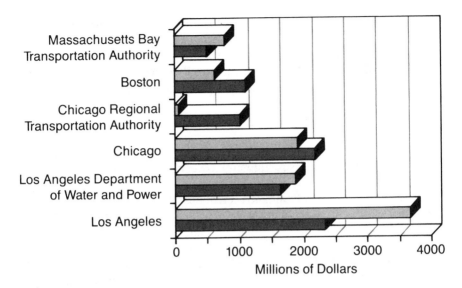

Total General Revenue
Debt Outstanding

Figure 8.3. Fiscal Data for Three Large Authorities and Three Cities, 1985–1986 Authority data are for Fiscal 1986; city government data are for the fiscal year ended June 30, 1985. Authority debt outstanding includes all long-term debt outstanding; city government debt outstanding is gross outstanding debt. (*Sources:* Data on authorities is from *City & State,* February 1987; data for cities is from *Statistical Abstract of the United States 1988,* 108th ed. Washington, DC: U.S. Department of Commerce, Bureau of the Census, 1987.)

authorities, with comparative budget data for related cities. The Massachusetts Bay Transportation Authority (MBTA) is responsible for mass transit in the Boston metropolitan area. Its total revenues are about half that of the city of Boston, but its outstanding debt is even greater than that of the city of Boston, presumably reflecting a substantial history of capital investment. Like the MBTA-Boston relationship, the Chicago Regional Transportation Authority shows about half the total revenue of the city of Chicago, but it does not have a notable volume of outstanding debt. The Los Angeles Department of Water and Power serves as a quasi-autonomous authority providing water and electricity for the city of Los Angeles. Like the others, the financial activities of this authority are dwarfed by those of the city of Los Angeles. Considering its narrow mission relative to the general purpose Los Angeles city government, however, it is by no means a trivial enterprise. Notice also that this last authority has as much outstanding debt as the city of Chicago and half again as much total revenue as the entire city government of Boston.

Although these very large authorities are among the most visible and best-known authorities and the infrastructures that they manage are familiar to many Americans, it is important to acknowledge the large number of authorities of more modest size found across the country. Figure 8.4 provides a sampler of these smaller authorities that suggests the range of activities in which they are engaged.

Viewed in the most positive light, authorities are important organizational innovations for getting infrastructure projects completed without the limitations that hamstring regular government departments. One of the strong currents behind the initial wave of authority creations in the 1930s was the belief that some aspects of government activity would be more efficiently handled if they could be split off from regular government operations. But why should these quasi-governmental bodies be more efficient and effective than regular government departments or agencies? Three answers can be given to this question. One emphasizes the *insulation from politics,* another emphasizes the *large powers* of these authorities, and a third focuses on the *coordination potential* of authorites.[62]

Insulation from Politics. The most familiar of these three answers is the one that emphasizes insulation from politics, perhaps because the proponents of the authority form emphasize this argument. According to the rhetoric, authorities are more efficient than traditional operations because they can be "run like a business." What does it mean to be run like a business? As we have already noted, it means avoiding the red tape and delays and bureaucratic rules that characterize government agencies. Many of these rules exist for purposes of ensuring accountability to the public. But proponents of the authority form argue that such rules are often too extensive, too burdensome, and altogether too likely to stifle activity.

It is not only procedural rules and rigidities that stifle efficiency but political patronage and the other complications of electoral politics. Authorities have an efficiency advantage because they are insulated from political forces that distract attention from merit and productivity. Even in reformed settings, where partisan politics is held in check, authorities can be important devices for insulating operations from pressures to be responsive to various constituency groups. Regular bureaus of government must be concerned about the reactions of neighborhood organizations, environmental groups, taxpayer associations, and a variety of other interests because the elected officials to whom they report must be concerned about those reactions. Because elected officials control their budget, the regular government bureau is not in a position to ignore the interest groups and political sensitivities that are relevant to elected officials.

By contrast, the typical authority is concerned with a much narrower range of interests, the most important of which are "the private financial institutions which must certify its investment and revenue plans as 'profitable'

UTILITIES

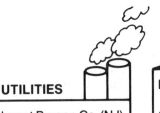

Northwest Bergen Co. (NJ)
   Utility Authority 10,339
N. Minnesota Municipal
   Power Agency 00
Klickitat Co. (WA) Public
   Utility District 2,076

HOUSING

Bradford Co. (FL) Housing Finance
   Authority 00
Somerville (MA) Housing Authority 250
Jackson Co. (IL) Housing Authority 41
Ft. Wayne (IN) Housing Authority 11
Qualla (NC) Housing Authority 00
Chilicothe (OH) Metro Housing Authority 3,668
Portland (OR) Housing Authority 7,937

WATER AND SEWER

Milwaukee Metro (WI) Sewer District 69,279
W. Carolina (SC) Reg. Sewer District 4,320
Scranton (PA) Sewer Authority 1,132
Pequannock–Lincoln Park–Fairfield (NJ)
   Sewerage Authority 622
Central Arizona Water Conservation
   District 00
Fresno (CA) Irrigation District 857
Campbell Co. (KY) Water
   District #1 337

SCHOOL CONSTRUCTION

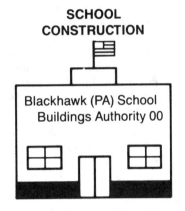

Blackhawk (PA) School
Buildings Authority 00

AIRPORTS

Burbank–Glendale–
   Pasadena (CA) Airport
   District 1,213

HOSPITALS

Thomas (AL) Hospital Board 6,018
Colquitt Co. (GA) Hospital Authority 00
Rockdale Co. (GA) Hospital Authority 38
Geisinger (PA) Medical Center Authority 13,600
Northeast (TX) Hospital Authority 3,024
Palo Pinto Co. (TX) Hospital District 00
Petersburg City (VA) Hospital Authority 1,180

OTHER

Orange County (CA) Civic Center Authority 00
San Bernardino (CA) Public Safety
   Authority 00
Oklahoma Development Authority 00
E. Pennsboro Township (PA) Authority 00

Figure 8.4. A Sampling of the Nation's Authorities (Numbers are dollar amounts of capital outlay, in thousands, for 1982.) (*Source:* Bureau of the Census, 1982 Census of Governments, *Finances of Special Districts,* Table 14.)

and its bonds therefore as saleable."[63] Since the authority is not subject to the budgetary control of elected officials, it has much greater autonomy from many of the political interests and constituency concerns that are important to regular government bureaus.

Insulation from the pressures of multiple constituencies thus frees authorities to concentrate on only that constituency which demands efficiency and successful projects. Insulation from everyday electoral concerns also permits authorities to act with a longer time horizon, rather than the limited time horizon imposed by electoral constraints. This is particularly important when public works projects are at issue. Some of the most important infrastructure problems may require investments in very large, long-term projects that cannot generate political benefits quickly enough to motivate politicians facing election within two or four years.

Large Powers. Authorities have advantages from a slightly different point of view as well. It is not just that they are insulated from politics, with all that this means for efficiency. It is also that they are by design given flexibility and relatively open agendas. They are freed from many of the conflicting mandates and restrictive rules that stand in the way of innovativeness in the typical local government department. For all these reasons, authorities may have the advantage in attracting talented, aggressive, ambitious managers. According to Doig, the notable leaders who accomplished great projects with authorities such as New York's Triborough Bridge and Tunnel Authority and the Port Authority of New York and New Jersey were attracted to those authorities because such an organizational setting provided them with the chance to exercise comparatively large powers. Furthermore, these talented, ambitious leaders are then able to "attract and keep at those public authorities coteries of skilled planners, engineers, and other specialists who can . . . feel assured that their carefully developed programs to raise bridges, raze buildings, or lay down water mains will go forward to completion."[64]

Coordination. Finally, authorities are sometimes claimed to have clear advantages over traditional government agencies because of their coordinative capacity. The logic of this argument is clearest when we consider regional or at least metropolitan authorities that are created to deal with an infrastructure problem that confronts a set of neighboring jurisdictions. For example, before the creation of the Port Authority of New York and New Jersey, a variety of local governments and two state governments all had interests in the development of the port, but they were not necessarily capable of collaborating on port projects and resolving turf battles and rivalries.[65] A single overarching authority, with a mandate to focus on the port as a whole, is one vehicle for breaking out of the stalemate that can arise when general purpose governments have partially competing interests in a region. Similarly, mass transit systems would be almost impossible to develop if we had to rely on the fragmented networks of local government that exist in many metropolitan areas. Many regional authorities are created to overcome the fragmentation, inertia, and conflict that can stymie progress at the local level.

The coordination argument rests on the assumption that, despite their fragmented and competing interests, leaders of general purpose local government will find a way to cooperate just long enough to agree to the creation of a regional authority. In some cases, initiative or pressure for the creation of regional authorities may come from state government.

Having acknowledged the arguments *for* authorities, it is only fair to acknowledge the arguments *against* them. Critics of the authority form have raised essentially two sorts of critiques. One focuses on a variety of public accountability problems; the other focuses on the corruption potential of authorities.

Accountability Problems. Public authorities are, almost by definition, problematic on accountability grounds. The very features that insulate them from politics—their freedom from red tape, removal from normal oversight by elected officials, and the greater discretion provided to their top management—all short-circuit the usual channels for accountability to the public. More specifically, because authorities rely heavily on financing instruments like revenue bonds, they avoid both direct popular controls (such as voter approval requirements for tax-supported bonds) and the sort of public scrutiny that occurs in the budgeting process for government agencies that are tax supported. Finally, because authorities are typically not subject to the full range of open meetings requirements that regular city agencies face, their operations can be cloaked in a veil of secrecy that effectively prevents accountability to the public.

Some critics allege that this lack of accountability translates into arrogance and policy bias:

> Public authorities also have been criticized for . . . their alleged insensitivity to the needs of their clients (for example, tenants in their housing projects) or of citizens who live near their airports, power plants, or other facilities. The argument here is that the agency's insulation from elected officials (and therefore from the voters), coupled with its self-perception as responding legitimately only to "efficiency standards". . . sometimes makes its officials arrogant and leads to authority actions which ride roughshod over important community values.[66]

More generally, the political insulation of authorities, coupled with the revenue basis for authority operations, is sometimes said to create a bias toward building rather than preservation and toward building facilities that are most likely to generate a handsome revenue stream from user fees. These biases are precisely the grounds for criticism of Robert Moses, whose highway and urban redevelopment projects in the New York metropolitan area became very controversial when neighborhoods were destroyed with apparent heartlessness.[67]

Corruption Potential. Finally, there has been some concern about the corruption potential of authorities. Henriques, for example, argues that public authorities are particularly susceptible to corruption for two reasons.[68] First, they are functioning in a realm in which incentives for corruption may be quite high. The awarding of contracts for construction, the siting of major facilities that will affect nearby land values, and many other decisions that are part of infrastructure development create huge financial stakes for those making the decisions and those affected by the decisions. Second, public authorities are dangerously likely to fall prey to these incentives for corruption because they are often structured without the fiscal control and oversight mechanisms, disclosure rules, and similar management controls that are forced on governmental bureaus. Authorities, as we have seen, are meant to be freed of stifling red tape and are expected to develop their own more flexible and innovative management practices. In many cases, Henriques argues, an overly lax and free-wheeling management style in authorities creates an "enticing environment" for corruption.[69]

SUMMARY

This chapter has explored the alleged crisis in America's urban infrastructure and various proposals for doing better in the area of infrastructure development. Urban America may not be completely in ruins, but there is ample evidence that public works is a problem area. A variety of competing methods for assessing the actual state of needs in public works is presented in this chapter. A review of these methods shows that, although urban managers and policymakers must go beyond occasional reports of sensational infrastructure failures, it is difficult and costly to obtain high-quality information about infrastructure needs.

The chapter also explores a variety of alleged reasons for the infrastructure problem. Blame has been placed in the hands of local officials, who quietly sacrifice public works maintenance in times of fiscal stress and who permit capital spending projects to suffer from chronic waste and the costs of delay. Blame has also been placed on the federal government for not doing enough to finance local infrastructure needs. This chapter emphasizes the limitations of many of these arguments and the important role that local officials must play in building coalitions of support for capital spending programs.

Finally, the chapter considers a host of reform proposals, each involving a form of privatization for infrastructure provision. These include arrangements in which the private sector builds facilities and leases them to the public sector, arrangements in which the public sector demands private sector provision of infrastructure as a condition of approving development plans, and arrangements in which quasi-governmental authorities are created to pursue infrastructure goals with freedom from the constraints under which traditional governmental units must operate. As is often the case with reform proposals, each of these arrangements can lead to unintended, negative consequences in addition to, or instead of, the improvements for which they are intended.

DISCUSSION QUESTIONS AND EXERCISES

1. Design an assessment strategy for infrastructure needs that a medium-sized city could realistically use in planning for capital improvements. Discuss your proposed strategy. What compromises on information quality must be made because of time or cost constraints?
2. Under what circumstances are authorities more appropriate than government bureaus for infrastructure provision? Always? Or is the case for using an authority more compelling for certain *types* of infrastructure than others?
3. To do this exercise, you will need access to the publication called *City Government Finances,* published annually by the U.S. Bureau of the Census as part of its government finances series. See if you can find this in the government documents section of your library. Choose two or more cities of interest to you that are large enough to be included in the Table 5 section, which provides financial information on cities with a population of 50,000 or more. Compare each city's infrastructure spending, called *capital outlay,* for each year from 1974–1975 to 1985–1986. Describe the results of your research, perhaps based on a simple time-series figure like Figure 8.1. Have your study cities been increasing or decreasing their capital spending over this period? Are there any periods of dramatic but temporary increases in capital spending? What might that signify? Do both cities show the same trends over the period? If not, can you speculate about the reasons for observed differences?

NOTES

1. Joel Tarr, "The Evolution of the Urban Infrastructure in the Nineteenth and Twentieth Centuries," in *Perspectives on Urban Infrastructure,* ed. Royce Hanson (Washington, DC: National Academy Press, 1984), p. 4.
2. Michael A. Pagano and Richard J.T. Moore, *Cities and Fiscal Choices* (Durham, NC: Duke University Press, 1985), p. 6.
3. Ibid., p. 8.
4. Robert Cook Benjamin, "From Waterways to Waterfronts: Public Investment for Cities, 1815–1980," in *Urban Economic Development,* ed. Richard Bingham and John Blair (Beverly Hills: Sage, 1984), pp. 23–46.
5. Pagano and Moore, *Cities and Fiscal Choices,* p. 11.
6. Herman Leonard, *Checks Unbalanced: The Quiet Side of Public Spending* (New York: Basic Books, 1986), p. 167.
7. Pat Choate and Susan Walter, *America in Ruins* (Durham, NC: Duke University Press, 1983), pp. 2–3.
8. This outline of approaches to assessing infrastructure problems is drawn from Pagano and Moore, *Cities and Fiscal Choices,* pp. 13–18; it in turn derives from the earlier formulation by George Peterson, "Finance" in *The Urban Predicament,* ed. William Gorham and Nathan Glazer (Washington, DC: Urban Institute, 1976), pp. 35–118.
9. Pagano and Moore, *Cities and Fiscal Choices,* p. 13.
10. Ibid., p. 15.
11. George E. Peterson, "Financing the Nation's Infrastructure Requirements," in *Perspectives on Urban Infrastructure,* ed. Royce Hanson (Washington, DC: National Academy Press, 1984), p. 116.

12. Kelly O'Day and Lance A. Neumann, "Assessing Infrastructure Needs: The State of the Art," in *Perspectives on Urban Infrastructure,* ed. Hanson (Washington, DC: National Academy Press, 1984), p. 71.

13. Pagano and Moore, *Cities and Fiscal Choices,* p. 16.

14. Ibid.

15. Peterson, "Financing Nation's Infrastructure Requirements," p. 113.

16. Choate and Walter, *America in Ruins,* p. 8.

17. Leonard, *Quiet Side of Public Spending,* p. 169.

18. Peterson, "Financing Nation's Infrastructure Requirements," pp. 115–116.

19. U.S. Congress, Joint Economic Committee, *Hard Choices: A Report on the Increasing Gap Between America's Infrastructure Needs and Our Ability to Pay For Them* (Washington, DC: U.S. Government Printing Office, 1984), p. 119.

20. Leonard, *Quiet Side of Public Spending,* p. 170.

21. Pagano and Moore, *Cities and Fiscal Choices,* pp. 40–45.

22. Ibid., p. 48.

23. Heywood T. Sanders, "Politics and Urban Public Facilities," in *Perspectives on Urban Infrastructure,* ed. Hanson (Washington, DC: National Academy Press, 1984), pp. 150–151.

24. Ibid., pp. 154–166.

25. Ibid., p. 164.

26. Information for this case was obtained from James Fitzpatrick, "Capital Improvements," *Kansas City Times,* March 5, 1988, pp. F1, F2; Kevin Murphy, "Who Won? Vote Pleases Both Sides," *Kansas City Star,* March 9, 1988, p. 7A; James Fitzpatrick, "They'll Go It Alone Next Time," and Steve Farnsworth, "City Sees Mandate on Station," *Kansas City Times,* March 10, 1988, pp. 1, 16.

27. Sanders, "Politics and Urban Facilities," p. 161.

28. U.S. Congress, Joint Economic Committee, *Hard Choices,* p. 85.

29. Ibid.

30. Richard P. Nathan and Fred C. Doolittle, "Federal Grants: Giving and Taking Away," *Political Science Quarterly* 100 (Spring 1985): 55.

31. Peterson, "Financing Nation's Infrastructure Requirements," p. 118.

32. U.S. Congress, Joint Economic Committee, *Hard Choices,* p. 85.

33. Executive Office of the President, Office of Management and Budget, *Special Analyses. Budget of the United States Government, FY 1989* (Washington, DC: U.S. Government Printing Office, 1988), p. G-40.

34. U.S. Congress, Joint Economic Committee, *Hard Choices,* p. 84.

35. Royce Hanson, ed., *Rethinking Urban Policy* (Washington, DC: National Academy Press, 1983), p. 89.

36. U.S. Congress, Joint Economic Committee, *Hard Choices,* p. 119.

37. Pagano and Moore, *Cities and Fiscal Choices,* p. 70.

38. Peterson, "Financing Nation's Infrastructure Requirements," pp. 118–119.

39. U.S. Congress, Joint Economic Committee, *Hard Choices,* p. 116.

40. Paul Peterson, *When Federalism Works* (Washington, DC: Brookings Institution, 1986), pp. 11–13.

41. Choate and Walter, *America in Ruins,* p. 40.

42. Sam Roberts "Westway II: A Delay Costing $90,000 a Day," *New York Times,* July 16, 1987, p. 15.

43. Choate and Walter, *America in Ruins,* pp. 42–45.

44. Ibid., p. 43.

45. Ibid., p. 46.
46. Ibid., pp. 50–54.
47. The survey was conducted by ICMA in 1984.
48. Leonard, *Checks Unbalanced*, pp. 180–185.
49. This explanation of leasing and the Oakland Convention Center example that follows are from Leonard, *Checks Unbalanced*, pp. 189–191.
50. J. C. Raub, "The Impacts of Proposition 13 on New Development," Costa Mesa, CA, mimeo, cited in John Kirlin and Jeffrey Chapman, "Active Approaches to Local Government Revenue Generation," *Public Interest* 2 (Fall 1980): 88.
51. Douglas C. Henton and Steven A. Waldhorn, "The Future of Urban Public Works: New Ways of Doing Business," in *Perspectives on Urban Infrastructure*, ed. Hanson, p. 192.
52. Betsy Strauss, Marjorie Mikels, and Donald Hagman, "Description of Propositions 13 and 4," in *Tax and Expenditure Limitations: How to Implement and Live with Them*, ed. Jerome Rose (Rutgers: State University of New Jersey Press, 1982), p. 24.
53. Ibid.
54. Kirlin and Chapman, "Active Approaches to Local Government Revenue Generation," p. 89.
55. Bryan Jones and Lynn Bachelor, *The Sustaining Hand* (Lawrence, KS: University Press of Kansas, 1986).
56. Strauss, Mikels, and Hagman, "Effect of Propositions 13 and 4 on Land Use and Development," in *Tax and Expenditure Limitations: How to Implement and Live with Them*, ed. Rose (Rutgers: State University of New Jersey Press, 1982), p. 46.
57. Kirlin and Chapman, "Active Approaches to Local Government Revenue Generation," p. 89.
58. Diana B. Henriques, *The Machinery of Greed: Public Authority Abuse and What To Do About It* (Lexington, MA: Heath, 1986), pp. 3–4.
59. Annmarie H. Walsh, *The Public's Business* (Cambridge: MA: MIT Press, 1978).
60. James Bennett and Thomas DiLorenzo, *Underground Government: The Off-Budget Public Sector* (Washington, DC: Cato Institute, 1983), pp. 41–45.
61. U.S. Bureau of the Census, *Finances of Special Districts*, 1982 Census of Governments (Washington, DC: U.S. Government Printing Office, 1984), p. x.
62. This section relies heavily on Jameson W. Doig, "'If I See a Murderous Fellow Sharpening a Knife Cleverly . . .': The Wilsonian Dichotomy and the Public Authority Tradition," *Public Administration Review* 43 (July/August 1983): 292–301, especially for the emphasis on the "large powers" argument. See also Irene Rubin, "Municipal Enterprises: Exploring Budgetary and Political Implications," *Public Administration Review* 48 (January/February 1988): 542–550.
63. Doig, "'If I See a Murderous Fellow . . .'," p. 297.
64. Ibid.
65. Jameson W. Doig, "Coalition-Building by a Regional Agency: Austin Tobin and the Port of New York Authority," in *The Politics of Urban Development*, ed. Stone and Sanders (Lawrence: University Press of Kansas, 1987), pp. 76–77.
66. Doig, "If I See a Murderous Fellow . . .'," p. 299.
67. Robert Caro, *The Power Broker* (New York: Random House, 1975).
68. Henriques, *Machinery of Greed*, pp. 19–36.
69. Ibid.

PART III
Economic Development

CHAPTER 9

The Meaning of Economic Development

What is economic development? Without worrying too much about what the concept technically includes, communities across the country are engaged in a variety of activities for the sake of economic development. Consider the following examples.

In 1987, a billboard cleanup campaign got under way in Houston, Texas. The campaign, budgeted at $7.5 million, was financed by the Houston city government, in partnership with Houston Lighting and Power, the Texas Department of Highways and Public Transportation, and many local businesses. The purpose of the billboard cleanup, according to a local developer, was to make sure that businessmen visiting Houston would not be put off by the trashy appearance of the very gateways of the city.[1]

In early 1988, officials in Kansas City, Missouri, were smarting from the failure of their efforts to get the national headquarters of the Presbyterian Church (USA) located in the city. City officials and private leaders had devoted several years of research and preparation to the effort, culminating in a $13 million proposal that included the renovation of a downtown hotel for use as the headquarters site. Late in the decisionmaking process, the Kansas City proposal was overshadowed by a $20 million proposal from Louisville, Kentucky, that included the provision of two vacant buildings and a parking garage, plus a $25 million low-interest loan. At its convention, Presbyterian Church leaders chose to go with the Louisville proposal, a choice that was estimated to bring 580 jobs and $52 million in new spending to Louisville.[2]

Kansas City's failure to win the Presbyterian Church national headquarters might not have been so deflating for city leaders had it not been for other losses occurring at about the same time. In January 1988, for example, General Motors

215

officials announced that the Leeds auto assembly plant would be indefinitely shut down. The impact of that shutdown included the loss of 1,600 jobs and a $66 million payroll, the potential loss of 2,200 additional jobs in related supportive industries, and the loss of about $1.5 million in tax payments to the city.[3] It was unclear what the city or nongovernmental leaders could do to alter this outcome.

Meanwhile, the tiny community of Irwindale, California (population 1,038), was celebrating its successful effort to lure the Los Angeles Raiders to the community. The city agreed to help with the building of a sixty-five-thousand seat stadium for the Raiders, offering a $115 million financial package to do so. In a similar fashion, officials had aggressively used bonds and other development financing tools to get the Miller Brewing Company and other industries to locate in Irwindale.[4]

Rockford, Illinois, has pursued an economic development strategy that involves the use of computers to help manufacturers to develop products and improve sales. The Rock Valley College Technology Center, a publicly financed research facility that companies can use for product testing and display, is the site for the computer integrated manufacturing cell. The $8.7 million center, financed completely with local taxes, has a state-of-the-art demonstration site that models manufacturing processes, enhances product design, and enables demonstrations of new products.[5]

Each of the foregoing instances is an example of the challenge of economic development, which for the moment can be roughly defined as enhancing growth and sustaining vitality of the local economy, or re-energizing the local economy if it has been subject to decline. As the preceding examples suggest, however, an extremely broad array of activities and goals are pursued under the rubric of economic development—so much so that the topic may seem to lose any distinctive focus or meaning.

To add to the confusion, the term *economic development* is used to refer to economic outcomes, economic processes, and government activities. Figure 9.1 diagrams these major differences in meaning of the term. For example, the term is sometimes used as a way of characterizing the status of a community's economic base—that is, how much vitality, sophistication, resilience, or size that local economy has. From this perspective, economic development is an outcome or goal: Underdeveloped communities wish to achieve a greater level of economic development. At other times, economic development refers to a process or series of processes. Economic development in this sense means growth and change in local economies, with emphasis on the economic factors that are central to those processes. From yet a third perspective, economic development is a government function. As Bowman states, for example, "Economic development is defined operationally as a city's policy actions (promotional strategies and market interventions) aimed at creating jobs and increasing capital investment in the jurisdiction."[6]

Chapter 10 considers the types of policies that local governments pursue under the banner of economic development and the question of whether these

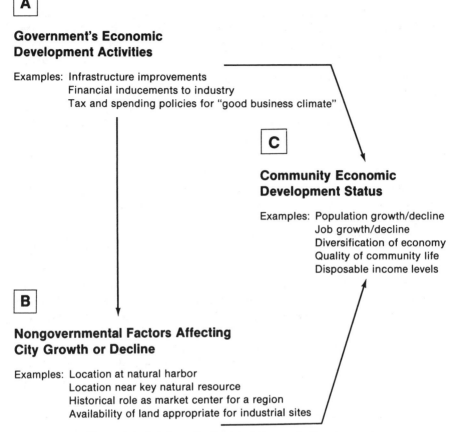

A

Government's Economic
Development Activities

Examples: Infrastructure improvements
Financial inducements to industry
Tax and spending policies for "good business climate"

C

Community Economic
Development Status

Examples: Population growth/decline
Job growth/decline
Diversification of economy
Quality of community life
Disposable income levels

B

Nongovernmental Factors Affecting
City Growth or Decline

Examples: Location at natural harbor
Location near key natural resource
Historical role as market center for a region
Availability of land appropriate for industrial sites

Figure 9.1. A Schematic Model of Economic Development

policies can have the desired impacts on economic development processses and outcomes. This chapter focuses on the other two elements of Figure 9.1—the meaning of economic development as a goal or outcome and the closely related issue of economic development processes—from the perspective of general theories of urban growth and decline.

MEANINGS OF ECONOMIC DEVELOPMENT AS AN OUTCOME

Even when individuals refer to economic development as a goal or desired end state, there is not always consistency in the meaning of the term. This section briefly explores these contrasting meanings.

First, economic development is often equated with growth. Development is assumed to mean more industry, more jobs, more people, and more tax dollars.

This is evident from the land use perspective as well. To develop land means to transform vacant land by building on it or to intensify the use to which the land is put. From this perspective, a lot with a home on it has been developed whereas a vacant lot has not; a lot with an apartment building on it is more highly developed than a lot with a single-family home on it; and a lot with a multistory office tower on it is more highly developed than a lot with a single small store on it.

In one sense, this perspective on economic development is undeniable. An office tower means more jobs and tax dollars for the community, and this is indirectly expected to contribute to enhanced quality of life. However, in a number of settings, challenges to the growth assumption have occurred, and the costs as well as the benefits of growth are being emphasized. Some would argue that economic development does not necessarily mean merely growth in the local economy; it might instead be defined as attainment of an acceptable or appropriate level or mix of economic activity. (See Box 9.1).

Economic development is also frequently linked to job availability. From this perspective, a community is economically developed if plenty of new jobs are available. This "boom town" concept is often criticized for its limitations. Albert Shapero, for example, draws on Jane Jacobs's classic contrast between Manchester and Birmingham, England, to illustrate why economic development is more than just job creation.[7] In the midnineteenth century, Manchester seemed to have everything going for it; it had all the features necessary to boom as a cotton textile manufacturing center. Birmingham, on the other hand, seemed less economically developed because it had no industrial specialty. However, with twentieth century hindsight, we can see that Birmingham

---

BOX 9.1   Growth as Economic Development?

Nashua, New Hampshire, provides an example of the strains that may occur when an influx of population and jobs occurs—strains that may mean a decline in quality of life. Nashua's population, now about 80,000, has tripled in the last two decades. In 1987, *Money Magazine* rated Nashua as the best place in America to live, a rating based in part on the city's low crime rate, healthy economy, and accessibility to beaches and mountains. However, local residents are concerned that Nashua's rapid growth is eroding its quality of life. There is debate over the growth issue, especially since traffic jams have become a problem. Housing prices have ballooned, a change that is welcome news to sellers but a problem for would-be, young homebuyers. Some locals complain about the loss of the city's small-town, personalized character, while others argue that homelessness, pollution, and traffic are the main problems.

Source: "Nashua, N.H., Shrugs At a High Compliment," *New York Times,* August 2, 1987, p. 26.

succeeded economically because of its innovativeness and economic flexibility, while overreliance on textile manufacturing has limited Manchester's development. Shapero uses this example to suggest a broader meaning for economic development:

> What we really want for an area . . . is to achieve a state denoted by *resilience*—the ability to respond to changes in the environment effectively; *creativity* and *innovativeness*—the ability and willingness to experiment and innovate; *initiative taking*—the ability and willingness to begin and carry through useful projects.[8]

In other words, economic development means more than simply creating more jobs at any given time; it means having the capacity to respond successfully to changes in economic activity that may have an adverse effect on existing jobs.

Viewed as an end-state, then, economic development can mean many things. It evokes images of fast-growing communities, communities with an abundance of job opportunities, communities with particularly attractive (i.e., higher income) types of jobs, communities that, whatever their current mix of jobs, have a diversified, resilient base to adapt to changing economic circumstances, and communities in which the general quality of life is high.

Despite the variety in these conceptualizations of economic development and even the apparent inconsistencies between some of them, they all have a common thread of meaning. Each incorporates the perspective that communities are economically developed if they have healthy, vibrant economies that provide opportunities for individuals to make a good living and to live a good life.

THEORIES OF URBAN GROWTH AND DECLINE

But what are the processes that lead some cities to attain the goal of economic development while others lag behind? As Figure 9.1 suggests, the term *economic development* is often used to refer to those processes that generate the jobs, quality of life, resiliency, and other outcomes that we have discussed. The economic development policies and programs of government that are discussed in the next chapter can be viewed as interventions that are intended to enhance the forces of economic growth and to counter the forces of economic decline. But what are the general dynamics of economic growth and decline?

This section reviews a variety of theories and general principles that have been offered as explanations of urban growth and decline. Although some of these are relatively antiquated, and none are totally satisfactory explanations, all offer important insights and concepts that are highly influential in urban planning and economic development practice. Adopting a framework suggested by Alfred Watkins, the section begins with the models of urban development suggested by classical location theory and central place theory, reviews the principle of growth suggested by the distinction between basic and nonbasic industry, and concludes with a theory of urban growth vis-à-vis changing economic stages.[9]

Classical Location Theory

The oldest of the theories to be considered is classical location theory, which emphasizes the importance of "spatial variations in cost."[10] To minimize its costs of operation, a firm must not only determine the ideal mix of factors of production (land, labor, and capital) at a given site, but it must also consider that each factor will vary in costs in different locations. In considering the trade-offs among different locations, the firm must consider the costs of transporting materials to the assembly site and final products to market. For example, a firm might consider whether, by locating closer to a market center where population is concentrated, it could sell at lower costs because, although land, rent, and labor costs are higher, these are more than offset by lower costs of transporting the final product to the buyer.

Differential types of economic activity have different types of cost considerations, leading to different least-cost locations. For example, some industries, like steel production, are material-oriented, meaning that bulky, expensive-to-ship raw materials (like iron ore and coal for steel producers) are key cost factors for the industry. Consequently, material-oriented industries minimize costs by locating near raw materials rather than near markets. By contrast, some industries find it more advantageous to locate nearer to their market because the product being produced has higher transport costs than do the raw materials, or because of other advantages of proximity to consumers.[11]

The upshot of this discussion is that cities have different *locational advantages* and consequently attract different types of economic activity. Cities that are near critical raw materials have a unique advantage, as do cities uniquely sited on natural transport routes, like river confluences or ports. Other cities have the advantages of being market centers.

As this description suggests, classical location theory is less an explicit theory of urban growth and decline than it is an explanation of the spatial distribution of economic activities. By implication, however, it suggests reasons for urban growth and decline. Some cities have a variety of locational advantages, others have fewer or none. Those that have locational advantages relevant to a set of rapidly expanding economic activities will prosper while those with locational advantages relevant only to stagnant sectors of the economy will not prosper.

A city's initial locational advantages can be compounded through agglomeration economies—that is, considerations that "lower processing costs when several firms or industries congregate in one region."[12] For example, there is a tendency for firms in a particular industry to cluster around the site of an initially successful firm, partly because of imitation and partly because the development of a pooled labor market and other pooled resources provides cost advantages.[13] The principle of agglomeration economies suggests that locational advantages that initially cause particular cities to attract a particular type of industry will also cause concentrated growth of that industry in a few locations.

In sum, classical location theory provides some basic conceptual tools to account for the growth of particular cities in the industrial era and to explain why urban development occurs so unevenly. In a more updated form that takes account of locational considerations that are relevant to newer types of business and industry, the theory can form the backbone for strategic assessment of the community's strengths for use in developing relevant public policy initiatives.

Central Place Theory

Another classic theory of urban development, central place theory, is important because it introduces the idea of a hierarchically ordered classification of cities. According to Watkins:

> It [central place theory] assumes that some cities, or central places, contain a wide variety of activities including many higher-order industries while other central places possess only a few lower-order industries. As a result, the larger central places occur less frequently while the smaller central places are dispersed throughout the region. This distribution of hierarchically ordered central places promotes uneven, although uniformly patterned, development.[14]

What is meant by higher-order and lower-order industries? Higher-order industries or facilities are those that are viable only with a relatively large population to provide a threshold level of demand, whereas lower-order industries can be supported by smaller population centers. Stated another way, higher-order industries or facilities are those producing goods that people will be willing to travel relatively far to get; lower-order industries produce goods for which demand diminishes dramatically with distance.[15] For example, a full-scale natural history museum will not be located in every community, nor will every community be able to support a major medical center. However, even relatively small communities will have grocery stores, doctors' offices, and clothing stores. Central place theory, in short, depicts cities as occupying various positions in a hierarchy, with the few cities at the top of the hierarchy providing a full range of goods and services, with the array of goods and services becoming increasingly limited through the lower ranks of cities.

As we will see later, more contemporary treatments also make distinctions among economic activities although the distinctions are based on industrial-service distinctions and on level of technology used rather than on the more simplistic conceptions of range or minimum necessary population bases for goods and services that characterize central place theory.

Basic Industry, Nonbasic Industry, and the Growth Multiplier

One of the most influential models of urban growth hinges on the distinction between basic and nonbasic industry. This distinction stipulates that some economic activities create goods or services that are exported rather than totally consumed within the local economy. As a result, they add to the local economy in two important ways.[16] First, they bring new money into the community when outsiders purchase the community's goods and services. In Kansas City, for example, Hallmark Cards can be considered a basic industry. Its products are not simply purchased by locals, leading to a recycling of local dollars; instead, its products are purchased throughout the region and nation, thus adding to jobs, income, and wealth in the community.

Second, basic industries typically require a variety of supportive industries. As a result, the presence of a basic industry is envisioned as creating a host of jobs in related supportive industries as well. For example, the existence of a large manufacturing establishment such as Hallmark Cards creates the need for firms producing a variety of goods and services consumed by Hallmark's employees (e.g., dry-cleaning establishments, food stores, clothing, entertainment, medical services) as well as goods or services needed directly by the Hallmark plant (e.g., cardboard boxes, freight handling, insurance).

The distinction between basic and nonbasic industries leads to the concept of a growth multiplier. That is, by examining the ratio of nonbasic to basic employment in various settings, analysts have created quantitative assessments that have been used to predict how many new jobs in nonbasic industry would be created for each new job in basic industry. As Watkins observes, this model of urban growth treats the industrial sector as the source of growth, with consumption-oriented goods and services treated as passive sectors that follow along after growth in the industrial sector. This assumption can be questioned, however.

> But if we assume that a city's export base is transient and subject to constant alterations, then long-run prosperity does not depend upon a single export activity. Instead, with a basic sector that changes periodically, long-run local prosperity depends upon a city's ability to generate new basic activities. . . . Especially important in this respect are . . . urbanization economies . . . they are essentially residentiary, nonbasic services. In other words, in the long run a region's prosperity and ability to maintain a viable export base depend on the nonbasic services that it can offer prospective entrepreneurs. If this is true, then a city is branded by its residentiary industries and not by its export activities.[17]

Stage Theories of Urban Growth and Development

Economic development is sometimes conceptualized as a process with distinct stages. Cities, regions, or even entire nation-states are observed to occupy economically one or another of the stages along a continuum from less to more advanced. A good example of this approach can be found in Daniel Bell's classic study, which identifies three stages of development: preindustrial, industrial, and postindustrial.[18] Preindustrial societies (Asia, Africa, and Latin America by Bell's classification) are characterized by reliance on extractive industries such as agriculture, mining, fishing, and timber. Industrial societies (Western Europe, the Soviet Union, and Japan by Bell's classification) have economic sectors dominated by goods processing, or manufacturing, and show the occupational centrality of semiskilled workers and engineers. The United States is the only postindustrial society identified by Bell. It is characterized by the importance of economic sectors such as trade, finance, insurance, real estate, health, education, research, government, and recreational services, and by the occupational centrality of professional and technical workers and scientists.

Although one might argue over Bell's typology and regional classifications, it is the underlying concept that is of interest. The notion that economic development means advancing from more primitive economic stages to more sophisticated, complex economic arrangements is very powerful and is applicable to subareas within nation-states as well. Many state and local leaders reflect a concept like this when they express a desire to attract high-tech industry, although they may not be all that clear about the precise meaning of high-tech industry. It is not just the desire for diversification, however, that underlies the push for educational, recreational, finance, and similar industries in areas that have previously been dependent on manufacturing industries. It is the notion that some economic activities represent an advance toward a more developed future, while others—sunset industries—represent the less developed past.

If the United States as a whole is a postindustrial nation, what are the important characteristics of the national economy, and what are the implications for various types of cities within the postindustrial economy of the United States? This section outlines four important and interrelated features of this postindustrial economy: (1) the decline of goods manufacturing relative to service industries; (2) the internationalization of the American economy; (3) the importance of information, or knowledge-intensive jobs; and (4) the significant diversity within the American economy, with some cities specializing in knowledge-intensive work, others sustaining more traditional manufacturing sectors, and others dominated by low-wage industries.

The first element of the postindustrial society that must be understood is the declining importance of traditional manufacturing industry. Observers have pointed to substantial corporate disinvestment in many industries that have long been considered basic. Disinvestment is apparent in the wave of layoffs, scalebacks, and total plant closings that have occurred nationally, especially in industries such as steel manufacturing, auto assembly, and the like. Much discussion focuses on the movement of industrial jobs from the Frostbelt to the Sunbelt, but perhaps the more important trend is the loss of these industrial jobs to other countries as American corporations shift their investments to foreign plants. Barry Bluestone and Bennett Harrison document the scope of the change:

> Between 1950 and 1980, direct foreign investment by U.S. businesses increased *sixteen times,* from about $12 billion to $192 billion. Over the same period, gross private domestic investment grew less than half as rapidly, from $54 billion to about $400 billion. . . . The total overseas output of American multinational corporations is now larger than the gross domestic product of every country in the world except the United States and the Soviet Union.[19]

In a larger sense, America's preeminent role as an industrial power has been altered by a new international industrial order in which Third World nations play an important role.

> As recently as the mid-1960s the inhabitants of Taiwan, Hong Kong, South Korea, Mexico, and Brazil primarily made basic products—like clothing, shoes, toys, simple electronic assemblies—that called for cheap labor but little in the way of sophisticated capital equipment. . . . By the mid-1970s several of these countries had followed Japan's lead into steel and other basic capital-intensive processing industries. Japan, meanwhile, had become an exporter of steel-making equipment as well as basic steels, and had moved its industrial base into products . . . requiring technical sophistication as well as considerable investment in plant and equipment.[20]

Although jobs in many manufacturing industries are disappearing overseas, other kinds of industries involving other kinds of jobs have gained importance in the U.S. economy. Within the manufacturing sector itself, jobs involving the manufacture of sophisticated products that reflect new technologies are growing as other manufacturing jobs disappear. Table 9.1, for example, shows the top ten and the lowest ten industries, measured in terms of growth in shipments from 1972 to 1987. As the table makes clear, extraction industries (like primary zinc) and industries representative of the old industrial age (like clothing and footwear manufacture and machine making) are on the wane. U.S. companies are now shipping half or less the volume of these products that they did in the mid-1970s. Meanwhile, the manufacture of products representative of high technology—new biological products, medicinals and botanicals, and electronics—are showing dramatic increases.

Ironically, the emergence of new high technologies contributes to the internationalization of the U.S. economy, a process that includes the siphoning off of some economic activities from U.S. locations to overseas locations. Manuel Castells gives several reasons for this development.[21] For one thing,

TABLE 9.1. PERCENTAGE GROWTH IN SHIPMENTS OF SELECTED INDUSTRIES,
1972-1987 (1987 SHIPMENTS AS A PERCENTAGE OF 1972 SHIPMENTS)

Lowest Ten	Percentage	Top Ten	Percentage
Turbine Generator Sets	7	Semiconductor Devices	5094
Photoengraving	29	Optical Devices/Lenses	854
Primary Zinc	33	X-Ray Apparatus	509
Cigars	34	Biological Products	382
Sewing Machines	39	Medicinals/Botanicals	361
Leather-lined Clothing	41	Lithographic Services	327
Building Paper/Board Mills	45	Electronic Connectors	326
Women's Footwear	46	Radio/TV Communication Equipment	304
Metal-forming Machines	50	Wood Pallets & Skids	296
Textile Machinery	50	Surgical Appliances	278

Source: David R. Barton, "Highlights of the 1987 U.S. Industrial Outlook," in 1987 U.S. Industrial Outlook, U.S. Department of Commerce (Washington, DC: U.S. Government Printing Office, 1987), p. 7.

high-tech industries involve a hierarchical division of labor, with research and design processes separable from assembly operations. Many high-tech products are small and lightweight, thus enabling production anywhere in the world where labor costs are favorable, without shipping costs being a deterrent. Furthermore, new telecommunication technologies help to make such globally dispersed operations possible. As a result, communities in the United States that wish to compete for the jobs that high-tech manufacturing operations can bring are not competing with other U.S. communities only. They are competing in a worldwide labor market and an internationalized form of industry.

Change in the composition of the U.S. manufacturing sector is only a part of the picture of our postindustrial economy—and the smaller part of the picture at that. Even more important is the shift in the economy from manufacturing to nonmanufacturing industries. "An analysis of U.S. non-agricultural employment for the period 1970-1985 shows that a total of 26.7 million jobs were created in that period and also that virtually all employment growth occurred in the non-manufacturing industries."[22]

But what are these nonmanufacturing industries that have taken up the slack as manufacturing industries decline? And how much has the manufacturing sector declined relative to other sectors of the economy? Using very broad Census Bureau categories, Figure 9.2 shows that in the period 1970 to 1984 manufacturing jobs declined from nearly one-quarter of the total to less than one-fifth of all jobs. There are now more jobs in the trade sector, which includes both wholesale and retail sales, than there are in the manufacturing sector; and a greater share of jobs are in the Census Bureau services category than there are in the manufacturing sector.

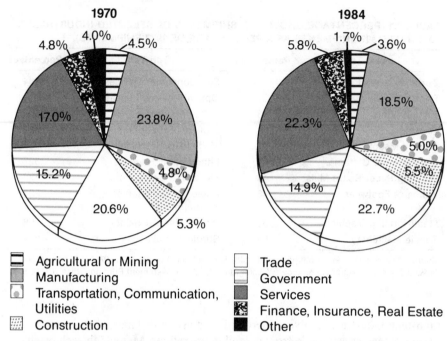

1970

4.8% 4.0% 4.5%
17.0%   23.8%
15.2%   4.8%
20.6%
5.3%

1984

5.8% 1.7% 3.6%
18.5%
22.3%
5.0%
5.5%
14.9%
22.7%

▤ Agricultural or Mining	☐ Trade
▨ Manufacturing	▦ Government
◉ Transportation, Communication, Utilities	■ Services
▨ Construction	▨ Finance, Insurance, Real Estate
	■ Other

Figure 9.2. Percentage of Total Employment in Selected Industries, 1970 and 1984 (*Source:* U.S. Department of Commerce, Bureau of the Census, *Statistical Abstract of the United States 1987.* Adapted from Table No. 661, p. 389.)

As Daniel Bell observed some time ago, "A postindustrial society is based on services."[23] The Census Bureau categories in Figure 9.2 actually underplay this fact. In addition to the designated service category, several other categories in the table involve service rather than manufacturing industries—like finance, insurance, and real estate, government, trade, transportation, and communications. Combining these categories with the designated service category, we find that two-thirds (66.7 percent) of all jobs in 1984 were in the service sector, compared with only 24 percent in manufacturing or construction and less than 10 percent in all other categories (such as agriculture or mining).

Very different sorts of jobs are implied by the rise of a service-dominated economy. Some "traditional centers of white collar employment,"[24] like real estate and insurance, are included. Compared to the 0.5 percent growth in manufacturing jobs between 1970 and 1984, the number of jobs in real estate grew 67.4 percent, jobs in banking grew 59.9 percent, and the number of jobs in the insurance field grew 34.9 percent.[25] Many low-status, low-wage sectors—for example, restaurant workers, hotel workers, retail clerks, and the like—are also involved. Again, by comparison with the 0.5 percent increase in manufacturing jobs, the 1970 to 1984 period saw a 28.2 percent increase in jobs in the retail trade sector and a 77.3 percent increase in jobs in hotels and lodging places.[26]

Analysts of postindustrial society have been most attentive to other categories of jobs, however. For example, the contemporary U.S. economy is said to be much more characterized by "information workers." One study estimates that, even before 1970, one-quarter of the Gross National Product (GNP) of the United States consisted of the production, processing, and distribution of information goods and services, including "computer manufacturing, telecommunications, printing, mass media, advertising, accounting, and education . . ." and another 21 percent of the GNP is derived from information workers functioning within goods-producing sectors.[27] Others characterize the postindustrial economy as being dominated by knowledge-intensive activities that ". . . involve working with knowledge, technology, or information such as applying, servicing, and advancing technology, adapting technology to new situations, to new problems and to new markets."[28]

Census Bureau industry classifications are not as useful at revealing growth in knowledge-intensive jobs. Hospital jobs, for example, increased 60.3 percent between 1970 and 1984, but this lumps together relatively low-skilled jobs such as maintenance with traditional skilled professions ranging from nursing to anesthesiology to radiology that involve the use and extension of highly sophisticated new technologies. Perhaps a better indicator of the increasing importance of knowledge-intensive activity in postindustrial society is the scope of higher educational attainment. Although the total population in the United States increased 14.1 percent between 1971 and 1984, enrollment in institutions of higher education increased 45.2 percent for roughly the same period (1970 to 1983). As of 1985, nearly one-fifth (19.4 percent) of the population had completed at least four years of college. The number of master's degrees conferred per year increased 23.3 percent between 1971 and 1984. Roughly 33,000 doctoral degrees have been conferred *each year* since 1979.[29]

Much diversity remains within a postindustrial economy. Not everyone is a knowledge-intensive worker. Rather, those with education and professional credentials become a "new intelligentsia" with status claims that conflict with other communal and populist impulses.[30] Similarly, not all jobs are in the nonmanufacturing service sector, although stagnation in the manufacturing sector and growth in the service sector mean that the economy is more and more predominantly based on services. Nevertheless, those communities with histories of preeminence in a particular type of manufacturing will still see their future tied in part to that industry. Many leaders in the Kansas City area, for example, believe that as long as there is any auto assembly going on in the United States, they must be in the running for the action because they have a labor force with skills in that area and services and related industries to support it. Such commitments are understandable because the manufacturing jobs at issue typically have paid high wages relative to many of the service sector jobs that are not knowledge-intensive. Other communities with a lesser labor force stake in the old industrial order are quickly developing economies based on recreation, education, health, finance, and other service industries.

Just as older theories of urban growth and change (like central place theory and classical location theory) lead to conclusions of uneven development, analysis of the postindustrial economy also suggests uneven development across cities and regions in the United States.[31] A number of analysts, for example, have developed classifications of U.S. cities showing their role in the new postindustrial order and the consequences of their role. In comparison with the hierarchy of cities that is suggested by central place theory, these six classifications suggest a hierarchy based on the niche that a city fills in a complex postindustrial international economic order.

One such classification groups metropolitan areas into six categories.[32] Nodal cities have diverse service sector economies, including arts and recreation, government services, and business support services. Corporate headquarters are typically located in such nodal centers. Examples of nationally significant Nodal centers include New York City and Chicago; regionally significant Nodal centers include Atlanta and Houston.

By contrast, Functional-Nodal centers do not have a predominantly service-oriented economy. Rather, they rely on a combination of manufacturing production and a special range of related service functions like research and development. Detroit is a prototype of the Functional-Nodal city.

The third type of metropolitan economy is dominated by a Government-Education mix by virtue of the fact that the community is either a state capitol, the site of a major institution of higher education, or both. Albany, New York, is an example. In yet a fourth type, Education-Manufacturing, a city that has been a traditional manufacturing center also has important local universities that can help in the transition to postindustrial economic functions. Examples of this type include Ann Arbor, Michigan, and Pittsburgh, Pennsylvania.

Fifth are Production centers, which specialize in routine manufacturing processes or mining and which have not developed corporate research or administrative functions as have the Functional-Nodal centers. Buffalo, New York, and Charleston, West Virginia, are examples of this type. In an important variant of the Production center, the Industrial-Military city owes its economic well-being to some military presence like a base or shipyard. Norfolk, Virginia, is an example of this subtype. Finally, the sixth category is the Resort-Residential center, which is either a retirement and vacation area or a specialized residential enclave for a nearby Nodal center. Examples include Tampa, Florida, and Nassau-Suffolk, New York.

This is by no means the only classification of cities according to economic function. Logan and Molotch, for example, offer a typology that contrasts headquarters cities (like the Nodal cities considered here) with innovation centers oriented to research and development (roughly corresponding to the Functional-Nodal category), "module production"places (similar to the Production center), Third World Entrepôt cities that serve as immigration entry points and specialize in low-wage labor activities, and retirement centers (like the Resort-Residential category).[33]

The important point about these classifications is that the types of cities are having very different experiences with economic development in at least two senses. Recall that economic development is often understood as a phenomenon of stages, with some types of activities considered to be more advanced than others. In this sense, cities with economies still largely dependent on routine manufacturing or mining operations (the Mining-Industrial or Production centers) would be considered less developed than cities with economies that are dominated by postindustrial services (e.g., Government-Education centers) or that have substantial components of knowledge-intensive research and development activity (e.g., Functional-Nodal centers).

The categories of cities have also had various levels of success based on the bottom-line standard of job creation. Table 9.2 shows rates of employment growth for the various categories of cities for the period 1976 to 1983. Apart from the special case of Industrial-Military centers, which have clearly prospered in recent years, cities with industrial processing economies have fared the worst in generating jobs over the period in question. By contrast, employment has been growing dramatically in Residential-Resort centers, although many of the jobs in these centers are likely to be low-wage, unskilled service jobs. There has also been substantial growth in employment in those metropolitan areas that specialize in postindustrial services (e.g., Government-Education centers) and Nodal centers, particularly those smaller than New York and Los Angeles.

The classifications of local economies that have been considered here suggest not only important differences across cities but a clear hierarchy, with some

TABLE 9.2. AVERAGE ANNUAL RATE OF EMPLOYMENT GROWTH, BY TYPE OF LOCAL ECONOMY, 1976–1983

Type of Urban Economy	Employment Growth
National Nodal (4)	1.37
Regional Nodal (19)	2.64
Functional Nodal (24)	1.04
Government-Education (14)	2.50
Education-Manufacturing (5)	1.36
Manufacturing (22)	.63
Industrial-Military (12)	3.14
Mining-Industrial (12)	1.06
Residential-Resort (11)	4.95

Numbers in parentheses are the numbers of metropolitan areas classified in each category.

Source: Manuel Castells, *High Technology, Space, and Society* (vol. 28), p. 128, copyright 1985 by Sage Publications, Inc. Reprinted by permission of Sage Publications, Inc.

types of communities faring much better than others. A community's capacity to attract new jobs, its overall quality of life, and many of its internal challenges all depend on the role that it plays in a postindustrial economy. A privileged few cities with the desirable roles of Nodal, or headquarters, cities and innovation centers will have predominantly better-educated labor forces, many cultural amenities, and a generally high quality of life. By contrast, cities specializing in routine production tasks are vulnerable to corporate decisions made elsewhere and are pressed to maintain low-wage labor forces and generally low expectations for quality of life.

Given the greater desirability of some types of local economies, it should not be surprising that civic leaders in many communities are actively attempting to transform the local economic base. Using a variety of the economic development policies and programs that will be detailed in Chapter 10, traditional centers for manufacturing are attempting to bring more knowledge-intensive, technology-development activities to their area, or to attract corporate headquarters. Other communities have staked their future on the building of some version of a service economy. For example, while sustaining a commitment to retain and attract traditional manufacturing industries, Baltimore leaders have pursued a vision of the city as a convention and tourism center, complete with a new convention center and a revitalized Inner Harbor with an aquarium, shops, and the like.[34] Indianapolis has opted for a sports theme for its postindustrial future, focusing resources and more than $125 million in investments on sports and fitness facilities such as the Hoosier Dome, which helped bring the National Football League's Colts to Indianapolis from Baltimore, and which will be the location for the NCAA basketball championship tournament in 1991. The city has already hosted the Pan-Am Games, an international athletic event that contributed about $175 million to the city's economy.[35]

Can cities purposively transform their local economies to achieve a more desirable role in the postindustrial order? There is considerable controversy about this question, with some theorists emphasizing the helplessness of communities in the face of structural forces in a capitalist system, and others emphasizing "the role of individual actors in resisting, modifying, or conforming to these structures."[36] The extent to which cities can transform their economies is in part dependent on local political considerations that shape the adoption of the policy interventions. The political dimensions of economic development are treated in Chapter 11.

On a more practical level, the old saying about making a silk purse from a sow's ear applies. The Silicon Valley in California and the Route 128 area near Boston are postindustrial versions of boomtowns, and the professional, high-paying jobs that characterize these high-tech boomtowns were the envy of many a community in the U.S. (at least until the downturn in the microchip industry). But the circumstances that created them were unique and are unlikely to be easily reproduced in other communities. Communities that do not have universities with strengths in high-tech fields and strong ties to sources of federal funding have no real capacity to transform themselves into Silicon Valleys.[37] By contrast, Indianapolis's effort to key economic development to the theme of amateur sports and fitness makes sense in the context of the community's history and resources, which include a strong basketball tradition, the Indiana University School of Medicine's health and fitness activities, and the Eli Lilly pharmaceutical company's activities in the health field.[38] Development strategies are likely to fare better if they build on what the community has been and take advantage of natural assets that the city has rather than striking out in directions that have little connection to the community's resource base.

The Strategic Approach to Economic Development

The Indianapolis example illustrates what might be called the strategic approach to economic development, which draws on a number of the insights from the theoretical models discussed in this chapter. The strategic approach recognizes uneven development and competition among regions and cities for economic growth and acknowledges possibilities for developmental success if the actions of entrepreneurs and public policymakers are consistent with the economic assets and capacities of the community. For example, McGowan and Ottensmeyer argue that state and local economic development specialists are increasingly stressing the need for strategic planning processes that involve analysis of the "distinctive competencies" that they can provide for specific firms and industries.[39] Like classical location theory, the strategic approach assumes that communities have particular locational advantages. However, classical location theory is too mechanistic. It assumes that economic enterprises will naturally gravitate toward those places with the locational advantages of relevance to them. The strategic approach places more emphasis on the need for planning and initiative on the part of community leaders, so that potential locational advantages are exploited.

Strategic models also offer an important perspective on economic competition among communities. Most theories of urban growth and decline imply that there is structural competition among cities and regions—that is, that the processes of urban growth outlined in the theory will create some places that are winners and some that are losers with respect to economic development. As noted earlier, however, most of these theories are mechanistic, suggesting naturally unfolding processes that are relatively immutable to strategic intervention.

The strategic approach recognizes and incorporates many of the growth principles suggested by those theories, but it adds an emphasis on intentional action. Competition, from this point of view, is not simply an organic process. Competition also includes the strategic choices that community leaders make or fail to make. Explanations for urban growth or stagnation must include consideration of the extent to which community leaders recognize a competitive environment and act accordingly.[40]

The strategic approach also emphasizes the importance of identifying and overcoming barriers to development.[41] The concept of barriers to development is actually a component of the stage theory of economic development discussed earlier in this chapter. It is used to explain why cities that grew to prominence with the economic activities characteristic of the industrial era might have a difficult time transforming themselves to attract the newer economic activities that characterize postindustrial society. As Perry and Watkins explain the problem of developmental barriers:

> [T]hose cities which had previously crafted a set of barriers to insure their dominance in a particular sphere of economic activity become trapped by their own actions. Unless they can overcome their addiction to these old activities and transform their economies so that they are once again in harmony with the requirements generated by the succeeding wave of capital accumulation, their local economy will ossify and their position as growth leader will wane. The benefits flowing from their initial advantage during one developmental phase are thus transformed into barriers which inhibit the emergence of a new generative industrial base.[42]

From the perspective of strategic models of economic development, these barriers to development are not necessarily immutable. For example, transportation networks that are structured to accommodate heavy industry may diminish in importance relative to fiber-optic cable and other telecommunications investments that are important for many newer economic activities. Zoning and other regulations for land use that reflect the needs of an older industrial order may need to be revised to reflect the needs of postindustrial economic activities. This is not to say that removal of developmental barriers is either easy or inexpensive. However, from a strategic approach, barriers to development cannot possibly be removed unless they are first acknowledged.

In sum, the strategic approach incorporates emphases on assessment of the community's unique assets, identification and removal of obstacles to development, and the importance of strategic leadership to undertake these planning tasks in a competitive environment. But are local government officials, in collaboration with private sector officials, in a position to exercise such leadership? What public policy tools can be used to influence economic development in desired directions, and what are the strengths and limitations of these policy tools? The following chapter takes up these questions.

DISCUSSION QUESTIONS

1. Choose some community with which you are familiar or about which you would like to do some background research. If you are researching a community about which you do not have personal knowledge, you might consider sources such as *County and City Data Book* and several of the Census Bureau sources from which it is compiled

(such as the Census of Manufactures, Census of Wholesale Trade, Census of Retail Trade, and Census of Service Industries). What are the five largest employers in the community? Does each of the five firms appear to be basic industries, or are some of them nonbasic? Explain.

2. How many of the five leading industries in your study community are extractive industries (mining, forestry, etc.)? How many are industrial-era enterprises (goods processing, traditional manufacturing)? How many are postindustrial in character (i.e., either high-tech manufacturing or service industries)? Can your study community be comfortably classified as having a preindustrial, industrial, or postindustrial economy? Explain.

3. Has your study community lost or gained population between 1970 and 1980? Was it losing or gaining population in the decade before that? If it was losing population, how would you account for the decline? If it was gaining population, how would you account for the growth?

4. What locational advantages does your study community have? If it is difficult to answer this question in general terms, consider again the five largest employers in the community. Does the community have strengths or advantages that would be of particular relevance to those industries? What two economic enterprises have most recently either newly located in the community or substantially expanded operations in the community? What locational advantages may have been relevant for those decisions? Are there other potential strengths or assets that are not currently being exploited?

NOTES

1. Robert Reinhold, "Freeway Billboards Imperiled as Houston Rethinks Growth," *New York Times,* June 15, 1987, p. 8.
2. Andy Oakley, "Kansas City a Meek Competitor," *City & State,* September 1987, p. 44.
3. Rod Perlmutter, "GM to Shut Down Leeds," *Kansas City Times,* January 20, 1988, pp. A-1, A-10.
4. William Fulton, "Tiny City Picks Off Raiders," *City & State,* September 1987, p. 2.
5. John G. Falcioni, "Tech Center Aids Rockford, Ill., Economy," *City & State,* April 11, 1988, p. 41.
6. Ann O'M. Bowman, "Competition for Economic Development Among Southeastern Cities," *Urban Affairs Quarterly* 23 (June 1988): 512.
7. Albert Shapero, "Entrepreneurship in Economic Development," in *Shaping the Local Economy,* ed. Cheryl A. Farr (Washington, DC: International City Management Association, 1984), pp. 12-24.
8. Ibid., p. 14.
9. Alfred J. Watkins, *The Practice of Urban Economics* (Beverly Hills: Sage, 1980).
10. Ibid., p. 28.
11. Ibid., pp. 42-46.
12. Ibid., p. 55.
13. Ibid., p. 60.
14. Ibid., p. 107.

15. Ibid., pp. 107–108.
16. Werner Z. Hirsch, *Urban Economic Analysis* (New York: McGraw-Hill, 1973), pp. 186–192.
17. Watkins, *Practice of Urban Economics,* pp. 125–126.
18. Daniel Bell, *The Coming of Post-Industrial Society* (New York: Basic Books, 1976), p. 117.
19. Barry Bluestone and Bennett Harrison, *The Deindustrialization of America* (New York: Basic Books, 1982), p. 42.
20. Robert B. Reich, *Tales of a New America* (New York: Vintage Books, 1987), p. 43.
21. Manuel Castells, "High Technology, Economic Restructuring, and the Urban-Regional Process in the United States," in *High Technology, Space, and Society,* ed. Manuel Castells (Beverly Hills: Sage, 1985), p. 30.
22. David R. Barton, "Highlights of the 1987 U.S. Industrial Outlook," in *1987 U.S. Industrial Outlook,* U.S. Department of Commerce (Washington, DC: U.S. Government Printing Office, 1987), p. 6.
23. Daniel Bell, *Coming of Post-Industrial Society,* p. 143.
24. Ibid., p. 128.
25. U.S. Bureau of the Census, *Statistical Abstract of the United States: 1987,* 107th ed. (Washington, DC: U.S. Government Printing Office, 1987), p. 389.
26. Ibid.
27. John Naisbitt, "From an Industrial Society to an Information Society," in *Shaping the Local Economy,* ed. Cheryl Farr (Washington, DC: ICMA, 1984), p. 10.
28. Richard Knight and Gary Gappert, "Cities and the Challenge of the Global Economy," in *Urban Economic Development,* ed. Richard Bingham and John P. Blair (Beverly Hills: Sage, 1984), p. 72.
29. Figures are from U.S. Bureau of the Census, *Statistical Abstract of the United States: 1987,* pp. 138, 121, 147, and 147 respectively.
30. Bell, *Coming of Post-Industrial Society,* p. 128.
31. Castells, "High Technology, Economic Restructuring, and the Urban-Regional Process in the United States," in *High Technology, Space, and Society,* ed. Manuel Castells (Beverly Hills: Sage, 1985), p. 28.
32. Thomas M. Stanback, Jr., "The Changing Fortunes of Metropolitan Economies," in *High Technology, Space, and Society,* ed. Manuel Castells (Beverly Hills: Sage, 1985), pp. 126–127.
33. John Logan and Harvey Molotch, *Urban Fortunes* (Berkeley: University of California Press, 1987), pp. 258–277.
34. Bernard Berkowitz, "Economic Development Really Works: Baltimore, Maryland," in *Urban Economic Development,* ed. Richard Bingham and John Blair (Beverly Hills: Sage, 1984), pp. 201–221.
35. Rodd Zolkos, "A Realized Vision of Business Revival," *City & State,* August 29, 1988, p. 27.
36. Robert Beauregard, "Structure, Agency, and Urban Redevelopment," in *Cities in Transformation,* ed. Michael Peter Smith (Beverly Hills: Sage, 1984), p. 62.
37. Annalee Saxenian, "Silicon Valley and Route 128: Regional Prototypes or Historic Exceptions?" in *High Technology, Space, and Society,* ed. Castells (Beverly Hills: Sage, 1985), p. 99.
38. Zolkos, "Realized Vision of Business Revival," p. 27.

39. Robert McGowan and Ed Ottensmeyer, "Technology and Economic Development Strategies: A Foreword," *Policy Studies Review* 6 (February 1987): 508.
40. Bowman, "Competition for Economic Development," pp. 512–513.
41. McGowan and Ottensmeyer, "Technology and Economic Development Strategies," p. 510.
42. Alfred Watkins and David Perry, "Regional Change and the Impact of Uneven Urban Development," in *The Rise of the Sunbelt Cities*, ed. D. Perry and A. Watkins (Beverly Hills: Sage, 1977), p. 26.

CHAPTER 10

Tools for Economic Development

Considerable debate rages about the capacity of city governments to shape their economic future. One extreme view holds that city government leaders are helpless in the face of much larger economic forces that range from the decisions of OPEC oil ministers to ever-changing communications and transportation technologies that may make previous geographical advantages irrelevant, to the choices of distant corporate capitalists. At the other extreme, public officials are portrayed as key players in economic development decisions, and their policies are often either touted as contributing to local economic revitalization or blamed for worsening economic decline.

The truth of the matter is likely to lie between these two extremes. The truth of the matter is also much more difficult to find if the question is posed at a highly abstract level (such as "To what extent can local public policies affect the economic future of the community in desirable ways?") than in particular terms. Perhaps some local development policies can have an impact, whereas others are limited. An effort to swim directly against the tide of economic trends (for example, policies designed to revitalize the ailing steel industry) may be much less likely to succeed than policies designed to fit existing trends or features of the local economy that are already promising. What is needed is a more specific set of organizing questions, like the following: What sorts of strategies and policy tactics are local governments using for economic development goals? What are the strengths and limitations of these strategies and tactics? What are the circumstances under which particular economic development policies are more and less effective?

The *goals* of economic development are extremely varied, as the preceding chapter on cities in a postindustrial economy suggests. *Strategies* refer to

236

the broader operational approaches that cities choose in pursuit of their economic development goals. By contrast, *tactics* are the narrower, more specific actions or programs that cities may adopt to implement a given strategy. For example, retention of existing manufacturing industries appears to be an important economic development goal for many older cities, despite the advent of the postindustrial age, because the local labor force consists of workers skilled in particular manufacturing industries and used to the relatively high wages involved. One strategy for retention might be the provision of financial incentives to convince existing industry to expand in the community rather than relocate. Specific tactics reflecting this strategy might include property tax abatements and provision of low-interest or no-interest loans. In practice, of course, there is not a hard and fast line distinguishing strategies and tactics. Some very broad strategies involve increasingly more specific strategies, ultimately shading into narrowly programmatic tactics.

With this distinction in mind, however, we can see that there are many ways to answer the question: What public policies are cities using for economic development purposes? The question can be answered by describing various classifications of strategies or by giving much more detailed listings of specific tactics.

One important method for categorizing economic development strategies focuses on differences in the relationship between the public sector and the private sector. The public sector can be involved in (1) "promotion" of the private sector, (2) "cooperation" with the private sector, (3) "inducement" of the private sector, or (4) "coercion" of the private sector through regulation or control.[1] This particular categorization is useful for several reasons. First, it provides an organizing framework for a host of specific economic development programs or tactics. Second, because each strategy implies a particular relationship between the public and the private sector, the typology suggests some important things about the conditions under which one rather than another approach is appropriate. For example, the inducement strategy assumes that the private sector is pursuing goals other than those desired by government leaders. Consequently, policies are designed to restructure private sector incentives so that activity is more in line with the goals of the public sector. The inducement strategy would not be appropriate in cases where private sector incentive systems already operate to make private and public sector goals correspond. For example, if public officials want downtown office development and the private market for such development is already strong, inducement strategies like tax abatements would be unnecessary.

The following section considers each of the economic development strategies, describes some of the more important programs, or tactics, that are a part of each strategy, and explores what is known about the effectiveness of each. There is also systemmatic evidence about the extent to which city governments nationwide use many of the specific programs, or tactics. This information is from a survey of city governments and economic development conducted by the

International City Management Association (ICMA) in 1984, and the survey is reported where relevant throughout the chapter.[2]

PROMOTION AS AN ECONOMIC DEVELOPMENT STRATEGY

Promotion of the private sector includes public sector provision of some of the preconditions for economic activity in the hope that economic activity will follow. In contrast with strategies like inducement or cooperation, promotion does not involve "prior agreement with private sector representatives about their subsequent actions."[3] Rather, under a promotion strategy, the public sector provides facilities and services believed to be important for a fairly broad range of economic activities, publicizes the availability of these facilities and the attractive features of the community, and hopes thereby to attract or generate new economic activity.

This section considers three tactics that fit the promotion strategy:

1. Infrastructure investments, such as the construction of facilities needed to sustain economic development.
2. Developmental land management activities, such as the clearance, acquisition, sale, or donation of land to developers.
3. Public relations activities designed to attract or retain business.

Table 10.1 shows the percentages of cities responding to the ICMA survey that engage in each type of promotional activity.

A key promotional tactic involves construction of facilities that can encourage economic development. This may include the provision and upkeep of basic infrastructure, from roads and bridges to sewage treatment plants, that are necessary for business activity. In addition, cities provide specialized infrastructure developments, such as industrial parks where roads, utilities, and the like are placed in a spatial arrangement believed desirable for industry. Two-thirds of the city governments responding to ICMA's 1984 survey have undertaken construction or improvements to city facilities primarily to encour-

TABLE 10.1. FREQUENCY OF CITIES' USE OF PROMOTIONAL ACTIVITIES FOR ECONOMIC DEVELOPMENT

Type of Promotional Activity	Percentage
Construction or Improvement of Facilities to Encourage Economic Development	67
Developmental Land Management Activities	60
Publicity Efforts Designed to Attract or Retain Business and Industry	80

Source: International City Management, National Sample Survey on Economic Development Activity, 1984.

age economic development. Most typically this activity involved improvements to streets, sidewalks, or bridges (50 percent of the cities had undertaken these improvements for economic development) or to sewage collection or treatment facilities (41 percent had done this for economic development purposes).

Another set of promotional tactics consists of various developmental land management activities. Three-fifths of the city governments responding to ICMA's survey reported some such activities. For example, 26 percent had consolidated lots to create sites suitable for large-scale development. Local government can also identify parcels of land suitable for the type of economic activity desired and either stand ready to assist private sector actors in assembling them efficiently for development or buy and hold them against the possibility of future private sector development.[4] Two-fifths of the cities responding to the ICMA survey have acquired land for development purposes; 39 percent have sold land to private developers; 17 percent have leased land; and 6 percent have donated land to private developers.

Finally, the promotional strategy includes outright publicity campaigns designed to get out the word about the virtues of the community as a place to do business. This can be done through advertising or distribution of printed material and by having city officials make field visits or meet personally with managers of prospective new businesses. Four-fifths of the cities in ICMA's survey reported some activity of this kind (see Table 10.1).

Publicity campaigns have historically been associated with the civic boosterism of local Chambers of Commerce. In recent years, however, there have been more and more elaborate promotional campaigns, often conducted as a joint venture of local government and the local Chamber of Commerce, a local convention and tourism bureau, or other private development organizations. For example, the relatively small city of Lawrence, Kansas (population approximately 55,000), has for some years undertaken an economic development marketing program led by a staff member of the Chamber of Commerce whose salary is jointly supported by Lawrence city government and the Chamber of Commerce. Between March and October, 1987, this program led to the creation of an industrial facts book about the community, a directory of high-tech business in Lawrence, contacts with more than seven-hundred firms in a direct mail campaign designed to inform businesses about the advantages of Lawrence as a site, visits by thirty-one firms interested in locating in the community, and contacts with more than one hundred existing businesses in the community to promote expansion possibilities.[5] Meanwhile, even a community such as Overland Park, Kansas, which has been enjoying a growth boom in recent years, invests in promotional activities. Its full-color brochure boasts that it is "the premier suburb of Kansas City—unique in its combination of business community and comfortable residential setting."[6] The impressive brochure provides statistical detail on government, taxes, employment and population trends, education, recreation and other facilities, housing, and weather.

Programs of promotional strategy are often viewed as passive, low-level, relatively weak approaches to economic development. They involve investments or actions taken in the hope that private economic investment will follow but with no advance commitment from any particular private sector enterprise. Any number of empty fields with "Industrial Park" signs at the entryway testify to the fact that supplying some of the preconditions for economic activity does not necessarily mean that economic activity will follow. Publicity campaigns can all too easily be viewed as no more than symbolic action, with slick brochures substituting for real dealmaking with business prospects. Furthermore, because promotion involves no direct, prior commitments from particular private sector investors, evaluating the impact of promotional activities is difficult. When new economic activity does come to the community, local officials are likely to credit the promotional strategy for the new investment, but there is plenty of room for skepticism and little hard evidence to settle the matter. Since we cannot know what private sector investment *would have occurred* even without local promotional strategies, a cloud of uncertainty hangs over promotional efforts.

On the other hand, promotional-style economic development activities appear in a more favorable light if we recognize that they do involve the provision of *preconditions* for economic activity—no more and no less. They may not be sufficient conditions for economic development, but many of them are something like necessary conditions. For example, as Chapter 8 suggests, economic activity is premised on the availability and at least minimal quality of local public infrastructure. Without adequate sewer and water capacity, for example, certain types of industry simply cannot locate in a community and existing industry cannot expand. Similarly, without appropriate sites for new construction or expansion, various industries, particularly those that are space intensive, cannot locate in a community. Even simple advertising campaigns can be viewed as necessary, if not sufficient, conditions for attracting new economic activity. Potential business prospects cannot be expected to find out all about the community on their own. The costs of information gathering are large, and the number of cities that could meet a business establishment's needs is also large. Given these facts, most communities want to take a proactive role in making their communities' virtues widely known to potential investors. The promotion kinds of economic development policies are perhaps best viewed as important, but not necessarily definitive, activities toward achieving goals of economic development.

INDUCEMENT AS AN ECONOMIC DEVELOPMENT STRATEGY

A second strategy for economic development involves some form of inducement, which means a conscious attempt to alter the incentives of private sector actors to get them to make decisions that are more in line with public sector development goals.[7] The presumption here is that, left as is, incentive systems, such as the existing market for residential land or the private retail market downtown, are perverse. They lead business interests to underinvest in the sorts of development that public planners believe are important to the economic future of the community. Consequently, government must offer inducements to make it worthwhile for business interests to make more of the desired investments.

A wide range of specific programs, or tactics, are part of the inducement strategy. This section considers several of the more important, widely used, and controversial ones, including (1) tax abatement, (2) the provision of low-cost capital through issuance of industrial development bonds, and (3) the provision of low-cost capital through direct loans, loan guarantees, subsidized loans, direct grants, or in-kind contributions. Table 10.2 shows the extent to which these various financial inducements are used by cities responding to ICMA's 1984 survey.

1. Tax incentives typically involve programs to abate, or forgive, various sorts of taxes on business for a specified number of years. Although there is some variation in the nature of abatement programs, the typical program is quite straightforward. In Ohio, for example, municipalities can designate areas suffering from blight and deterioration to be exempted from property tax payments on improvements or new development. The precise amount of the abatement is determined through a process of negotiation with a developer, and the developer receiving the abatement must promise that, after the period of the abatement is over (typically about ten years), tax payments will be at least as much as they were prior to the abatement.[8] The direct negotiation and advance commitment that are involved highlight the contrast between the inducement approach and the promotion strategy discussed earlier.

TABLE 10.2. FREQUENCY OF CITIES' USE OF FINANCIAL INDUCEMENT FOR ECONOMIC DEVELOPMENT[a]

Type of Financial Inducement	Percentage
Property Tax Abatement	21
Industrial Development Bonds	52
Direct Loans	16
Subsidized Loans	14
Loan Guarantees	7
Direct Grants for Development Projects	10
In-kind Contributions to Development Projects	11

[a] In cities above 10,000 population.

Source: International City Management, National Sample Survey on Economic Development Activity, 1984.

At the local level, property tax abatements are perhaps the most significant because the property tax is typically the most substantial local tax on business. As of 1985, thirty-three of the fifty states had adopted programs enabling their localities to provide property tax abatements for economic development purposes.[9] Twenty-one percent of the city governments responding to ICMA's 1984 survey indicated that they use tax abatement as an economic development tool.

2. Another financial inducement is the provision of low-cost capital through publicly subsidized loans or bonds. Just as tax abatement reduces one presumed disincentive to investment (i.e., taxes), programs that make capital available to business at below-market interest rates are meant to make the incentive structure for investment more attractive. Because the bonds issued by states and cities are typically tax exempt, these governments can borrow money at a lower interest rate than would be the case if persons buying the bonds had to pay federal taxes on the interest they earn. By issuing bonds for various industrial development purposes, state and local governments effectively provide below-market capital that business enterprises can use to expand operations, build new facilities, and so forth. The bonds are then paid off by the business enterprises for which they were issued, just as those businesses might pay off a private loan. In this arrangement, however, the federal government indirectly provides the subsidy for business development because the bonds are technically issued by local government and therefore have tax-exempt status. Although there have been federal policy changes designed to limit state and local governments' use of tax-exempt bonds for essentially "private" purposes (i.e., subsidy of private economic activity), the extent of state and local use of this tactic for economic development has been substantial.

[T]he value of industrial revenue bonds shot up during this period from $0.1 billion in 1970 to $3.6 billion in 1983. While there is general agreement that this development is irrational and costly from the point of view of the nation as a whole, it must nonetheless be conceded that from the point of view of the state and locality it is almost irresponsible not to use such incentives. This is because such financing constitutes a subsidy from the federal government to industry in the taxing jurisdiction of the state or locality.[10]

Not surprisingly, over half (52 percent) of the cities responding to ICMA's survey reported that they had issued Industrial Revenue Bonds (IRBs) or Industrial Development Bonds (IDBs) for private facilities.

3. Low-cost capital as a financial inducement can also be provided through the use of grant programs, various sorts of loans, and loan guarantees. Sixteen percent of the cities responding to ICMA's survey provide direct loans to private businesses, and 14 percent of the cities subsidize loans by making a payment to private lending institutions to decrease the interest rates of loans made to private developers. In addition, 7 percent of the cities guarantee the loans that private

lending institutions make to particular borrowers. Finally, 10 percent of the cities in ICMA's survey have made direct grants to development projects, and 11 percent have made various in-kind contributions like providing labor for land clearance.

Municipalities have become adept at putting together financial incentive packages for economic development using a variety of federal and state grant and loan programs as well. Some cities have used federal Community Development Block Grants as part of such a financial inducement package.[11] The city of Detroit put together an impressively varied financial incentive package in its drive to get General Motors to build a new automobile assembly plant in Detroit. Sources of revenue to support the financial incentives package included grants and loans from the federal Department of Housing and Urban Development, the Economic Development Administration, and the Urban Mass Transportation Administration, and monies from various programs of the state of Michigan.[12] In fact, city governments responding to ICMA's survey not only made widespread use of federal and state grant-in-aid programs for development purposes, but they identified these intergovernmental aids as the most important source of revenue for economic development purposes.

The inducement strategy has been widely used in American cities. Existing research suggests that cities facing economic distress are especially likely to use financial inducements as a strategy for economic development. Rubin and Rubin, for example, find that economic development tools such as tax abatement and direct loans to business are more likely to be used in cities with lower median incomes, in cities with higher percentages of families in poverty, in cities with higher unemployment rates, in cities with higher property tax rates, and in cities with smaller tax bases. These results do not hold for industrial development bonds, however. The propensity to use bonds for industrial development purposes is unrelated to the various measures of economic need and fiscal stress.[13] Feiock and Clingermayer suggest that the political structures of the community may be more important than economic need or fiscal stress in accounting for the propensity to use financial inducements. That is, cities with unreformed institutions are more likely to offer financial inducements such as tax abatement. Feiock and Clingmayer find that tax abatement is more frequently used as a development tool in cities with partisan elections than in cities with nonpartisan elections, more frequently used in cities without the council-manager form of government than in cities with city managers, and more frequently used in cities where the chief executive has veto power. Feiock and Clingermayer interpret these results as showing the importance of financial inducements as credit-claiming devices that elected officials use to "provide some form of visible—if only symbolic—benefits to a great array of potential supports."[14]

Many analysts have argued that financial inducement as an economic development strategy is popular *despite* its ineffectiveness and inefficiency, not because of its demonstrated successes. In particular, a rather substantial literature on the impacts of financial inducement programs suggests that these programs fail because they are directed to relatively unimportant factors for business.

> In general the literature shows that business decisions on location and investment are primarily determined by such factors as proximity to markets, transportation, chief executive's homes, raw materials, and low cost nonunionized labor in roughly that order of importance. The levels and types of taxes play a minor role in some studies, and government services and targeted business incentives have virtually no role in any of the studies.[15]

This does not mean that business decisionmakers will decline to take advantage of financial inducement packages. It means only that the inducement strategy is a waste of resources because location and expansion decisions are not really affected by the availability of those financial inducements.

Such a conclusion is something of an overgeneralization. Financial inducements such as tax abatements are likely to be more important in the locational decisionmaking of some types of firms than in others. Some firms are relatively footloose whereas others have substantial locational ties because of the importance of specific raw materials, unique labor markets, or spatial arrangements that are difficult to replicate. The footloose industries would presumably be more susceptible to financial inducements, whereas the locational decisions of other firms are too dominated by other considerations.

In addition, the importance (or unimportance) of financial inducements seems to depend on whether cross-regional or intraregional moves of business firms are at issue. There is a great deal of consensus that "taxes and fiscal incentives play little or no role in a firm's choice of location among regions. This results partly because market and cost variables vary more among regions than do fiscal variables."[16] On the other hand, some studies show that fiscal inducements such as tax abatements are important factors in industrial firm location *within metropolitan areas.*[17] Even so, such inducements are not the most important of locational factors.

What little importance financial inducements do have within a metropolitan area is minimized by an important phenomenon—the competition among localities for economic development. The effect of financial inducements is lessened, or even erased, if all jurisdictions are offering inducements. As one observer notes, "tax competition among the states tends to narrow differentials in the long run, as retaliatory tax cuts cancel out any temporary advantage one state may gain over another."[18] A similar narrowing of differences through the competitive use of financial inducements occurs at the local level. For example, when Fort Wayne, Indiana, and Springfield, Illinois, competed directly with financial inducement packages to garner an International Harvester truck assembly plant, each community's inducement strategy nullified the other. When International Harvester ultimately announced its decision, its "press release stated that the financial incentives offered by the two cities were so comparable as not to be a factor in the final decision."[19]

Another form of failure involving financial inducements occurs when firms that have accepted these financial bonuses to locate or expand in a locality later close down, scale back, or transfer their operations. There is no guarantee, of course, that a business will be forever healthy simply because it has been given tax breaks or other financial inducements. On the other hand, city officials may legitimately perceive that they have been taken advantage of if a firm benefits from public inducements without delivering on the jobs or other economic development gains that it promised.

In response to this difficulty, some cities have begun to write the responsibilities of private firms receiving financial inducements into the fine print of legal documents involving low-cost funds, tax breaks, and the like. Subsequently, business firms have been challenged in court when these economic development deals go aground. For example, the city of Duluth, Minnesota, has sued Triangle Corporation, a manufacturer of tools, which was provided $10 million in low-interest loan money to keep the local Diamond Tool and Horseshoe Company and its 350 jobs alive. After taking the financial help, the corporation scaled back work at the Duluth plant and has indicated that it might close down all or part of it. Similarly, the city of Chicago sued a toy manufacuring company in 1985 for shutting down a plant that had benefited from public funds. In an out-of-court settlement, the city got the manufacturer to spend half a million dollars to aid workers who would lose their jobs.[20]

In general, the inducement strategy works best when public sector officials have very strong information about private sector locational considerations, so that the relevance, appropriate level, and likely impact of any incentives offered by government can be accurately judged.[21] Unfortunately, in many cases public officials do not have good information about private sector motivations and likely behaviors. This is not simply due to a lack of understanding across sectors. Rather, there is a structural reason for the information gap. It is to the advantage of business leaders to keep public officials from knowing precisely how various considerations operate in their investment decisionmaking. Because public officials from a number of cities are typically competing with one another for the firm's investment, there will be a tendency for any particular city to oversupply financial inducements, rather than to undersupply them, just to be sure that their financial package is not so low as to be uncompetitive. When cities are competing with one another for economic development, and competing without explicit knowledge about what amount of inducements it will take to tip a private firm's locational decision, the result is likely to be a "corporate surplus"—that is, financial inducements "beyond what would be strictly necessary to attract the facility."[22] The corporate surplus means that public sector resources have been inefficiently used.

COOPERATION AS AN ECONOMIC DEVELOPMENT STRATEGY

There are subtle but important differences between inducement as an economic development strategy and public-private cooperation. In the case of inducement, conflicting goals between the two sectors are presumed, and incentives are used to divert private decisionmaking toward public goals. Relatively similar incentive packages may be offered to a number of firms, there may be little direct interaction between public officials and private sector decisionmakers, and little in the way of a longer-term relationship is presumed. By contrast, the cooperation strategy involves situations in which the two sectors collaborate on specific plans or projects in which both have an important stake.

> [T]he public and private sectors may cooperate in specific joint venture projects. Each agrees to undertake specific activities, and the public sector may agree to assume a portion of the cost. This may resemble the inducement approach, but unlike that approach it involves extensive negotiations and planning for specific projects rather than a more impersonal restructuring of market incentives.[23]

The cooperation strategy is evident in large-scale development projects that have the public and private sectors sharing costs and in other ways playing mutually supportive roles. An example of the cooperation strategy at work is provided in Jones and Bachelor's description of the relationship between General Motors and government leaders in Flint, Michigan, as the plans for a new Buick City complex unfolded.

> Until that project [Buick City], companies routinely requested aid by using the implied or actual threat of relocation as a resource in the bargaining process. Buick City involved something new. . . . Buick . . . is not only using corporate persuasion to attract suppliers to the Flint region but is also working directly with local government to do so. By supplying information on the financial and operating status of suppliers, the corporation is handing the city a major bargaining chip in its dealing with suppliers. This has the effect of disadvantaging other localities that are interested in attracting suppliers.[24]

In this case, both city government and GM's Buick division officials have a strong stake in the success of the new Buick production system. This has led to a sustained, collaborative relationship in which the two institutions work together to successfully bring in other businesses that are necessary for advancing their shared conception of the economic future of this center for auto manufacturing.

Public-private cooperation for economic development is often institutionalized in special organizations similar to the authorities that were described in Chapter 8. These quasi-public, quasi-private corporations are particularly attractive when civic leaders wish to pursue large-scale development projects with maximum flexibility and freedom from the many accountability controls that normally characterize government operations. In the ICMA survey, 15.2 percent of the cities reported that a local development corporation is the organization most active in fostering economic development in the community.

Many good examples of public-private collaboration through quasi-public corporations can be found in the transformation of Baltimore's inner harbor into a successful, large-scale redevelopment project. The Charles Center/Inner Harbor Management, Incorporated is a quasi-public corporation with designated responsibility for development of the Inner Harbor and the related Charles Center area. The city-owned National Aquarium is a centerpiece of the Inner Harbor redevelopment, attracting large numbers of visitors, creating 2,950 jobs for the region, and generating $1.9 million in local taxes and $3.3 million in state taxes in 1984.[25] Another quasi-public corporation, Baltimore Aquarium, Incorporated, runs the aquarium.

Individual development projects by public-private development groups can create impressive-sounding numbers of new jobs for the community, as the foregoing examples show. However, recent research offers a cautionary note concerning the effectiveness of quasi-public development groups. Drawing on a nationwide survey of directors of industrial development organizations, researchers have found that the successes of these organizations must be tempered by acknowledgement of their limited impact:

> While industrial development groups . . . have some success in generating jobs and do so with very limited internal financial resources, the question remains as to whether their efforts have produced a significant positive impact on their service area economies. The small number of new jobs generated by the typical group suggests that its impact on its service area may be negligible and overshadowed by broader economic forces that influence the service area economy.[26]

Nevertheless, quasi-public development organizations have become popular devices for large-scale development projects. Because they are not regular government entities and not subject to rules and procedures like public hearings, budget approval requirements, civil service rules, and the like, they can operate more quickly and quietly without as much likelihood of getting caught up in the political wrangling and public controversies that seem to dog traditional public projects. They can also use very flexible and innovative financing arrangements. Private sector leaders frequently prefer to have collaborative relationships carried out by these organizations because collaboration can proceed under organizational arrangements and operating rules that are more familiar to business leaders. And when it is to the advantage of the quasi-public organization to assert its "publicness" (for example, when receipt of state or federal grant funds is at issue), the organization can do so.[27]

The implication of these observations is that public-private collaboration, particularly as carried out within quasi-public corporations, is a powerful prescription for economic development. But like any powerful prescription, it can have undesirable side effects. In this case, the undesirable side effects have to do with the potential for business interests to dominate, rather than to work hand in hand with, public sector interests.[28] For this reason, the forms of public-private collaboration described here are perhaps most appropriate when (1) collaboration is preceded by a meaningful planning process that identifies genuinely mutual goals, (2) the public sector side of the collaboration is represented by strong political leadership, and (3) the collaboration focuses on a joint venture whose costs and benefits can be objectively assessed.

REGULATION AS AN ECONOMIC DEVELOPMENT STRATEGY

On the surface, regulation of the private sector may seem more like a strategy for miniminizing rather than maximizing development. In fact, various forms of regulation have been used to prevent undesired growth. But regulation is a relevant strategy for economic development. From the earlier discussion of the meaning of economic development, we have seen that in and of itself growth may not qualify as economic development. Many conceptualizations of economic development focus on particular desired sorts of new economic activities rather than growth of any kind, regardless of its negative side effects. However, to encourage desirable development often means discouraging undesirable development, and the latter requires regulation.

Local government's use of its land-use powers is the central focus of a regulatory strategy. Two particular types of land-use regulation are especially important. First are subdivision regulations, which control the conversion of property into blocks of land for building purposes. Subdivision regulations usually require that the owner submit a map of the property (called a *plat*) to the city, showing streets, lot lines, utility rights of way, and so forth. Before approving the plat for building, the city government can insist on particular improvements like sewer or water infrastructure consistent with local standards or street connections.[29]

In addition to subdivision regulations, city zoning ordinances are a powerful mechanism for land-use control. In the most basic sense, zoning means the authoritative mapping of the community into subareas, with the stipulation of which types of land uses (such as single-family residential, heavy industrial, and so forth) are permitted in each subarea. Modern zoning ordinances are typically quite detailed, including requirements such as the following: minimum lot size, minimum distance from building to lot line, maximum height and number of storeys, and required parking places for various types of buildings.[30]

The logic behind zoning suggests why this form of regulation also can serve as an important economic development strategy. Zoning is one of local government's police powers—that is, its power to act for the health, safety, and well-being of its citizens. In the law, zoning is related to the concept of nuisances. An offensive land use, like a tannery, has impacts on surrounding properties. It is, as it were, a nuisance. Local government's right to regulate how private land is used is an acknowledgment of the fact that some land uses if not suitably separated from others can have harmful effects.

The harmful effects that are of greatest concern from an economic development perspective are those that devalue property for uses that might be important to the economic future of the community. At one extreme, for example, tourist-related uses such as upscale retail stores, eating establishments, and the like, cannot thrive next to smokestack industrial uses. However, even manufacturing uses, which are by no means esthetically fragile, still can be harmed by adjacent noncomparable uses. In an example from Chicago, a steel-fabricating establishment has been affected by an influx of new, upscale housing and stores as old industrial areas adjacent to it have been redeveloped. The clash of the divergent uses has created numerous problems for the factory, ranging from increased automobile traffic to the threat of demands for more severe noise abatement at the plant from residents in the newly redeveloped area, to annoying intrusions as people wander into the open doors of the plant from nearby restaurants and bars, attracted by the beauty of the steel-pouring process.[31]

Finally, cities have a variety of other regulations that affect private decisionmakers who are planning to locate or expand a business or industry. Building codes include many requirements relating to materials and methods of construction. Fire codes carry stipulations concerning how facilities must be constructed, and they limit how buildings can be used. Noise control ordinances and environmental regulations constitute additional forms of regulation with implications for business and industry. In addition to the potentially restrictive content of these regulations, the time-consuming process of obtaining necessary permits that show compliance with regulations can be a costly hassle for potential investors.

Many communities have conducted reviews and found that existing regulations serve as unnecessary obstacles to the kind of development that the community desires. Reforming these regulations can be a tool for economic development. The experience of Beaumont, Texas, illustrates the problems that are often tackled with zoning reform efforts:

> New types of development were being discouraged and, in many instances, development costs were being inflated by unnecessary and excessive regulation. . . . Many new developments and uses were not provided for in the list of permitted uses. This meant that the zoning officer could not always immediately respond to informational requests from potential developers. . . . Compounding this problem was the fact that no list of permitted uses existed for the heavy industrial district and each and every proposed heavy industrial use had to be approved by the board of adjustment. The uncertainty and delay caused by this situation had an adverse effect on the city's ability to compete for industrial prospects.[32]

Beaumont is by no means an exceptional city in terms of its development-oriented regulatory reforms. Three-fifths of the cities responding to ICMA's survey report that they have undertaken some effort to reform building or zoning regulations to facilitate economic development.

Regulatory reform is similar to the promotion strategies discussed earlier. By streamlining permit processes and updating zoning, cities are ensuring the basic preconditions for development but not working one-on-one with *particular* investors concerning *particular* development projects. Like promotion strategies generally, regulatory reform is a relatively passive tool for economic development. However, zoning and other land-use regulations can be used in a much more aggressive manner. To understand the more aggressive use of land-use controls requires attention to flexible, negotiated zoning practices. These include incentive zoning, development rights transfer programs, development agreements, and exactions.

Incentive zoning means an arrangement in which local government allows a potential developer to build at a greater height or higher density, or otherwise exceed zoning requirements in exchange for the developer's provision of certain desired project features. For example, office development that exceeds traditionally allowable densities might be permitted if the developer also provides "a plaza in front of the entrance to the building, a direct entrance to a subway station, or a 'vest pocket' park or sitting area."[33]

The policies concerning the transfer of development rights make up a system in which private landowners can, and indeed are encouraged to, exchange development rights with one another. Suppose that a city government wishes to radically restrict the amount of development in subarea *A* (perhaps because of historic preservation concerns or the existence of other land uses in the subarea that would be damaged by new growth) and to encourage development in subareas *B* and *C*. Severely curtailing development in subarea *A* through traditional zoning might lead to legal challenges in which property owners argue that the allowable uses of their land are so limited as to amount to government expropriation of their property rights. If such a "taking" could be shown, government would have to reimburse all landowners for the loss of their development rights.[34] Programs of transferable development rights are intended to avoid these legal limitations of traditional zoning, while still accomplishing goals like those posed earlier. Property owners in subarea *A* who agree not to develop their property can be reimbursed by selling their rights to develop to potential developers in subareas *B* and *C*.[35]

Although it may seem odd to think of buying or selling a right to development, such rights are very real and values can readily be determined. Imagine a landowner with a site that could in principle accommodate a twenty-story office building in a city where the existing real estate market shows that office buildings typically are worth $10 million per storey. Now imagine a regulation that limits development to ten floors in that location. The regulation effectively costs the landowner $100 million. A landowner so regulated might be sorely tempted to sue to get the $100 million in compensation from the city by challenging the regulation. Under a transferable development rights program, landowners in a sector of the city where city officials wish to encourage more intense development could be given automatic authorization to build, providing they buy development rights from a landowner such as the one who would otherwise be out $100 million. One potential development reimburses the other, and development occurs in the location that is consistent with city government's economic development plans, not elsewhere.

Development agreements are much like incentive zoning. They are arrangements under which city government negotiates directly with a potential developer toward an agreement that allows the developer to go beyond certain zoning limitations in exchange for certain desired actions that the developer agrees to take. For example, the developer of one office complex in Santa Monica was allowed to build higher than the usual forty-five-foot restriction in the zoning ordinance and to include some property uses in the complex that were not usually allowed. In return, the developer agreed to build low-income housing at another location and to provide a park and child-care center at the site of the complex.[36] In ICMA's 1984 survey, 29 percent of responding cities reported that they engage in administrative negotiation with developers on regulatory requirements.

In some cases, development agreements fade into innovative but nonnegotiable requirements placed on developers. For example, New York City recently changed its zoning ordinance in order to protect the city's garment district. The ordinance provision stipulates "that developers and building owners who convert manufacturing space into office space must then set aside an equivalent amount of manufacturing space elsewhere in the district.[37]

Finally, a host of bargained regulations go under the name of *exactions.* Exactions typically involve various sorts of payments that developers agree to make to city government, often because of the argument that development imposes some costs on the community even though it also brings desired economic activity.[38] For example, the developer might be asked to make a lump-sum payment to the jurisdiction in an amount that covers all or part of the costs that the municipality will have to take on for improvements in water, sewage, transportation, or other facilities. As an example, Budweiser paid the city of Fairfield, California, $13 million in a lump-sum payment as part of the approval process preceding its construction of a major brewery in the community. The payment was to cover estimated additions to the community's sewage and wastewater treatment facilities occasioned by the addition of the brewery.[39]

Incentive zoning, programs for transferable development rights, development agreements, and exactions are important extensions of traditional land-use regulations and are intended to add flexibility to what are otherwise rather ponderous, rigid, and unimaginative regulations. Each of these policy tools has considerable potential for enhancing economic development. Furthermore, as many of the examples suggest, that potential is being realized in many settings. However, there are some important limitations and contingencies that must be appreciated as well.

First, these regulatory tools largely depend on negotiated arrangements between the public and the private sectors. In locations that are already very attractive for business activity, the public sector will be in a good position to negotiate. However, communities that are declining and desperate for new economic activity are hardly in a good position to negotiate.[40]

Second, although local government has substantial land-use powers, there are important legal limits on these powers. Most particularly, government cannot regulate too restrictively without running afoul of the Fifth Amendment's stipulation that private property not be taken for public use without "just compensation." In situations where government needs land for a particular public facility, such as a fire station, it may use its condemnation powers to acquire land from private owners if it provides just compensation to those landowners. In the case of economic development efforts, however, local government wishes to use its regulatory powers to influence what private landowners do with their property, but does not wish to be so intrusive as to be required to reimburse the private landowner.

However, land-use regulations create substantial amounts of litigation, and local government must be prepared to deal with the costs and potential consequences of such litigation. Recently, the stakes have been raised for local government. In June 1987, the United States Supreme Court decided that a local government that is found to have engaged in such a "taking" cannot remedy the situation simply by rescinding the overly restrictive land-use regulation. Instead, local government will have to compensate the landowner for the losses incurred while the offending regulation was in place.[41]

Finally, it must be recognized that the effectiveness of these innovative land-use regulations in enhancing economic development depends on the capacity of public officials to foresee appropriate investment possibilities for the community. Zoning in general, as well as particular development agreements, have validity only if they are based on a comprehensive plan that realistically assesses the community's potential and sets forth a design for future development. This requires substantial knowledge about a wide range of matters, including population trends, composition of the labor market, retail markets, current and projected demand for water, sewage, transit, and other capital facilities, the housing market, and so forth. Ideally, development agreements and other uses of the community's land-use regulatory powers should be undertaken in a coordinated fashion so that development is predictable, mutually reinforcing, and consistent with the long-range commitments of public agencies. Regulatory decisions that are contradictory generate a hodgepodge of potentially conflicting new land uses, uncertainties for potential developers, and a variety of unintended consequences for public authorities.

Unfortunately, communities are not equally endowed with the resources and professional talent to develop high-quality, comprehensive plans. Many a comprehensive plan has been prepared by an outside consultant, then left to gather dust on city hall shelves. To the extent that planning is taken seriously, it tends to engender intense politicization, as citizens and interest groups become concerned about matters of great consequence to them. The planning profession has historically been ambivalent about such political involvement, and in some cities, planning staff are technically adept but incapable of dealing with the politics of planning.[42] In short, effective use of land-use regulatory powers for economic development is contingent on both the technical and political capacities of the public sector. Limited knowledge and limited public consensus are the two primary obstacles to effective use of land-use regulation for economic development purposes.

SUMMARY

Local government has a vast repertoire of policy tools that can be used to enhance economic development, including such diverse items as tax abatements, developer exactions, promotional campaigns, joint venture arrangements, infrastructure investments, subsidized loans, and incentive zoning. Given this great array of programs and policy tools, highly generalized statements about the capacity of city government to influence its economic future are perhaps less useful than more limited generalizations about the effects of particular types of policy tools under particular circumstances. Grouping particular policy tools or programs into broader categories that reflect unique *strategies* for economic development can help to structure these limited generalizations.

In this chapter, we have seen that some economic development programs are more passive and disengaged from particular economic enterprises, whereas others are quite aggressive and involve intense interaction between the public sector and individual investors in the private sector. The former characterization largely fits the promotion strategy and the traditional versions of regulatory strategies. The latter characterization largely fits the cooperation strategy and the more innovative, negotiated forms of land-use regulation such as development agreements. The inducement strategy can be tailored to either characterization. For example, tax abatements at a prespecified level can be legislated for any industry that meets stated criteria. The community then waits to see what prospects respond to the stated policy. Alternatively, tax abatements and other financial inducements can be individually negotiated with particular economic enterprises, as when complex financial packages are arranged to accommodate the needs of significant employers who are threatening to leave the community.

Which strategy is preferable? There is no simple answer to this question. Rather, each strategy has unique advantages and limitations, and the appropriateness of each is dependent on circumstances. For example, more aggressive, interactive, bargaining approaches like those in the collaborative strategy and some forms of the inducement strategy require strong political leadership, considerable technical knowledge on the public sector side, and a capacity for flexible and prompt response. These are not always hallmarks of the public sector. To the extent that communities have these features, more aggressive, interactive approaches to economic development are possible. Where these features do not exist, some communities attempt to approximate them by creating special quasi-public corporations to carry on economic development projects.

Another important contingency is the current position of the community with respect to potential investors. Communities that are suffering from long-term economic decline and that are not very attractive for most investment will find that both passive approaches, like those in the promotional strategy, and aggressive regulatory approaches designed to direct private investment to appropriate channels may be inappropriate. Communities in this situation may need to pursue targeted inducement strategies and complex, cooperative strategies in order to have any impact at all on the community's economic future.

It is also important to acknowledge that combinations of strategies are possible and that there may be important interactive effects when more than one strategy is used. A promotion strategy might be used to good advantage hand in hand with an inducement strategy. For example, a community that has adopted an innovative set of financial inducements to encourage business investment will need a promotion strategy to advertise the availability of these inducements to appropriate prospects. Alternatively, a community that has chosen a promotional strategy geared toward heavy investment in basic infrastructure might explore the possibility of limiting its offering of tax abatements on grounds that the infrastructure spending should be expected to leverage some private investment.

Interesting combinations of land-use regulatory approaches and inducement approaches can also be envisioned. For example, tax abatements or low-cost loans might be coupled with a transferable development rights program in a way that targets substantial financial incentives toward development of a particular type in a particular location. The publicly provided inducements supplement the private market incentives for development that are created in the transferable development rights program, and the impact of both would presumably be strengthened. Alternatively, a community must intelligently consider the relationship between developer exactions and financial inducements for development. The former are typically meant to force developers to bear a suitable share of the infrastructure costs that new development brings. Financial inducements like tax abatements are intended to encourage new development, even if the price is a period of forgone tax revenues that might have contributed to the building of necessary new infrastructure like roads, sewage treatment capacity, and water lines. In general, simultaneously offering tax abatements and demanding exactions for the same types of development does not make sense—one hand gives financial inducements while the other takes away some or all the value of those inducements. On the other hand, communities might offer tax abatements to particularly desirable industries that would create minimal added infrastructure costs, such as firms with high-wage jobs that are capable of locating in an existing underused industrial park. Investors wishing to develop parcels in areas where new sewage lines would have to be run and where new road construction would be required might, on the other hand, be subject to developer agreements or exactions.

Pressures to realize gains from economic development are such that government decisionmakers can be tempted to deploy any and every development policy that other communities are using. However, contemporary trends emphasize a more contingent approach to development policy, stressing the fit between community context, local goals, and policy tools. Research on the limits of various development policies has also led to a reappraisal of the appropriateness of development policies. For example, the presumption that tax abatements and other financial inducements should be broadly used is being replaced with consideration of the circumstances under which financial inducements will generate net benefits for the community. Each of these developments may be viewed as part of a trend toward a more sophisticated, strategic approach to economic development planning at the local level.

DISCUSSION QUESTIONS

1. How are economic development planning and policymaking conducted in your community? Is there a special office in city government that handles this function? Who staffs it? How is it financed? Is the Chamber of Commerce or some other private organization involved in economic development activity? What is the range of its activities? If local government and one or more private organizations are simultaneously involved in economic development activity, what is the relationship, if any, between their efforts? Are there any arrangements for coordination, joint planning, and so on?

2. What financial inducements, if any, has your community used to attract or retain business and industry? Is there a general policy concerning the issuance of tax abatements and other financial inducements? Or does the city issue inducements completely on a case-by-case basis?

3. Imagine that you have been appointed to serve on a task force on economic development for your community. What economic development goals should you suggest for the community? What suggestions would you make about each of the broad categories of development strategies: promotion, inducement, cooperative arrangements with the private sector, and the use of regulatory policies for development purposes? Are there particular development policies within each of these categories that you would wish to emphasize? Deemphasize? Explain.

NOTES

1. Harold Wolman and Larry Ledebur, "Concepts of Public-Private Cooperation," in *Shaping the Local Economy,* ed. Cheryl Farr (Washington, DC: ICMA, 1984), pp. 26–27.
2. A write-up of most of the survey results can be found in ICMA's publication "Facilitating Economic Development" in *Baseline Data Report,* vol. 16 (November/December 1984).
3. Wolman and Ledebur, "Concepts of Public-Private Cooperation," p. 29.
4. Real Estate Research Corporation, "Urban Infill: Its Potential as a Development Strategy," in *Shaping the Local Economy,* ed. Farr (Washington, DC: ICMA, 1984), pp. 102–116.
5. Economic Development Marketing Program, Major Marketing Activities, March 1, 1986–September 22, 1987 (Lawrence, KS: Lawrence Chamber of Commerce, 1987), pp. 1–2.
6. *Overland Park, Kansas, Welcome Home* (Overland Park, KS: Chamber of Commerce), p. 10. Undated.
7. Wolman and Ledebur, "Concepts of Public-Private Cooperation," p. 29.
8. Todd Swanstrom, *The Crisis of Growth Politics* (Philadelphia: Temple University Press, 1985), p. 137.
9. National Association of State Development Agencies, *Directory of Incentives for Business Investment and Development in the United States,* 2nd ed. (Washington, DC: Urban Institute Press, 1986).
10. Paul Peretz, "The Market for Industry: Where Angels Fear to Tread?" *Policy Studies Review* 5 (February 1986): 629.
11. Paul Dommel, "Local Discretion: The CDBG Approach," in *Urban Economic Development,* ed. Richard Bingham and John Blair (Beverly Hills: Sage, 1984), pp. 101–114.
12. Bryan Jones and Lynn Bachelor, "Local Policy Discretion and the Corporate Surplus," in *Urban Economic Development,* ed. Bingham and Blair (Beverly Hills: Sage, 1984), p. 248.
13. Irene Rubin and Herbert Rubin, "Economic Development Incentives: The Poor (Cities) Pay More," *Urban Affairs Quarterly* 23 (September 1987): 37–62.
14. Richard Feiock and James Clingermayer, "Municipal Representation, Executive Power, and Economic Development Policy Activity," *Policy Studies Journal* 15 (December 1986): 218–224.
15. Peretz, "Market for Industry," p. 624.
16. Michael Wasylenko, "The Location of Firms: The Role of Taxes and Fiscal Incentives," in *Urban Government Finance,* ed. Roy Bahl (Beverly Hills: Sage, 1981), p. 186.
17. Ibid.
18. Peter Fisher "Corporate Tax Incentives: The American Version of Industrial Policy," *Journal of Economic Issues* 19 (March 1985): 15.
19. John P. Blair and Barton Wechsler, "A Tale of Two Cities: A Case Study of Urban Competition for Jobs," in *Urban Economic Development,* ed. Bingham and Blair (Beverly Hills: Sage, 1984), pp. 274–275.
20. Patrick Houston, "When a City's Deal to Save Jobs Sours," *New York Times,* June 24, 1988, pp. 25, 27.

21. Wolman and Ledebur, "Concepts of Public-Private Cooperation," pp. 29–30.
22. Jones and Bachelor, "Local Policy Discretion," p. 247.
23. Wolman and Ledebur, "Concepts of Public-Private Cooperation," pp. 31–32.
24. Bryan Jones and Lynn Bachelor, *The Sustaining Hand* (Lawrence: University Press of Kansas, 1986), pp. 191–192.
25. Robert Stoker, "Baltimore: The Self-Evaluating City," in *The Politics of Urban Development*, ed. Clarence Stone and Heywood Sanders (Lawrence: University Press of Kansas, 1987), pp. 253–258.
26. Craig R. Humphrey, Rodney A. Erickson, and Edward J. Ottensmeyer, "Industrial Development Groups, Organizational Resources, and the Prospects for Effecting Growth in Local Economies," *Growth and Change* 19 (Summer 1988): 11.
27. Stoker, "Baltimore," p. 252.
28. Wolman and Ledebur, "Concepts of Public-Private Cooperation," p. 31.
29. John M. Levy, *Contemporary Urban Planning* (Englewood Cliffs, NJ: Prentice Hall, 1988), p. 102.
30. Ibid., p. 103.
31. William E. Schmidt, "Chicago Plan Seeks to Prevent Loss of Factories," *New York Times*, December 10, 1987, p. 1.
32. Bruce McClendon, "Reforming Zoning Regulations to Encourage Economic Development," in *Shaping the Local Economy*, ed. Farr (Washington, DC: ICMA, 1984), p. 146.
33. Levy, *Contemporary Urban Planning*, p. 115.
34. William Fischel, *The Economics of Zoning Laws* (Baltimore: Johns Hopkins University Press, 1985), p. 45.
35. Levy, *Contemporary Urban Planning*, pp. 115–116.
36. Ibid., p. 119.
37. William E. Schmidt, "Chicago Plan Seeks to Prevent Loss of Factories," op. cit., p. 1.
38. Levy, *Contemporary Urban Planning*, p. 119.
39. John Kirlin and Anne Kirlin, "Public/Private Bargaining in Local Development," in *The Entrepreneur in Local Government*, ed. Barbara Moore (Washington, DC: ICMA, 1983), p. 156.
40. Susan Clarke, "More Autonomous Policy Orientations: An Analytic Framework," in *The Politics of Urban Development*, ed. Clarence Stone and Heywood Sanders (Lawrence: University Press of Kansas, 1987), pp. 105–124.
41. Stuart Taylor, Jr., "High Court Backs Rights of Owners in Land-Use Suits," *New York Times*, June 10, 1987, pp. 1, 17. The case is *First English Evangelical Lutheran Church of Glendale* v. *County of Los Angeles*, 85–1199.
42. Levy, *Contemporary Urban Planning*, pp. 77–85.

CHAPTER 11

The Politics of Economic Development

The preceding chapter discussed a number of public policy tools that government managers use to pursue economic development goals. Effectiveness considerations are a major concern in that discussion, but it is important to acknowledge that the choice of economic policies and programs is not an objective, politically neutral, goal-directed process. Rather, the initiation, choice, and implementation of economic development policies and programs is affected by various interested parties and takes place in a context of power relationships. In short, economic development is a political process, not simply a policy analytic process.

Describing the nature of economic development politics is hampered by an important difficulty: There is no consensus on the matter. In fact, the political aspects of economic development are the subject of some of the most interesting and pointed debates in all of urban analysis. The power of these debates stems from the fact that the task of characterizing economic development politics is more than a straightforward, descriptive one. Instead, important theoretical and normative issues are involved.

This chapter is organized around a pair of questions that encompass many of the issues, themes, and controversies of economic development politics. The first question seems deceptively simple: Are the politics of economic development unique? That is, does economic development policy involve a sphere of politics that is different from the politics of other policy domains? The first section of this chapter gives the argument of those who respond affirmatively to this question, the implications of the argument, and the objections to it that can be raised.

The second organizing question for this chapter is: How much variability is there in economic development politics? Here, there is a substantial debate.

The debate is not over whether economic competition is a major constraint on the making of development policy—clearly it is. The debate is over whether the economic imperative is a single, overriding imperative, or whether there are multiple "imperatives" that public officials must balance.[1]

For example, are private economic interests necessarily dominant, or can local governments maintain autonomy from those economic powers? If there is variability, under what conditions do different types of arrangements emerge? As we will see, the two organizing questions for this chapter are interrelated. Depictions of a unique sphere of economic development politics include the premise that economic notables are invariably dominant in that sphere. Challengers to this deterministic point of view suggest that the politics of economic development is affected by various local contexts with various interest groupings and various governing coalitions. The result, these challengers argue, is that economic development politics are different in different communities and many of the alleged features of economic development politics are not universally applicable.

ECONOMIC DEVELOPMENT: A UNIQUE POLICY DOMAIN?

A number of urban analysts argue that economic development is not only one of several key functions of local government but also a special policymaking sphere with its own special blend of political characteristics. Paul Peterson, for example, divides local policymaking into three spheres:

1. An "allocational policy" sphere involving distributional, basic housekeeping functions like snowplowing and garbage collection.
2. A "redistributional policy" sphere involving programs targeted to benefit disadvantaged citizens.
3. A "developmental policy" sphere involving efforts to enhance the competitive economic position of the community relative to other communities.[2]

The third sphere incorporates essentially the same activities that we have so far referred to as economic development programs or policies.

Peterson goes on to argue that local politics is distinctively different for each policy domain. The differences have to do with openness, level of conflict, and elite domination in the three spheres. The politics of allocation, according to Peterson, can be characterized as open-ended, conflictual, and pluralistic:

> There is no end to the politics of allocation. It is a continuing, thriving, potentially explosive political arena that . . . often subjects decisionmakers to intense political heat. . . . The widely held view that local politics is an arena of bargaining, compromise, cross-cutting cleavages, and changing political issues is not incorrect. On the contrary, such a view depicts and characterizes the most visible aspects of local political relationships.[3]

In short, the allocational sphere is said to have many of the hallmarks of local democracy in action: widespread citizen involvement, a variety of issues being heatedly debated, mechanisms of popular accountability, and a system of counterbalancing interests that prevents any one interest from systematically dominating others.

By contrast, Peterson argues that the redistributional sphere is severely atrophied and borders on irrelevant at the local level.

> Because redistributive policies are usually at odds with the economic interests of the city, proponents will find difficulty in gathering support for them. Since the policies are manifestly unrealistic economically, even those groups which themselves would in the short run benefit from redistribution lend little support to such proposals.[4]

The result is the absence of a meaningful politics of redistribution, except in the most sporadic sense. Redistributional issues rarely are raised, and when raised they are easily diverted from the agenda. The accuracy of this characterization has been taken up in Chapter 6 in the context of equity questions at the local level.

Given the purposes of this chapter, the most important contrast Peterson draws is between the allegedly pluralistic politics of allocation and the politics of developmental policy, which he claims to be more closed, elite-dominated, and nonconflictual:

> [Developmental policies] . . . are often promulgated through highly centralized decision-making processes involving prestigious businessmen and professionals. Conflict within the city tends to be minimal, decision-making processes tend to be closed until the project is about to be consummated, local support is broad and continuous, and, if any group objects, that group is unlikely to gain much support.[5]

According to Peterson, then, decisionmaking about allocational policies involves a style of politics that fits the pluralist model of community power quite nicely, whereas developmental policies are formulated in a way that better fits elitist theories of community politics. Similar arguments are offered by Thomas Dye, who describes allocational politics in the following way:

> Community power structures are seldom directly interested or active in allocational policy. The allocational policy arena is pluralist in character . . . [public

officials] are responsive to the expressed demands of many varied and often competing groups within the community. Participation in decision-making is open. . . . Interest and activity rather than economic resources are the key to leadership in allocational policy.[6]

By contrast, Dye argues that the community power structure, including "the mortgage lending banks, real estate developers and builders, and landowners" are very much involved and dominant in developmental policies. Power structure theorists who focus on developmental policies and use reputational methods are not inappropriately skewing their results, according to Dye, because "Reputations for power correlate with the 'reality' of power when the issues specified are developmental issues."[7]

Table 11.1 summarizes the model of local politics that is suggested by the work of Peterson and Dye. For our purposes, we refer to it as the "bifurcated politics" model because it draws such sharp contrasts between the allocational and developmental domains of local politics.

The bifurcated politics model is appealing in many ways. It helps to clarify the long-standing question of "who rules?" in American communities. According to the bifurcated politics model, an appropriate counter question to "who rules?" is "who rules what?" in American politics. The question cannot be adequately answered without stipulating which domain for the exercise of power is at issue.

TABLE 11.1. THE BIFURCATED POLITICS MODEL

	Allocational Politics	**Developmental Politics**
Illustrative Issues	Fairness of Existing Police Patrol Allocation	Revitalizing the Central Business District
	Adequacy of Snow Removal	Creation of an Industrial Park
	Allegations of Improper City Hiring Practices	Public-Private Alliance to Attract New Business
	Proposal to Contract Out for Trash Collection	Subsidies to Attract New Business
		Construction of New Harbor Facilities
Typical Participants	Neighborhood Organizations	Banks
	Public Sector Bureaucracies	Developers
	City Council Members	Downtown Business
	Mayors	Corporate Leaders
Visibility of Decisionmaking	High	Low
Involvement by Economic Elites	Low	High
Level of Controversy	High	Low
Overall Pattern of Power	Pluralistic	Elitist

The bifurcated politics model is also consistent with many observable differences in local decisionmaking. The model's characterization of developmental decisionmaking as quieter, less visible, and more dominated by economic interests is consistent with observations that many development projects are handled by quasi-public corporations. As explained in Chapter 10, these entities are governed by boards of directors that include important corporate interests, and they are not subject to the same accountability requirements that place traditional government decisionmaking in a fishbowl.

Different financing and spending arrangements tend to prevail in the allocational and developmental spheres. These differences suggest some reasons why developmental politics may be quieter, more consensual, and less subject to the hurly-burly of public debate than allocational politics. The distributional services of the allocational sphere are typically financed with tax revenues, supplemented perhaps by user fees and a few other minor sources of revenue, and expenditures for such services are part of the regular budgetary process. For this reason, the many popular accountability controls and requirements that are part of mainstream, public sector budgeting come into play with full force for allocational decisionmaking. Even the construction of physical facilities that support allocational services, like fire stations, solid waste incineration facilities, and police stations, is most typically financed with tax-supported general obligation bonds. When an expansion or improvement in one of the basic services of the allocational realm is at issue, therefore, tax consequences are quite often at issue, too. This typically brings on the full range of required hearings, public debate, and politically charged position taking by elected officials.

By contrast, many economic development projects involve financial arrangements on the "quiet side" of public finance.[8] These include financing strategies such as revenue bonds, which are freer from public accountability controls (see Chapter 7), and state or federal grants or loans. On the spending side, economic development frequently involves invisible sorts of commitments, like loan guarantees, tax abatements, and land cost write-downs. For these reasons, the actual scope of what local government is doing in economic development may be much less obvious, much less subject to voter scrutiny, and consequently much less controversial than what local government does with respect to police services or snow removal.

There are other reasons to agree with the claim of the bifurcated politics model that developmental politics is much more consensual than the conflictual politics of allocation. For one thing, there is a powerful ideology encompassing ideas of growth, investment, and well-being that supports action in the developmental sphere. This ideology may effectively serve to maintain consensus and prevent threats and challenges. Molotch, for example, describes the pervasiveness of the local growth ideology:

> Government funds support "boosterism" of various sorts . . . city-sponsored parade floats, and stadia and other forms of support for professional sports

teams carrying the locality name. The athletic teams in particular are an extraordinary mechanism for instilling a spirit of civic jingoism regarding the "progress" of the locality. . . . This enthusiasm can be drawn upon, with a glossy claim of creating a "greater Cleveland," "greater Baltimore," etc., in order to gain general acceptance for local growth-oriented programs. Similarly, public school curricula . . . help build an ideological base for local boosterism and the acceptance of growth.[9]

A number of commentators have argued that the politics of development is comparatively noncontroversial for another reason as well: It is all too easy for interested parties to divert public attention from development activities by whipping up needless controversy over allocational policies. For example, Logan and Molotch describe how the local media can seize on crime as an issue because it is easy and sensational news and how local politicians feed the issue because it gives them opportunities for symbolic crusades. Moreover, attention to something like crime allows politicians to avoid issues that might be sensitive for the powers-that-be in the developmental sphere. As a result, a series of hubbubs over crime, snowplowing, city hall hiring practices, and any number of other allocational matters keep public attention diverted from the plans, policies, and programs being pursued in the developmental sphere.[10] In short, the development sphere may be more quiet and consensual than the allocational sphere because the strategic activities of some political participants make it so.

Furthermore, when attention is drawn to economic development, it is often in a congratulatory or credit-taking mode, rather than a controversial one. The nature of the economic development enterprise facilitates this.

> Such projects have one supreme advantage over most other public decisions: by definition they produce something new. Adding to the budget of the police department may be a useful thing to do, but it is less likely to be seen as innovative. By contrast, a major downtown mall or convention center can be advertised as taking the city into the new metropolitan age.[11]

This is not to say that the accomplishment of economic development projects and goals is necessarily easy. However, positive attention can be drawn to projects and credit can be claimed for them, even at initial planning stages. This practice has been called "the politics of announcement."[12]

LIMITATIONS OF THE BIFURCATED POLITICS MODEL

Many observers of urban affairs will be somewhat puzzled by the bifurcated politics model, however. Its claim that the developmental sphere is more consensual than conflictual is particularly likely to raise eyebrows. After all, much of what we know about the politics of economic development is based on case studies *of development controversies.*

For example, in their case study of economic development politics in Detroit, Jones and Bachelor document the controversy surrounding the redevelopment of the Poletown neighborhood as a site for a new General Motors auto assembly facility.[13] In this case, the Poletown Neighborhood Council was unable to prevail. But in the process of trying, the group engaged in street demonstrations, made use of a variety of avenues for redress through the courts, were visible at public meetings and hearings, lobbied local, state, and federal officials involved with the project, and got a great deal of media exposure. Despite the ultimate failure of the citizens' group to overcome General Motors and city officials sympathetic to GM, this is surely an instance of economic development being conflictual.

In Kalamazoo, Michigan, citizen opposition stymied important development initiatives in the 1960s. Sanders documents the controversy that surrounded downtown redevelopment plans in Kalamazoo and argues that citizen concerns about debt and taxes, coupled with the existence of strong mechanisms for popular review of development proposals, led to the failure of those development initiatives:

> [T]he reality in Kalamazoo has been a history of initiatives blocked, failed policy entrepreneurship, and a public reaction against the cost of specific public policies. Those failures came despite the attempt to link downtown revival and capital improvements to the symbols of community economic growth and job gain, as well as to a persistent rhetoric of city-wide necessity and advantage.[14]

Yet another case example of a development project that created controversy and became bogged down in local conflicts is the Chicago North Loop Redevelopment project.[15] This project initially involved a plan to clear a substantial tract of land just north of the downtown loop. In place of some of the older retail uses in the area, the project would have created a series of newer retail establishments, a site for a new central library, and a convention hotel. However, by 1979 preservationist groups began objecting to the scale of demolition that the plan involved, partly because several architecturally important old theatres were in the area. Then, approval of the part of the project's financing package that involved tax abatement got caught in a political tug of war between two factions of the Democratic party. In addition, neighborhood groups began to exert opposition on the grounds that the tax abatement was too big a subsidy to Hilton Hotels, Inc., compared to the attention neighborhood problems get. As a result of these and other difficulties, the project has been modified a number of times and has dragged on for fifteen years without being completed.

These and other case studies of conflict and controversy over development projects suggest that the realm of economic development politics is not necessarily quiet and consensual. More generally, the characterization of economic development politics that the bifurcated model gives us (see Table 11.1) clashes with a number of analyses of conflicting interests concerning economic development. Description of these conflicting interests, along with evidence that the conflicts can embroil the community in development controversies, are at odds with a portrait of economic development as an insulated, noncontroversial realm of politics.

What are the lines of political conflict over economic development? The case examples just discussed give some clues to answers to this question. But is there some more general way of categorizing the ways groups and interests are aligned with respect to economic development? Logan and Molotch provide one that differentiates those groups and institutions with an interest in the "exchange value" of property and those groups and institutions with an interest in the "use value" of property:

> For some, places represent residence or production site; for others, places represent a commodity for buying, selling, or renting to somebody else. The sharpest contrast . . . is between residents, who use place to satisfy essential needs of life, and entrepreneurs, who strive for financial return, ordinarily achieved by intensifying the use to which their property is put.[16]

A consideration of some specific groups and institutions should help to clarify this important observation. First, consider the typical homeowner. Other things being equal, homeowners presumably prefer to have the value of their property increase rather than decline over time. The Proposition 13 property tax revolt in California suggests, however, that rapid increases in housing value, coupled with reassessment methods that quickly translate into higher property taxes, imposed harsh costs on homeowners. This was particularly true of the homeowner with no plans to sell and, hence, no way of cashing in on the increased value of the house. Furthermore, the growth dynamic that makes houses in the community increase in value brings with it important costs *from the perspective of the homeowner as a current user of the property.* Growth means increased congestion, traffic, noise, pollution, school crowding, and so forth.

Understandably, the typical homeowner is not only uninterested in the intensification of land use but is often actively hostile to such intensification. For example, owners of single-family homes frequently resist proposals to rezone adjacent properties for apartment construction or commercial uses such as offices or stores. Such uses are perceived as creating noxious side effects that interfere with homeowners' ability to enjoy their property (i.e., use value).

Some residential groupings, particularly in poorer neighborhoods, have even more dramatic reasons for opposing the intensification of land use in the community. Growth and redevelopment of properties can mean that some of these residents totally lose use value through forced relocation, either because of condemnation of their property to make way for new infrastructure or urban renewal, or because they are priced out of the market as the area "gentrifies."[17]

By contrast, consider the interests of developers, speculative landowners, and banks with property investments. Each of these groups is a key part of the local "growth machine."[18] Each has an important financial stake in having property in specific locations be more "built-up." Each then realizes financial gain when the property is sold or rented. The encroachment of their development activities on areas often brings use and exchange values into conflict.

A number of other groups and institutions have more indirect stakes in growth and intensification of property uses. These include politicians, some of whom will make careers based on civic boosterism and credit claiming about community growth. Also included are the local newspapers, which benefit from increased circulation and advertising, and utilities like power and water companies, which have a stake in increasing the number of utility users. Organized labor is also typically supportive of growth goals, largely because of the jobs that growth is expected to bring.[19]

So far, we have seen that residential groupings frequently resist growth and development initiatives when those initiatives bring exchange values into conflict with residential use values. Neighborhood and community organizations like the Poletown Neighborhood Council described earlier, often emerge to champion residential use values in such conflicts. By contrast, there are a variety of groups and institutions that have direct or indirect stakes in community growth and exchange values, and consequently they are aligned in support of development initiatives. There is yet another sort of group or institution with mixed stakes in the conflict between use values and exchange values. For these groups, reactions to development depend on the specific form and location that it takes. For example, smaller retailers and professionals such as dentists and doctors may worry that redevelopment projects will displace the groups of patrons and clients that they have built up over the years. On the other hand, growth of other kinds might mean a net increase in sales and clients for them.[20] Some business establishments benefit more directly from increased population and traffic than do others. For example, "on reaching a certain size, markets become more attractive to higher-volume, national retailers, such as McDonald's or chain department stores and the malls that house them."[21] Consequently, many small entrepreneurs will have mixed reactions to growth, despite the ideology of civic boosterism to which they are attracted.

In short, the politics of development includes a wide variety of interests and groups, some solidly aligned behind growth goals, some characteristically opposed to growth in the form of intensified land uses, and some with mixed stakes. Given these many and conflicting interests, it is not surprising that economic development projects and proposals regularly erupt into full-scale controversies. Whether conflict and controversy are as frequent and visible as conflicts involving allocational policies is difficult to judge precisely. The level and extent of conflict over developmental projects is far from trivial, however. This fact is inconsistent with the general theme of the bifurcated politics model.

The bifurcated politics model also contains a normative perspective that should be evaluated. So far, we have considered whether that model is an accurate rendition of what allocational and developmental politics are actually like. But the model is also in part an implied standard of what should be.

In his contributions to the bifurcated politics model, for example, Peterson claims that development policies are in the best interests of the community as a whole. Unlike allocational services, which can in principle distribute benefits to some groups more than others, developmental projects, Peterson claims, constitute a "unitary interest" of cities. From this perspective, objections to development, like those of promoters of residential use value, are a matter of narrow, special interests. Citizens who attack tax abatements or other development policies that could bring new business to the community are ignoring the big picture of what the community needs to remain economically competitive. Furthermore, placing development decisionmaking in the hands of a more centralized and politically insulated business elite is an appropriate approach, not the least because it protects important development projects from the whims of popular sentiment and the vagaries of normal politics.

Critics have been quick to attack this normative face of the bifurcated politics model on several grounds. One line of attack focuses on the presumption that activities conducted in the name of economic development will necessarily contribute to the well-being of the community as a whole. Stone argues that this "seems to assume the very point that is at issue."[22]

Furthermore, although economic development is easily portrayed as a community imperative and a unitary benefit for the city, many programs sold under the label of economic development actually fail to generate benefits for the community. For example, local economic initiatives may lead to business location or expansion in the community, but the jobs that are supposed to result may not be forthcoming for community residents because local governments cannot prevent the leakage of jobs outside the jurisdiction:

[F]irms will employ residents of any locality, and may often recruit highly skilled employees from entirely different regions or low-wage employees from different countries. Some types of economic development are even predicated on the assumption that regeneration will displace low-income residents and replace them by commuting labor and new, high-income residents.[23]

As we saw in Chapter 10, this is only one of a number of limitations or ineffectiveness problems that plague various policy tools for economic development. Given the weaknesses of many tools for economic development, the riskiness of many strategies, and the possibilities that the public sector will find itself taken advantage of in a desperate competition to gain private sector investment, many observers are not inclined to agree that developmental policies are necessarily in the unitary interest of the city.

Another line of attack argues that even if an economic development project or policy is successful from the perspective of some individuals in the community, the benefits it creates are unevenly distributed. Economic development projects or policies also carry costs, also unevenly distributed, that are all too often downplayed. Furthermore, although some of these costs can be viewed as sacrifices that a few must bear for the greater good of the community, there is also evidence of costs to the community as a whole. In an analysis of Houston, for example, Feagin finds that economic growth has a substantial downside. Industrial growth and associated rapid population growth created a substantial toxic waste disposal problem, sewage and garbage disposal challenges, flooding in some areas of the city, and subsidence, or the sinking of properties in other areas resulting from increased pumping of water. Air pollution and traffic are also substantial and growing problems. Finally: "Market-dominated growth has destroyed one major black community in the central city area, and is about to destroy another."[24]

STYLES OF ECONOMIC DEVELOPMENT POLITICS

So far, we have seen that the bifurcated politics model emphasizes the consensual, business elite–dominated, noncontroversial aspects of the politics of development. However, a look at the conflicting interests that are at stake in economic development decisionmaking, coupled with case study evidence of actual economic development controversies, suggests that this characterization may be exaggerated. It is more likely that the politics of economic development takes different forms, depending on a variety of local circumstances. In some settings, the politics of development may indeed fit the characterizations of the bifurcated politics model. But not always.

For example, in some cities economic development decisionmaking is insulated from normal politics by having private or quasi-private organizations handle economic development activities, a pattern consistent with the bifurcated politics model. But in many cities, economic development policymaking is primarily handled by city government itself, rather than being siphoned off to less accountable private or semiprivate organizations. Some evidence of this can be gleaned from a survey of cities conducted by the International City Management Association (ICMA) in 1984.[25] As Table 11.2 shows, economic development activities are primarily handled by a private sector organization such as the Chamber of Commerce in nearly one-third of these cities and by a quasi-private development corporation in another 15 percent. However, in more than half of the cities, city government is the most active in promoting economic development.

Similarly, in some communities, economic development decisionmaking is more visible and involves more popular participation than it does in other communities. All city leaders responding to the ICMA survey were asked if the community had a formal economic development plan and, if so, which groups

TABLE 11.2. WHO IS INVOLVED IN ECONOMIC DEVELOPMENT?

Most Active Group or Institution in Fostering Economic Activity		Citizen Input Methods Used in Economic Development Planning	
City Government	55%	Citizen Surveys	30%
Private Business Group	30	Appointed Advisory Committees	56
Local Development Corporation	15	Open Meetings/Public Hearings	51
Tol...	100		

Source: National Sample Survey on Economic Development (Washington, DC: International City Management Association, 1984).

were involved and which methods were used in the planning process. Many ₊he cities that had economic development plans used various methods for popular involvement in the planning process (see Table 11.2). For example, 30 percent had used citizen surveys to find out about the public's preferences on development issues, more than half (56 percent) had used appointed advisory committees representing the entire community, and about half (51 percent) had used open meetings or public hearings as part of the planning process.

In many cases, the use of particular methods for popular involvement is mandatory and cannot be taken to reveal the orientation of the local regime. For example, many state and federal grant programs require public hearings or other methods for getting local public input; communities using such funding sources for economic development projects are forced to open their decision-making to public input. Similarly, many states require public hearings and similar accountability devices before communities can issue some of the bonds used for redevelopment purposes (see Chapter 7). It is also important to note that the methods of popular involvement reported in the ICMA survey have to do with development planning. Whether citizen involvement is that widespread in the implementation of development projects is an open question. For all these reasons, there is no guarantee that the use of various devices for popular involvement makes economic development decisionmaking a model of popular democracy. However, cities using such methods for broad public involvement presumably exhibit a different style of development politics than cities that do not. There is at least the potential in these communities for a more pluralistic, high-visibility, and popularistic mode of economic development decisionmaking.

If the *process* of economic development decisionmaking varies from one community to another, is it also possible that the *policy orientation* or bias of development decisions differs across communities? Stated another way, is it always the case that the politics of development is dominated by the interests and preferences of economic elites, or are there contexts in which other interests dominate?

A number of authors give us reason to believe that there are contexts in which other interests dominate. Swanstrom, for example, describes the emergence of urban populist regimes in a number of cities. Urban populist regimes are characterized by mayors who seek to focus attention on differences between the haves and the have-nots in the community and to steer policy in directions that benefit the have-nots. Rather than assuming that economic development is beneficial to the community as a whole, urban populist regimes are mobilized around the problems of uneven benefits from economic development. A key theme in these regimes is "spreading the wealth of downtown to the neighborhoods."[26]

According to Swanstrom, Cleveland during the mayoralty of Dennis Kucinich (1977 to 1979) was a prototypical example of an urban populist regime. It drew its political strength from lower-middle and lower-income ethnic residents and neighborhood activists whose needs were not being served by the development of gleaming office towers and condominiums in Cleveland.

> Kucinich's urban populist program turned growth politics inside out: instead of spending public money on attracting wealthy investors and residents, government would concentrate on basic benefits and services for the neighborhoods. Constituencies that might be divided on social, ethnic, or racial issues could be united, Kucinich argued, on economic reforms.[27]

Similarly, Clarke argues that some cities, under some circumstances, have economic development policy orientations that exhibit autonomy from the alleged dominance of business and economic elites. The agenda of these communities includes a call for "the more equitable allocation and distribution of the risks and costs of investment, as well as more equitable distribution of benefits."[28] An example is Chicago under the administration of Harold Washington. In this regime, special conditions were placed on potential developers of downtown sites to ensure that needs for low-income housing would receive attention as a byproduct of the developers' desires to cash in on profitable downtown development efforts.

One of the most interesting cases of urban populism in recent times is Santa Monica, California, after the emergence of the Santa Monicans for Renters Rights (SMRR) as a governing coalition in 1981.[29] Originally mobilized in reaction to sharply rising rents, condominium conversions, and similar aspects of a heated real estate market, SMRR activists attracted national attention for the tough rent-control ordinance that they were instrumental in getting adopted. Once in control of the city council, however, SMRR activists promoted a variety of other populist policies as well, including some that have an important bearing on the city's style of economic development politics. These included public improvements to keep the Santa Monica pier as a model of human-scale use rather than high-rise, luxury development, and an aggressive program of affordable housing policies. As part of the latter policy emphasis, Santa Monica began to demand that developers of commercial, industrial, or apartment projects also provide low-cost housing either at the site of their proposed project or at an adjacent site. In addition, the SMRR regime was responsible for expanding social services in the community, in contrast to the reductions in social services that other California communities were experiencing in the wake of the tax revolt. Finally, the SMRR leaders had a strong commitment to principles of participatory democracy—a commitment that resulted in the creation of a staggering array of citizen task forces and commissions and a very politicized, vocal style of politics.

In contrast with these examples of populist approaches to economic development, there are many examples of cities that *are* dominated by the interests of business elites with respect to economic development and that have the other features described in the bifurcated politics model of economic development. For example, Dallas in the period from the Depression to the mid-1970s has been characterized as a "pure entrepreneurial" political economy.

> The links between public officials and business leaders were extensive and well developed. . . . The extensiveness of the links is suggested by the fact that for a substantial portion of the period of the pure entrepreneurial economy, leading business figures were also the principal elected officials. . . . More important, public officials, both elected and appointed, had views in common with leading businessmen.[30]

As a result of this close linkage, economic development in Dallas during this period was vigorously pursued in ways that fit the interests of business elites and in ways that insulated development decisionmaking from public accountability and from any competing interests. The city manager system of government was institutionalized as part of this regime, a fiscally conservative stance was emphasized, and a commitment to growth through annexation and the maintenance of a good business climate was sustained.[31]

Baltimore, Maryland, is also an excellent example of a city with an economic development sphere that is dominated by the business elite.[32] Baltimore relies on a host of quasi-public corporations for the formulation and implementation of economic development projects. These corporations, like Charles Center/Inner Harbor Management, Incorporated and the Baltimore Economic Development Corporation, along with the trustees who control the city's loan fund for city development initiatives, constitute a shadow government that has considerable impact on the economic development ventures that the city undertakes. Economic elites and business interests are well represented in this shadow government, and public scrutiny and the politicization of development issues are minimized.

In addition to cities that have a style of development politics dominated by the business elite and cities that have a more populist style, there are also cities in which conflict between these two alternative styles has not yet been resolved. Hartford, Connecticut, is an example of such a situation.[33] In Hartford the politics of development has historically been dominated by the coalition of interests that is familiar from earlier descriptions of entrepreneurial communities dominated by the business elite. In Hartford, the Chamber of Commerce, corporate leaders (especially from the insurance industry), and real estate investors have long been key players in economic development in collaboration with city government. These actors constitute a downtown-oriented growth coalition that has been instrumental in generating a downtown development boom.

However, Hartford's downtown boom has primarily benefited the finance, insurance, and real estate sectors of the community, along with those relatively affluent individuals who work in or are associated with those sectors. As a result, challenges to the prevailing development orientation have been raised by low-income residents and the neighborhood organizations that represent them. These challenges have been powerful enough to yield some movement in the populist direction. A new policy shifted the property tax burden more heavily toward commercial property, at least for a limited time. As in Cleveland under Kucinich, critics of development as usual were able to block further tax abatements for downtown office development on the grounds that they constituted tax breaks for the rich and were unnecessary subsidies. Finally, neighborhood groups forced the city to at least consider a linkage policy, such as those in Chicago, Boston, and elsewhere, that would exact financial commitments for nonluxury housing and other programs of benefit to low-income groups in exchange for rights to develop in profitable areas like the downtown.

However, these challenges to the preexisting system of development politics dominated by the business elite are not yet fully institutionalized, and the outcome of the push for a more populist approach is still in doubt. Furthermore, there is substantial conflict, as mobilized neighborhood organizations continue to make demands for a change in direction. Hartford, in short, might be described as having a "challenged elite" style of economic development politics, which is much more conflictual than the characterization offered in the model of bifurcated politics.

Whelan's description of New Orleans suggests that in that city, too, economic development politics has settled into neither a business-elite mode nor a purely populist mode.[34] The city has, instead, some of the elements of each style coexisting somewhat uneasily. Although business interests are important, neither the downtown business community nor land-use interests generally have been as dominant as they are in other cities. During the 1970s mayoralty of "Moon" Landrieu, for example, downtown redevelopment projects and development projects relating to the tourism industry were launched with the usual range of incentives and public-private partnerships. Simultaneously, however, the Landrieu administration improved city services in residential neighborhoods and in other ways catered to white homeowner groups. It also emphasized the incorporation of blacks into city government.

Briefly, the politics of development appears to come in at least three different styles: (1) a style dominated by the business elite, and approximating the description in the bifurcated politics model; (2) a populist style in which features typically ascribed to the politics of allocation are also characteristic of the economic development realm; and (3) a mixed style in which elements of each of the pure styles coexist but in an unsettled fashion.

Under what circumstances does one rather than another style take hold? Are there situational factors or community characteristics that influence whether the city will have the elite-dominant style, the populist style, or the challenged-elite style? The following section suggests five situational factors or community characteristics that may be expected to affect the character of economic development politics:

1. Economic trends that create visibly unequal economic circumstances for different subgroups of the population.
2. Use of public policies that accentuate the extent of business subsidies.
3. The existence and strength of reform institutions.
4. Quality and unity of leadership among business elites.
5. Degree of mobilization of neighborhood organizations, trade unions, and local environmental organizations.

Table 11.3 summarizes the arguments concerning the relationship between each situational factor or characteristic and the style of economic development politics.

TABLE 11.3. FACTORS AFFECTING COMMUNITY STYLE OF ECONOMIC DEVELOPMENT POLITICS

	Expected Style of Economic Development Politics	
	Economic Elite-Dominant	*Populist, or Challenged Elite*
When the community has:		
Visibly unequal economic circumstances	x ---------->	x
Public policies visibly subsidizing business	x ---------->	x
Strong reform institutions	x	
Strong, unified leadership of economic elites	x	
Weak or nonexistent neighborhood organizations, trade unions and environmental organizations	x	

SOURCES OF A CITY'S STYLE
OF ECONOMIC DEVELOPMENT POLITICS

First, populism, or at least the challenged-elite situation, may be more likely to emerge whenever unequal outcomes of economic development are particularly visible. For example, "juxtaposition of lavish corporate growth in downtown Hartford and economic deprivation in the city's neighborhoods has been the central factor" in the emergence of challenges to the elite-dominated system there.[35] Cleveland, too, is a community in which the prosperity of the revitalizing downtown in the latter 1970s offered a striking contrast to the economic stagnation that many blue-collar residents in the neighborhoods continue to face. The juxtaposition of growth and decline is particularly likely to occur in cities that are attempting to transform themselves from historic roles as industrial centers to newer, postindustrial service roles. In such situations, "there is a mismatch between the types of jobs that are being located in the city and the job qualifications of city residents."[36] Resident populations are, in these circumstances, left on the sidelines while outsiders either commute in to take advantage of the new, white-collar jobs or price residents out of the housing markets in neighborhoods that they gentrify.

If populist politics are an outgrowth of visibly uneven consequences of development, then by logical extension populist styles or challenged-elite situations are more likely to emerge when economic development policies visibly redistribute resources to already advantaged groups and interests. For example, resentment of tax abatements for already profitable investments like downtown office construction was a key element in Dennis Kucinich's rise to power in Cleveland.

However, tax abatements and other subsidies of business interests are not always visible. In many communities, substantial commitments of the community's financial resources can be made without creating populist mobilizations because the rules governing popular oversight of development decisions differ from place to place. In places where state law or local policy requires voter approval of bond issues even for redevelopment purposes, public hearings for development planning, and formal, city council approval of tax abatements on a case-by-case basis, it is much more likely that development decisions will be politicized. In places where those devices for popular accountability are not required and where there is enabling legislation that encourages the creation of politically insulated, quasi-public entities to handle economic development projects, politicization of development decisions and the emergence of populist reactions is less likely.

Similarly, the form of city government may have an important bearing on the form that economic development politics will take. In particular, the city manager form of government is said to be consistent with an elite-dominant mode of development politics.[37] Elkins' analysis of the entrepreneurial, business-dominant regime in Dallas emphasizes the importance of the city-manager plan in such a regime.

> From the beginning, leading local business figures viewed the city-manager system as a form of government that would best suit their concerns. Local business leaders were willing to see that some sustained effort was made to recruit candidates for office who would be committed to the perpetuation of a local government that was efficient, professional, and administered by experts.[38]

Because it emphasizes professionalism and expertise more than political linkages between government and citizenry, the city-manager form of government lends itself nicely to the economic development approach that the bifurcated politics model describes. Economic development decisions and projects are more insulated from both public scrutiny and from patronage demands. An emphasis on efficiency and fiscal constraint rather than political responsiveness also links the city-manager form with the growth interests of business elites.

The quality of economic leadership in the community is also important in shaping the character of economic development politics. An elite-dominant form of politics, like that described in the bifurcated politics model, is much more likely to emerge if economic notables in the community recognize common interests and have the talent and willingness to take on leadership roles in economic development. These preconditions are not always present.

> As with other groups, growth elites can be ridden with internal dissension, weighted down by incompetent leaders, or afflicted with diversionary agendas. . . . A long history of economic prosperity can mean that a given area has in place a well-worked-out system of intraelite communication. . . . In other instances, a conservative patrician past may hinder development, as old families with social pedigrees suffocate dynamic growth initiatives.[39]

Elite-dominant styles of economic development are also constrained in settings where certain political interests are especially strong. In particular, and under some conditions, neighborhood organizations, trade union groups, and environmental interests can alter the agenda of economic development politics. Much of the attention that has been given to the rise of urban populism focuses on the role of such groups. Neighborhood organizations are the most commonly implicated in the rise of populist challenges. This should not be surprising because these "territorial" organizations typically represent use values that are threatened by the exchange values of the growth coalition.[40] In addition, many community organizations are active in poorer neighborhoods, a situation that gives rise to mobilization around the problem of uneven benefits of development, as previously mentioned.

The emergence of a populist version of economic development politics is by no means guaranteed simply because of the existence of neighborhood organizations, a strong trade union tradition, or mobilized environmental interests. The existence of these political interests may instead yield stalemate or continuing conflict—something like the challenged elite style described earlier. At a minimum, the existence of strong neighborhood organizations, trade unions, or environmental interests is likely to be a key factor in preventing the evolution of a full-blown, elite-dominant approach to economic development along the lines suggested by the bifurcated politics model. This is the lesson drawn by Keil, for example, in his study of Wilkes-Barre and Luzerne County, Pennsylvania, where strong, working-class union organization was a key factor thwarting the economic development agenda of the local business elite.[41]

SUMMING UP: THE BIFURCATED POLITICS MODEL REVISITED?

This chapter began with a description of a bifurcated politics model. That model is appealing for a variety of reasons, not least of which is its offering of a definitive description of the nature of politics in the economic development realm. Economic development decisionmaking, according to this model, is typically consensual, noncontroversial, and insulated from the tumult of allocational politics. Furthermore, economic development decisionmaking is elitist. Business elites and economic notables are directly and indirectly involved, and their interests are paramount on the economic development agenda.

This characterization is not universally applicable, however. In a variety of case studies, urban analysts have found situations in which economic development is neither limited to the processes nor to the business elite bias that the bifurcated politics model suggests. In some communities, the politics of economic development takes on a populist style that ironically has many of the features that the bifurcated politics model would reserve for allocational decisionmaking concerning routine urban services. That is, economic development issues are visible and engender controversy that brings a multitude of conflicting interests into the fray. In still other communities, the politics of economic development fits neither the characterization offered in the bifurcated politics model nor the description of urban populism.

Admittedly, the alternative styles of economic development politics may not be as common as the style described in the bifurcated politics model. Urban populism in particular appears to be a rather fragile style. It emerges only in special circumstances and does not seem to be durable. The unsettled style of challenged elitism, in which economic development issues regularly create conflict between opposing groups of interests, may be only a transitory style that resolves itself into some other style. The style described in the bifurcated politics model may, in other words, be the most typical style of economic development politics in American cities. Nevertheless, the bifurcated politics model can be faulted for distracting attention from the considerable variety that there is in the politics of economic development.

What are the implications of this acknowledgment of diversity? First, the political aspects of economic development become more prominent. If there is no single uniform arrangement of political interests for purposes of economic development decisionmaking, the implication is that there are shifting patterns and strategic efforts to mold suitable arrangements. Stated another way, acknowledgment of diversity renews interest in the coalition-building activities of local politicians. The competing interests that have been identified in this chapter can be integrated in a variety of ways by skillful politicians. As a result, the conflicts that economic development engenders will be approached in a number of different ways, depending on the nature of the governing coalition that can be constructed by political entrepreneurs.[42]

More specifically, diversity in styles of economic development politics means that the interests of the business elite do not necessarily dictate what a community's economic development policies will be like. This is not to say that the interests of business elites are irrelevant, or even that they are no more important than other interests. But it does underscore the point that the power of business elites varies from place to place and that the variation is far from trivial.

Finally, diversity in styles of economic development opens the way for a richer characterization of urban regimes overall. Different styles of economic development politics may combine with different styles of allocational politics to yield a number of possible combinations. These different combinations may be conceived of as types of urban regimes. Something like this has been proposed by Elkin, who argues that urban regimes, or political economies, actually vary along three dimensions.[43] One of these dimensions is the city's particular form of growth coalition, which is much the same as what we have been calling "style of economic development politics." In addition, Elkin argues that cities differ in terms of the electoral coalitions that local politicians construct—that is, the shifting alliances of racial, ethnic, and neighborhood groupings that serve as the base for the party or reform group in power. Third, cities differ in the degree of power and autonomy that city bureaucracies have. Elkin argues that these three dimensions of difference can be used to construct several kinds of regimes, or urban political economies.

In short, the bifurcated politics model offers an interesting but standardized description of the politics of economic development. The bifurcated politics model may be the most common style, but a closer look shows that there is *diversity* in styles of economic development politics based on interesting exceptions to the bifurcated politics model.

DISCUSSION QUESTIONS

1. Consider two of the most recent development decisions or economic development policies handled in your community. Did they involve conflict? If so, who was involved? Why was there conflict? If there was no conflict, can you explain why not?

2. Consider the following hypothetical case example: Your community has been approached by a group of investors who wish to develop a major amusement park adjacent to the community. They have an option to purchase a large block of vacant land and are requesting that the city rezone the land to allow for an amusement park. One corner of the vacant land is adjacent to a residential area, but the remainder is surrounded by agricultural land or light industry. The investors are also asking the city to widen one of the streets that would carry traffic from the interstate highway exit to the amusement park site and to issue industrial revenue bonds to subsidize the city's building of a large parking facility for the amusement park. The investors are arguing that the amusement park will generate many construction jobs for the community, dozens of year-round jobs, and hundreds of summer jobs for youth. Would this proposed development be controversial? If so, identify the groups and institutions most likely to be involved in the controversy. Identify the particular stakes or interests that each group or institution would have in the controversy. If you believe that the proposed development would not be controversial, explain why it would not. How would decisionmaking about the proposed development unfold?

NOTES

1. Clarence Stone, "The Study of the Politics of Urban Development," in *The Politics of Urban Development,* ed. Clarence Stone and Heywood Sanders (Lawrence: University Press of Kansas, 1987), p. 12.
2. Paul Peterson, *City Limits* (Chicago: University of Chicago Press, 1981).
3. Ibid., pp. 165-166.
4. Ibid., p. 167.
5. Ibid., p. 132.
6. Thomas Dye, "Community Power and Public Policy," in *Community Power,* ed. Robert J. Waste (Beverly Hills: Sage, 1986), pp. 43-44.
7. Ibid., p. 41.
8. Herman B. Leonard, *Checks Unbalanced: The Quiet Side of Public Spending* (New York: Basic Books, 1986).
9. Harvey Molotch, "The City as a Growth Machine: Toward a Political Economy of Place," *American Journal of Sociology* 82 (1976): 309-330, 314-315. On the ideology supporting developmental politics, see also Michael Peter Smith and Dennis R. Judd, "American Cities: The Production of Ideology," in *Cities in Transformation,* ed. Michael Peter Smith (Beverly Hills: Sage, 1984), pp. 173-196.
10. John Logan and Harvey Molotch, *Urban Fortunes: The Political Economy of Place* (Berkeley: University of California Press, 1987), p. 64.
11. Stephen Elkin, *City and Regime in the American Republic* (Chicago: University of Chicago Press, 1987), p. 37.

12. Clarence Stone and Heywood Sanders, "Reexamining a Classic Case of Development Politics: New Haven, Connecticut," in *The Politics of Urban Development*, ed. Stone and Sanders (Lawrence: University Press of Kansas, 1987) p. 178.

13. Bryan D. Jones and Lynn W. Bachelor, *The Sustaining Hand* (Lawrence: University Press of Kansas, 1986).

14. Heywood Sanders, "The Politics of Development in Middle-sized Cities," in *The Politics of Urban Development*, ed. Stone and Sanders (Lawrence: University Press of Kansas, 1987), pp. 196–197.

15. Case details are from Larry Bennett, Kathleen McCourt, Philip Nyden, and Gregory Squires, "Chicago's North Loop Redevelopment Project: A Growth Machine on Hold," in *Business Elites and Urban Development*, ed. Scott Cummings (Albany: State University of New York Press, 1988), pp. 183–202.

16. Logan and Molotch, *Urban Fortunes*, pp. 1–2.

17. Ibid., pp. 112–115.

18. Molotch, "City as a Growth Machine," p. 310.

19. Logan and Molotch, *Urban Fortunes*, pp. 66–82.

20. Ibid., pp. 82–83.

21. Ibid., p. 83.

22. Clarence Stone, "The Study of the Politics of Urban Development," in *The Politics of Urban Development*, ed. Clarence Stone and Heywood Sanders (Lawrence: University Press of Kansas, 1987), p. 7.

23. Andrew Kirby, "Nine Fallacies of Local Economic Change," *Urban Affairs Quarterly* 21 (December 1985): 211.

24. Joe Feagin, "Tallying the Social Costs of Urban Growth Under Capitalism: The Case of Houston," in *Business Elites and Urban Development*, ed. Scott Cummings (Albany: State University of New York Press, 1988), p. 225.

25. The survey was sent to all cities of 10,000 or more population. A total of 1,140 cities responded.

26. Todd Swanstrom, "Urban Populism, Uneven Development, and the Space for Reform," in *Business Elites and Urban Development*, ed. Scott Cummings (Albany: State University of New York Press, 1988), p. 123.

27. Ibid., p. 129.

28. Susan E. Clarke, "More Autonomous Policy Orientations: An Analytic Framework," in *The Politics of Urban Development*, ed. Stone and Sanders (Lawrence: University Press of Kansas, 1987), p. 107.

29. The description that follows is from Mark E. Kann, *Middle Class Radicalism in Santa Monica* (Philadelphia: Temple University Press, 1986).

30. Stephen L. Elkin, "State and Market in City Politics: Or, The 'Real' Dallas," in *The Politics of Urban Development*, ed. Stone and Sanders (Lawrence: University Press of Kansas, 1987), p. 28.

31. Ibid., pp. 29–39.

32. The following description is from Robert Stoker, "Baltimore," in *The Politics of Urban Development*, ed. Stone and Sanders (Lawrence: University Press of Kansas, 1987), pp. 244–265.

33. The descriptive material that follows is from Kenneth J. Neubeck and Richard E. Ratcliff, "Urban Democracy and the Power of Corporate Capital: Struggles over Downtown Growth and Neighborhood Stagnation in Hartford, Connecticut," in

Business Elites and Urban Development, ed. Cummings (Albany: State University of New York Press, 1988), pp. 299–328.

34. The description that follows is adapted from Robert K. Whelan, "New Orleans: Mayoral Politics and Economic-Development Policies in the Postwar years, 1945–1986," in *The Politics of Urban Development,* ed. Stone and Sanders (Lawrence: University Press of Kansas, 1987), pp. 217–228.

35. Neubeck and Ratcliff, "Urban Democracy and the Power of Corporate Capital," p. 300.

36. Swanstrom, "Urban Populism, Uneven Development, and Space for Reform," pp. 127–128.

37. Richard Feiock and James Clingermayer, "Municipal Representation, Executive Power, and Economic Development Policy Administration," *Policy Studies Review* 15 (December 1986): 211–229.

38. Elkin, "State and Market in City Politics," p. 29.

39. Harvey Molotch, "Strategies and Constraints of Growth Elites," in *Business Elites and Urban Development,* ed. Scott Cummings (Albany: State University of New York Press, 1988), p. 31.

40. Clarke, "More Autonomous Policy Orientations," p. 112.

41. Thomas J. Keil, "Disinvestment and Economic Decline in Northeastern Pennsylvania: The Failure of a Local Business Elite's Growth Agenda," in *Business Elites and Urban Development,* ed. Cummings, pp. 269–295.

42. This point is forcefully made by Clarence Stone in "The Study of the Politics of Urban Development," in *Business Elites and Urban Development,* ed. Stone and Sanders (Albany: State University of New York Press, 1988), pp. 9–11.

43. Elkin, *City and Regime in the American Republic,* pp. 36–54.

PART IV

Future Roles and Issues

CHAPTER 12

Urban Politics and Administration: Into the 1990s

This book has presented an overview of urban politics and administration that is based on contemporary research, theory, and examples. As we contemplate the beginning of a new decade, however, questions naturally arise about the contours of urban politics and administration in the 1990s. Should we expect that the trends identified in this book will continue into the 1990s? Or should we expect interruptions and reversals of some of these trends? Are there likely to be substantially new developments affecting urban politics and administration? What areas of urban governance are most likely to be characterized by change?

Neither social scientists nor professionals in government have a reliable crystal ball for assessment of what the future holds. However, for several reasons, it is possible to make informed judgments about continuity and change in urban affairs.

First, urban history demonstrates that there are substantial continuities in the nature of cities and city politics that can reasonably be expected to shape future developments. For example, cities have long been sites for economic opportunity and for cultural assimilation of new immigrant groups. One can reasonably expect that these roles will continue. City governments have taken on more responsibilities and service functions over time as cities have grown in size and complexity. For example, in colonial times, the policing function as we now know it did not exist. Rather, each community relied on a combination of nightwatch duty by individual citizens and a constable chosen by the citizens to keep the peace.[1] This system is a far cry from the full-time, paid, professionalized police forces of American cities today. Such processes of public service professionalization may be expected to continue as well.

Continuities like these help with assessment of change because they suggest the general direction of developmental processes. The present can, in other words, be projected into the future. However, discontinuities must also be expected. Contemporary trends may be interrupted or even reversed. Wholly new developments unexpectedly arise. For example, the era of "creative federalism" during President Lyndon Johnson's administration generated a flurry of urban-oriented federal programs the scope, character, and extent of which were unprecedented in American urban history. The emergence of this era of creative federalism and its substantial implications for federal-urban relations surely could not have been foreseen by even the most astute of urban observers.

On the other hand, some discontinuity is patterned. Judgments about the nature of future developments can and should be based on awareness of such patterned discontinuity. Of particular relevance is the American tendency to push strongly in one direction of reform, only to have it followed by a wave of reaction as the limits and unintended consequences of the policy direction become manifest.[2] Acknowledgment of this pendulum-like process of reform and reaction provides a useful diagnostic tool for assessing likely developments in urban service delivery and economic development in the 1990s. As we will see in the next section, other phenomena, such as innovations, exhibit somewhat different yet predictable patterns over time, providing a basis for assessment of future developments.

In addition to continuities and patterned discontinuities, there are concepts of enduring normative significance in the study of urban governance that might be called *orienting concepts.* For example, efficiency, effectiveness, equity, responsiveness, and accountability are all important orienting concepts. Not surprisingly, they have played an important role in setting the agenda for the materials covered in this book. In this final chapter, they also suggest important questions that should be asked as part of an assessment of future trends.

SERVICE DELIVERY AND ECONOMIC DEVELOPMENT: DIVERGENCE?

One starting point for an assessment of urban politics and administration in the 1990s is the issue of divergent trends for basic urban service delivery and economic development. As noted in Chapter 1, these two areas seem to have been on separate trajectories in the 1980s. With respect to the delivery of traditional urban services such as snowplowing and sanitation, local governments have been under pressure to privatize more. And in the face of financial pressures and an intellectual climate particularly favorable to market-like arrangements, local government officials have responded. As Chapter 5 shows, substantial numbers of cities are contracting out or otherwise privatizing services that have traditionally been provided by local government agencies. Meanwhile, with respect to economic development, local governments have been under pressure to "publicize"—that is, to take on responsibilities and risks that have traditionally been characteristic of private investors. Attention to city governments' role in enhancing the local economy has increased markedly in the 1980s, and as Chapter 10 shows, city governments have implemented a variety of development policies ranging from tax abatement to promotional advertising to investment in capital improvements.

There is reason to expect that these divergent trends will not be sustained through the 1990s. This is not to say that there will be a wholesale abandonment of privatization arrangements and a denial of local government's role in economic development. However, for several reasons, a leveling off in the upsurge of attention to economic development might be expected, coupled with leveling off in the fervor for more privatization in basic service delivery.

The increased attention to economic development in the 1980s reveals that economic development is an "idea in good currency"—that is, a concept that has particularly widespread legitimacy and that evokes broad support for programs undertaken under its banner.[3] The reasons for the rapid rise of interest in economic development during the 1980s are not entirely clear. The Reagan administration's emphases on economic growth, on the stimulation of business, and on cooperation between the public and private sectors are typically suggested.[4] The important point, however, is that the rapid upsurge in interest in economic development spawned a flurry of state and local policies, programs, and activities that may not have been adequately planned or analyzed. As Chapter 10 suggests, questions are already being raised about some of the policy tools that have been used in the name of economic development. Across the country, cities are encountering the fallout from the frenzied decade of economic development activity. Empty industrial parks created in great hopes with public funds, controversies over the wisdom of particular tax incentives, and public-private joint ventures that have gone sour all stand as testimony to the fact that not everything done in the name of economic development is appropriate. Because economic development has served as an idea in good currency, it swept into place both good and bad policy ventures in the 1980s. A reaction to the inappropriate policy ventures attempted in the name of economic development is therefore likely.

With respect to the delivery of basic municipal services, the trend toward privatization is likely to level off for several reasons. First, privatization is an innovation—a "process" innovation in the language introduced in Chapter 3. Innovations often follow a distinctive, S-shaped pattern of diffusion over time.[5] That is, innovations are initially taken up by only a few communities or individuals who are in a position to be particularly venturesome. In the second phase of innovation, there is a dramatic upturn in the number of communities adopting the innovation because everyone can draw on the leadership and benefit from the experience of the early innovators. The second phase is, in other words, the time for the bandwagon effect to set in. Finally, in the third phase, the pace of new adoptions slacks off. Most communities that are going to adopt the innovation have already jumped on the bandwagon, and there are no new developments to alter the position of reluctant communities.

If privatization is viewed as an innovation, the 1980s could be said to constitute the second phase of its adoption cycle. As Chapter 5 shows, contracting out with private firms for provision of traditional urban services has become especially widespread. Privatization is no longer a particularly innovative idea used only by the most progressive and venturesome communities. It is, instead, an institutionalized part of urban management across a broad array of municipalities. In this sense, we can expect a leveling off in the trend toward privatization if for no other reason than that privatization as an innovation has already experienced the frenzied second phase of rapid diffusion.

There is a second reason to expect that the trend toward privatization in the 1980s will be tempered in the 1990s. Like economic development, privatization served as an idea in good currency in the 1980s. As noted earlier, ideas in good currency are powerful concepts, capable of providing legitimacy to many programs and activities that are sold under the banner of the idea in good currency. As a result, many poorly conceived programs and activities that might not otherwise be justified can be swept quickly into place. But the special legitimacy of the idea in good currency eventually wears off as the limitations of the idea become evident in practice. The 1990s are likely to witness this process of reassessment of the privatization concept as well as the economic development concept. As noted in Chapter 5, scholars have already begun to ask questions about the appropriateness and limits of privatization, particularly with respect to the accountability problems that privatization can create and the threat to constitutional protections that privatization can pose. This is likely to be supplemented by a more realistic assessment of management problems with private contractors and other limits of privatization that communities discover through experience.

In short, basic service delivery and economic development are unlikely to remain on the divergent paths suggested in Chapter 1. There was pressure for increasing privatization of the one and increasing public involvement in the other during the decade of the 1980s. But for the reasons suggested, these pressures can be expected to abate if not to totally reverse themselves.

ESCALATING SERVICE DEMANDS

Apart from the leveling off of privatization fervor, several other developments or enduring issues regarding urban service delivery might be expected for the 1990s. It is reasonable, for example, to expect continuing demands for more and better services. This is consistent with the long-term historical development of city government's role. More specifically, it is possible to isolate at least four sources of increased demand for urban services: (1) demands for amenities;

(2) demands for services to deal with the problems created by growth and economic activity; (3) demands for services to deal with unmet social problems; and (4) demands for more services of the order-maintenance variety to deal with conflict resulting from social diversity.

Demands for Amenities

Many cities will face pressures for more services of the amenities type. Amenities refer to services beyond the traditional basic services provided by government as necessities. For example, sanitation and sewage treatment and policing are typically viewed as essentials in the sense that they are necessary to ensure the public safety and health. But the provision of elaborate recreational facilities, including weight-lifting rooms, areas for aerobics dance classes, and whirlpools is far from a basic traditional service of local government. Yet many cities are facing increasing pressure for these and other amenities. Increasing levels of income and education, especially when coupled with increased leisure time, create pressures for such amenities. At the same time, there is likely to be increasing justification of amenities on grounds that they can contribute to particular visions of economic development. Many cities are attempting to attract high-tech companies or are pursuing postindustrial economic roles as tourism or cultural centers. Quality-of-life factors, including the presence of a full array of local public services, can be of considerable importance in the pursuit of such economic development goals.

Dealing with the Effects of Growth

Another source of increased demand for urban services is the set of problems created by growth and increased economic activity. Some of these problems have long been recognized but have also been long-ignored consequences of growth. Los Angeles is the prototypical example in this regard. Los Angeles is confronting alarming levels of traffic congestion and air pollution. These are not new problems. However, the power of the idea of economic growth, coupled with the complexity of the problems has sustained a long period of political inertia. As Los Angeles enters the 1990s, however, traffic congestion, pollution, and other problems of growth are squarely on the public agenda. Demands for new transportation alternatives and other public policies to ease the fallout from growth are a part of the agenda.

In addition to renewed attention to classic but long-ignored problems of growth, the 1990s are likely to witness increased demands for city government intervention into wholly new areas of regulatory activity. Environmental protection has for some time been viewed as an appropriate policy domain for the federal government and for the states, not for local government. This is so because the scope of most environmental problems, such as air and water pollution, is larger than the jurisdiction of the typical local government.

Environmental protection at the local level has traditionally been limited to the regulation of very localized nuisances, such as brush piles on residential property and unauthorized trash dumping. However, the 1980s have already witnessed a spate of attention to environmental problems such as toxic wastes and transportation of hazardous materials. In the 1990s, increasing numbers of cities are likely to attempt policy initiatives designed to regulate storage and transportation of hazardous materials within city limits. Similar initiatives may be expected concerning noise abatement and esthetic regulations, such as ordinances restricting the size, character, and placement of commercial signs. In short, growth and increased economic activity tend to generate conflicts between commercial or industrial land uses and residential land uses, as well as a host of more general public safety and esthetic issues. The result is increased pressure on city government for additional regulatory services.

Dealing with Unmet Social Problems

In Chapter 6, we considered the argument that local governments are, by virtue of the mobility of taxpaying individuals and businesses, constrained from doing much in the way of redistributive services. As a result, social services targeted for the disadvantaged, who are not substantial contributors to the local tax base, must be the responsibility of the federal government and the states.[6] Chapter 6 acknowledges that although local governments do spend state and federal funds on social service programs and facilitate the work of a network of nonprofit social service agencies, they devote a very limited amount of locally raised revenues to social services for the disadvantaged.

Although arguments and evidence about local government's limited role in redistribution are compelling, one might nevertheless expect a trend toward increased local spending on social services in the 1990s. America's cities are the focal point for a variety of unresolved social problems, ranging from drug abuse to homelessness to juvenile delinquency to family violence. A variety of federal and state programs exist, but none appears to be adequate to the task at hand. Continuing local pressures for more substantial federal and state resources to deal with these social problems may be expected. In addition, there are two reasons that local governments can be expected to devote more local resources to social service programming: (1) interpretation of some social problems as threats to the existing social order and (2) perceptions that unmet social problems can interfere with economic development efforts.

While the theory is still controversial, Piven and Cloward offer a compelling interpretation of surges in redistributive social service spending (see Chapter 6). Their thesis suggests that governments provide more generous welfare benefits in response to threats to the social order, such as those posed by the urban riots of the 1960s. If Piven and Cloward's thesis is correct and if threats to the social order include the tremendous surge in drug-related violent crime that many cities experienced in the 1980s, then it is reasonable to expect increased local commitment to drug counseling, job training, and other social services in the 1990s.

In addition, unresolved social problems may increasingly be recognized as counterproductive from an economic development viewpoint. In small ways, this already occurs. Retailers place pressure on city hall to "do something" about the homeless, because the presence of street people on the sidewalks of the downtown is believed to be bad for business. But in larger ways, problems of poverty, lack of job skills, substance abuse, and illiteracy are an obstacle to economic development. In many areas, labor markets are very tight. Potential developers are deterred when there are shortages of workers to staff retail stores, serve as hotel workers, and fill a variety of other unskilled or semiskilled positions. Cities are unlikely to become the dominant partners in an intergovernmental system that places the primary responsibility for job training, welfare, and other social services in the hands of the federal government and the states. But cities may be expected to move more aggressively in the 1990s to supplement state and federal programs with initiatives of their own in order to transform problem segments of their population into a viable labor force.

Demands for Maintenance of Order

Crime, violence, and other threats to the social order may be expected to generate demands for expanding police service as well as demands for social services. As the 1980s close, problems of violent, drug-related crime are already overburdening law enforcement and corrections institutions. More important, the amount of attention paid to drug-related crime in the media, in sources of popular entertainment, and by politicians indicates that this is an item with very high status on the agenda. One might confidently predict that the 1990s will include a strong surge of state and local government responses in the form of heightened spending for policing, courts, and correctional facilities.

There is nothing particularly new about demands for additional urban services. Periods of pressure for new or expanded city services are a continuing feature of American urban history. Consequently, it is not particularly risky to forecast that, as America's cities move toward the year 2000, they will be confronting such service demands. However, this section has discussed some particular sources of demand and the types of service demands that they are likely to engender: amenities; regulatory services in response to negative, spillover effects of growth and economic development; social services and maintenance of order. But how will cities manage to respond to these demands? To do more, cities must either develop new revenue sources, draw more heavily on existing revenue sources, or do more with available resources through productivity-enhancing innovations. The next section suggests that the first two of these are highly likely because only a modest role can be expected for municipal innovation.

MUNICIPAL INNOVATION

Technological innovations for productivity improvement are likely to continue at a pace of adoption that is slower than optimal from the viewpoint of proponents of innovation. Two factors, however, may enhance technological innovation in the 1990s. First, as Chapter 3 showed, there is evidence of a greater diffusion of innovations in municipal government in the late 1970s and 1980s. One possible reason for this jump in adoption of innovations is that city governments were responding to the fiscal strains of that period (i.e., fiscal caps inspired by the tax revolt, inflation, and recession) partly by searching for innovations to hold down costs. If this interpretation is correct, then the pace of municipal innovation in the 1990s depends partly on whether fiscal strain escalates again.

Second, cities' enhanced experience with privatization in the 1980s may also provide an impetus for greater use of technological innovations in the 1990s even if the concept of privatization itself undergoes critical reassessment. As noted in Chapter 5, private firms have been found to have a greater propensity to use state-of-the-art equipment. When cities contract out for particular services from such firms, they in effect create a local demonstration project for technological innovation. Municipal agencies responsible for other types of services may be encouraged to adopt similar technologies for their work under these circumstances. For example, the existence of a private contractor using computers and software to efficiently route and schedule crews for garbage collection might serve to inspire the municipal street department to adopt similar technology to route and schedule its crews for street repair.

The service demands discussed in the preceding section may also constitute an impetus for greater innovation. Pressures to meet new service demands, when coupled with fiscal constraints, could constitute a potent motivator for innovation. For all these reasons, one might reasonably expect that the progress in innovating that cities exhibited in the late 1970s and the 1980s will continue in the 1990s.

Nevertheless, productivity-enhancing innovations cannot be expected to close the gap between municipal capabilities and service demands. Even at its best, municipal innovation occurs gradually and has an incremental impact on local government's performance. As a result of fiscal pressures ranging from populist tax revolts to inflation to erosion of the local tax base to cutbacks in intergovernmental aid, many U.S. cities have been attempting to do more with less for some years now. Increased service demands in the 1990s are unlikely to be met with still more doing more with less. Instead, the 1990s are likely to be the decade of revenue enhancement, including both increases in existing sources of revenue, such as sales taxes and property taxes, and a scramble for new, less visible sources of revenue that are not politically sensitive. As Chapter 7 indicated, the scramble for new revenue sources has already begun. User fees, for example, have already attracted considerable attention as a potential revenue alternative. City officials in the 1990s may be expected to exercise ever more creativity in devising new sources of revenue. In short, innovation with respect to revenue raising is likely to be at least as important as innovation in service delivery technologies.

CITIZEN PARTICIPATION
AT THE MUNICIPAL LEVEL

What trends and developments concerning citizen participation should be expected as cities move toward the year 2000? Should we expect extensive or limited citizen participation? And what forms will citizen participation take?

As Chapter 4 shows, there is no agreement on whether the extent of citizen participation in the 1970s and 1980s has been hopelessly low or on an encouraging upward trend. This is because definitions of what meaningful participation includes vary enormously. A focus on levels of voting turnout and electoral interest may lead to very different forecasts for participation than would a focus on neighborhood organization activity or a focus on individual service demands.

It is possible to conceptually aggregate the many forms of citizen participation and to consider whether trends in overall participation exhibit any interesting patterns. Hirschman has done precisely this sort of analysis that has yielded an intriguing thesis of a "private-public cycle."[7] According to this thesis, citizen involvement in public affairs follows a pendulum-like pattern. Periods of private orientation characterized by a lack of interest in public affairs and an emphasis on consumption of goods and services are followed by periods of public orientation marked by outbreaks of participatory fervor and intense involvement in public affairs. Inevitably, however, the period of public orientation is displaced by yet another turn toward private consumption and neglect of civic involvement. Hirschman speculates that the dynamic driving this pendulum-like pattern is disappointment. The private orientation is eventually abandoned because of a variety of consumer disappointments, and the public orientation is abandoned because of the many frustrations of collective participatory activity.

Hirschman's thesis provides one intriguing basis for developing a citizen participation prognosis for the 1990s. Hirschman acknowledges popular characterizations of the 1950s as a period of preoccupation with individual economic advancement, the 1960s as a period of "sudden and overwhelming concern with public issues," and the 1970s as a period of return to private economic concerns.[8] Popular characterizations include the 1980s along with the 1970s as a period of private orientation dominated by concerns for consumption, material acquisition, and personal success. If these characterizations are accurate and if Hirschman's thesis of a public-private-public cycle is accurate, we are due for a period of renewed interest in public affairs accompanied by high levels of citizen activism and participatory fervor.

From an alternative perspective, what changes is not so much the aggregate volume of citizen involvement in public affairs but the character of that involvement. One might argue, for example, that the 1970s and 1980s were far from quiescent in terms of political participation. Rather than a change from a public orientation in the 1960s to a private orientation, the 1970s, and 1980s witnessed a shift in the forms of political participation. From this point of view, the 1960s are best characterized as an era of visible protest activity. In the period that followed, citizen involvement in public affairs did not necessarily die off; rather, it moved off the streets and into interest groups. In particular, the rise of the neighborhood movement, the emergence of a variety of environmental interest groups, and increasing political mobilization of public sector unions are broadly acknowledged phenomena of the latter 1970s and 1980s. Similarly, the 1970s and 1980s witnessed an upsurge in the use of the tools of direct democracy—that is, the initiative and referendum at the state and local levels. These devices were particularly important in campaigns involving the issues of tax limitation and environmental protection.[9] Having demonstrated their power and potential, interest organizations like neighborhood organizations and tools for direct democracy are likely to be of continuing importance in local affairs.

It is also important to acknowledge that citizen demand-making is an important form of participation, whether it is channeled through interest groups such as neighborhood associations or whether individually registered with city officials. Ironically, the same period (1970s and 1980s) that is sometimes characterized as lacking in public orientation and citizen participation also witnessed a surge of attention to the problem of demand-overload on governments.[10] Governments in advanced postindustrial societies are said to be facing deadlock or crisis brought on by the flood of competing demands for government services. At the local level, city governments are said to be swamped in "street-fighting pluralism" characterized by an overload of competing demands from conflicting interest groups.[11]

There is little reason to expect that this rising tide of demands will abate in the 1990s. Rather, as earlier sections in this chapter explain, there are good reasons to forecast a continuing, perhaps even escalating, flow of demands for urban services in the 1990s. As acknowledged in these earlier sections, however, the content of these demands may differ from the content of demands in earlier decades. An increased flow of demands for amenities, regulatory services dealing with the negative consequences of growth, social services, and social control services is likely to be added to the more traditional demands for distributive, residential services such as snow removal, trash collection, and street repair.

In short, Hirschman's thesis of pendulum-like shifts in the degree of public involvement is not the only basis for forecasting substantial levels of citizen participation in the 1990s. From an alternative point of view that acknowledges a steadily increasing proliferation of interest groups and a rising tide of demands through the post-1950s period, the prognosis is for relatively high levels of citizen participation in the 1990s. The decade may be expected to include substantial amounts of citizen participation, *not* because the citizenry is returning to a public orientation after a period of private absorption but because of ongoing processes by which interest groups have proliferated and citizen involvement in public affairs has been institutionalized. Hirschman's thesis allows for the possibility that the urban future holds the promise for a convulsive period of regular large-scale protest activity and intense mass-based citizen participation. A more conservative forecast suggests that the future of citizen participation lies in a continuation of existing trends toward more institutionalized forms of making demands, using devices such as neighborhood organizations, urban complaint-handling units, and direct democracy devices such as the initiative and referendum.

ECONOMIC DEVELOPMENT

Finally, what prognosis might be made with respect to urban economic development activities? Several responses to this question are already evident from prior sections of this chapter. As noted at the outset, the strong upsurge in attention to the economic development function that we have seen in the 1980s can be expected to moderate, in part because the glamour and persuasiveness of economic development as an "idea in good currency" will suffer the fate of all such concepts—that is, a partial loss of legitimacy as the limitations and unintended consequences of activities carried out in its name become manifest. In addition, many economic development policies may be viewed as innovations, the proliferation of which can be expected to follow the S-shaped pattern discussed earlier. This, too, suggests that the 1990s will witness a leveling off in the adoption of economic development initiatives that were considered innovative in the 1980s. Finally, ever-increasing demands for a variety of services, ranging from amenities to social services, can be expected to help divert local decisionmakers from disproportionate attention to economic development. This is not to say that state or local governments will abandon their concerns with economic development or totally reverse their commitment to it, for economic development is an enduring function of governments in capitalist societies.[12] However, economic development may not have the privileged position vis-à-vis other government responsibilities that it seemed to attain in the 1980s.

One might also expect increasing differentiation in the content of local governments' economic development activity. American local governments have collectively gone through a period characterized not only by increased attention to economic development but by substantial copycat activity. Like all processes of innovation, the diffusion of economic development activities has involved considerable emulation of successes, perhaps without adequate attention to the workability of particular activities in alternate settings. The proliferation of convention center plans, industrial parks, and financial inducement packages are all examples of the emulation of economic development policy. However, as noted in Chapter 9, a more strategic approach is already beginning to emerge. The hallmarks of a strategic approach are realistic assessment of the community's unique economic assets and selection of development policies specifically tailored for the community's unique development goals and circumstances. The result is likely to be a much less standardized approach to economic development policy in the 1990s.

Economic development is also likely to be the focal point for increased conflict in the 1990s, at least in communities that are experiencing substantial growth. Growth in economic activity frequently brings unwelcome side effects such as pollution, traffic congestion, and strains on everything from schools to water-supply systems. As noted in previous sections of this book, these negative consequences of growth are likely to be the focus of increased citizen activism in the 1990s, particularly in the form of organized pressure for local government to provide new or expanded regulatory services. Economic development may also be expected to generate increasing levels of conflict as a result of the not-in-my-backyard syndrome, as communities struggle with controversial siting decisions for airport expansions, new landfills, and other facilities that are objectionable to nearby residents but made necessary by growth.

SUMMARY

This venture into forecasting the urban future suggests that in many ways continuities and patterned discontinuities are helpful in assessing likely changes in urban affairs. Long-term trends, such as increases in demands on government, may be expected to continue. Other phenomena follow patterned discontinuities, such as the pendulum-like movement of reform-reaction and the S-shaped pattern of diffusion of innovations. Perhaps most important, orienting concepts such as equity, responsiveness, and efficiency are of continuing relevance in discussing the quality of urban governance. These concepts suggest a durable set of questions that can be asked about the future of urban affairs: (1) Are the outcomes of urban governance more or less equitably distributed? (2) Do various avenues for citizen participation make a difference in the pattern of local government responsiveness to various interests? (3) Is local government making progress with respect to efficient allocation of public resources? It requires no special boldness to forecast that these and similar questions will continue to preoccupy urban leaders and urban scholars beyond the year 2000.

NOTES

1. James Levine, Michael Musheno, and Dennis Palumbo, *Criminal Justice: A Public Policy Approach* (New York: Harcourt Brace Jovanovich, 1980), p. 162.
2. Allan J. Cigler and Elaine B. Sharp, "The Impact of Television Coverage on City Council," *Journal of Urban Affairs* 7 (Spring 1985), p. 65.
3. Barbara Nelson, "Setting the Public Agenda: The Case of Child Abuse," in *The Policy Cycle,* ed. Judith May and Aaron Wildavsky (Beverly Hills: Sage, 1978), p. 21.
4. Richard D. Bingham and John P. Blair, "Introduction: Urban Economic Development," in *Urban Economic Development,* ed. R. Bingham and J. Blair (Beverly Hills: Sage, 1984), p. 12.
5. Richard D. Bingham, *The Adoption of Innovation by Local Government* (Lexington, MA: Heath, 1976), p. 199.
6. Paul Peterson, *City Limits* (Chicago: University of Chicago Press, 1981), pp. 182–183.
7. Albert O. Hirschman, *Shifting Involvements* (Princeton, NJ: Princeton University Press, 1982), p. 3.
8. Ibid.
9. Harlan Hahn and Sheldon Kamieniecki, *Referendum Voting* (New York: Greenwood Press, 1987), pp. 2–3.
10. Samuel Huntington, "The Democratic Distemper," *Public Interest* 41 (Fall 1975): 9–38; Roger Benjamin, *The Limits of Politics* (Chicago: University of Chicago Press, 1980); Helen Ingram and Dean Mann, "Policy Failure: An Issue Deserving Analysis," in *Why Policies Succeed or Fail,* ed. Helen Ingram and Dean Mann (Beverly Hills: Sage, 1980), pp. 11–32.
11. Douglas Yates, *The Ungovernable City* (Cambridge, MA: MIT Press, 1977), p. 33.
12. James O'Connor, *The Fiscal Crisis of the State* (New York: St. Martin's Press, 1973).

Index